*The Search
Begins*

Introduction

Man is always curious about what lies beyond the places he knows, and there are always adventurous men who go to see. This is a story of the earliest adventurous men. Their known world, small as it was, was imperfectly understood. Yet there were those who still wanted to go beyond. For who could say what wonders might exist, what miracles might await them? Here is the ceaseless human effort to find out, from the nameless Egyptians who left some records, at least, to Magellan, whose men circled the globe and brought back maps of where they had gone.

That is what exploration is: not only venturing into the unknown, but returning with information about what has been discovered. We have the stories here of the men who came back. Thousands of others simply disappeared with their hard-won knowledge of their travels.

For a long, long time the most difficult part of each journey was the return trip. Getting to virgin territory was easy enough when the known world extended for only a few days' travel. The problem was to find out where you were in that territory, and—most important—where your home lay in relation to it. So throughout this book, the infant science of navigation gradually grows as the explorers of the time grapple with the problem of recording location. Each explorer who returned brought a piece of information. Some, such as Marco Polo, brought such a big piece that they were simply not believed.

The first part of this book tells of the fragmentary accounts of the very first journeys. The art of writing was new, and the records have been copied over many centuries. So we are left with many questions. Where was Punt? What was Thule? The questions tantalize us today as much as they must have intrigued the first hearers. The fascination lingers even in the sketchiest story: the first explorers were amazing, mysterious men who set off deliberately into the black unknown—and came back to tell us about it.

A HISTORY OF DISCOVERY AND EXPLORATION

The Search Begins

Aldus Books / Jupiter Books

London

Contents

This edition published in 1973 by
Aldus Books and Jupiter Books, London

SBN 490 00290 0

Distributed by Jupiter Books
9-13 Cowcross Street, London EC1M 6DR

© 1971 Aldus Books Limited, London

Printed and bound in Yugoslavia by
Mladinska Knjiga, Ljubljana

Part 3 The Great Age of Exploration

Below: an artist's impression of a group of
Neanderthal people roaming through rugged
country. Migrating tribes of prehistoric
families had made their way across all the
continents except Antarctica before civilization really began in about 4000 B.C. Such
tribes were the true "first explorers."

PART ONE
The First Explorers

BY FELIX BARKER
in collaboration with Anthea Barker

Below: a painted bas-relief from the temple at Thebes, in Egypt, showing boats being loaded for the journey to Punt. Like many accounts of early voyages, the story of the expedition to Punt is remarkably complete in some ways, but deficient in others. For example, we are never told where Punt was.

Into the Unknown

1

As the high-prowed Egyptian ships sailed south down the coast of East Africa, their captains searched for signs of life. The sandy foreshore, backed by thick jungle, seemed unending. Monkeys chattered in the trees, and on moonlit nights the sailors could see the distant shadowy forms of wild animals. But there was no sign of people. Did the land of Punt really exist? How much farther must they sail before they reached that legendary country?

Many months had passed since the small fleet had left Egypt and set out down the Red Sea. To the 30 Sudanese slaves pulling on the oars of each vessel in the tropical heat, it must have seemed an unendurably long journey. And to what end? Simply to bring back a cargo of trees.

Nearly 1,500 years before the birth of Christ, Queen Hatshepsut, the powerful and beautiful ruler of Upper and Lower Egypt, had issued a decree. A temple was to be built at Thebes, on the banks of the Nile, to the glory of Amon-Re, king of the gods. Like no other temple in the land, it was to be approached by a terraced garden

Below: the temple at Thebes. Queen Hatshepsut sent her expedition to Punt for myrrh trees, unobtainable in Egypt, to plant on the temple terraces.

Above: the Egyptian explorers in procession carrying palm leaves. This is one of the bas-reliefs from the temple at Thebes, telling the story of the expedition to Punt. When Queen Hatshepsut had a record of the voyage made in her temple, she little imagined that more than 3,000 years later it would be studied by scholars trying to fit together all the details of the journey.

Right: the world's first explorers were the numerous generations of pre-historic men who migrated huge distances in search of better places to live or to escape from danger. Trudging across continents, paddling down rivers and even across seas, they moved gradually through Asia, Europe, Africa, the Americas, and even southwest into Australasia. This map shows the routes they probably followed.

Probable migration routes of the earlie

© Geographical Projects

where the spirit of the god could walk at leisure for all eternity.

Hatshepsut ordered that the garden be planted with fragrant myrrh trees, which would provide incense for the altar of Amon-Re. But these trees did not grow in Egypt. To obtain them, it was necessary to send an expedition south down the Red Sea to the distant land of Punt. Five hundred years earlier, other Egyptian voyagers had sailed to this country. But now the route to Punt was forgotten, its exact whereabouts uncertain, and the place itself hardly believed in.

Suddenly, when the Egyptians had almost given up hope of ever reaching their goal, they caught sight of some people on the fore-shore. And in the shade of the palm trees that reached almost to the water's edge, they could see the cone-shaped huts of a small village.

The explorers dropped anchor and went ashore. The people on the shore clustered around them in amazement. "How came you to this land that people know not of?" they asked. "Did you come along the paths of heaven, or have you traversed the sea and the waters of the land of the gods? Or have you come on the beams of the sun?" This was indeed Punt. The country was no mere legend.

Now the voyagers would be able to accomplish their mission.

The Egyptian expedition was outstandingly successful. Not only did the explorers return with myrrh trees for Queen Hatshepsut, but their vessels were loaded with gold, ivory, jewels, ebony, incense, and other treasures from the land of Punt. Their momentous journey had taken the Egyptians far from their native land. In frail ships, with no charts to guide them, they had sailed through vast stretches of unfamiliar sea. And in these same ships they returned in triumph to Egypt. There, on the walls of her temple, their grateful queen recorded their achievement in pictures and inscriptions that can still be seen today.

The voyage to Punt took place nearly 3,500 years ago. But it was a comparatively recent enterprise in the long story of exploration. For thousands of years before the Egyptians put out to sea, men had been making tentative journeys into the unknown.

Far back in the remote beginnings of their existence on earth, men began to roam across the world. Seeking food and shelter, or fleeing from danger, they traveled farther and farther from their original homes. Generations of prehistoric men drifted across the great land masses through Europe, Asia, Africa, and the Americas. Trudging through trackless lands and paddling down rivers in hollowed-out logs, the men of the Stone Age were the world's

Above: a prehistoric rock painting of hunters, found in what is now Rhodesia, in Africa. Prehistoric tools and weapons, and rock paintings such as this one, have been found in various parts of the world. They are the only surviving record of the wanderings of these first explorers.

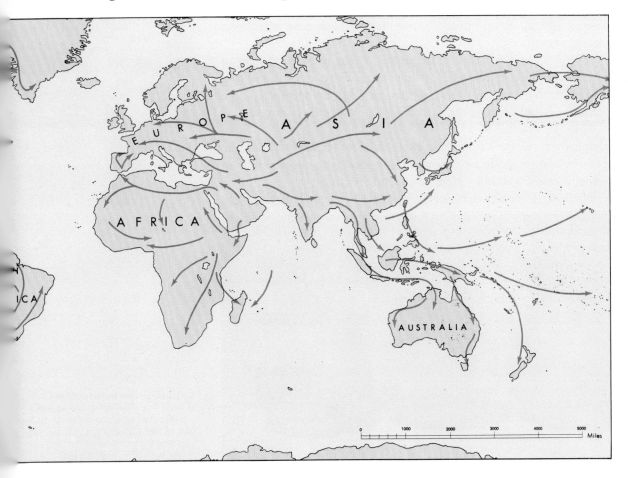

first explorers. Some of them settled where the land and climate were favorable. Others preferred the nomadic life and continued to journey on. But these men left no records of their travels. Time passed, and men began to settle in permanent communities. Then they began to explore beyond these settlements. But their ancestors' journeys had long been forgotten, and the new explorers had to learn for themselves about the lands beyond.

Defying danger, and often for scant reward, these early men left the comparative safety of their small communities and made their way into the unknown. They had no idea of the size or shape of the earth. And they lacked all but the most primitive equipment to guide them.

As soon as the early explorers put out to sea, they were at the mercy of unfamiliar currents and sudden, unpredictable squalls. Once they were out of sight of land, they were in immediate danger of being lost. By day, their course could be judged roughly in relation to the position of the sun. At night, they could navigate by the stars. But in winter the sun was often hidden by clouds, and in the dark there was the constant danger of running onto rocks. Slowly and hesitantly, these early mariners sailed and rowed their vessels into unknown seas. The shortest voyage was filled with hazard. Mariners dared not go far out of sight of land, and always carried enough food and water for the journey back to known waters. Every mile of coastline and each new island was dearly won.

Travel by land was equally hazardous. Apart from the danger of attack from wild beasts and hostile peoples, the land explorer, too, was venturing into the absolute unknown. He could carry only a limited amount of provisions, and, unless he followed a river, or established a series of water holes behind him, he ran the risk of dying from thirst. Without the example of other explorers before him, he had to decide for himself how to deal with every new situation, and every strange thing he encountered.

Many early peoples were forced to travel by need. They hoped to

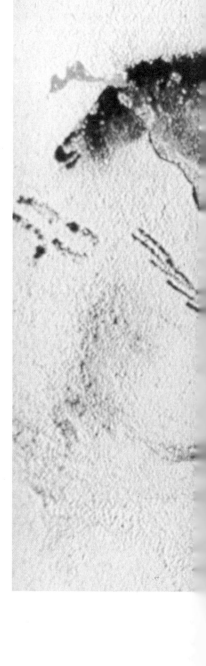

Left: bell-beaker pottery of the Early Bronze Age. The bell-like shape and the method of decoration are characteristic of the work of a group of people from the Rhineland and The Netherlands, who later migrated to Britain.

ind a land of plenty beyond the distant mountains, or a richer island just over the horizon. Sometimes the threat of attack by stronger neighbors forced them to flee their homes. At other times, they themselves went in search of conquest. Gradually, the growth of civilization brought another reason for travel. Man ceased to be content with bare necessities. If the materials he needed were not available near home, he set off to find them elsewhere.

The first explorers were mainly materialists, self-preservationists, aggressors, and fortune hunters. Even so, it is possible to discern another strong quality in their makeup. They possessed a streak of adventure. They could not repress a curiosity about the unknown. Behind their opportunism and varying motives lay the same rash and inexplicable desire that has inspired explorers throughout history. They wanted to be the first to set foot in new territory.

Above: some of the early rock paintings are very beautiful and full of movement. This horse comes from the famous Lascaux Cave in France, discovered in 1940. Below: a seal from around 3000 B.C., from Sumer in Mesopotamia, showing a boat with a passenger. This is one of the earliest records of boats. By this time, the Sumerians had already sailed as far as the Persian Gulf.

Above: the Nile at Aswan. The regular flooding of the river has made this valley an oasis in the surrounding sterile desert. On the fertile lands of the Nile Valley grew a civilization of great wealth and power.

Archaeological evidence provides interesting clues to the possible movements of the earliest explorers. But there are no written accounts of their travels. Only with the growth of civilization and the beginnings of written records is it possible to trace the story of the first journeys of exploration and of the men who made them.

Civilization first grew up between 5,000 and 6,000 years ago in Egypt and in Sumer. Sumer lay in southern Mesopotamia, the land between the Tigris and Euphrates rivers in what is now Iraq, eastern Syria, and southeastern Turkey. Both Egypt and Sumer depended for their livelihood on their rivers, and it was along these rivers that the people of these countries made their first voyages. In Egypt, river vessels traveled up and down the Nile, and in Mesopotamia the Sumerians navigated the Tigris and Euphrates.

The Sumerians are the first people who are known to have put out to sea for the purpose of exploration. In about 4000 B.C., Sumerian ships were sailing the waters of the Persian Gulf and had even begun to travel southward along the Asian coast to trade with India. Later, the Sumerians probably established trading contacts with Egypt.

In time, Egypt too began sending expeditions abroad. The wealth of Egypt, like that of Sumer, was mainly agricultural, and the Egyptians were forced to import many of their raw materials. One of the most important of these materials was timber, needed not only in building temples and palaces but also for constructing the ships on which Egyptian trade depended. Egypt was a land without forests. The only trees common in Egypt were palms, the wood of which is unsuitable for building seaworthy vessels. At first, the Egyptians built their boats from reeds. Later, they brought timber from the mountainous regions of the Sinai Peninsula, which lies between the two northern arms of the Red Sea. Then they discovered a source of supply in Phoenicia. This country, which corresponds approximately to the coastal areas of present-day Syria, Lebanon, and Israel, was the land of the famous cedars of Lebanon. The Egyptians soon found that these trees could provide them with an abundant source of excellent timber. So eager were the Egyptians to take advantage of this discovery that on one occasion they brought 40 shiploads of cedarwood from the Phoenician port of Byblos in a single expedition.

This voyage to Byblos, about 800 miles there and back, was made in 2600 B.C. and is the earliest recorded sea-going voyage. Many other expeditions were probably being made at this time and even before, but archaeologists have found only fragmentary evidence of them. The date at which voyaging and exploration began to take place on a significant scale may be fixed at around 2000 B.C. And in order to appreciate the achievements of those expeditions, it is important to picture the world as it appeared to the explorers of that time.

The world as it was known in 2000 B.C. was centered on the

Right: an Egyptian wall-painting of a boat of about 2000 B.C. By this time, Egyptian sailors had reached Phoenicia, and were making trading voyages to the land of Punt.

15

Mediterranean Sea, extending from the coastal fringes of the Middle East to the narrow Strait of Gibraltar. In this area existed the three great civilizations of Egypt, Phoenicia, and Crete. Of these, Egypt was the most powerful and influential. And it was the rise of her wealthy rulers that first stimulated trade in the Mediterranean world.

Egypt was a long, narrow country stretching south for 680 miles from the Mediterranean Sea to Aswan, just below the First Cataract (a series of rapids) on the Nile. Bounded on the east by the Red Sea, and on the west by the Libyan Desert, it drew the whole source of its life from the fertile valley of the Nile.

Mediterranean sailors entered Egypt through the marshy lagoons and sandy islands of the Nile Delta. As they sailed on up the Nile, they passed the sacred city of Heliopolis, an important religious and cultural center where work had just begun on a great temple to the sun god Re. Soon afterward, they had their first glimpse of the three pyramids at Giza (now Al Jīzah). Each nearly 500 feet high, and built from some 2 million stone blocks, the pyramids served as tombs for the kings of Egypt, and were taller than any building known to man until modern times. The largest of the three was the Great Pyramid, built in around 2600-2500 B.C. Near it stood the Sphinx. This 240-foot-long monument with the head of a king on the body of a lion was probably made in about 2600 B.C.

Twelve miles farther south was Memphis. The sailor traveling up the river reached the city just as he left the Nile Delta and set out up the mighty main stream of the river. Memphis was one of the five cities from which, at different times, the Egyptian kings ruled their land. Enclosed by a defensive wall of gleaming white limestone,

Right: the gold mask of Tutankhamon—this mask covered the face of the pharaoh's *mummy* (preserved body) in his tomb. It shows clearly the artistry of the Egyptian craftsmen.

Below: the Sphinx at Giza (Al Jīzah), with the Pyramid of Chephren behind it. These enormous stone monuments, built some 4,500 years ago, were then —and remain—wonders of the world.

it was a city of magnificent temples and fine houses.

After sailing 300 miles farther up the Nile, ships arrived at Thebes (just across the river from present-day Luxor). At that time, Thebes was an unimportant village. It was, however, destined to become the richest and most powerful city in the world. Nearby, in the barren Valley of the Kings, generations of pharaohs (rulers of Egypt after about 1370 B.C.) would be buried.

By 2000 B.C., Egypt had an estimated population of 750,000. Under King Amenemhet I, the country was entering its most prosperous period. To this Middle Kingdom (2050–1800 B.C.) belongs the finest of Egyptian craftsmanship by jewelers, carpenters, carvers, and glaziers, who worked in gold, silver, colored stones, rare woods, ivory, ebony, and glass. It was also a period when literature, art, and building flourished in the 15-mile-wide strip of land down the long course of the Nile.

About 260 miles northeast of Egypt lay the narrow strip of fertile coast occupied by the Phoenicians. Bordered by the Lebanon Mountains to the east and the Mediterranean on the west, Phoenicia

Below: the Middle East, showing the cities and empires of the ancient world. It was here, and in particular in Egypt on the banks of the Nile and in Sumer between the Tigris and the Euphrates, that civilization first grew up between 5,000 and 6,000 years ago.

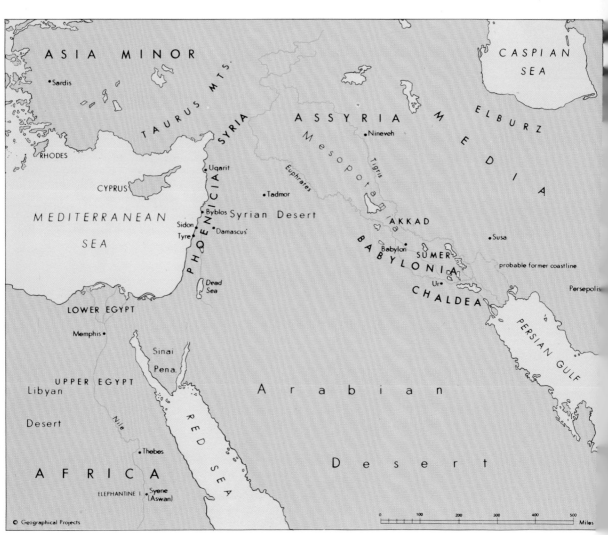

was about 200 miles long and 12 miles wide. At various times the country lay under the influence of Egypt, Babylonia, and the Hittite Empire (in what is now central Turkey), and it did not become independent until about 1100 B.C. Already in 2000 B.C., however, the Phoenicians were a formidable and enterprising people, though their civilization was very different from that of their Egyptian neighbors. They looked seaward for their livelihood, and their coastline was dotted with ports. The largest of these ports were independent city-states ruled by merchant kings. But although not formally united, the Phoenicians cooperated against common enemies. Their main activity was commerce and their greatest skill lay in sailing.

Following the Mediterranean coast to Phoenicia, Egyptian ships came first to the small coastal towns where Phoenician ships lay at anchor. When the sailors saw the snow-capped mountains of Lebanon, they knew they were approaching the important city of Tyre. Built mainly on an offshore island, and partly on the mainland, Tyre was a characteristic Phoenician port. Cities sited on rocky headlands and islands protected by chains of rocks were ideally suited to a maritime people who preferred to fight their battles on the sea. Tyre had two harbors, and the town, closely packed with houses rising to several stories, had been constructed on the rocks. Within this island fortress lived an expanding population of sailors, ship-builders, weavers, cloth dyers, and timber merchants.

Above: ruins of Tyre, the Phoenician seaport built largely on an island, and partly on the adjoining mainland. Below: a clay tablet inscribed in cuneiform (wedge-shaped) letters. The tablet is a letter from the King of Byblos to the ruler of Egypt, asking for help against invaders. Part reads, "...if no troops come, then the territory is lost." In fact, the troops did not come.

Some of Tyre's earliest inhabitants had moved to the city from the nearby port of Sidon, 25 miles farther up the coast. Together, the cities of Sidon and Tyre became famous for their cloth, which was dyed a red-purple color. They exported it to Egypt, and, later, to Greece and Rome where it was made into royal robes.

Yet another hundred miles north lay Byblos, the center of export for the cedarwood that was brought down from the forests on the slopes of the mountains of Lebanon. Byblos was an important trading center, not only for the Egyptians, but also for the peoples of Mesopotamia who traveled regularly to the land of cedars. These people were the Babylonians, descendants of a Semitic race who had conquered the inhabitants of Sumer.

The Babylonians also traded at Ugarit, possibly the most im-

portant of the Phoenician cities. The most northerly Phoenician port, Ugarit was situated opposite the eastern tip of Cyprus. In its royal palace were kept the state archives—clay tablets that recorded the extensive commercial activities of the Phoenicians. But, unlike Tyre and Sidon, the city of Ugarit fell into decay. In time, it was forgotten and only by chance rediscovered in A.D. 1927.

Like the Egyptians, the Phoenicians imported ivory, gold, and other raw materials. In their city workshops, these materials were turned into manufactured goods for export. But, unlike the Egyptians, the Phoenicians were wholesalers, retailers, and deliverers. By carrying their goods across the seas, the Phoenicians gained the experience that enabled them to become the greatest of the world's first explorers.

Above: the Octopus Vase, an elegant example of Minoan pottery. It was made in about 1500 B.C., and shows the octopus among seaweed and coral.

Left: the Throne Room at Knossos. The throne is alabaster, and stone benches are placed against the walls. The paintings of griffins in a landscape are modern reconstructions based on original fragments found in the ruins.

21

In contrast to the heavily fortified Phoenician ports, the towns of the Minoans of Crete—the third great Mediterranean civilization—were unprotected. The island of Crete provided its own defense. Four hundred miles from Egypt, 500 miles from Phoenicia, and about 80 miles from Greece, Crete was, at this time, unassailable. The Minoans also possessed a fleet quite capable of dealing with any marauders who might attempt an attack from the sea. Minoan prosperity, like that of the Phoenicians, depended on trade. During the Middle Minoan period (1900–1580 B.C.), commerce with Egypt, Italy, Spain, and the Middle East made Crete rich. Arriving at the southern port of Komo, ships from Egypt unloaded their cargoes of linen and gold destined for the palace cities of Phaestos, a few miles away, and Mallia and Knossos on the north of the island. From Komo, a well-established road led through the mountains to Knossos.

Knossos was already a busy city which, with its port, had an estimated population of 100,000. It had a royal palace with modern comforts that included bathrooms and flushing water closets. At Knossos lived the king of the region, who united with the rulers of other parts of the island to form a strong federal government. The kings controlled the agriculture, industry, and trade of Crete.

The Cretan standard of living may not have been as high as that of the Egyptians, but, nevertheless, theirs was a civilization which employed the skills of gem cutters, fresco painters, and spinners of delicate glass ornaments. The beautifully painted pottery of the Minoans was renowned. It was their chief export, and was shipped all over the Mediterranean.

Apart from the Egyptians, Phoenicians, and Minoans, no other Mediterranean people who are concerned with the story of exploration were sufficiently advanced by 2000 B.C. to be regarded as a civilization. But the early voyagers from Egypt, Phoenicia, and Crete brought their knowledge and ideas as well as their goods to other communities living around the Mediterranean at this time. And as these communities developed, they produced their own explorers.

Between 2000 B.C. and the first centuries after the birth of Christ, as one great civilization after another rose to power and then declined, the early explorers extended the frontiers of the known world. They journeyed throughout the Mediterranean and into the Atlantic Ocean. They explored the continent of Africa. They crossed the Indian Ocean, and they probed the interior of Asia. In the face of seemingly insurmountable handicaps, they accomplished amazing feats of exploration. They were the forerunners of many great discoverers of far later times, who, without knowing it, were often following the heroic pioneers, the world's first explorers.

Right: the continents of the Old World—Europe, Africa, Asia, and Australia—showing the main physical features and the chief cities of today.

The Egyptians Explore

2

Foreign trade made Egypt the wealthiest country of the ancient world. A civilization of such magnificence could not have come into existence if the nation had been content to rely entirely on its own natural resources. The well-irrigated delta and valley of the Nile provided wheat to feed the people. And there was flax for linen clothing. But these were basic necessities. The standard of luxury reached by the kings and the ruling class by the time of the Old Kingdom (2700–2200 B.C.) required more exotic commodities.

Gold and silver, needed for works of art in palaces and pyramid tombs, were brought from the mines of Syria, Nubia (in present-day Sudan), and from Punt. Copper for making tools and weapons, malachite (a green mineral used for ornaments and mosaics), and turquoise came to Memphis in the saddle-packs of donkeys which followed the caravan routes across the desert from Sinai. To obtain tin, voyages were made to Spain. To provide granite for the great temples of Karnak and Thebes, there were long journeys to the quarries at the First Cataract, more than 100 miles away. Even a vital raw material such as wood had to be brought from Phoenicia.

To obtain these products, the Egyptians had to become ship-builders and sailors. Although they were never such accomplished mariners as the Phoenicians (whom they were later to employ), they learned to navigate their main highway, the Nile, in boats of their own construction. These were combined rowing and sailing ships with curved, pointed prows, designed to land on the riverbanks and to negotiate lagoons and rapids. When the Egyptians ventured into the rougher waters of the Mediterranean, and had to make their way through the coral reefs in the Red Sea, their ships were enlarged, on much the same pattern, into 70-foot-long vessels with oblong sails.

Above: a caravan of Amorite nomads, from a tomb painting of one of the later Egyptian pharaohs. The Egyptian civilization was enriched by goods brought to its cities from distant places. But only some of the luxuries the Egyptians craved could be bought from nomad merchants. For others, they had to travel themselves. Below: a wall-painting of Egyptian goldsmiths (bottom) and carpenters at work.

Above: King Pepy II, who came to the throne when only six years old, seated on his mother's lap. This statue dates from about 2230 B.C. Rulers under the Old Kingdom (2700-2200 B.C.) sent expeditions abroad for the luxuries they could not obtain at home.

For traveling overland, the Egyptians used pack donkeys and bullock carts. Camels, which are commonly associated with Egypt, were not used as carriers until about 500 B.C. Great caravans of pack animals set out regularly from Syene, the most southerly Egyptian town, on journeys into the Sudan lasting for some months. Several such expeditions were made around 2270 B.C. during the reigns of Mernere and his successor, Pepy II (who came to the throne as a child of six), by an explorer named Herkhuf, governor of Egypt's southern province. Herkhuf returned to Egypt with many of the luxuries the Egyptians longed for—ivory, ebony, frankincense, and skins. But from one expedition he brought back a special treasure—a Pygmy from one of the Sudanese tribes. The Pygmy caused a sensation in Egypt, and Herkhuf was rewarded with splendid gifts.

Herkhuf, like the other governors of southern Egypt, was concerned with defending the frontier from attack by Sudanese tribes and protecting Egypt's trading expeditions in Sudan. The governors also organized voyages to Punt, the "land of the gods" at the south of the Red Sea. This country had a legendary fascination for the Egyptians, who believed it to have been the home of their earliest ancestors. And from this land came one of the most highly sought products in all Egypt—incense. To obtain this sweet-scented substance, used in the worship of the gods, the Egyptians undertook some of their longest and most dangerous expeditions.

In about 2500 B.C., King Sahure sent ships to bring back incense from the distant land of Punt. The success of the voyage was proudly recorded. Sahure's ships returned laden, not only with incense, but with quantities of other priceless treasures from the land of the gods. Eighty thousand measures of myrrh, 6,000 weights of electrum (a gold-silver alloy), and 2,600 logs of costly wood (probably ebony) were brought from Punt to Egypt. These figures sound impressive, even though it is not known what the measures represent. The fleet also took back a number of "dwarfs" (Pygmies), who, like Herkhuf's Pygmy after them, were employed as dancers at religious festivals and court entertainments.

Egyptian ships had probably visited Punt before the time of Sahure, but his was the first expedition to have been recorded. Even so, there are no details of the port from which the fleet set out, nor of how many ships there were, nor of how far they traveled. Nor do any of the inscriptions mention where the land of Punt was situated.

For hundreds of years, scholars have tried to discover the whereabouts of this mysterious country which was of such importance to the ancient Egyptians. It now seems certain that Punt was somewhere on the Red Sea coast of Somaliland, but exactly where no one knows. Many other locations have, however, been suggested. Temple inscriptions describe Punt as lying "on both sides of the sea." This has been taken to refer to the point at which the Red Sea narrows to a 20-mile channel between the east coast of Africa and present-day Southern Yemen. Slightly farther south, the land on either side of the Gulf of Tajura near Djibouti in the French Territory of Afars and Issas also fits the description. Because some of the Egyptian expeditions to Punt brought back antimony (used in the making of rouge and for hardening copper), it has been suggested that Punt may have lain as far south as Mozambique—probably the only part of Africa where antimony could have been mined at the time of the Egyptian voyages. But, if so, the Egyptians would have had to travel 4,000 miles down the African coast to reach their destination.

During the centuries after Sahure's expedition, at least 11 further

Mentuhotep sent a trading expedition to the land of Punt.

Right: this map of ancient Egypt shows the voyage to Byblos, the great voyages down the Red Sea to Punt, and Herkhuf's journey into the Sudan.

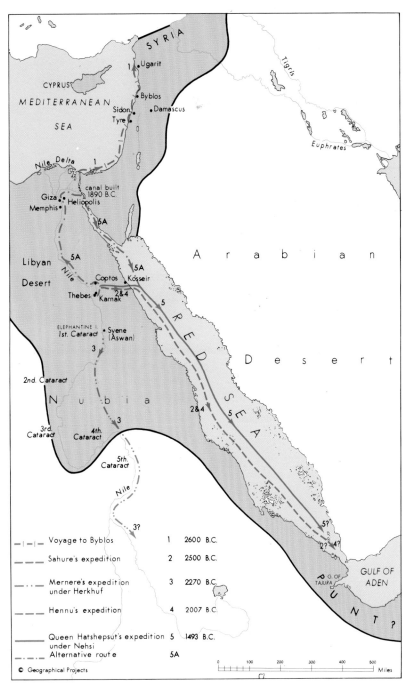

—·—·—	Voyage to Byblos	1	2600 B.C.
— — —	Sahure's expedition	2	2500 B.C.
—···—	Mernere's expedition under Herkhuf	3	2270 B.C.
— — —	Hennu's expedition	4	2007 B.C.
———	Queen Hatshepsut's expedition under Nehsi	5	1493 B.C.
—··—··—	Alternative route	5A	

© Geographical Projects

0   100   200   300   400   500   Miles

Above: the men of Punt bringing their myrrh trees as gifts for the Egyptians. Among all the riches that the explorers brought back from Punt, these trees were valued most highly. The incense they provided was used in ceremonies in the Egyptian temples.

voyages were made to Punt. But nearly 500 years passed before the next expedition of which we have a detailed record. This took place in 2007 B.C., when an Egyptian called Hennu was ordered to send a ship to Punt for myrrh. "I left the Nile," wrote Hennu, "with 3,000 men." Why so many? Apparently only one ship set sail down the Red Sea for Punt. The great majority of the men were probably slaves needed to carry the materials necessary for building ships across the 90 miles of desert from one of the Nile cities to the sea. Until a canal was dug between the Nile Delta and the Red Sea by Sesostris II in about 1890 B.C., this was Egypt's only way of transporting ships to its eastern seaboard. Hennu records that he sank 15 wells for drinking water on the journey, and issued each man with 2 jars of water and 20 small loaves a day during the march. Then, writes Hennu, "I reached the sea, built the ship, and sent it off."

After Hennu's expedition, the Egyptians appear to have lost interest in seafaring and travel. Concerned with their own internal prosperity, religious cults, and civilized living, they were content to let the ships and caravans of other countries carry their goods for them. But the use of these middlemen inevitably led to an increase in the cost of merchandise. This may well have been one reason for

Left: Hennu, who in 2007 B.C. took a ship to Punt for myrrh. In the 500 years before Hennu's voyage, no detailed records were kept of Egyptian journeys to Punt. Hennu, however, left details of his expedition, and of the organization of the trip.

the greatest of all the Egyptian expeditions to Punt, which was carried out by order of Queen Hatshepsut in 1493 B.C.

Queen Hatshepsut was the first woman to rule Egypt. Officially coregent, first with her husband and then with her stepson, she gradually assumed all the powers of state, and adopted the titles of ruler for herself alone. She was a gifted, ruthless, and beautiful woman. Her profile portrait, preserved among the rock carvings of her temple at Thebes, shows her with almond eyes, full lips, a finely modeled nose, and a graceful neck.

At the time of Hatshepsut's rise to power in about 1500 B.C., more than 500 years had passed since the last Egyptian voyage to Punt. The vital supplies of incense, which Egypt imported from abroad, were in greater demand than ever. One temple alone is reported to have burned over 300,000 bushels of incense on its altars in a single year. This incense was brought in heavily guarded caravans from the Hadhramaut in southern Arabia, and by the time it reached Egypt it had become extremely expensive. At the same time, the mines of Nubia, Egypt's chief source of gold, had been worked out, and the country was running short of funds with which to purchase such costly imports. Hatshepsut desperately needed to find a way of breaking the Hadhramaut's incense monopoly and of replenishing her stocks of gold.

It was probably Hatshepsut's ambitious chancellor and chief adviser, Senmut, who suggested that the queen should organize an expedition to the land of Punt. Senmut may have gained some knowledge of Hennu's expedition to Punt from inscriptions on the rocks of a tomb in the Wadi Hammamat, a stone-quarrying center to the northeast of Thebes between the Nile and the Red Sea. At all events, Senmut knew that both incense and gold were to be found in Punt and that, if Hatshepsut could succeed in repeating the journey of her forebears, it would add greatly to her prestige as queen.

Although economic necessity and personal ambition may have been the primary motives for the expedition, a less material inspiration was Hatshepsut's devotion to Egypt's state god Amon-Re. To the glory of this king of gods, Hatshepsut built a magnificent new temple at Thebes. Cut into the massive yellow cliffs on the west bank of the Nile, this temple remains today in a fair state of preservation. It is possible to visualize the great stepped terraces leading up to the temple where Queen Hatshepsut planted the myrrh trees that her sailors brought back from Punt.

As no Egyptian ships had sailed to Punt for so long, there was some doubt about the wisdom of the expedition. But the oracle of the god was consulted, and it pronounced firmly that the route was to be re-explored. Ships were prepared for the voyage and the crews were carefully chosen. The expedition was placed under the leadership of a man named Nehsi.

Left: Egyptians rowing to Punt, from the temple at Thebes. Although the ships had sails, for much of the time they relied on slaves to row them.

Right: Queen Hatshepsut in the form of a sphinx. She was a forceful, ambitious woman who came to power first as the wife of her half-brother Thutmose II. After his death, she took over his power, and her monuments show a truly regal dignity.

The carvings in Hatshepsut's temple at Thebes show five ships departing for Punt, but this may be symbolic. It seems probable that 20 or more vessels set sail for the south. Their port of departure is a matter of speculation. Like Hennu's ship, the vessels, or the materials for building them, were probably carried across the desert from Coptos (modern Kuft), on the east bank of the Nile, to the Red Sea port of Kosseir (modern Al Qusayr), about 300 miles south of Suez. But possibly Queen Hatshepsut had reopened the Nile-Red Sea canal which had been allowed to silt up since its creation by Sesostris II 400 years earlier. If so, the ships would have set out from Thebes, sailed north down the Nile to the delta, turned east into the canal, and been hauled or rowed through this man-made waterway to the head of the Gulf of Suez. Depending on the exact location of Punt, the whole voyage may have taken as little as 14 months or as long as 3 years.

On arrival, the fleet anchored offshore, and the Egyptians presented King Perehu and Queen Eti of Punt with gifts of knives, necklaces, and glass beads. During this ceremony, it is recorded, the Egyptian sailors could hardly conceal their laughter at the extraordinary appearance of Queen Eti. With her broad shoulders, stunted torso, and thick, misshapen thighs, she was unlike any woman they had ever seen.

The people of Punt prepared a banquet for Nehsi and his crew, and friendly relations were soon established between the two peoples. Then, the business of trading began. The Egyptians probably exchanged glass beads and trinkets for the incense trees and other treasures that were carefully counted out or weighed. Thirty-one saplings, each in a special wooden tub, were carried to the ships and stowed on board. Soon the Egyptian vessels were "very heavy with marvels of the land of Punt; all goodly fragrant woods of God's Land, heaps of incense-resin, fresh incense trees, ebony and pure ivory, gold . . . cinnamon wood, eye cosmetic, baboons, monkeys, dogs, skins of the southern panther. . . ." The Egyptians also took with them some of the people of Punt, "natives and their children,"

Above: a model of an Egyptian sea-going ship. Originally, the Egyptians built their ships from reeds because there was little wood in Egypt. But reed boats were often unseaworthy, and the Egyptians began to use wood from the Sinai Peninsula. Later, they imported Phoenician cedarwood.

Below left: the Egyptian party giving the gifts they had brought with them to King Perehu and Queen Eti of Punt.

together with portraits of Punt's rulers, King Perehu and Queen Eti.

The return of Nehsi and his crew to Egypt was greeted with a wave of popular enthusiasm. A public holiday was proclaimed and the explorers marched through the streets in procession, carrying the treasures of the land of Punt for all to see. There were speeches, banquets, and religious celebrations. The mariners were given a royal reception in Queen Hatshepsut's palace, where Hatshepsut sat on her throne with Nehsi and Senmut at her feet. All around her lay piles of exotic goods, incense, and precious metals. "Such a treasure," the temple inscription ends, "was never brought for any king who has ruled since the beginning."

No other Egyptian expedition was on a comparable scale. After Queen Hatshepsut's death in 1482 B.C., her stepson and successor Thutmose III engaged in a series of military campaigns to expand the Egyptian Empire. Under his leadership, Egyptian armies pushed north and east through Palestine and Syria. When they reached the Euphrates River, it is recorded, elephant hunts were organized in which as many as 120 animals were killed for their tusks. On this occasion, Thutmose, who had come unscathed through all his military adventures, narrowly escaped death when a huge elephant charged him.

During his reign, which lasted until about 1436 B.C., Thutmose commissioned the Minoans of Crete to do much of the fetching and

Below: a procession of Egyptians carrying palms, from the records of the expedition at Thebes.

Above: Thutmose III (right), the stepson and successor of Hatshepsut. This portrait is on a colonnade at Thebes. Thutmose spent much of his reign fighting in Palestine and Syria, and under him the Egyptian Empire reached its greatest size.

carrying of Egyptian trading goods. At that time, the Minoans were masters of the Mediterranean, and their ships were to be seen in every port from Byblos to the shores of southern Spain. But the power and civilization of Crete came to a sudden and dramatic end soon after it had reached its greatest heights. In about 1400 B.C. Crete lay in ruins. Possibly an earthquake destroyed the island, but it may have fallen before invading forces from the city of Mycenae in southern Greece.

Five hundred years later, Egypt, torn by internal strife and weakened by foreign invaders, had also lost much of its former greatness. This decline in Egypt's power was recorded in the travel diary of Wen-Amun, an envoy sent to the Phoenicians in 1080 B.c.

The Egyptians were going to Phoenicia for cedarwood as they had done ever since that first recorded expedition in 2600 B.C. Wen-Amun had been commissioned to obtain the wood for the temple of Amon-Re at Thebes. But the high priest of the temple had supplied him with only limited goods for exchange, and Egypt no longer possessed the prestige to compensate for this lack of funds.

Wen-Amun was treated badly. He was robbed and insulted. "The prince of Byblos sent to tell me, 'Get out of my harbor,' " he wrote. For 19 days Wen-Amun was kept waiting before being summoned to see the prince, who asked him haughtily, "What kind of beggar's journey is this that you have been sent on?"

Vainly did Wen-Amun remind the prince of happy historical precedents. It had no effect until a messenger who had been sent back to Egypt returned with sufficient goods to exchange for the cedars. Even then, Wen-Amun was harried during the loading of the timber, and, as a final insult, the prince told him: "See that you get on your way, and do not make the bad time of the year an excuse for remaining here."

The star of Egypt was in decline. Rising now to dominate the whole scene of exploration were the Phoenicians. These daring and accomplished sailors embarked on more distant and ambitious voyages than any undertaken by the mariners of Egypt. The Phoenicians made themselves the masters of the Mediterranean Sea and became the first explorers to venture through the Strait of Gibraltar into the vast and unknown waters of the Atlantic Ocean.

Above: a pendant from Byblos, inlaid with semiprecious stones. Dating from about 2000 B.C., this pendant was probably made by a local artist, influenced by Egyptian craftsmen.

Left: an Egyptian wall-painting of two figures, identified as Minoans, carrying ingots. Thutmose III hired the Minoans of Crete to do much of the transportation of Egyptian goods.

Below: Phoenician *hippoi*—river craft
—shown on a wall relief in a palace
at Khorsabad, Iraq. The Phoenician
boats, which are manned by oarsmen
are carrying cedar logs for trading.

Phoenician Pioneers

3

About 600 years before the birth of Christ, a fleet of vessels set out on an extraordinary 23,000-mile journey into the unknown. Manned by Phoenician sailors, these ships were embarking on one of the greatest voyages in the history of exploration—the first circumnavigation of Africa.

This was a voyage so extraordinary for its time that many people doubt whether it could ever have taken place. There is evidence that the Phoenicians were making trading voyages as early as 2700 B.C. Their prowess as sailors is recorded in the Old Testament and in classical writings. From tools, weapons, and other such remains discovered in various places, archaeologists have been able to plot the extent of many of the Phoenician voyages. But no trace has ever been found of their feat of circumnavigation. Is it possible that the Phoenicians could have made such a journey over 2,000 years before the generally accepted first rounding of the African continent by the Portuguese? And what kind of people were the Phoenician explorers who might have undertaken such a daring expedition?

Above: an old map showing Phoenicia, on the eastern coast of the Mediterranean.

37

Above: Phoenician pendants, glass beads in the shape of heads, modeled on a sand core in Carthage before 300 B.C. The Phoenicians established their colonies all around the Mediterranean.

Below: a goddess carved in ivory, from what is now Syria. It shows the influence of similar figures from the Aegean area, particularly in the flounced skirt and bare chest, and demonstrates the Phoenician aware-ness of the world in which they traded.

The Phoenicians were the Canaanites of the Old Testament. They were a Semitic race, believed to have originated in the Persian Gulf area. In about 3000 B.C., they settled in the land between the mountains of Lebanon and the Mediterranean Sea. There they founded the cities of Sidon and Tyre, probably naming Tyre after their original home on the island of Tyros (modern Bahrain in the Persian Gulf). Their 200-mile coastline was fertile but they were prevented from expanding eastward by hostile neighbors. As the Phoenician population grew, their small country became over-crowded. It was logical that when this happened they should turn increasingly to the sea for their living.

Ideally situated for trade halfway between two prosperous nations—Egypt and the land of the Hittites—the Phoenicians began to make their living by fetching and carrying merchandise by both land and sea. Phoenicia was on the main caravan routes between northern Africa and the Mesopotamian countries, and the Phoenicians carried goods overland as far as Babylon. As the earliest traders to operate according to an organized plan, they spread out farther and farther from their great seaports, founding small colonies all over the Mediterranean. Phoenician colonies grew up in Sicily and Cyprus, and as far west as Cádiz in southern Spain. They even had a small trading post at Memphis in the commercial heart of Egypt.

The Phoenicians combined their abilities as traders with other skills. They were miners, metallurgists, shipbuilders, and dyers. The cedar forests of Lebanon gave them timber which they sold abroad, and another valuable export was the transparent glass that they made from the white sand of their seashore. The alphabet which they invented around 1000 B.C. formed the basis of the Greek alphabet, on which were later founded the Roman and all western alphabets.

The Phoenicians' fame as dyers probably gave rise to their name Phoenician comes from a Greek word meaning red-purple, an allusion to the special dye that they used. The dye came from a shellfish found on the Syrian shore that gave off a defensive juice called purpura. Cloth dyed in this juice was in great demand all over the East, where the color became a mark of rank and dignity.

It might have been hoped that so versatile a race, and the inventor of the alphabet, would have left records of their early exploration But the Phoenicians appear to have been deliberately secretive keeping all knowledge of their sea routes and discoveries to them selves. If they wrote down their achievements, nothing has survived In later centuries, they even went so far as to wreck one of their ow ships rather than give away its destination to a Roman competitor.

Because of this mystery about their voyages, stories of th Phoenicians' achievements are not as widely believed today as on they were. And the theory that for hundreds of years the Phoeniciar held absolute trade monopolies all over the Mediterranean has als encountered some opposition. Archaeological findings indicate th

the Minoans rather than the Phoenicians must be given greater
credit for pioneering voyages in the Mediterranean. But with the
decline of Crete in about 1400 B.C., the Phoenician ascendancy began,
and the Phoenicians have a strong claim to being the first people to
have explored the whole Mediterranean from one end to the other.

Historians believe that Phoenician sailors were the first to learn
how to navigate by the Pole Star. Their maritime accomplishments
were so widely recognized in ancient times that other nations often
found it more profitable to employ Phoenician sailors as carriers
than to build their own fleets.

In about 950 B.C., the Phoenicians supplied ships and sailors for
a great expedition ordered by King Solomon of Israel. Their voyage
is recorded in the Old Testament: "And King Solomon made a navy
of ships in Ezion-Geber [Elat, at the head of the Gulf of Aqaba] on
the shore of the Red Sea. . . . And Hiram [king of Tyre in Phoenicia]
sent in the navy his servants, shipmen that had knowledge of the sea,
with the servants of Solomon. And they came to Ophir, and fetched
from thence gold, four hundred and twenty talents, and brought it
to King Solomon. . . ." The Old Testament also mentions the bringing back of "gold and silver, ivory and apes and peacocks" from
Ophir.

Ophir was famous for its fine gold, and it could possibly have been
the same land of Punt to which the Egyptians had traveled.
Solomon's fleet may have ventured far beyond the Red Sea, for the

39

Right: a kneeling bronze figure of King Necho. According to Herodotus, he sponsored an expedition which sailed around the continent of Africa.

Below: the servants of Hiram of Tyro with King Solomon, from the Great Bible of King Henry VIII of England. Hiram and Solomon sent a fleet to the land of Ophir—probably in southern Arabia—to bring back gold and other precious goods.

voyage is said to have taken three years. The peacocks that they brought back could have come only from India or Ceylon, and it is possible that the fleet reached the shores of India. It seems probable, however, that Ophir lay in southern Arabia, a region that had grown immensely wealthy on the proceeds of the incense trade and where Indian merchants also came to exchange their wares.

The Phoenicians played a major part in the voyage to Ophir. Solomon's people did not care for the sea and had little experience of sailing. When they tried, on another occasion, to make a voyage to Ophir on their own, their ships are said to have fallen apart soon after being launched. The success of such an expedition depended on the shipbuilding and navigational skills of the Phoenicians. If the Phoenicians did indeed make a voyage around the African continent in about 600 B.C., those skills would have been tested to the utmost.

It is said that the Phoenician voyage around Africa was commissioned by King Necho of Egypt, who wanted to find out if he could establish a sea route from the Red Sea to the Mediterranean. At that time, no one had the faintest idea of the extent of the African continent. If King Necho did indeed sponsor such a voyage, he must have believed that if ships sailed beyond Punt, they would soon circle around the southern land mass, and so find themselves at the western end of the Mediterranean. In any case, neither he nor the sailors could have had any conception that this would mean a journey of about 23,000 miles.

The only record of this fantastic exploit is this short account by the Greek historian Herodotus, who was writing 150 years after the event:

"As for Libya [Africa], we know that it is washed on all sides by the sea except where it joins Asia, as was first demonstrated, so far as our knowledge goes, by Necho, the Egyptian king, who, after calling off the construction of the canal between the Nile and the Arabian Gulf, sent out a fleet manned by a Phoenician crew with orders to sail west-about and return to Egypt and the Mediterranean by way of the Strait of Gibraltar. The Phoenicians sailed from the Arabian Gulf into the southern ocean, and every autumn put in at some convenient spot on the Libyan coast, sowed a patch of ground,

ight: a Phoenician silver bowl. The
terior is decorated with gilt, while
e friezes around the outside show
enes of combat between warriors and
ns, sphinxes, and winged griffins
abulous animals, part lion, and part
gle). At various times, Phoenicia
y within the empires of Egypt and
abylonia, and the Phoenician culture
ars strong traces of their influence.

41

Left: Herodotus, the great Greek historian and traveler, who came to be known as "The Father of History." His is the only account of the Phoenician voyage around Africa, and many scholars doubt the truth of his report. One point in Herodotus' story indicates that such a voyage had taken place—but this point Herodotus himself did not believe. He records that the sailors reported that when they sailed west around the south of Africa, the sun was on their right—that is, to the north. When sailing west in the Southern Hemisphere, the sun does appear on the right at noon.

ΗΡΟΛΟΤΟΣ

Above: coral islands in the Red Sea off the coast of Ethiopia. By 600 B.C., the canal between the Red Sea and the Nile had fallen into disuse. Necho may have ordered a voyage around Africa to find a new way from the Red Sea to the Mediterranean Sea.

and waited for next year's harvest. Then, having got in their grain, they put to sea again, and after two full years rounded the Pillars of Hercules [Strait of Gibraltar] in the course of the third, and returned to Egypt. These men made a statement which I do not myself believe, though others may, to the effect that as they sailed on a westerly course round the southern end of Libya, they had the sun on their right—to northward of them. This is how Libya was first discovered to be surrounded by sea. . . ."

Tantalizingly inadequate though it is, Herodotus' account has become a central part of the belief that the Phoenicians are among the greatest sailors in history. For, if this voyage did take place, it must rank as one of the most amazing feats of seamanship ever accomplished.

Herodotus himself apparently accepted the circumnavigation as a fact, except for the Phoenicians' story about the position of the sun. Yet, if anything, this is the most authentic detail of the account. For ships sailing in a westerly direction in the Southern Hemisphere would indeed find that, at noon, the sun was on their right, that is, to the north of them. The very remark which made Herodotus' report seem incredible in his own time indicates that daring sailors did make a successful voyage around the African continent at a very early date.

There have been many attempts to amplify Herodotus' brief statement and to reconstruct the details of the Phoenician voyage. Those who believe that the voyage really took place point out that King Necho had a good reason for promoting it. He was eager to stimulate Egyptian trade and had been trying to reopen the ancient canal between the Red Sea and the Nile which had fallen into disuse over the centuries. But this work was halted when Necho was warned by an oracle that the canal would help enemies to invade his country. He was therefore anxious to know if there was any route other than the Nile canal by which ships could get from the Red Sea into the Mediterranean. He was curious to discover how long it would take to travel by such a route, and to find out what trading possibilities existed beyond Punt. An added incentive for such a voyage was the report that gold was to be found in what is now Rhodesia.

It is interesting to see just how the Phoenicians could have carried out this long and hazardous voyage. They would probably have made the voyage in the same large compact vessels, with a high convex prow and stern, that they used for trading voyages. These ships may have been as much as 130 feet long and 33 feet across. They had covered decks and a single large sail. They were manned by 30 to 50 oarsmen. In addition, they must have carried a few replacements in case of illness or death, and possibly a certain number of soldiers, together with a group of officers under the captain.

With their fragile ships, and primitive equipment, the Phoenicians would have seized gratefully on the natural advantages of wind or current to help them on their way. Any reconstruction of their voyage can therefore best be based on just those same natural conditions. The expedition would have set out from the Gulf of Aqaba, probably in late November. The ships must have been fully equipped for a long voyage and, according to Herodotus, they carried a fast-growing wheat which could be planted and reaped for food during the journey.

The autumn start meant that the northeast monsoon was against the Phoenician sailors, and they would have had to row until they were out of the Red Sea. But, when they had rounded Cape Guardafui on the northeastern tip of Somaliland, the same monsoon would have helped them down the coast of Somaliland as far as the equator. In spring, they could take advantage of the southeast trade wind to reach the Mozambique Channel between mainland Mozambique and the Malagasy Republic. Once the ships were in this channel, the swift-

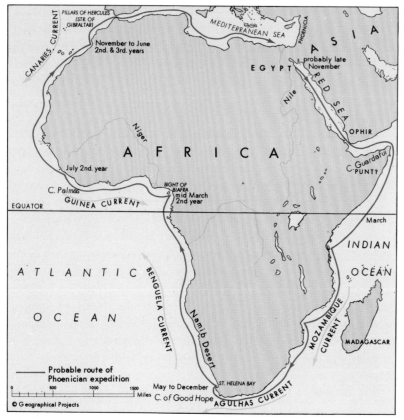

Left: the African continent, showing the probable route of the Phoenicians on their 23,000-mile expedition around Africa, 600 years before the birth of Christ. The map also shows the main currents which would have helped or hindered the Phoenicians on such a long and perilous voyage.

flowing South Equatorial Current would have borne them south-ward, and the Agulhas Current helped to carry them around the southern tip of Africa.

At this point in their voyage, the Phoenicians would have entered dangerous waters. The passage around the Cape of Good Hope is a treacherous one, where sudden squalls are frequent and the belt of westerly winds now known as the "roaring forties" can sweep vessels far out to sea. The Phoenicians must have edged their way slowly along 1,000 miles of coastline between what are now Port Elizabeth and Cape Town.

As they rounded Cape Agulhas, they would have found that at last the coastline was running northward. In May or June, they may have landed, probably about 150 miles up the west coast of Africa in

Above: a Phoenician galley, of the kind used for long voyages. It has two banks of oars with a deck above, and along the deck are hung the warriors' shields. Although such ships had a single sail, they were often rowed. Necho's men would have used ships like this.

45

St. Helena Bay. There, they would have sown their first crop of wheat, repaired their vessels, and rested while they waited for the wheat to ripen. In the subtropical climate of southern Africa, seed sown in early June would have been ready for reaping by November. With fresh grain in their holds, the ships would have started northward in December. They would now have been away from Egypt for over a year.

With the aid of a favorable south wind and the Benguela Current, the Phoenician ships could have made steady progress up the West African coast. But soon they would have faced another hazard—lack

Below: reaping wheat, shown in an Egyptian painting on papyrus. According to Herodotus, Necho's expedition took a fast-growing wheat which the men planted and harvested during the voyage.

of water. Along the coast of South West Africa lies the Namib Desert—1,000 miles of desolate shore which receives less than an inch of rainfall a year. Because of the threat of death from thirst, the Phoenicians must have left this part of the coast behind them as quickly as possible.

With wind and current still in their favor, they would probably have reached the Bight of Biafra, off present-day Nigeria and Cameroon, in mid-March of the second year. But, as the explorers advanced into the Gulf of Guinea, they would have met with a combination of contrary winds and currents, interspersed with unexpected calms. For 2,000 miles, they must have battled against these grueling adversities, pulling hard on their long oars in the heat of the tropical sun. As the weeks and months went by, their voyage must have seemed endless. It was probably late June by the time they rounded Cape Palmas in what is now Liberia, only to find that now the Canary Current was against them.

The Phoenicians may have made their second long stop on the coast of Senegal, or continued as far as the Atlantic coast of Morocco, where they could have sown their wheat in December and reaped it the following June. From there, it was a relatively short haul up the Moroccan coast and through the Strait of Gibraltar. Once in the Mediterranean, the Phoenicians would have been in familiar waters.

Above: sunset at Lanzarote looking toward the island of Fuerteventura in the Canaries. Necho's expedition would have sailed near here on their way to the Strait of Gibraltar.

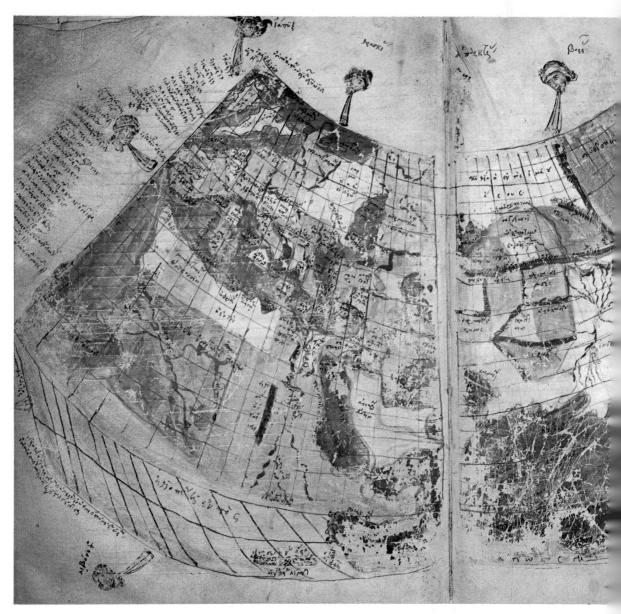

Above: a map of the world drawn in the 1200's. This map is based on the writings of the Greek geographer Ptolemy, who summed up what the ancient world knew about geography. The map pictures Africa as part of a great southern land mass, which seems to indicate either that Ptolemy knew nothing about the Phoenician expedition, or that he did not believe Herodotus' account.

The terrible uncertainties and sufferings of their long voyage were over. Neutral winds, generally favorable currents, and the sailors' own enthusiastic efforts on the home stretch would have carried the fleet safely along the north coast of Africa to the mouth of the Nile, and Egypt.

On their journey around the African continent, the Phoenicians would have had to follow every indentation of the 22,921-mile-long coastline, except in the familiar Red Sea and Mediterranean. They probably completed their journey in about three years, which (if two six-month harvesting periods are deducted) works out at a reasonable daily average of about 30 miles.

There was probably no great celebration for the returning heroes. They had brought no gold or treasure back, and their momentous

voyage had only served to prove that the route around Africa was far too long and dangerous to be considered for trading purposes. As they told the story of their voyage, one of the main points of discussion must have been the size of the African continent.

Why did Herodotus not mention this in his account? He believed, like others of his time, that the east coast of Africa turned west not far below the Gulf of Aden. The great southward extension of Africa would therefore have been one of the expedition's most remarkable discoveries. There are other questions that provide evidence for those who doubt the reality of the Phoenician voyage. Why did Herodotus fail to name the leader of the expedition? Why does he give no details of the lands that the explorers visited, or the wild beasts and the men that they must have encountered? Why are there no parallel accounts of the voyage? Later historians—Greek, Arabian, or Roman—do not confirm it. Was such a voyage remotely feasible in such early ships and without a compass? Would the Phoenicians have embarked on a long voyage in an area where they knew nothing of the prevailing winds and currents?

The most likely explanation of why Herodotus, normally an excellent reporter, was brief in his account is that his information was based on hearsay. It is possible that King Necho died before his expedition got back, and because the voyage had achieved none of its commercial aims, his successor failed to keep an official record of it. But it is equally possible that the whole incident was a fiction—a traveler's tale exaggerated over the decades. Even thorough sifting of the evidence leaves the verdict open. The Phoenician circumnavigation of Africa remains the greatest unsolved mystery in the history of exploration.

Right: a painted Egyptian pot showing giraffes. It is upon remains such as this that scholars must base their theories about ancient times. For example, this vase can be taken to prove that the Egyptians had penetrated deep into Africa, for giraffes only live south of the Sahara.

West from Carthage

4

With their eyes ever looking out to sea, the Phoenicians were ill prepared to defend themselves against attack from the rear. Their cities, built on islands off the coast or on inaccessible headlands, gave them some protection from invaders. But as a people they were not unified nor collectively strong, and they eventually fell victim to the powerful armies of their Mesopotamian neighbors. When the Assyrians from the northern part of Mesopotamia swept down on Phoenicia in the 800's B.C., the Phoenician city-states withstood long sieges, but could not hold out indefinitely.

Tyre resisted longest, but in 668 B.C., even this island fortress was forced to capitulate to King Ashurbanipal of Assyria after a nine-year siege. Just under 100 years later, this "crowning city whose merchants are princes," as it is described in the Old Testament, was conquered again, this time by King Nebuchadnezzar II of Babylonia. This defeat, which was achieved after a siege of 13 years, brought the whole of Phoenicia under Babylonian rule.

The time had come for the Phoenicians to find a new home. Moreover, now that the whole Mediterranean had been opened up, a site farther west would be better placed geographically than Phoenicia as a trading center. They chose a small port on the north coast of Africa in what is now Tunisia, where there had been Phoenician settlers for some 200 years. They developed it into their new city-state of Carthage.

To the Phoenicians, Carthage seemed an ideal spot for their new capital. Like Tyre, it was well situated for defense. It was built on a triangular peninsula joined to the mainland by a narrow strip of land, and was backed by the Lake of Tunis. Besides, according to Phoenician legend, Carthage had a royal history. Dido, a princess of Tyre, was said to have fled there with some of her people. Grandniece of the notorious Jezebel of the Bible, Dido was a fugitive not from the Assyrians, but from her tyrannical brother, King Pygmalion. She sailed first to Cyprus, and then along the desert shores of Libya to the Tunisian headland nearest Sicily.

Above left: an artist's reconstruction of Carthage as the city would have appeared at the height of its power. Notice particularly the inner harbor, with its circular enclosing wall. Left: the ruins of Carthage today, with the sea in the distance.

Above: Ashurbanipal, the Assyrian king who captured Tyre after a nine-year siege, shown taking part in a lion hunt. He was the last great king of Assyria.

Right: a mosaic from Carthage, showing the earth goddess of the city. After the fall of Phoenicia in the 500's B.C., Carthage became the center of the Phoenician world. It grew into a capital whose riches and luxury were a legend in ancient times.

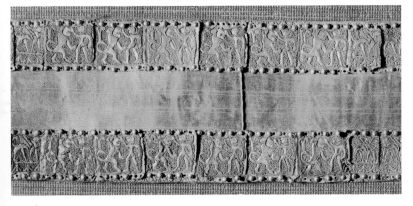

Left: a gold belt, showing Phoenician craftsmanship with fine metals. Like many Phoenician treasures, this belt shows foreign influence, probably that of the Etruscans who lived in Italy.

There, according to colorful legend, Dido asked Iarbas, the local king, for land on which to settle, and he derisively agreed to let her have as much as she could cover with an oxhide. But he was no match for a Phoenician. Dido cut up the hide into thin strips, and with these was able to encircle all the land she needed for a fortress. Her city was called *Kart-hadasht*—Carthage—meaning *New Capital* or *New City*.

The earliest archaeological remains found at Carthage date from about 750 B.C., although according to tradition it was founded in 814 B.C. Little is, however, known about the city until it was chosen as the new Phoenician capital. Within 300 years, Carthage had become a capital far greater than Tyre or Byblos, a city of gleaming white buildings and rich palaces overlooked by a marble temple. At the height of its power, the main city covered 30 square miles. About 70,000 people lived within a surrounding wall, some 40 feet high and 18 miles long. Determined never to suffer the fate of Tyre, Carthage maintained a garrison of 20,000 infantrymen and 4,000 cavalry. In its stables stamped and trumpeted 300 elephants of war— like those which Hannibal was later to make the most famous in history.

The most impressive feature of Carthage was its harbor. Divided into an inner and an outer section, this was a remarkable piece of maritime architecture. The inner harbor was circular, and built around a small central island. It was about 1,000 feet in diameter, and there was docking space for 200 ships. On the island was the naval headquarters, a tall building commanding a view of the sea. The harbor entrance, about 70 feet wide, could be closed against a marauding enemy by chains, and the whole harbor was surrounded by a wall so that it was possible to keep secret the number of vessels at anchor.

Out of this harbor sailed the Carthaginian warships. They patrolled the narrowest neck of water in the Mediterranean—the 00-mile wide Strait of Sicily—and so controlled all seaborne trade between east and west. From Carthage, their long ships set out for even more distant horizons. From about 550 B.C., their attention was fixed on the "outer sea" beyond the Strait of Gibraltar. The Atlantic offered them new trade routes and fresh sources of wealth.

The West African coast awaited development. From a new found port in Spain they explored farther west and discovered Madeira, the Canary Islands, and the Azores.

Carthaginian ruthlessness in trade can be seen in the way they dealt with the Tartessians, a wealthy seagoing people who occupied a large area of southern Spain. These people knew one of the greatest secrets of the "outer sea"—the way to the Tin Islands. These islands were a source of mineral wealth lying somewhere in northern waters as yet unknown to the Carthaginians. The Phoenicians were at first content to act as carriers, taking silver and tin from Tartessus across to the eastern end of the Mediterranean. But after 500 B.C., no more is heard of the Tartessians. It is thought that the Carthaginians destroyed them and seized their trade.

To develop this trade for themselves, the Carthaginians needed a good port on the Atlantic seaboard. They decided on Gades (modern Cádiz), where there had been a small Phoenician settlement since about 1100 B.C. Gades lay off the southwest coast of Spain in a typically strategic position at the end of a long island, which today

is attached to the Spanish mainland by a narrow arm of land.

It was from Gades that a Carthaginian navigator named Himilco set out in about 450 B.C. on the first recorded voyage into the North Atlantic. According to the Roman historian Pliny, Himilco's orders were "to explore the utmost bounds of Europe," a brief which undoubtedly included a search for the Tin Islands. Although some tin was mined in Spain, the supply was inadequate for the growing needs of the Mediterranean peoples, who needed it as an ingredient of bronze. Bronze—a mixture of nine parts of copper to one part of tin—was vital for making strong, durable weapons and tools as well as utensils and ornaments.

Himilco's voyage lasted for four months, but the records of his achievements are sparse. His expedition is referred to in Pliny's *Natural History*, which was published in A.D. 77, and in a poem called *Ora Maritima,* which was based on a Greek legend and was written by the Roman poet Avienus in the A.D. 300's. It seems likely that Himilco followed a route given to the Carthaginians under duress by the defeated Tartessians. This route is thought to have

Above: one of the H-shaped ingots of Cornish tin which were exported to the Mediterranean area. Tin was a very valuable commodity, needed to mix with copper to produce bronze.

Below: a Phoenician round ship, of the type used for trading voyages. It was smaller than the galley, but, like galleys, had two banks of oars.

Map labels

24°   50° 16°   8°   0°   8°

NORTH SEA

ATLANTIC

OCEAN

BRITISH ISLES

Land's End · Cornwall
SCILLY IS.   ICTIS

ENGLISH CHANNEL

Rhine

Loire

Danube

Rhone

Rhône

Massalia
(Marseilles)

Antipolis
(Antibes)

CORSICA

C. St. Vincent

Tartessus

BALEARIC IS.

SARDINIA

(Alicante)

M E D I T E

STR. OF SICILY

ADEIRA

PILLARS OF HERCULES
(STR. OF GIBRALTAR)

Gades
Cádiz

(Málaga)

Carthage

STR. OF SICILY

Thymiaterium

Sebou

(Mogador)

G R E A T   A T L A S

CANARY IS.

to Cerne

(Agadir)

Draa

Legend

Egypt during Middle Kingdom c.2000 B.C.

Phoenicia & her colonies 1200–573 B.C.

Greece & her colonies (greatest extent) 750–350 B.C.

Carthage & her colonies (greatest extent) 550–140 B.C.

.... Egyptian trade routes

– – – Minoan trade routes

——— Phoenician trade routes

——— Greek trade routes

– – – Carthaginian trade routes

8°   © Geographical Projects

TROPIC OF CANCER   0°   8°

0   100   200   300   400   500   Miles

Above: the Mediterranean world between 2000 B.C. and 140 B.C. This map shows the civilizations which, in succession, dominated the area, controlling trade and initiating exploration. Earliest of these civilizations were those of Egypt, Crete, and Phoenicia. At first the Minoans of Crete held power in the Medi-

Vistula

Dnepr

Don

CASPIAN

SEA

CAUCASUS

42°

BLACK SEA

Danube

BOSPORUS

DARDANELLES

AEGEAN

SEA

GREECE

Phocaeas

Ephesus

SAMOS

Miletus

(Messina)

Peloponnesus

Mycene

(Syracuse)

Knossos   Maltia

CRETE Komo   Phaestos

ASSYRIA

Tigris

Mesopotamia

34

Euphrates

Ugarit

PHOENICIA

CYPRUS

Babylon

Byblos

Sidon

Tyre

A N   E A N   S E A

Cyrene

Naucratis

Giza

(Al-Jizah) Heliopolis

Memphis

Ezion-Geber

(Elat)

Sinai

Pena.

L i b y a n

EGYPT

26

Nile

RED

SEA

D e s e r t

Kosseira

Coptos

Thebes

to

Ophir

& Punt

TROPIC OF CANCER

24°   32°   40°

...erranean but, after about 1400 B.C., the Phoenicians succeeded them. The Greeks
...nd the Carthaginians—last of the great Mediterranean powers before the rise
...f the Roman Empire—existed alongside one another. The Greeks were mainly
...ctive in the eastern Mediterranean, while Carthage controlled trade in the west.

taken him up the Atlantic coast of Spain in search of the northern lands from which the Tartessians obtained their supplies of tin.

At the start of the voyage, Himilco encountered calms, shallows, and seaweed, which entangled oars and keels, and slowed down his ships. This has been interpreted as meaning that he went as far southwest as the Sargasso Sea, a large tract of water in the North Atlantic, about 2,000 miles west of the Canary Islands, notorious for its abundance of thick seaweed. But it seems unlikely that Himilco could have been driven so far off his course, and he may have been referring to the large quantities of seaweed that still collect in high summer off Cape St. Vincent, at the southwest corner of present-day Portugal.

Himilco probably followed the Spanish and French coastlines until he reached the shores of Brittany, which were mainly uninhabited. Then he may have struck northwestward across the English Channel and reached the Scilly Islands, off Cornwall in southwest England. Were these the mysterious Tin Islands? The Scilly Islands themselves may not have produced a great deal of tin, but they could have served as a depot to which tin from Cornwall was brought and then re-exported. The most controversial speculation of all is that Himilco actually reached Britain, and mistook the Cornish peninsula at Land's End for the tip of a group of islands. The rich deposits of tin found near the surface of the ground and in streams could easily have led him to think that he had discovered the so-called Tin Islands. If this did happen, it would make him the instigator of the subsequent Cornish-Mediterranean tin trade.

Unfortunately, the whole question of whether the Phoenicians or Carthaginians ever reached Cornwall remains tantalizingly unanswered. There is evidence, however, that Cornish tin did reach the Mediterranean by two different routes. It was smelted into H-shaped ingots and taken by wagon to the Island of Ictis (St. Michael's Mount, a small island off the Cornish coast which can be reached by a causeway at low tide). There, it was loaded into traders' ships. These ships may have carried the tin all the way to the Mediterranean. Alternatively, they may have unloaded the ingots on the coast of France for overland transportation to Marseille and thence by ship to the East. There are records of this route being used by 300 B.C., but it may well have existed for hundreds of years before that time.

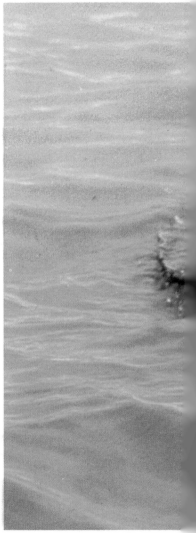

Another Carthaginian sailor has left a far more detailed account of a voyage that he made down the western coast of Africa. His name was Hanno, and he may have been the king of Carthage. The purpose of his expedition was to set up a number of Carthaginian colonies on the African coast beyond the Strait of Gibraltar. Possibly these colonies were intended to safeguard the approaches to Madeira and the Canary Islands, where the Carthaginians had discovered an important new source of raw material for the dye trade. The colonies could also be of assistance to Carthaginian ships sailing in that part of the Atlantic, and the settlers would be able to search as well for new sources of gold and precious metals in the African interior.

Hanno set out from Carthage with 60 ships in about 450 B.C. Each ship was large enough to carry 500 immigrants and all their provisions, and was rowed by 50 oarsmen. Hanno's account of this extraordinary voyage of 30,000 settlers was recorded on a bronze tablet which was set up to commemorate the event in the temple of Saturn (Baal Hammon) in Carthage.

Having sailed through the Strait of Gibraltar, and around Tangier, Hanno's ships made their way down the Moroccan coast. A landing was made at Thymiaterium (modern Mehedia, 70 miles north of Casablanca), and the first colony was founded there. Six more towns, including one on the site of modern Essaouira and another on that

Left: some of the excavations at Mogador (present-day Essaouira) on the coast of Morocco. On his voyage down the coast of Africa, Hanno founded seven colonies on the Moroccan coast, one of them at Mogador.

Below: during their voyage, Hanno and his men sailed up a big river, where they found crocodiles and hippopotamuses. The river is now thought to have been the Senegal, because both animals are found there.

Left: Mount Cameroon. It has been suggested that this volcano is the "Chariot of the Gods" mentioned by Hanno, who might have seen the volcano erupting. But some scholars believe that Hanno did not sail so far south, and that what he saw was Mount Kakulima, on the Guinea-Sierra Leone border, with its slopes ablaze.

Above: a decorated ostrich egg bowl. Such bowls were apparently one of the most popular of Phoenician trading goods, as similar ones have been found on the sites of nearly all the known Phoenician settlements.

of Agadir, were set up about 300 miles farther south in the coastal strip at the foot of the Grand Atlas mountains.

Near the southern border of Morocco, the Carthaginian explorers made friends with the nomadic people who pastured their flocks on the banks of what was probably the Draâ River, and they stayed there for some time. Then, taking some of the nomads as interpreters, they continued south along the coast of Spanish Sahara until they came to a small offshore island at the top of a gulf. This island, which Hanno called Cerne, has been variously identified as Herne Island off Spanish Sahara, Arguin Island about 50 miles below Cape Blanc off Mauritania, or one of the small islands near the mouth of the Senegal River. Perhaps attracted to the island because it resembled the classic Phoenician defensive sites, Hanno landed all the remaining settlers there to establish what was to be the most important West African trading colony for the next 400 years.

His mission accomplished, Hanno might well have turned back, but the true spirit of exploration made him continue the voyage. Having reached the mouth of a big river which interested him, he decided to sail inland. He went up the river until he came to some high mountains which, he says, "were inhabited by forest dwellers who were attired in the skins of animals and who sought to stop us from landing by hurling stones at us." The sailors then found themselves in another river full of crocodiles and hippopotamuses. They had probably reached a fork in the Senegal River—the only river in this part of Africa where these animals are found.

The ships sailed back down the river and returned to Cerne. Then

they headed south again. Fourteen days later they reached the estuary of the Gambia River, where they stopped to take on supplies of water. After another five days' sailing, they landed on an island in a large bay. This was probably one of the Bissagos Islands off the coast of what is now Portuguese Guinea. There they found a salt lake that contained a smaller island. "We made our way there. In the daytime we could see nothing but forests, but at night we saw many fires. We heard the sound of pipes and cymbals, the rumble of drums and mighty cries. This instilled fear in us, and our soothsayers ordered us to leave the island." This account is the earliest description of the beating of African tom-toms. The arrival of the expedition probably coincided with a festival, for even today Hanno's description still fits such events.

Hanno continues: "We passed with great speed, and sailed along a burning yet sweet-smelling region where streams of fire ran out into the sea. We could not go ashore because of the heat. In the grip of fear, we made all haste from this place also. On the four nights following we saw land covered in flames. In the center of the land was a high pyre, larger than the others, which seemed to reach to the stars. In the daytime it proved to be a high mountain which is called the Chariot of the Gods."

The "land covered in flames" which apparently frightened Hanno and his sailors has a simple explanation. Along the Guinea coast it was an annual occurrence after the harvest for the farmers to burn loose straw and stubble to prepare the ground for the next year's planting of grain. But the "Chariot of the Gods" is not so easily explained.

Above: a beautiful necklace of glass beads and gold, of Carthaginian design. Hanno probably took various trading goods with him on his voyage, and used them to barter with friendly peoples he met. Glass beads were almost always included among such goods, but a finely-wrought necklace such as this would have been considered too precious for trade with primitive peoples.

Possibly Hanno was describing the volcanic Mount Cameroon in eruption, but it is difficult to understand how he could have got as far south as Cameroon in the sailing time he mentions. Another explanation is that Hanno and his crew saw Mount Kakulima, near the frontier between Guinea and Sierra Leone, with its slopes ablaze for some reason.

During the voyage Hanno probably tried to trade with friendly inhabitants along the coast. The Carthaginians developed a method of silent barter for which they became well known in Africa, and which later explorers have found extremely useful. The first move was made by the visitors. They landed on the coast, unloaded their cargo, and laid it along the water line. Then they lit a fire and returned to their ships. The Greek historian Herodotus describes the next stages: "The people of the country see the smoke, and, coming to the sea, they lay down gold to pay for the cargo and withdraw away from the wares. Then the Carthaginians disembark and examine their gold; if it seems to them a fair price for their cargo, they take it, and go on their way; but, if not, they go aboard again and wait, and then the people come back and add more gold till the ship's crew are satisfied."

But there was no chance of silent barter for Hanno at the most southerly point of his voyage. Three days after seeing the Chariot of the Gods, Hanno landed on an island. This may have been Sherbro Island, off the coast of Sierra Leone, although it was possibly as far south as Cameroon or even Gabon. The inhabitants of the island, like the people of Senegal, greeted Hanno and his men with stones. But these "forest dwellers" were very strange. Hanno says that they were mainly "women with long-haired bodies, and our interpreters called them 'gorillas.' We pursued them, but were unable to seize any because they fled and climbed steep cliffs and defended themselves with stones. We captured three women, but they bit and scratched their captors and would not go with them."

It has been suggested that Hanno may have been describing Pygmies, who have yellow skins, red-brown woolly hair, and hairy bodies. But were these "forest dwellers," in fact, human beings at all? The most likely explanation is that the unfriendly islanders were chimpanzees, smaller than gorillas and tailless. But Hanno obviously thought them human or he would hardly have used the word "women" in his report of their capture. And they must have been unusual trophies, for he adds, "We killed and skinned them, and took the hides to Carthage with us."

Hanno's account of this remarkable voyage ends abruptly. "We did not journey farther than this," he says, "since our provisions were beginning to run low." There is no record of the return journey, but Hanno and his crew would certainly have stopped to see how the settlers in each of the new colonies were faring. History tells little of the development of these colonies in the years and decades that followed. There are no accounts of subsequent visits by other navigators or of regular trade with Carthage. Of all the places

Below: during the last stop of his journey, on an island off the African coast, Hanno encountered some very strange people. He described them as "forest dwellers" and obviously thought they were human. The most likely explanation is, however, that these "forest dwellers" were chimpanzees. The Carthaginians would never have seen such animals before, and their similarity to human beings could well have led the sailors to believe that the apes were human.

mentioned by Hanno, only Cerne appears to have become important, probably because it was dealing in gold. Even this trade ended with the fall of Carthage in 146 B.C. Neither the Greeks nor the Romans seem to have profited from Hanno's great pioneering achievement.

For nearly 2,000 years, the stretch of West African coast explored by Hanno sank back into oblivion, from which it did not emerge again until the late Middle Ages. Then the Portuguese took half a century to rediscover the places that the Carthaginians had found and colonized in a few months.

The Greek Adventurers

5

Even after he had landed the last of his settlers on the African coast, Hanno continued his journey southward. What made him go on? He had done what he set out to do. Now he was leading his men farther into unknown waters and possibly into danger. Yet he continued just the same. His reason can only have been a desire to know what lay beyond the horizon.

Hanno was experiencing the excitement of discovery—the lure of sailing unknown waters and seeing unknown places. Up to his time travelers nearly always had a good, practical reason for their journeys. They wanted to establish colonies or trade. Now there was another motive—the spirit of adventure. That spirit was given an added boost with the emergence of the Greeks as a great seafaring people.

A glance at a map showing their colonies in the 500's B.C. reveals that the Greeks were great sailors and persistent explorers. Already they were rivaling the Phoenicians. As well as establishing trading settlements, they, too, were starting colonies and building independent city-states where enterprising men emigrated with their families to start a new life.

A desire for freedom, a love of adventure, a curiosity about th

unknown—all these factors combined with economic necessity to make them migrate. It led them to rediscover areas which the Phoenicians, with their anxiety to safeguard their trade routes, had done so much to keep secret. By 500 B.C., the Greeks had established ports all over the Aegean and central Mediterranean. They had crossed to North Africa, and colonized Cyrene on the coast of present-day Libya. They had spread to the eastern extremities of the Black Sea, and as far west as Malaga in Spain. They had even ventured beyond the Strait of Gibraltar which was then called the Pillars of Hercules. They infiltrated Egypt, and established a Greek trading center in the Nile Delta. This caused a contemporary writer to complain that "the islands were restless." The Greeks, he went on to say, "were disturbed among themselves; they poured out their people all together. No land stood before them . . . they advanced upon Egypt. . . ."

Although it is known that more than a hundred Greek colonies existed, no descriptions have survived of the voyages that led to their foundation, and historians have been unable to discover exactly when these voyages took place. The sagas of the great Greek poet Homer—the *Iliad* and the *Odyssey*—probably provide indirect

Above: Odysseus and his men embark on their voyage home from the Trojan War, shown here in a picture from an Italian manuscript of the 1300's. In Homer's poem, the *Odyssey,* Odysseus was the king of Ithaca and a Greek leader in the war. It took him 10 adventure-packed years to reach home. Below: head of a Libyan from Cyrene.

65

accounts of the early Greek journeys. The legendary travels of Homer's hero Odysseus, which are so minutely described that they may well have a basis of truth, seem to speak for the wanderings of all the sailors of ancient Greece.

The existence of Greek colonies is mentioned in passing by Herodotus in about 450 B.C. and by Strabo, a Greek historian and geographer who lived around the time of the birth of Christ. But, by the time these authors were writing, some of the settlements had been in existence for hundreds of years. The details of their establishment had been forgotten. The brief references to Greek colonization made by these historians are supplemented by buildings which have survived and by archaeological finds. The magnificent temples at Paestum in southern Italy and Agrigento in Sicily, which are believed to date from around 600 B.C., provide evidence of Greek expansion. So do the hoards of Greek coins found at Marseille—the

former Greek colony of Massalia—on the southern coast of France.

Some of the colonizing voyages must have been dramatic and daring, but the colonies really owed their existence to exploration spread over centuries. As the years passed, mariners learned about the Mediterranean and the sailing conditions there, and they passed their knowledge on to the would-be colonists. From the various accounts of early sailors, the settlers could build up for themselves a reasonably accurate picture of the lands they were aiming for, and the sea they would have to cross to reach them.

The first Greeks are thought to have come from the steppe lands of southern Russia soon after 2000 B.C. Displacing the Pelasgians and other native inhabitants, they settled in groups of villages on the Greek mainland and the islands of the Aegean Sea. During the centuries that followed, they were increasingly influenced by the civilizations of Crete and Phoenicia, whose traders were frequent

Above: Stonehenge in Great Britain, which resembles the buildings of the distant Mycenaeans in the way the stones were cut and erected. At the peak of their power, the Mycenaeans were a great seafaring nation.

Above left: a wall-painting of Greek soldiers from Paestum, Italy. Paestum was the most northerly settlement th Mycenaeans made in Italy, commanding a wide agricultural area. Bu it had no strategic advantage, and w soon taken over by the Italians.

visitors to the southern shores of Greece. Gradually the Greek villages grew into cities. The largest and most important of these was Mycenae in the Peloponnesus (the peninsula forming the southern part of mainland Greece). Mycenae became so rich and powerful that, by about 1500 B.C., it was challenging the might of Crete itself.

In the next 200 years, the Mycenaean Greeks developed into a great seafaring nation. They traded throughout the Aegean and exported their wares to Egypt and Asia Minor (the peninsula of western Asia between the Black Sea and the Mediterranean, which is now occupied by Turkey). It is probably to this period of Mycenaean power that many of the Greek legends of seafaring heroes belong. But there followed a confused period of invasion and migration that gradually sapped the strength of the Mycenaean civilization. By the end of the 1200's B.C., Mycenae was in decline.

By the 1100's B.C., a number of migrating peoples had found their way into mainland Greece. Aeolians from the north moved into east central Greece and, in the Peloponnesus, other migrants settled and intermarried with the inhabitants to form a group known as the Ionians. In the late 1100's B.C., the Aeolians and Ionians were driven out in turn by a great wave of invading Indo-European tribes called the Dorians. These people, who were probably of much the same racial origin as the earliest Greeks, swept across the Greek mainland, conquering most of the Peloponnesus, and finally destroying the city of Mycenae.

It was with the invasion of the Dorians that the first great era of Greek colonization began. Fleeing before the invaders, Ionian and Aeolian refugees crossed the Aegean to the shores of Asia Minor, where they founded new settlements. Three hundred years later, there was another exodus when the population grew so large that Greece could no longer produce enough food for all its people. Economic shortages, together with a desire for freedom, drove the Greeks to emigrate throughout the Mediterranean and Black seas.

Sometime after 750 B.C., the Ionian Greeks established 12 cities in Asia Minor, which they organized into a confederacy. At Ephesus, they built the Temple of Artemis (Diana), one of the Seven Wonders of the Ancient World. Miletus, in Asia Minor, was the richest city in the Greek world until the 400's B.C., and the Greek city most concerned with exploration. It was at Miletus that the first maps and writing on navigation were produced. From its harbor sailed the ships that ventured into the Black Sea to trade with the nomadic Scythians of southern Russia.

So extensive was the colonization of Sicily and southern Italy, that this area was given the name of Magna Graecia. Places such as Naples, Messina, Syracuse, and Ischia owe their existence to the migrations of the Greeks after the middle of the 700's B.C. Present-day Antibes, Monaco, and Marseille were three among innumerable

Greek towns which dotted the Mediterranean coasts of what are now France and Spain as far west as Alicante.

Marseille (Massalia to the Greeks) was a colony of a colony. It was founded in about 600 B.C. by the inhabitants of Phocaea, yet another Greek settlement on the coast of Asia Minor. It is not surprising that the Egyptians, contemplating all this activity, described the Greeks rather sourly as "restless." They had firsthand evidence. There was a Greek colony, known as Naucratis, right in the Nile Delta.

The Greeks were lucky as well as restless. Prosperity grew out of a minor disaster that overtook one of their sea captains named Colaeus in 630 B.C. On a voyage from the Aegean island of Samos to Egypt he was swept off his course. An east wind drove his ship across the Mediterranean and past the Pillars of Hercules. Thus he became the first Greek to penetrate the narrow gateway into the "outer sea"—the Atlantic Ocean.

Above: a fragment of pottery with the autograph of Herodotus on it. It was found at Naucratis, where travelers used to write their names on vases, just as people today sign the visitors' book when stopping at a monument.

Colaeus brought his ship safely to shore at Tartessus, in southern Spain, where he sold his cargo. He carried back the news of what he had seen to Asia Minor, and for the next hundred years the Greeks benefited from his accidental discovery. The Phocaean Greeks opened up the silver trade from Spain to the Aegean with organized expeditions in 50-oared galleys. Marseille was obviously founded to serve as an intermediate port of call during these voyages.

Even more important than the penetration into the Atlantic was the gradual exploration of the Black Sea, the inland sea which,

Above: a gold buckle which belonged to Darius I of Persia. The Persian Empire retained its wealth and splendor until it was conquered by Alexander the Great in the late 300's B.C.

Right: the tomb of Darius I of Persia in the center of the cliff at Naqsh-i-Rustam, near Persepolis in what is now Iran. Darius' conquests greatly enlarged the Persian Empire.

because of its dense fogs and winter ice, the Greeks called the *inhospitable sea*. Even getting to it was difficult. Greek sailors had to learn to navigate the treacherous narrows of the Bosporus and the Dardanelles, which lie between the Aegean Sea and the Black Sea. For nine months of the year, strong currents run through these straits, backed by fierce northeast winds.

Exploration of the Black Sea probably began in the period between the 1100's and the 800's B.C. when the Carians, who occupied a region known as Caria in the southwest of Asia Minor, established colonies on its northern and western shores. But the Carians left no records of their voyages, and it was the people of Miletus who began the true opening up of the Black Sea in the 700's B.C. Tradition has it that the first settlements of people from Miletus were on the Dardanelles and the northern coast of what is now Turkey. From there, the colonists exported fish, metal, and wheat. They also possessed a far more exotic commodity—golden fleeces. These fleeces, which explorers brought back from the Caucasus, were produced by hanging sheepskins in gold-bearing streams, so that particles of gold clung to the wool. The sheepskins (fleeces) were later burned and the gold

Below: a horseman in the costume of the Scythians, a group of nomads who lived in the region of the Black Sea. By 300 B.C., when this statue was made, the Greeks had known the area for nearly 400 years, and Greek influence is apparent in this work.

was recovered. Here legend and fact may well go hand in hand. One of the most famous of the Greek myths tells the story of Jason, who sailed to the land of Colchis in search of the golden fleece. Colchis lay on the shores of the Black Sea, and it is possible that mariners' tales of the golden fleeces of the Caucasus could have given rise to the legend of Jason's golden fleece.

The first recorded exploration by a Greek mariner was made in about 510 B.C. By this time, the Greek colonies in Asia were under Persian domination, and it was on behalf of King Darius I of Persia

Ain el Beda. 1913.454

that the voyage was undertaken. Darius ruled an empire that stretched from Thrace in the Balkan Peninsula and Cyrene in northern Africa to northeast India. He was curious to learn the course of the Indus River, of which he knew only the upper reaches. To discover where the river entered the sea, Darius commissioned a Carian Greek named Scylax to sail down the Indus to its mouth. According to Darius' orders, Scylax was then to continue westward into the Arabian Sea, across the entrance to the Persian Gulf, and sail around Arabia and up the Red Sea to Egypt, which had been conquered by the Persians in about 525 B.C.

At the time when Scylax made his journey, the Greeks knew very little about the Red Sea or the Arabian Sea. Until about 600 B.C., the Egyptians had denied them a passage through the Red Sea and the Arabians blocked shipping farther eastward. Although sea routes from India to Arabia had probably been explored before, Scylax is the first Westerner who is known to have made the voyage.

Scylax came from the town of Caryanda, to the south of Miletus in Asia Minor, and was probably a commander in the Persian fleet. He probably traveled overland from Asia Minor to India, and built his ship at the point where the Indus becomes navigable. That is about 1,400 miles from the Indian Ocean.

Herodotus, the only recorder of the voyage, says that Scylax sailed down the river "toward the east and the sunrise." But this is inaccurate. The Indus makes its way south-southwest through what is now Pakistan. This might seem to throw doubt on the authenticity of the whole account, except for the fact that, when Herodotus was writing, the shape and size of Asia were unknown. He still thought of the world as a disk, and it was natural for him to visualize so distant a river as flowing east toward the outer edge of the disk.

Scylax left no account of his journey, but he is assumed to have been responsible for several strange tales about the peoples of India that were repeated by later writers. He came back with descriptions of the Shadowfeet People who used their feet to ward off the sun, of people who slept in the shelter of their own huge ears, and of men with only one eye. Of more scientific value was his success in completing his 2½-year voyage down the Indus, around southern Arabia, and up the Red Sea.

Once Darius knew that a sea route existed between his eastern domains and Egypt, he ordered the clearing of the old canal that linked the Red Sea with the Nile, and marked the event by raising a monument on its banks which proclaimed that ships "sailed through it from Egypt all the way to Persia as was my will."

More than a hundred years after the epic voyage of Scylax, another Greek, this time a soldier, led a land and sea expedition that ranks as one of the greatest feats in history. Xenophon brought 10,000 Greeks from the middle of the Persian Empire back to their native land.

Xenophon was an Athenian, a man of action, and a historian. By

Above: a seal showing Jason carrying the Golden Fleece. This famous legend may be based partly on fact—the Greek colonists in the Caucasus traditionally produced golden fleeces.

Above: a man with huge ears, one of
the fabulous people apparently based
on Scylax's tales. These stories had
a powerful influence on the imagination of western Europe. When the
book containing this woodcut was
published in 1544, the tales were
still thought to be true.

the time he was 20, he had fought in battle and studied under the philosopher Socrates. Though skeptical about Athenian democracy, he was extremely patriotic and wanted to see Greece united against the Persian Empire. This aim, combined with the hope of possible honor and booty, led him to Asia Minor. There, he joined an army of Greek mercenaries being raised by Cyrus against Cyrus' brother, Artaxerxes II of Persia.

The army left Sardis (near present-day Izmir, in eastern Turkey) and marched southeastward through the mountains of Cilicia, past Aleppo in northwestern Syria, and down the Euphrates River into Babylonia. The Greeks covered a distance of about 1,700 miles in five months. At Cunaxa, on the Euphrates River north of Babylon, they routed the Persians, but Cyrus was killed, and the army, far from home and stranded deep in unknown country, elected Xenophon to lead them back to Greece.

To avoid returning by the same long overland route through Asia Minor, Xenophon decided to strike north and try to return to Greece by way of the Black Sea. Even today, with a knowledge of the country, and modern equipment such as maps, compasses, and mechanized transportation, such a journey would be formidable. In 400 B.C., to lead 10,000 battle-weary and dispirited soldiers and their camp followers on a 2,000-mile journey was a feat little short of superhuman.

Xenophon's route took the Greeks northward up the east bank of the Tigris River to Nineveh (about 230 miles north of present-day Baghdad, in Iraq), and then through the mountains of Armenia. To avoid attack from hostile inhabitants, they traveled over trackless hills. During the winter, they had to march through snowstorms, and at times wade waist-deep in rivers and mountain torrents. Exposed to bitter conditions and extreme hunger, many did not finish the journey. In his memoirs, Xenophon recounts that some lost toes through frostbite and others were blinded by the snow. He urged his men on, forbidding them to rest except at night. Before they slept he ordered them to remove their footwear, so that their shoes would not freeze to their feet.

Once, the army made the mistake of taking a wrong route. For seven days they marched along the banks of a river, believing that it was carrying them toward the Black Sea. Then to his horror Xenophon learned that he had been misled because two different

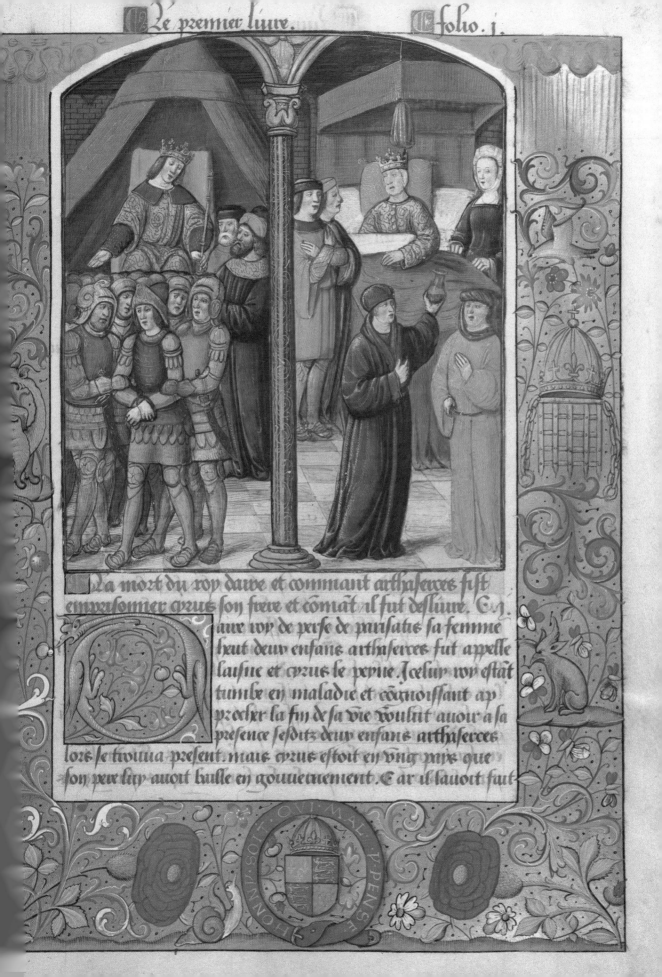

La mort du roy dauie et comment arthaseries fist
empuisonner cyrus son frere et comât il fut desliure. Et
aure roy de perse de parisatis sa femme
heut deux enfans arthaserces fut apelle
lausue et cyrus le peyne. Icelur roy estât
tumbe en maladie et cõgnoissant ap
procher la fin de sa vie voulut auoir a sa
presence sesditz deux enfans arthaserces
lors se trouua present. mais cyrus estoit en vng pays que
son pere luy auoit baulle en gouuernement. Car il sauoit fait

Left: Xenophon and his soldiers, an illustration from a French translation of his book made in the early 1500's. Xenophon is shown wearing a helmet, at the head of his men.

Right: Xenophon and his men on the shores of the Black Sea. The terrible 2,000-mile march had required every ounce of determination his weary men could muster. They had their reward when they saw the silvery gleam of the waters of the Black Sea in the distance. The Greeks believed that wherever there was salt water, the Greek language would be understood, and their way home certain.

rivers had the same name. The men were traveling in entirely the wrong direction. Weary and dispirited, they had to retrace their steps.

After a year of forced marches, local battles, and intense privation, the leading troops came to the head of a mountain pass. Xenophon, who was then with the rearguard, saw them waving their arms and heard excited shouts. Fearing that his men had been ambushed, Xenophon rode forward. Then he distinguished their cry: "The sea! The sea!" The army was at last within sight of its goal. Seven days later, Xenophon and his men reached the southeast coast of the Black Sea at Trapezus (Trabzon).

So Xenophon led his great army on the last stage of its journey. At Byzantium (Istanbul), on the Bosporus, he said good-by to his soldiers. He had brought them home through 2,000 miles of unknown and hostile territory. He had earned his future retirement with his wife and sons in Greece. There, on his country estate, he set a precedent for many future generals by writing his war memoirs. He gave them the modest, almost deprecating, title of *Up-Country March,* and possibly in terms of pure exploration the results were meager. But he had been where no Greek had traveled before and had taken notes of the country through which he had passed. His astonishing journey meant that more accurate maps could now be drawn. Xenophon had made a valuable contribution to the growing storehouse of geographical knowledge.

Alexander the Great

6

In 356 B.C., about the time of Xenophon's death in Corinth, a boy destined to become one of the greatest generals history has known was born at Pella, in Macedonia. The boy was named Alexander. History calls him "the Great." He was the son of King Philip II of Macedonia, an outstanding military leader and administrator, and Queen Olympias, a brilliant and ambitious woman. While Alexander was growing up, Philip was fighting to extend Macedonian power down into Greece, and to bring the Greek city-states under Macedonian rule. He aimed to lead a united army from Macedonia and the Greek city-states against their common enemy, the Persians, who were in control of the Greek colonies in Asia Minor. Philip was murdered before this could be accomplished, but Alexander was ready for the task. He was determined to follow his father's plan and free the Greeks in Asia from their Persian masters. He set out to conquer the Eastern world, and he founded an empire of $1\frac{1}{2}$ million square miles which stretched from Greece to India and included Egypt, Asia Minor, and Persia.

Alexander's success as a military leader was extraordinary. But he was not content with conquest alone. During the 11 years in which he created a vast new empire, he combined the role of explorer with that of conqueror. He possessed the one quality essential to the explorer—an insatiable curiosity about the unknown world.

Left: the head of Alexander the Great. This head is known as the Azara Herm. It is a Roman copy, made in the late 100's B.C., of a portrait head by the Greek sculptor Lysippus.

Right: a pebble mosaic from Pella, the city where Alexander was born, showing the young Alexander hunting a lion.

Above: a page recounting a battle, from an illustrated edition of the *Iliad* dating from the A.D. 300's. The *Iliad*, like the *Odyssey*, is probably by the Greek poet Homer, and tells a story of the Trojan War. The work was obviously significant to Alexander, who carried a copy with him throughout his long travels.

As he penetrated deeper and deeper into the Orient, he sent back accounts of what he saw. Geographers, naturalists, and an official historian were important members of Alexander's staff. The writing of these scholars are now lost, but they were incorporated in the history of Alexander written by Arrian in the A.D. 100's. Some of their reports were also sent to the great Greek philosopher Aristotle.

Aristotle had been a leading influence in Alexander's education. King Philip had brought him from Athens to Pella when his son was 14. For three years, the philosopher had taught Alexander history, religion, science, and the theories of politics and monarchy. Together they read the Greek dramatists. Alexander was particularly influenced by the *Iliad*. He owned a copy of this work—marked with Aristotle's own notes—which had been given him by his teacher, and he carried this volume of Homer with him throughout his travels.

At the age of 20, Alexander succeeded his father as king of Macedonia. His father had died before the Greek states were completely subdued to Macedonian rule, and Alexander spent the first two years of his reign in making his authority felt in Greece. Then

Above: Troy, which Alexander visited at the beginning of his campaign. The ruins of Homer's Troy were no longer visible by this time, and all Alexander would have seen was a small town. The archaeologists who have excavated the site of Troy have named the city of Homer's story Troy VIIa. Alexander's Troy is called Troy VIII.

At last, he was able to turn his attention to the conquest of the Persian Empire. Early in the spring of 334 B.C., when he was 21 years old, Alexander set out on his great expedition. He was never to see his native country again.

Alexander's army consisted of 30,000 infantry and more than 5,000 cavalry. Along with his Macedonian troops were soldiers from Thrace and Thessaly, and men from many other Greek states. All the members of this force spoke some form of Greek. Alexander's troops made their first march at a speed which was to be characteristic of all their journeys. They covered the 300 miles to the Hellespont (Dardanelles) in only 20 days.

Once on the mainland of Asia Minor, Alexander visited the site of Troy, the ancient city made famous in Homer's *Iliad* and *Odyssey*. There, he made a sacrifice to the Greek goddess Athena and visited the supposed tomb of the legendary Greek warrior, Achilles, from whom he claimed to be descended. He exchanged some of his armor for a sacred shield said to have been used in the Trojan War. Thus, armed like one of the heroes of Greek legend, and believing himself

81

to be more a god than a man, Alexander was ready to face the Persians.

During the first year of his campaign, he overcame the enemy in many battles, and won back for the Greeks the Persian-occupied cities of Ephesus, Miletus, and Halicarnassus. Then he marched on to Syria. He defeated Darius III, the king of Persia, in a great battle at Issus, near the Turkish-Syrian frontier. But, although Persian losses at Issus were enormous, Darius himself escaped. Alexander then pushed on to occupy Phoenicia, and laid siege to the city of Tyre. As in the past, Tyre put up a strong and determined

Right: a head of Ptolemy I, founder of an Egyptian dynasty which lasted from 323 B.C., until the death of Cleopatra in 30 B.C. Under the Ptolemies—as the dynasty was called —Alexandria became the intellectual and religious center of the world.

Left: a detail showing Alexander at
the Battle of Issus, at the moment
when Darius III decided to retreat.
The mosaic was found in the House of
the Faun at Pompeii, and is a copy
of a painting of about 330 B.C.

resistance. While Alexander's troops were constructing a causeway across the half-mile of sea between the shore and the besieged island city, the Tyrians, perched high on their city walls, hurled missiles and red-hot sand down on the soldiers. On one occasion, a Tyrian ship ventured forth under the shelter of darkness and destroyed the part of the causeway that had already been built. It was only after seven months of laborious work and bitter fighting that the city finally fell to Alexander. With the capture of Tyre, which was the principal Persian port, Alexander became master of the Mediterranean.

Alexander was now free to travel south to Egypt, where he was crowned as pharaoh by a people grateful to be delivered from Persian rule. He visited the shrine of Zeus-Ammon, Egypt's chief god, at Siwah in the Libyan Desert, about 160 miles southwest of present-day El Alamein. There, the priests received him as the son of a god. On the edge of the desert, just west of the Nile Delta, Alexander founded the city that bears his name—Alexandria. Under Alexander's successors—the Greek Ptolemies—Alexandria was to become the chief city of the Mediterranean. With its renowned library containing 700,000 scrolls of parchment—the equivalent of 100,000 books—it grew into one of the most important cultural, as well as commercial, cities in the world. It was one of more than a hundred new cities, including 30 Alexandrias, that the young conqueror was to leave in his wake.

The next year was spent in pursuit of Darius. From Egypt, Alexander's army marched north again to Tyre, and then inland through Syria to the Euphrates and the Tigris rivers. At Gaugamela, near the ruins of the ancient Assyrian city of Nineveh, the Persians suffered their greatest defeat. But Darius constantly fell back across the desert plains and into the mountain regions of his immense empire. From Gaugamela, Alexander marched his army south through Babylon to the heart of the Persian Empire. There, he partially destroyed Persepolis, one of the great capitals of Darius.

Leaving Persepolis, Alexander followed Darius to Ecbatana (present-day Hamadan in Iran). The Greek Army covered an average of 36 miles a day, a punishing pace for the infantry. But Alexander never succeeded in catching the Persian king. In July, 330 B.C., somewhere near present-day Damghan (south of the Elburz Mountains), Darius was murdered by Bessus, a Persian general who

Above: one of the surviving examples of the elaborate stonework at Persepolis, the royal Persian city burned by Alexander. This carving on a gateway shows the Persian king fighting a lion.

ruled the province of Bactria in what is now northern Afghanistan. Pausing only to take the title of king of Persia and assume Persian dress (apparently to gain the good will of the local tribes), Alexander went in search of the murderer who had also claimed the royal title.

This meant an autumn and winter march of 1,700 miles south into Arachosia in Persia, and then northeast through the mountains to Kabul in Afghanistan in the face of ice and bitter weather. Blocked by snow, Alexander established a winter camp and waited until spring before attempting to cross an 11,000-foot-high pass over the formidable Hindu Kush mountain range. Once over the pass, the army descended into the valley of the Oxus River (today called the Amu-Darya). The river was swollen by melting snow, and the army had no wood to build boats to cross it. Alexander ordered his men to fill their leather tents with straw and use them as floats. By this means the army crossed the Oxus into Sogdiana and caught up with Bessus, whose supporters surrendered. Bessus himself was executed.

Now Alexander might well have called a halt to his expedition. But he announced his intention of marching on to explore the northern borders of his new empire. The comparatively small army of under 40,000 with which he had left Macedonia five years before was now 200,000 strong. With seasoned troops and auxiliaries who had either volunteered or been forced to join his army, Alexander marched over 300 miles from the Oxus River to Maracanda (modern Samarkand in the Soviet republic of Uzbek). Then, continuing northeastward, he reached the great Jaxartes (Syr-Darya) River, which had marked the northeastern boundary of the Persian Empire.

For two years, Alexander remained in central Asia, fighting and exploring, marching and countermarching across the desolate plains and uplands of present-day Afghanistan and the Uzbek and Turkmen regions of Russia. He toyed with the idea of exploring the northern shores of the Caspian Sea to discover whether it was an inland sea or the southern tip of a vast bay connected to the ocean then believed to surround the world. But the unknown regions of India attracted him more, and he turned his troops southward.

In the summer of 327 B.C., Alexander's men struck through the Khyber Pass and reached the upper part of the Indus River. Some of them plunged into the water for a refreshing swim. But, to their horror, they found that the river was infested with crocodiles believed at that time to be found nowhere but in the Nile. Alexander

began to wonder if this Indian river might somehow be joined to the Nile itself. After a few weeks' march over the plains of the Punjab in northwest India, the army arrived at another river, the Hydaspes (Jhelum), a tributary of the Indus. There, too, they found crocodiles. It therefore seemed to Alexander that both the Hydaspes and the Indus rivers must be the unknown sources of the Nile. He wrote a triumphant letter to his mother, announcing his great discovery. And he appointed a Cretan named Nearchus to build a fleet of ships, so that, whenever he chose, he could lead the army back to Egypt

Below: the Indus River near Attock. It was near here that Alexander had a bridge built so that his army could cross the river. The Indus River was the first place at which his men found crocodiles, only previously known to live in the Nile, in Egypt.

and the Mediterranean by sailing down the Indus to the Nile.

It was not long, however, before Alexander realized his mistake. Local Indians told him that the Indus and Hydaspes flowed into the "great sea," a huge expanse of water that lay somewhere to the south. Greatly disappointed, Alexander destroyed the letter to his mother, although he did not call off the construction of the fleet. Still on the banks of the Hydaspes, Alexander then engaged in battle with Porus, the ruler of a land to the east of that river, and defeated Porus' huge army which included a contingent of 200 elephants.

As he pushed on into the Punjab, Alexander was at the extreme limit of the known world. Even the Persians had traveled no farther. But Alexander had heard reports of fertile lands and an immense river (the Ganges) to the east, and he could not resist the challenge of the unknown. His men were not similarly inspired. They had just marched through 70 days of incessant rain, and their morale was at a low ebb. They were weary of battles, and they felt that they had traveled far enough. After eight years away, they longed for home.

Alexander called his rebellious troops together and, in an eloquent speech, he urged them to go on. "I beseech you," he exclaimed, "not to desert your king just at the very moment he is approaching the limits of the inhabited world." Alexander had no idea of the vast plains of northern Asia stretching away to China. He believed, as Aristotle had taught him, that his army was almost at the boundary of the world, on the edge of the great outer ocean which he thought surrounded the entire earth. Soon, he told his men, they would reach the eastern sea which would be found to join up with the Caspian Sea, the Indian Ocean, and the Persian Gulf. He promised them that "from the Persian Gulf our fleet shall sail round to Libya, right up to the Pillars of Hercules."

But the soldiers stood in defiant silence. They would not go on. Reluctantly, Alexander gave the order for the expedition to turn round and march back across the Punjab. They returned to the Hydaspes, where Nearchus and a team of shipwrights (including Phoenicians, probably brought from Tyre) had almost finished constructing a large fleet of ships. For now Alexander had a new plan. He would explore the Hydaspes and the Indus to see if they issued into the great outer sea. Perhaps he might yet reach the boundaries of the world. Sending part of the army by land along the banks of the river to ward off hostile tribes, Alexander and the rest of his men embarked in a large number of 30-oared galleys and cargo ships. Without guides, and knowing nothing about the depth of the river or the conditions they might encounter, they made their way downstream. Ahead of them lay a voyage of about a thousand miles.

The fleet sailed down the Hydaspes and the Acesines (Chenāb) rivers and on to the Indus, fighting occasional battles along the way. Then, one day, they reached a point at which the river widened to about 20 miles, and they could smell sea air. Their joy at the thought that the ocean was not far off suddenly turned to anxiety

Below: a woodcarving made by the Kafiri, a red-haired, blue-eyed people from the mountains of what is now Afghanistan. The Kafiri claim to be descended from Alexander's Greeks. Marco Polo, who visited them in the A.D. 1200's, reported this as a certainty.

87

Above: Alexander the Great addressing his men in the hope of persuading them to continue farther into India with him. This painting, from a manuscript of the late 1400's, captures the sullen stubbornness of his men. By this time, the Greek soldiers were tired of travel, and only wanted to return to their homes in Greece.

as they found the current turning against them, and the fresh water of the river becoming salt. The salt water was being carried upstream by the rising tide. But the Greeks, used only to the almost tideless Mediterranean, knew nothing of the rise and fall of tides. They dropped anchor and waited for an improvement in the weather. While they were waiting, the tide ebbed and left their ships stranded. Alexander's men were terrified. They had never encountered such a phenomenon. And when the river rose again and set their ships afloat, they were even more amazed.

Shortly after this, Alexander sailed out into the open sea at the end of his nine-month voyage down the Indus. According to Arrian, he took a few ships down the western arm of the Indus Delta and sailed some way out into the Arabian Sea to discover whether any land was to be found in it. He then went back to Pattala at the head of the Indus Delta, where he had left the majority of his army. After a further expedition down the eastern arm of the delta, he returned to Pattala and divided his forces into three groups. The sick and the wounded were placed under the command of Craterus and ordered

travel overland, with the baggage, to southern Persia. Alexander
himself set out at the head of the main part of the army on a long
march through hitherto unknown country along the shores of the
Arabian Sea and the Persian Gulf. The rest of the troops, under the
command of Nearchus, were sent by ship, with orders to explore the
sea between the Indus Delta and the Persian Gulf. The plan was for
Alexander to follow the coast and for Nearchus to touch land at
various points so that Alexander's forces could supply the ships with
food and water.

The plan failed. A range of hills forced Alexander's troops to
make a detour away from the sea. This meant that Nearchus kept
only one rendezvous with his commander during a voyage of 130
days from the Indus to the mouth of the Euphrates. The men at sea
suffered from hunger and thirst as well as from exposure. From time
to time, they landed but could find only the poorest of food.

One of Nearchus' most alarming experiences was an encounter
with a school of whales. These creatures terrified the sailors, who had
never seen a whale before. However, the monsters were successfully

Above: Alexander and his men caught
in the tidal waters at the mouth of
the Indus River. The Greeks, used to
the almost tideless Mediterranean,
could not understand why, near the
mouth of the Indus, the current turned against them, and the water became
salt. They were even more amazed when
the tide went out, and left them
stranded.

89

Right: the head of a man wearing a helmet of Grecian style, from a museum in Kabul, Afghanistan. Alexander's men took Greek art and culture with them to the lands they conquered, and the Greek influence persisted in Alexander's empire for many years.

Above: a vase decorated with Greek ships. These vessels are probably similar to those in which Nearchus and his men sailed from India to the Persian Gulf, while Alexander and his soldiers marched overland through the terrible Makrān Desert.

dispersed by a trumpet blast before they could damage the ships.

The problems facing Alexander on land were not so easily overcome. The inland detour meant that, for two months, Alexander and his followers were marching through the arid wastes and shifting sand of the Makrān Desert (in present-day Pakistan). Water holes were scarce, and, faced with starvation, men began to kill pack mules for food. Three-quarters of Alexander's company died in the fearful journey before reaching Bandar-e Shāhpūr (in southeastern Iran). The survivors followed a caravan route that led inland from Bandar-e Shāhpūr towards Persepolis. On the way they were joined by Nearchus, whose joy at finding his commander again was dashed at the sight of Alexander's ragged and depleted forces.

It was a sad climax to the otherwise triumphant journey of exploration and conquest, a cruel ending to the march of 25,000 miles which had been recorded with scientific precision by the *bematistae*—the *steppers*—as Alexander's road surveyors were called. Now only two years of life were left to the conqueror of the world. They were marked for Alexander by delusions of power and grandeur.

But, up to the time of his death at the age of 32, Alexander never lost his passion for exploration. He dispatched an expedition to explore the Caspian Sea. In the last few months of his life he made a personal voyage down the Euphrates River. He began assembling a great armada to sail to Arabia, which he intended to colonize. But

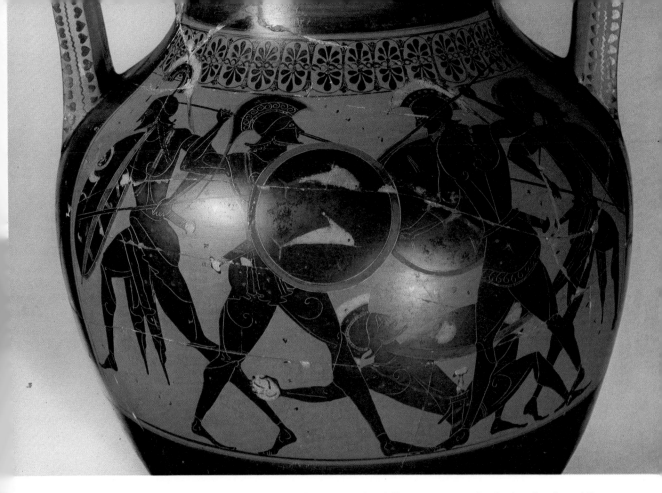

his plans were never to be realized. In the spring of 323 B.C., he fell ill with malaria. He died in the summer in the city of Babylon, which he had planned to make the capital of his great new empire.

Whatever his shortcomings in later life, Alexander's journeys confirmed him as one of the greatest explorers in history. Above all, he possessed a vision of what exploration could achieve in uniting a divided world. In 70 of the cities Alexander founded, Greek and Asian populations were deliberately mixed with the idea of uniting East and West into a single empire. At Susa (now in southwestern Iran), a year before he died, this internationalism took an even more personal form. This was a mass wedding in which 10,000 of his troops married Asian women, 80 of his Macedonian officers took Persian wives, and he himself took as his bride a daughter of Darius.

After Alexander's death, his empire was split up by his generals, and, before long, attacks from Gauls in the west and Parthians in the east divided it still farther. But Greek ideas and institutions continued to be a strong influence in the East. And the discoveries made by Alexander had vastly enlarged the known world of the Greeks. The lands that he had conquered or explored cover the modern countries of Greece, Bulgaria, Turkey, Iran, Afghanistan, West Pakistan, Iraq, Syria, Jordan, Israel, Egypt, and part of southern Russia. In the meantime, another Greek was pushing back the frontiers of the unknown in a different direction.

Above: a Greek vase, showing soldiers. The Greeks were used to difficult conditions, but even for them the march through the Makrān Desert was grueling. The heat and aridity of the region combined with hunger and thirst to cause many deaths among the men.

BLACK SEA

CAUCASUS

CASPIAN SEA

Thrace

3a from Pella

BOSPORUS
Byzantium
(Istanbul)

HELLESPONT (DARDANELLES)

Troy

ergamum

AEGEAN
SEA

Sardis

Ephesus

Miletus

Halicarnassus

Ancyra
(Ankara)

Trapezus
(Trabzon)

ELBURZ

Rhagae
(Teheran)

Issus

Euphrates

Aleppo

Ninoveh

Gaugamela

Tigris

Ecbatana

MEDITERRANEAN

SEA

Damascus

Tyre

Cunaxa

Babylon

Susa

Persepolis

Alexandria

Euphrates

probable former coastline

PERSIAN
GULF

wah

Libyan

Nile

Desert

RED

SEA

OPIC OF CANCER

0   100   200   300   400   500

Miles

30°   40°   50°

92

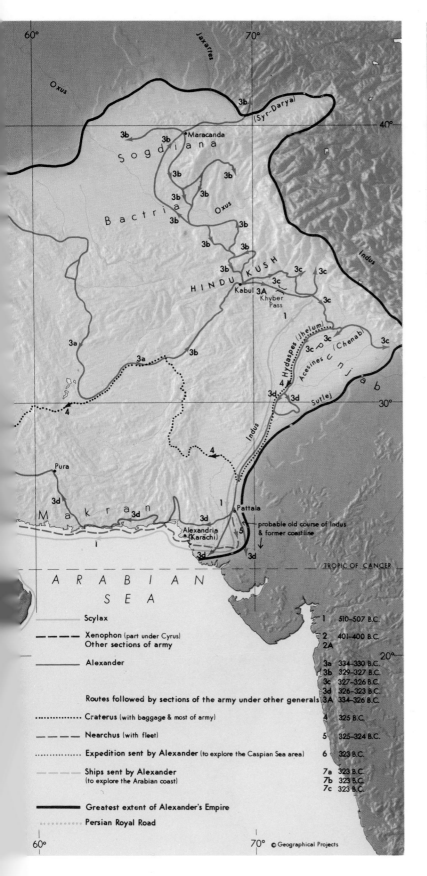

Above: the death of Alexander, from a Persian manuscript entitled *Alexander's Celestial Journey*. With Oriental splendor, Alexander is shown being drawn to heaven by birds.

Map labels

60°
70°
Jaxartes
Oxus
40°
3b
(Syr-Darya)
3b Maracanda
3b
S o g d i a n a
3b
3b
3b
B a c t r i a
Oxus
3b
3b
3b
3b
3b
H I N D U K U S H
Kabul 3A
Khyber Pass
1
3c 3c
3c
3c
3c
Indus
3a
3a
3b
3c 3c
Hydaspes (Jhelum)
Acesines (Chenab)
3c
P u n j a b
3d
3d Sutlej
30°
Indus
4
4
4
Pura
3d
M a k r a n
3d
1
Pattala
3d
Alexandria (Karachi)
5
probable old course of Indus & former coastline
3d
TROPIC OF CANCER

A R A B I A N
S E A

——— Scylax	1	510–507 B.C.
– – – Xenophon (part under Cyrus)	2	401–400 B.C.
Other sections of army	2A	
——— Alexander		
	3a	334–330 B.C.
	3b	329–327 B.C.
	3c	327–326 B.C.
	3d	326–323 B.C.
Routes followed by sections of the army under other generals	3A	334–326 B.C.
········· Craterus (with baggage & most of army)	4	325 B.C.
– – – Nearchus (with fleet)	5	325–324 B.C.
········· Expedition sent by Alexander (to explore the Caspian Sea area)	6	323 B.C.
Ships sent by Alexander	7a	323 B.C.
(to explore the Arabian coast)	7b	323 B.C.
	7c	323 B.C.
▬▬▬ Greatest extent of Alexander's Empire		
·········· Persian Royal Road		

20°

60°
70°
© Geographical Projects

Left: the Middle East, showing the routes of the Greek explorers, from Scylax in 510 B.C. to Xenophon in 401 B.C., and Alexander the Great and his generals between 334 and 323 B.C. The frontiers of Alexander's empire at its greatest extent are also shown.

93

New Horizons

7

Left: a Greek statue of a man found at Massalia – present-day Marseille. Greek emigrants founded Marseille in about 600 B.C., and within 300 years the city had become an important cultural and commercial center. It was from Massalia that the great navigator Pytheas set out on his long voyage into the unknown northern waters.

Below: a coin from Marseille. On the reverse side is a lion and the word *Mazza*, a name sometimes given to the city of Marseille.

About the time that Alexander and Nearchus were setting out from the mouth of the Indus, a Greek explorer left Massalia (Marseille) in southern France. He sailed past the Pillars of Hercules, and headed for northern waters on a voyage that was to take him around the island of Britain. The explorer's name was Pytheas. His expedition, like that of Alexander in the eastern parts of the world, is a demonstration of the spirit of inquiry and adventure that prevailed throughout the Greek-speaking world.

Pytheas was a mathematician and astronomer as well as a great navigator. He was the first Greek to suggest that tides were dependent on the moon. He upset the prevailing belief that the Pole Star was the center of the heavens, and that all other stars revolved around it. Using a sundial, he calculated the latitude of his native Massalia with only a fractional error. Pytheas' scientific inquiries support the claim often made for him that he was the first scientific explorer in history. But it is unlikely that his travels were made solely in the interests of discovery. He visited the tin-mining areas of Cornwall, and challenged the Carthaginian monopoly of Atlantic sea routes—a matter of great concern to the Greek colonists of Massalia at this time. The Carthaginians had achieved supremacy in the Atlantic by blockading the Strait of Gibraltar. So successful had they been that Pytheas is the first Greek known to have reached the Atlantic since Colaeus was accidentally blown there 300 years earlier.

Pytheas' voyage was so exceptional that most early geographers and historians disbelieved and ridiculed his reports of it. He wrote a book with the modest title *About the Ocean,* and this seems to have been enough for him to be accused of telling travelers' tales. The book has been lost, but it is referred to by classical writers. The Greek historian Polybius, who saw the original, condemned the author as "an arch-falsifier." But this has been the reward of many explorers, and today Pytheas' account is largely accepted.

The date of Pytheas' voyage may reasonably be fixed at about 325 B.C. The kind of ship he sailed in is unknown. Unless the merchants of Massalia were backing him for commercial reasons, he is unlikely to have been able to afford a large one. But it must have been a vessel capable of standing up to a year's voyage of at least 7,000 miles (about the distance of Columbus' voyage to America and back) in far rougher waters than those of the Mediterranean.

From the fragmentary evidence available, it is impossible to tell

Left: the rugged coastline of Brittany, along which Pytheas would have sailed on his journey northward. Sailors of his time, faced with the problem of determining their position on the open sea with virtually no navigational instruments, sensibly chose to hug the coastline on their voyages.

Below: cassiterite, crystals of tin ore. Cornwall was an important exporter of tin to the ancient world.

how Pytheas ran the Carthaginian blockade of the Strait of Gibraltar. He may even have avoided the strait altogether by traveling overland from Massalia on a trade route that ran north through France, and then sailing from Corbilo (St. Nazaire) at the mouth of the Loire River in northwest France. Alternatively, he may have slipped through the strait under cover of darkness and made his way around Cape St. Vincent, following much the same route as Himilco had done over 100 years before. His observations of latitude indicate that he passed what is now Oporto on the northwest coast of Portugal and continued northward through the Bay of Biscay to the island of Ushant off the tip of Brittany in northwest France. Leaving the French coast, he may then have struck across the English Channel directly to Land's End in Cornwall. Whatever his route, he passed beyond the northwestern limit of the world the Greeks knew as soon as he reached the waters north of Portugal. As he headed for the Cornish tin coast, he was making a daring trespass into the Carthaginian sphere of influence.

Once in Britain, Pytheas observed the way tin was extracted, smelted, refined, and cast into ingots for export. Then he probably rounded Land's End, and sailed up the west coast of Britain. There is no record that Pytheas landed in Ireland, but it is thought that he saw enough of the coastline to provide the Greek mathematician and astronomer Eratosthenes with the information he needed to locate it accurately on the map he drew a hundred years later.

Pytheas sailed all the way around Britain, which he judged to be triangular in shape. He placed Land's End (southwest England),

Right: ancient writers differ and mod
historians disagree about the exact
route followed by Pytheas, the Greek
explorer, in about 325 B.C. This map
of western Europe gives a number of
possible routes and the places he may
have visited on the way.

THULE
(ICELAND)

ATLANTIC

OCEAN

FAEROE IS.

SHETLAND
IS.

SCANDINAVIA

SCOTLAND

Duncansby Hd.

NORTH

SEA

BALTIC SEA

IRELAND

ENGLAND

HELGOLAND

E.N. Foreland

Lands End

Cornwall

ENGLISH CHANNEL

USHANT

Rhine

Corbilo
St. Nazaire Loire

BAY OF

BISCAY

Rhine

Rhône

Massalia

St. Vincent

HERCULES
(GIBRALTAR)

MEDITERRANEAN

SEA

© Geographical Projects

	Pytheas' route according to Stefansson & Broche
1a	Areas where Broche differs from Stefansson
2	Pytheas' route according to Markham & Synge
2a	Return journey where Synge differs from Markham
3	Pytheas' route according to Russian authorities
4	Pytheas' route according to Hermann

ARCTIC CIRCLE

ARCTIC CIRCLE

100   200   300   400   500
Miles

Above: an Anglo-Saxon map of the A.D. 900's, showing the ocean that was believed to surround the world. Although some Greek scholars had believed the earth to be round, the idea of a flat world surrounded by sea was again current by the A.D. 900's. It was to persist for centuries to come.

the North Foreland of Kent (southeast England), and Duncansb Head (northeast tip of the Scottish mainland) as the three extremities He estimated the distance around Britain as 4,684 miles (double th real length of the coastline) and the distance across the Englis Channel from Dover in southeast England to Calais in norther France as 11 miles (instead of 21). These inaccuracies are part of th reason why Pytheas' account of his expedition is not always believe today. But the difficulties of measuring distances at sea in his tim were considerable and many other sailors made similar mistakes.

Another misleading statement about Pytheas' voyage was made b Polybius, who says that the explorer "traveled all over Britain b foot." This probably means that Pytheas landed at various plac where he was able to make important observations about the cou try and the people. He noted that the Britons stored grain in cover buildings because of the rain, and, for the same reason, thresh indoors. He found the country extremely cold and observed that t large population led a primitive existence, living in log and re houses, eating simple foods, and drinking *curmi*, a type of beer.

To Pytheas' contemporaries, and to all geographers in the pr Christian era, it was a matter of the greatest interest to learn ho far north the world stretched. The notion that a sea—Oceanus—e circled the central land mass still persisted, and everyone w naturally curious to know where in the north sea and land wou meet. Pytheas brought back an answer. He said that he had been to about an island called Thule. Six days' sailing from the north Britain, this was the "outermost of all countries."

As an astronomer, Pytheas was fascinated by the information t

Above: ocean ice, now called pancake ice. Pytheas wrote that the sea beyond Thule (probably Norway or Iceland) was sluggish and congealed and that ships could not sail through it. This has been taken to mean that he encountered ocean ice. Pytheas described the ice as looking like a jellyfish.

Above: a coin of Euergetes II, who sponsored Eudoxus' voyage to India.

Right: a map showing Thule, which was first described by Pytheas. Whether Thule was what is now Iceland or part of Norway has never been determined.

in Thule the day was 24 hours long at midsummer. This indicates that Thule must have been either Norway or Iceland. But from the scanty information about Thule given by the writers who quote Pytheas, it is impossible to know for certain which of these two countries is meant. Pytheas is reported to have said that beyond Thule the sea became sluggish and congealed, and that men could neither sail through it nor walk over it. He also said that the inhabitants of Thule lived on wild berries and grain and made a mead-like drink from the honey of their bees. The congealed sea has been taken to refer to the sludge at the edge of the Arctic ice, which is more likely to be encountered off Iceland than Norway. Bees, however, are not found as far north as Iceland, and this has strengthened the belief that Thule was a part of Norway, even though Norway is not an island.

It is not certain whether Pytheas visited Thule, and little is known about the remainder of his travels. He may have followed the coast of Europe northeastward to explore beyond the Rhine. He is known to have landed on an island in northeast Europe where "in the Spring the waves wash up amber upon the shores." Perhaps this was Bornholm, 25 miles off the southern coast of Sweden. If so, Pytheas was the first man from the ancient world to enter the Baltic Sea. But the description could apply equally to the amber island of Helgoland off northwest Germany in the North Sea.

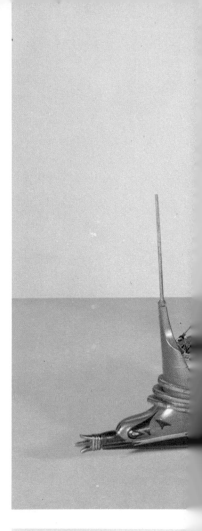

After Pytheas' return to Massalia, there were apparently no further Greek voyages to the north. The Carthaginians maintained their blockade on the Atlantic until Carthage fell to the Romans in 146 B.C. No one could verify Pytheas' discoveries, and this was certainly one of the reasons why his reports were open to the scorn of later historians.

Explorers' reports are a natural target for skeptics, and the story of Eudoxus, the first Greek to reach India by sea, was no exception. Eudoxus was a rich merchant from Cyzicus, a port in Asia Minor on the Sea of Marmara, which separates the Bosporus and the Dardanelles. His voyage was made in about 120 B.C. and started from Egypt. He was staying in Alexandria at the court of the Greek king of Egypt, Euergetes II, when some strange news was received. A shipwrecked Indian had been brought in from the Red Sea. He was nearly dead from drowning, but when he had been nursed back to health, Euergetes ordered that he was to be taught enough Greek to give an account of his voyage from his native country.

The rescued man's story was that he had been blown hundreds of miles from India across the Arabian Sea. This could not be corroborated as all his companions had been drowned. He insisted that they had been the victims of mischance, and if the king doubted the possibility of making such a voyage, he would readily act as a guide to take a ship back the way he had come.

Euergetes accepted the offer, and Eudoxus agreed to lead the expedition. With the Indian as his pilot, he set off down the Red Sea. All details of his voyage are lost, however. The story is wound up all

Above: a modern reconstruction of a
Greek trireme—a ship like those
probably used for the most ambitious
Greek voyages. As no complete contemporary sculpture or painting of a
trireme has been discovered, no one
knows exactly what these ships looked
like. It is known, however, that
they were propelled by 170 oars in 3
banks, and were some 150 feet long

Left: rough and cut gemstones from
India and Ceylon—sapphires, rubies,
and garnets. These treasures of the
mysterious East were a much-desired
luxury for the Mediterranean peoples.

too briefly by the historian Strabo. He merely recounts that, after
reaching India, Eudoxus "sailed away with presents, and he returned with a cargo of perfumes and precious stones. . . ." The pioneer explorer of one of the world's most important sea routes
received no honors or rewards. According to Strabo, "Eudoxus was
badly disappointed for Euergetes took from him his entire cargo."
Possibly the historian was exaggerating Eudoxus' reaction, for in all
such Egyptian state enterprises the king had a right to the cargo.

After the death of Euergetes, his wife Cleopatra, who had succeeded him as regent for their son Soter II, sent Eudoxus out again
to India with several ships. On the homeward journey, Eudoxus
was blown off his course and forced to land on the African coast
below Cape Guardafui, in Somaliland. When he finally made his way
back to Alexandria, all his cargo was once again taken from him.

Finding state voyages of such little profit, Eudoxus then embarked on a career of private exploration. While he had been on the
African coast, he had found a wooden prow in the shape of a horse
that had been washed ashore from a wrecked ship. The shipwrights
of Alexandria told him that this was a figurehead from one of the
small vessels of Gades that plied the West African shores as far as
northwest Morocco. Since Eudoxus had found the prow on the East

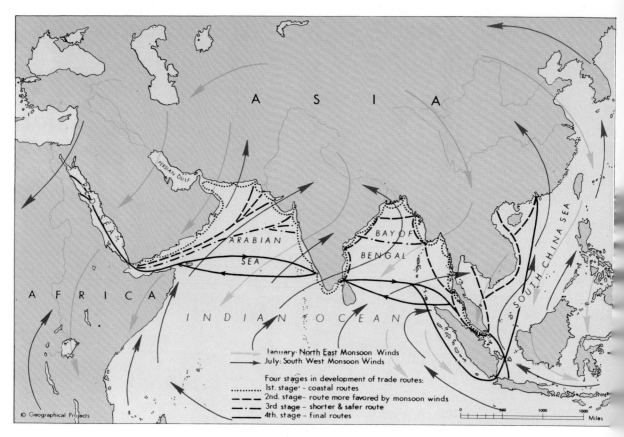

On the map:

ASIA

PERSIAN GULF

ARABIAN SEA

BAY OF BENGAL

INDIAN OCEAN

SOUTH CHINA SEA

AFRICA

© Geographical Projects

January: North East Monsoon Winds
July: South West Monsoon Winds

Four stages in development of trade routes:
.... 1st. stage - coastal routes
– – – 2nd. stage - route more favored by monsoon winds
–·–·– 3rd. stage - shorter & safer route
——— 4th. stage - final routes

0   500   1000   1500
Miles

Above: this map of the Indian Ocean shows the main direction of the monsoon winds—northeast in January and southwest in July. It also shows how the sailors of the ancient world used these seasonal winds to extend their trade routes as far east as China.

African coast, he concluded that it was possible to sail around Africa. He set out to try to reach India by rounding Africa from west to east, but abandoned the voyage when his ships ran aground on the Moroccan coast. Of his second attempt to circumnavigate Africa, nothing is known. He left Gades in about 105 B.C. and was never seen nor heard of again.

But Eudoxus' earlier voyages to India were not forgotten. For it seems probable that he brought back information that made long voyages across the open sea possible. The mysterious Indian guide may well have shown Eudoxus how to make use of the southwest summer monsoons. These winds would have blown the Greek captain's ship straight across the Arabian Sea to his destination. Eudoxus could then have used the northeast winter monsoon to make the return journey. For centuries, Arabian and Indian sailors had traveled between the Indian ports and the Red Sea with the aid of the regular seasonal winds of the monsoon. Nearchus, Alexander's lieutenant, had probably been the first Westerner to see the importance of these seasonal winds, which blow for six months from the southwest and for six months from the northeast. But, as far as is known, the Greeks of Nearchus' time ignored his discovery, and continued to make their voyages hugging the coast. The importance of the monsoons came as an immense revelation to Eudoxus.

Even after Eudoxus' discovery, the monsoon route to India was at first little used. In fact, its discovery has also been attributed to

Greek merchant called Hippalus who sailed from a port on the Red
Sea to the Malabar Coast of western India in about 45 B.C., nearly 80
years after Eudoxus' voyage. The southwesterly monsoon even
came to be called *hippalus* in his honor. But although Hippalus was
not the first to use the monsoons to make his voyage, his journey
played a vital part in establishing a trade route to India. Around the
time of the birth of Christ, as many as 120 ships a year were using the
monsoons to sail from Egypt to India across the open sea.

Before long, Greek sailors also found a more southerly route
across the Arabian Sea to the southern tip of India and Ceylon.
Venturing farther still, these unknown mariners made their way
around India into the Bay of Bengal, and explored the east coast of
India as far north as the mouth of the Ganges. In about A.D. 120, a
merchant named Alexander is reported to have used the monsoon
to sail across the Bay of Bengal from India to Malacca, on the
Malay Peninsula. He then continued his voyage around the southern tip of the peninsula, across the Gulf of Siam and northward
as far as the present-day frontier between North Vietnam and China.

If this is true, Alexander was the first man of the western world to
open up a sea route to China. As with so many of the early discoverers, little is known about this daring sailor. But his remarkable
achievement, and the pioneering voyages of those who first sailed
the seas between Africa and India, have a place of honor among the
world's great voyages of exploration.

ight: the head of the stone dragon
akara from the area that is now
ietnam. In about A.D. 120, a Greek
erchant called Alexander opened up
sea route to China. This was the
st recorded voyage to the Far East.

Hannibal Crosses the Alps

8

Above: Hannibal, on a silver shekel struck at Cartagena around 220 B.C.

Left: Hannibal crossing the Alps. This illustration is taken from a manuscript made centuries after Hannibal's journey. The artist clearly knew little more about elephants than the Roman soldiers of Hannibal's own time, who had been terrified by the sight of these huge beasts.

In the temple of Baal Shamin at Carthage, a nine-year-old boy stood beside his father, the great general Hamilcar Barca. He placed his hand on a sacrificed animal and swore to take vengeance on Rome, the enemy of his country. The boy's name was Hannibal. And his oath was the prelude to the most daring and unorthodox expedition of early times—a 940-mile march that took an army of men and elephants across the Alps. This was a journey of such difficulty and appalling hardship that it could never have succeeded without the outstanding abilities and iron will of a man like Hannibal. He was a brilliant strategist, a great leader, and single-minded in the pursuit of his aims.

Hannibal was born in 247 B.C. and grew up when Carthage was engaged in a death struggle with Rome. For 250 years, the Carthaginians had been masters of the western Mediterranean. Now the supremacy of Carthage, the largest and richest city in the world, was challenged by the new military power that had grown out of a confederacy of Italian tribes. During Hannibal's boyhood and early manhood, there was a complete change in the old Mediterranean spheres of influence. When Hannibal was six, the island of Sicily was wrested from Carthaginian control by the legions of Rome. The fall of Sicily in 241 B.C. ended the 23-year struggle between Carthage and Rome known as the First Punic War. The Carthaginian Navy was wiped out. Carthage was forced to accept humiliating terms for peace and to pay huge fines to the Roman victors. In 239 B.C., threatened by a fresh outbreak of war, the Carthaginians ceded Sardinia and Corsica to Rome.

Carthage itself stood in danger, but the Carthaginians' determination to resist Roman domination did not weaken. Soon after Hannibal had made his sacred vow in the temple, he set out with his father for Spain, where Carthage was to found an extension of its empire. For Hamilcar had already conceived the daring plan of marching overland from Spain and striking at the Romans from the north. Rome could mobilize a large army at short notice. Surprise was therefore essential. But Carthage had no navy with which to launch a seaborne invasion of Italy. Nothing could, however, be more unexpected than the arrival of an army across the Alps. Before he could undertake such an expedition, Hamilcar had to build up a strong base in Spain, recruit men for his army, and obtain enough money to finance his campaign.

At first, Hamilcar made the old Carthaginian town of Gades (Cádiz) his base. But soon he began the systematic occupation of southern and southeastern Spain. Copper mines were opened and agriculture flourished. An advance base was established near Alicante on the east coast. Spanish tribes were incorporated into a growing colonial army. When an alarmed mission from Rome arrived to discover what was happening, they were told that all this was in Rome's best interest. Why, it would ensure Carthage's steady payment of war debts!

When Hannibal was 18, his father was drowned in the course of one of his expeditions. Hannibal, who had already proved himself an outstanding soldier, continued to serve under Hamilcar's son-in-law Hasdrubal, who founded the city of New Carthage (Cartagena) on the southeastern coast of Spain. When Hasdrubal was murdered in 221 B.C., the 26-year-old Hannibal was unanimously elected commander in chief of the army. For three years, Hannibal worked to build up his forces, and continued to increase Carthaginian power in Spain. In 219 B.C., he attacked the city of Saguntum, in eastern Spain, which was allied to Rome. After a bitter seven-month siege, Saguntum fell to Hannibal. Rome at once declared war on Carthage, and the Second Punic War began. The time had come for Hannibal's long-pledged expedition of revenge.

In the spring of 218 B.C., Hannibal marched out of Cartagena with an army of 60,000 infantrymen, 12,000 horsemen, and a troop of

Below: Hannibal as a young boy making his solemn oath to take vengeance on Carthage's enemy, Rome. Watched by his father, Hamilcar Barca, Hannibal swore on the body of an animal that had been sacrificed to the gods.

37 elephants. His departure bore a distinct resemblance to that of Alexander, 116 years earlier. Here was another son fulfilling the plans of his father, a young general intent on the conquest of his enemies. Ahead of him lay a five-month march from Spain to Italy across the Pyrenees, the Rhône River, and one of the highest passes in the Alps.

The elephants added to the difficulty of the march. But they had an important role to play in Hannibal's campaign. Elephants were the tanks of ancient warfare. Ever since they had first been encountered in battle by Alexander's troops on the banks of the Hydaspes, their value as a substitute for war chariots had been recognized. They were extremely valuable pack animals and, although their behavior in battle was unpredictable, they could be useful against enemy cavalry that had not been trained to meet them. But, above all, they were a powerful psychological weapon. Hannibal knew that his elephants would create panic among the Roman soldiers, who would never have seen such creatures before.

At the start of the expedition, Hannibal did not reveal to his troops that their destination was Italy. But when the army was preparing to cross the Pyrenees, a number of the men must have guessed the daunting prospect ahead, for they mutinied. Hannibal decided to leave behind 7,000 of the more unreliable men. With the remainder of his army, he pressed on over the Pyrenees and marched into southern Gaul (France).

Above: a Punic coin with the head of Hamilcar Barca, minted at Cartagena late in the 200's B.C. *Punic* was the Roman name for the people of Carthage – in Latin it means *Phoenician*.

Below: the Pyrenees, which divide France from Spain, and which Hannibal's men had to cross at the start of their long march. The exact route they took cannot be determined from the accounts of the expedition.

Hannibal could then have followed the coast all the way through Gaul along the present-day French Riviera to Italy, thus avoiding the hazards of the Alpine passes and shortening his journey considerably. But the Greek colony of Massalia (Marseille), which lay on this route, was allied to Rome, and might have called for help. A head-on collision with a Roman army between the Basses Alpes and the Mediterranean Sea was too great a risk for Hannibal to take. So the Carthaginian general struck north up the Rhône Valley well west of Marseille.

The crossing of the Rhône was the first serious natural hazard. It was probably made at Fourques just above Arles. At this point, the river was shallow and the current not too swift. But the river was three-quarters of a mile wide. Hannibal took five days to obtain boats from the local inhabitants and assemble a fleet of rafts for the infantry. Some of the horses were embarked on boats. Others were pulled through the water by the men in the boats. The remainder swam across with their riders.

Getting the elephants to the far side was not so easy. Two 100-foot-long piers were built out into the river and attached to large rafts. Piers and rafts were covered with earth so that the elephants believed they were still on land when they were led onto them. As the rafts were towed away, some of the elephants took fright and a number of rafts capsized. But the river was shallow enough for the

Above: Hannibal and his men crossi
the Rhône River. Although the river
was shallow and the current did not
flow too swiftly, the crossing presen
ted considerable difficulties.

Left: the reverse side of two Carthaginian silver coins, showing elephar
The elephants that accompanied Ha
bal's army had been captured in the
foothills of the Grand Atlas, Morocc

elephants to wade across, keeping their trunks above the surface. All the elephants reached the far bank safely.

Historians who wrote of Hannibal's journey recorded no place names, and, as a result, his route over the Alps is subject to much speculation. Scholars have had to work mainly on the general descriptions provided by the Greek historian Polybius. He states that the actual crossing of the Alps took 15 days, and gives an account of each day's march. From the evidence provided by Polybius and other classical writers, the British historian Sir Gavin De Beer, whose book on Hannibal is the result of 40 years' research, concludes that Hannibal took the southern pass over the Col de la Traversette, east of the town of Gap.

According to Sir Gavin, after the crossing at Fourques, Hannibal followed the Rhône to a point north of Montélimar, where it is joined by the Drôme River. There, he turned his army east along the

Above: a detail taken from the above engraving, showing one of the rafts used to get the elephants across. The rafts were covered with earth so that the elephants would not be frightened.

valley of the Drôme, which winds its way to Die. Ahead lay the jagged peaks of the Alps, but Hannibal's troops were still traveling through valleys of trees and grassy slopes until they reached the Col de Grimone. In one of the low passes the convoy was attacked from above by a hostile local tribe. During the skirmish, Hannibal lost many animals which fell over the steep drop on one side of the narrow, uneven path.

After this encounter, which took place on the second day in the mountains, Hannibal's troops captured a town that was large enough to supply food for the men and forage for the animals. There Hannibal ordered a day's rest. But there was no time to waste. It was already October. The weather was getting colder and the ascent had still to be made into even more bitter altitudes. For two days after leaving the town all went well. But on the army's seventh day in the mountains, Hannibal was approached by more tribesmen.

These men came carrying olive branches to indicate peace, and offered guides. But Hannibal, suspicious of their intentions, put his elephants, cavalry, and pack animals at the front of the column, and his heavy infantry behind. This enabled him to fight a rearguard action when, just as he had anticipated, there was an attack. The enemy chose a narrow gorge with a wall of cliffs on one side and

a ravine on the other. They rolled down rocks on the Carthaginians, and for a while succeeded in splitting the column in two. But it joined up again, and, though he had suffered some losses, Hannibal pressed on.

The eighth and ninth days took him over the highest pass, 9,000 feet up and covered with snow. The going was hard and the troops were very near the end of their resources. Hannibal ordered a two-day halt to reassemble the convoy disorganized by the attack and to allow stragglers to catch up. Through gaps in the mountains it was possible to see the plain below, and Hannibal indicated to his men the direction of Rome. From now on, he promised them, the march was downhill and victory certain.

Above: "Snowstorm: Hannibal and his Army Crossing the Alps" by J. M. W. Turner (1775–1851). Turner was an English Romantic landscape painter, whose greatest works are studies of light, color, and atmosphere. As the title of this picture suggests, Turner was more interested in the snowstorm than in Hannibal. The figures of the Carthaginian conqueror and his men can barely be made out amid the swirling splendor of this fierce blizzard.

Above left: Punic armor of the type worn by Hannibal's soldiers. The pieces are decorated breast and back plates, with shoulder braces and belt

But the descent did not prove as easy as he hoped. The track down which the column began to wind its way was narrow and covered by a deceptive layer of snow. A false step to one side by soldiers or pack horses, and they slithered to their death down a precipice. This was a constant danger. But worse was to follow. The front of the column suddenly came to a halt. The track had disappeared. A landslide had obliterated it over a distance of more than 300 yards. With great difficulty, Hannibal's men were just able to scramble across the gap. But, for the horses and elephants, progress was impossible.

There was no alternative but to clear the snow and repair the track. A particularly large rock that was lodged directly in their path

had to be removed. To do this, the men felled trees, cut them up, an
lit a fire on top of the rock. Then they drenched the rock in vinega
or sour wine, until it split as a result of the heat and the chemica
action of the acetic acid. Pickaxes did the rest. The way was cleare
and sufficiently repaired for the army to make the final part of the
descent onto the Italian plain.

The figures for Hannibal's losses from the time he crossed th
Rhône until he reached Italy are conflicting. They have been place
as high as 36,000 men. This is an enormous number in proportion
the total strength of his army, which had already been considerab

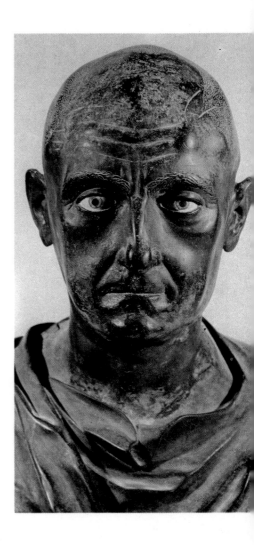

Left: the struggle to remove rocks from the path on Hannibal's descent, shown in a drawing of the 1600's by Pietro da Cortona. In the background, the army clambers through a gorge.

Right: a bronze bust of the Roman general Scipio Africanus, who finally defeated Hannibal's army at Zama.

eakened by the time it reached the Rhône. The march was a iumph of endurance, and not least for the elephants. All of them e said to have survived the mountain journey, but, with no chance getting natural foodstuffs at high altitudes, they suffered seriously. onsidering the difficulties, it was also a triumph of speed. The 15-y journey through the mountains was achieved at an average eed of 9 miles a day, or, if the rest-days are deducted, 12 miles a y.

The rest of Hannibal's story belongs more to the history of war an to an account of exploration. The strategy of surprise suc-

ceeded. He won a series of great victories: first at the Trebia River
northwestern Italy; then, after crossing the Apennines, at La
Trasimeno in central Italy; and then, in 216 B.C., at Cannae in t
southeast, where the Romans suffered the worst defeat they had ev
known. But although Hannibal remained in Italy for 15 years,
was never able to defeat the Romans decisively. After the Battle
Cannae, the armies met in numerous skirmishes, but they nev
again joined in open battle. In the autumn of 203 B.C., Hannibal l

Italy on receiving urgent orders to return home. Carthage was under siege by the Romans, and he was recalled to oppose the advance of the Roman general Publius Cornelius Scipio (later known as Scipio Africanus). Hannibal's army, so long undefeated on the Italian mainland, at last met its match. It was crushed by Scipio at Zama (Jama, 74 miles southwest of Tunis), and this defeat signaled the beginning of the twilight of Carthage. Just over 50 years later, the city was completely destroyed.

Hannibal did not live to see the end of the city to which he had dedicated his life. In 183 B.C., he died by his own hand rather than surrender to the Romans. Sometime before his death, he met the man who had defeated him at Zama. Scipio asked him whom he considered the greatest general in history. Without perhaps realizing it, Hannibal named the one leader comparable with himself as a military explorer. His reply was "Alexander the Great."

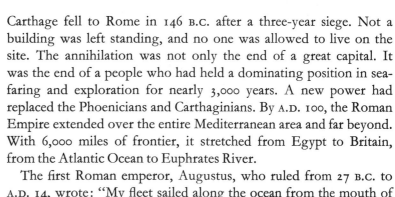

Rome's Exploring Legions

9

Carthage fell to Rome in 146 B.C. after a three-year siege. Not a building was left standing, and no one was allowed to live on the site. The annihilation was not only the end of a great capital. It was the end of a people who had held a dominating position in seafaring and exploration for nearly 3,000 years. A new power had replaced the Phoenicians and Carthaginians. By A.D. 100, the Roman Empire extended over the entire Mediterranean area and far beyond. With 6,000 miles of frontier, it stretched from Egypt to Britain, from the Atlantic Ocean to Euphrates River.

The first Roman emperor, Augustus, who ruled from 27 B.C. to A.D. 14, wrote: "My fleet sailed along the ocean from the mouth of the Rhine to the country of the Cimbri [a Germanic people] which no Roman before that time had penetrated by land or sea.... I advanced the boundaries of Illyria [in present-day Albania] to the banks of the Danube.... Many embassies were sent to the Indian kings... I added Egypt to my Empire...." These were the achievements of a single reign. During the 200 years from 100 B.C. to A.D. 100, the Romans also explored Britain; they went in search of the source of the Nile; they crossed the Grand Atlas mountains in Morocco and marched to the Persian Gulf; and they journeyed to Yemen and into present-day Crimea.

This might suggest that the Romans were the greatest of all the early explorers. Certainly they brought law and order, government, and civilization to far countries. But not all their campaigns can be regarded as true exploration. Some were purely military expeditions, made with the sole purpose of conquest. In others, however, the Romans did push back the frontiers of the known world. Julius Caesar's famous words from Zela (Zile) near the Black Sea—"I came, I saw, I conquered"—sum up the dual role of the explorer-general.

The Romans went into Asia in 192 B.C., and extended their influence as far as the Taurus Mountains in the south of modern

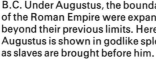

Left: a cameo of Augustus, the first of the Roman emperors. Augustus came to power after the death of Julius Caesar, and ruled as emperor after 27 B.C. Under Augustus, the boundaries of the Roman Empire were expanded far beyond their previous limits. Here, Augustus is shown in godlike splendor as slaves are brought before him.

Overleaf: the Mediterranean Sea showing the frontiers of the two rival powers, Rome and Carthage, in 218 B.C., the year in which Hannibal set out with his army on their great march. Hannibal's route, and the later expeditions of Aelius Gallus and Suetonius Paulinus, are also shown, together with Caesar's campaigns.

SCOTLAND

NORTH

SEA

BRITAIN

BAL

ATLANTIC

WALES

ENGLAND

Thames

BRITAIN

lost in A.D. 9

OCEAN

ENGLISH CHANNEL

Rhine

Danube

GAUL

A L P S

Col de la
Traversette

PYRENEES

Rhône

Massalia

LIGURIAN
SEA

ILLYR

Saguntum

CORSICA

L. Trasimeno

Rome

Canna

BALEARIC IS.

SARDINIA

Alicante

Gades
(Cadiz)

STR. OF GIBRALTAR

New Carthage
(Cartagena)

Caesarea

M E D I T E R R A

SICILY

MAURETANIA

Carthage

Zama

GREAT ATLAS

Ger

NUMIDIA

3

3

Roman Republic in 218 B.C.
Roman Empire at its greatest extent A.D. 117

Carthage & her colonies 218 B. C.

Hannibal   1 218-202 B.C.

Aelius Gallus   2 25-24 B.C.

Suetonius Paulinus 3 A.D. 42

Julius Caesar's campaigns in Gaul Spain, Britain & Armenia 61-47 B.C.
Julius Caesar's campaigns in the civil war against Pompey 49-45 B.C.

0   100   200   300   400   500
                                    Miles

© Geographical Projects

Turkey and the Halys River (modern Kizil Irmak) in central Turkey. But when Roman troops actually crossed the Taurus Mountains a century later, the military extension of the frontier also involved exploration. Similarly, the invasion of Armenia by the Roman general Lucullus in 69 B.C., and Pompey's advance across the Caucasus into the lands between the Black Sea and the Caspian at about the same period, were more than military expeditions. During both these campaigns, the Roman leaders observed the countries and the peoples they had conquered.

The Romans discovered which was the best pass over the Malyy Caucasus Mountains. They followed and mapped the course of the Cyrus River (now called the Kura). With the aid of a hundred interpreters, they recorded details of the trading methods of 70 tribes on the east coast of the Black Sea. Pompey made notes of trade routes from India which were to be of future use to the Romans. The explorers had a keen eye, too, for the unusual. They noted with amusement that the Armenians used toboggans for getting about on mountain slopes, and even a form of roller skate. This had spiked wooden wheels under the boots to prevent the wearer from slipping.

As the empire grew, the Romans were concerned mainly with securing their frontiers rather than embarking on far-flung campaigns in new lands. An exception was the expedition mounted by the Emperor Augustus in 25 B.C., to penetrate into the largely unknown and unexplored regions of southern Arabia. The aim was to reach Yemen and locate the city of Marib, near present-day San'ā'. From this great ancient capital, some people believed that the Queen of

Left: the Queen of Sheba fording a stream to meet King Solomon. The Bible story of the fabulously rich queen has long captured the imagination of the world, and many legends have grown up around it. This picture, from a prayer book of the 1400's, is based on the legend that Sheba refused to cross a stream by a bridge because she recognized the timbers as those upon which Christ would be crucified. None of the legends say exactly where Sheba's country was situated and several places claim the distinction of being her capital.

Right: a small Roman boat with its crew, from a mosaic found in a villa in Rome.

Above: the town of Marib in Yemen, viewed from the surrounding desert. Some believe it to be the capital of Sheba. In this belief Augustus sent out an expedition under Aelius Gallus to bring it under Roman rule.

Sheba had ruled, 900 years before. From Marib, she was said to have carried fabulous treasure to the court of King Solomon. Yemen was a land of gold, precious stones, myrrh, frankincense, perfumes, spices, and medicinal ointments. For too long, Augustus considered, Arab traders had come north with their caravans. They sold their treasures to Rome and went home rich, having bought nothing in exchange. Augustus resolved that Roman rule and a Roman shipping route would change all that.

In 25 B.C., an expedition under the leadership of Aelius Gallus set out from Cleopatris, a port near present-day Suez. Gallus' orders were to find and conquer the fabulous city of Marib and bring the rich Arabian trade route under Roman control. A force of 10,000 men embarked on the journey aboard 130 specially built ships. Besides Roman legions, the force included Egyptian troops, a contingent of 500 men supplied by King Herod of Judea, and 1,000 Nabataeans from Petra (in what is now Jordan). The Nabataeans were under the command of the Vizier Syllaeus. Gallus' ships sailed southward, keeping close to the Arabian coast. Navigation was difficult, and many of the vessels were wrecked on the coral reefs of the Gulf of Suez. When the men finally landed, about 300 miles down the Arabian coast, Gallus was forced to delay the overland march for many months because of illness among his men.

In the spring of 24 B.C., the 900-mile journey across the barren wastes of the desert of Arabia began. The army made frequent detours in search of wells and precious drinking water. They lived on local grain, dates, and butter. Camels carried only the most essential supplies. The Roman troops clashed with local tribes, but Roman superiority appears to have been overwhelming. The casualty figures read: Arabs killed, 10,000; Romans killed, 2.

During the weary trek south, several towns were captured by the army, but the city that was the main objective of the expedition withstood attack. It is not even certain that the city the Romans besieged was the famous Marib, the Queen of Sheba's capital. Its name is recorded as Mariba, but the reports of the expedition do not state specifically (as they surely would) that this was Sheba's city.

Exhausted by the march and dispirited after their defeat, the soldiers began the return journey. It was beset with difficulties. The explorers spent six hopeless months in the region of Yemen and Hadhramaut in southern Arabia. Misled by local guides, they were often lost in the trackless desert. It was even suggested that Syllaeus, the vizier from Petra, deliberately gave Gallus false directions to prevent the expedition from establishing new routes that would cut Nabataean profits from the trade caravans. It seems more likely, however, that Syllaeus was made the scapegoat for a campaign which had lost a great many men through disease and exhaustion, and was, by Roman standards, a disaster.

Considerably more rewarding and important for exploration were the Roman expeditions to Britain, made by Julius Caesar in 55 and 54 B.C., and by the Emperor Claudius 97 years later. After three

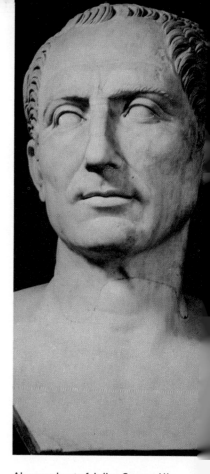

Above: a bust of Julius Caesar. His expedition to Britain in 54 B.C. was far more successful than his first invasion the previous year. In 54 B.C., Caesar landed in what is now Kent, and marched inland, fording the Thames probably above present-day London.

ears spent campaigning against the tribes of Gaul (present-day France), Caesar decided to invade the island of Britain. This was a country about which the Romans knew very little. Caesar had probably read that Pytheas the Greek had described Britain as a moist country. He was familiar with the tin trade. And he may also have hoped to find gold in Britain.

In the summer of 55 B.C., Caesar led 2 legions—about 10,000 men—across the English Channel in 80 transports. As the Roman ships approached the coast of Kent in southeast England, the Britons waded into the sea to oppose their landing. A bitter struggle followed, and the Britons were dispersed. The legionaries then made their way inland. But they did not proceed far. The Britons had resorted to guerrilla tactics. Time and again, they poured out of their dense forests and attacked the marching columns of Roman soldiers. The Romans had no cavalry reinforcements. The cavalry transports, which had left Gaul four days after the legions, were driven off shore by bad weather. To make matters worse, Caesar's own ships had been swept off the beach by rising tides, and a violent storm had destroyed many of them. Caesar was forced to give the order to retreat. His expedition lasted only two weeks.

The second invasion of Britain, the following year, was better planned. Caesar chose the month of July to land a force of 30,000 men near Sandwich, in Kent. Marching westward through Kent, he defeated the Britons in a battle near what is now Canterbury. He

Above: Roman soldiers in pitched battle with a Germanic tribe. Julius Caesar showed his brilliant military skill in his campaign to subdue the peoples of Europe, and he brought much of the western part of the continent within the Roman Empire.

Below: a helmet found in Britain of the type worn by Roman soldiers in the 100's. The Romans found the Britons determined adversaries who resorted to guerrilla tactics to defend themselves.

crossed the River Medway and then followed the River Thames, which he forded probably somewhere above present-day London. Leaving the Thames, he continued northward as far as Wheathampstead, near St. Albans (about 20 miles northwest of London). But after spending three months in Britain, Caesar learned that the Gauls were planning a rebellion against Rome. He made an uneasy peace with the Britons, and set sail again for Gaul.

By the time Caesar left Britain, he had formed a picture of the country and its people. Britain was thickly populated, he reported, and the people kept large numbers of cattle. The Britons lived in well-built homesteads and used gold coins or iron bars as money. Hares, fowl, and geese were reared "for pleasure and amusement," and it was considered unlawful to eat them. The climate was less cold than that of Gaul. Caesar had heard that Britain had a month of perpetual darkness, but, not surprisingly, could not confirm this.

Describing the people of the interior, Caesar noted that they did not grow corn, but lived on milk and meat, and clothed themselves with skins. "All the Britons dye their body with woad, which produces a blue color and gives them a terrible appearance in battle," Caesar wrote. "They wear their hair long, and shave the whole of their bodies except the head and upper lip."

Caesar's comments were based on hearsay as well as personal observation, and his facts do not always appear to be accurate. For example, grain is believed to have been widely cultivated in the interior of Britain, and the people used woven material for clothing. Caesar was, however, able to correct Pytheas' estimate of the size of Britain. He recorded that the south coast measured 475 miles, the west coast 665 miles, and the east coast 760 miles.

Claudius' expedition in A.D. 43 had the effect of speeding the growth of Britain as a trading center. His army conquered much of southern Britain and established a camp on the site of London as an advance base for the conquest of the entire island. Within 20 years, London had developed into a fortified town, and was crowded with merchants who came from all over Europe to buy British wares. Between A.D. 70 and 80, Romano-British civilization began in earnest under the Roman general Agricola, who conquered northern

Left: a detail showing a native Briton, from a mosaic floor of a Roman villa in what is now Somerset, in England.

Right: Hadrian's Wall, winding its way across the north of England. It was built at the command of the Emperor Hadrian at the northernmost limit of the territory under Roman control. The wall was to keep the still-unconquered Picts and Scots from invading England.

Left: after Carthage was defeated, Rome took over North Africa and established several Roman provinces there. These ruins are at Djemila, Algeria. Behind the columns can be seen the triumphal arch of the Emperor Nerva.

Below: a mosaic from Rome showing an imaginative picture of life on the Nile. The scene shows the people, the buildings, and local animals such as the hippopotamuses on the riverbanks.

England and North Wales and explored the coast of Scotland. The results of Roman occupation can still be seen all over Britain today, from the remains of forts and towns to the 70-mile-long wall across northern Britain built by the Emperor Hadrian in the A.D. 120's. Thousands of miles of straight Roman roads still exist to show another civil outcome of military exploration.

In Africa, at the other extreme of the Roman Empire, exploration took the Romans across the Grand Atlas mountains, on a search for the source of the River Nile, and probably into Kenya. North Africa had been annexed after the fall of Carthage, and Numidia (now part of eastern Algeria), and Mauretania (now in the northern parts of Morocco and Algeria) became Roman provinces after 46 B.C. Expeditions of Roman cavalry, mounted on fine Numidian horses, rode deep into the African interior south of Caesarea (Cherchel, on the Algerian coast). They brought back elephants, lions, leopards, and bears, which were shipped to Rome. There, the animals were used in one of the most popular entertainments of ancient Rome—fights between men and wild beasts. As many as 5,000 wild animals a day were required for these bloody spectacles in the Colosseum at Rome.

In Mauretania, the Roman consul Suetonius Paulinus became the first European to cross the Atlas mountains. In A.D. 42, he took an expedition 300 miles south from the Mediterranean coast to the mountains. He reported that the peaks were covered with snow even in summer. Ten days' journey took him through a pass to the River Ger (probably what is now the Wadi Guir) and "across deserts covered with black dust occasionally broken by projections of rock that looked as though they had been burned, a region rendered uninhabitable by heat." Where Suetonius crossed is uncertain, but the most likely route would have been between the peaks of the Grand Atlas to the west and the lower Saharan Atlas to the east.

Nineteen years later, in A.D. 61, the Emperor Nero ordered a journey of exploration to seek the source of the River Nile. The mysterious upper reaches of this great river had fascinated the people of the ancient world for centuries. The Egyptians themselves had never traveled farther up the Nile than Khartoum (in present-day Sudan). The Persians, under Cambyses, in 525 B.C., undertook an expedition up the river during which many men died from starvation. Herodotus recorded his journey to the First Cataract at Aswan in 460 B.C., and the Greeks in Egypt had many theories about the sources of the Nile. But in Nero's time the mystery was still unsolved.

Possibly exploration was not the only reason for Nero's expedition. It may have been a reconnaissance in preparation for a campaign against Ethiopia. But whether Nero had military intentions or not, his undertaking developed into an important journey of discovery. The small party of explorers, under the command of two *centurions* (commanders of a *century*, a group of about 100 men), pressed farther south than ever before in their attempt to reach the Nile's source.

The centurions probably followed a caravan route as far as the

Above: two Roman soldiers. It was men like these who tramped the long miles to the outermost edges of the world as it was then known. Much of the Roman expansion was in known countries, but in some of their military expeditions the Roman troops traveled right into the unknown.

Above: Murchison Falls in what is now
Uganda. The centurions of the Emperor
Nero's expedition reported seeing
"a great force of water" gushing from
two rocks. Exactly which waterfall
they saw has never been discovered.

Dunqulah bend of the Nile in present-day Sudan. During this par
of the journey, they found many abandoned Ethiopian towns or
the banks of the river. They saw parakeets and dog-faced baboons
and noticed traces of elephants and rhinoceroses. To save time
and to avoid following the Dunqulah bend, they then probably cu
across the desert to join the river again at a point just below wher
Khartoum now stands.

Still they pushed on until, they wrote, "we came to immens

marshes, the outcome of which neither the inhabitants knew nor anyone hopes to know. . . ." Progress on foot was impossible. And even the smallest of boats could not get far amid the thick tangle of weeds that choked the river. In this swampy region, the explorers saw "two rocks from which a great force of river water came falling." The Romans may have taken this to be the source of the Nile itself, but the Roman philosopher Seneca, who reported his conversation with the centurions after their return, wisely did not jump to that conclusion. It seems clear that the explorers had encountered the *sudd*—a mass of floating vegetable matter which can prevent boats sailing up the White Nile. Modern travelers have been unable to identify the two rocks and the great waterfall.

The discovery of the true sources of the Nile is claimed to have been made sometime between A.D. 60 and 70 by a Greek merchant named Diogenes. According to his story, he was sailing on the Indian route down the east coast of Africa when his ship was blown off course as far as what is now Dar es Salaam in Tanzania. Thence he traveled by an unidentified inland route until he "came in 25 days to the lake from which the Nile flows." Reporting Diogenes' discovery, the geographer Ptolemy states that Diogenes reached a place "where the Nile River becomes one from the union of rivers which flow from two lakes." He also mentions that these lakes were located at the extreme limits of a range called the Mountains of the Moon. These mountains, he adds, stretched 500 miles from east to west and were capped with snow, which melted into the lakes.

Ptolemy's account could mean that Diogenes reached the Victoria and Albert lakes. But the mountains that he saw are less easy to identify. There is no mountain range just south of these lakes where Ptolemy situates it. The name Mountains of the Moon is now applied to the Ruwenzori range, discovered by Henry Morton Stanley in 1889. But these mountains, which are frequently obscured by cloud, lie about 200 miles northwest of Lake Victoria and stretch from north to south, not east to west. It seems unlikely that Diogenes traveled as far as the Ruwenzori, although he may have been told about them. Possibly he passed near Mount Kilimanjaro during his journey inland and mistook its twin summits for a range of mountains, although he would have been wrong in thinking that snow from these peaks melted directly into lakes Victoria and Albert. Unfortunately, it is uncertain whether Diogenes saw these lakes and mountains personally. He may have relied on informants, and, indeed, some experts have doubted whether he can be believed at all. But although the geographic details of Diogenes' story do not fit in exactly with modern knowledge, Ptolemy must have had information on which to base his report. His map of the area is too near the truth to be wholly fabricated. The ultimate source of the Nile lies to the south of the Ruwenzori range, but melted snow from these mountains does flow into the Nile through Lake Albert. It was another 1,700 years, however, before anyone discovered how nearly right Ptolemy had been.

Above: a map of eastern Africa, drawn in the 1400's. This map still shows Ptolemy's Mountains of the Moon as the source of the River Nile. According to Ptolemy, the Greek merchant Diogenes was the first man to reach the mountains. Diogenes' report of his journey does not tally exactly with what is known today about the geography of Africa, and no one knows whether he saw what he reported, or whether he based his account on hearsay.

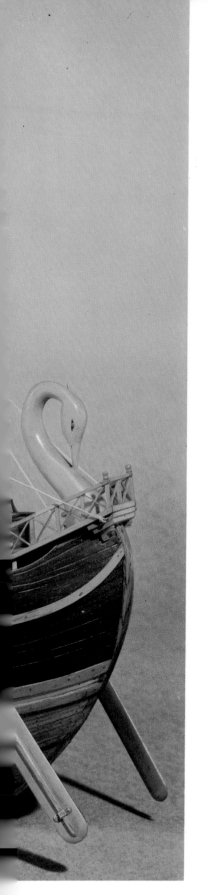

The Silk Road from China

10

During the 2,000 years in which Western culture was developing around the Mediterranean, another civilization was emerging on the other side of the world. This was the great Chinese Empire. Neither people knew much about the other's existence. Massive mountain ranges, the wide plateaus of Mongolia, and the barren Gobi Desert separated the early civilizations of East and West. The two cultures took shape independently, but shared many of the same basic ways of living which grew out of similar needs.

According to legend, there was civilization in China several thousand years before the birth of Christ. Around 1500 B.C., the earliest culture of which there is archaeological evidence arose in the valley of the Hwang Ho. This was the Shang dynasty. The Shangs were an agricultural people whose capital lay 300 miles south of present-day Peking. Like the Egyptians, the Shangs developed a form of writing which used drawings to represent words. Like the Greeks, they possessed books. Like the Carthaginians, they practiced human sacrifice. Like the Romans, they laid out their cities according to a regular plan. They evolved a system of rule consisting of king, government, and priests. Like most

Left: a model of a Roman merchant ship of the A.D. 100's. These ships carried Roman goods to the ports of Egypt and the Middle East, and returned to Ostia laden with treasures from the East. Although silk was highly prized and very expensive, the Romans did not attempt to voyage to China for it.

Right: a Roman glass jug. Roman glass was one of the commodities exported to the East in exchange for silk.

Above: a ceremonial Chinese bronze axhead, from the Shang period. The Shang dynasty is the first of which there is archaeological evidence.

Right: Ostia, the port of Rome. Ships from all parts of the Roman Empire brought their goods to this port.

ancient peoples, they indulged in a limited form of polygamy—the practice of marrying more than one husband or wife.

As their civilization developed, the Shangs forged bronze swords, built chariots, bred horses, and used stirrups to support their feet when riding. Ruling from their capital, the Great City Shang (present-day An-yang), the Shangs laid the foundations of the powerful nation of China. Under their successors, China began to expand. By 250 B.C., its frontiers stretched eastward to the China Sea and southward as far as the Yangtze River. Later in the 200's B.C., the Emperor Shih Huang Ti, a ruler of the Ch'in dynasty (221 B.C.–207 B.C.), built the Great Wall of China to protect the country's northern frontier from invaders from the rest of Asia.

Right: one of the mosaics found at Ostia. It shows the emblem of a shipping company, presumably based at Ostia when trade there was at its hei

The wall, which extends from present-day Lin-yu on the east coast to Kansu province in north central China, is over 1,500 miles long and about 25 feet high. It is believed to have been built by linking shorter walls that were already in existence. By the time of Shih Huang Ti, the Chinese had also set up an elaborate system of roads throughout their country.

China possessed a unique and precious commodity—silk. For centuries this was to be its most valuable export. Silk became one of the most fashionable and highly prized luxuries of the Mediterranean world, and it was by a silken thread that East and West were drawn together. To sell their profitable material, the Chinese needed to find routes to the West. Thus the silk trade opened the way for the exploration of vast areas of little known and hostile lands.

It might have been expected that the Romans would have found their way to the Far East. But no Roman of any consequence is known to have reached China until the A.D. 100's, and by that time the Chinese Silk Road had been established for over 200 years. Although they were forced to pay very high prices for the silk that they imported from China, the Romans appear to have been content to let the Chinese, the Parthians (inhabitants of a kingdom southeast of the Caspian Sea), and the Arabs act as their carriers. The Romans themselves were mainly concerned with bringing to Ostia, the port of Rome, those luxuries that could be obtained within the boundaries of the empire or at least no farther afield than India.

The Romans brought amber from Germany, ivory from Africa, and frankincense from Arabia. From Ceylon, they imported the pearls that were much sought after by Roman women. They looked to India for rice, cotton, coarse cloth, and the highly prized pepper from the Malabar Coast. Ships seeking cargoes for Rome followed the monsoon route to the west coast of India, sailed around Cape Comorin (the southernmost tip of India), called at Ceylon, and even ventured north into the Bay of Bengal. But apparently there was not enough incentive to voyage farther still and brave the Strait of Malacca between Malaya and Sumatra to bring back the soft, luxurious material and silk thread from China. Not that foreign traders would have been at all welcome. The Chinese guarded the secret of silk manufacture so successfully that they retained a world monopoly for thousands of years. So great a mystery surrounded the origin of silk that even as late as the 100's B.C. a Roman writer as well informed as Virgil imagined that it grew on trees.

The Chinese themselves have left little information about the early development of silk. An ancient legend tells that silk was discovered in about 2700 B.C. A Chinese empress was asked by her husband to find out what was damaging his mulberry trees. She found what appeared to be white worms eating the leaves and spinning shiny cocoons. When she accidentally dropped one of the cocoons into hot water a fine thread began to unwind. Delicately she unpicked it until she had unraveled 4,400 yards of silk.

Whatever the truth about the discovery of silk, very little of it,

Above: Chinese ladies preparing a length of newly-woven silk. Silk was one of the most sought-after luxuries for the Romans, but the Chinese held a monopoly of its manufacture for more than 3,000 years. This picture is actually painted on silk. It dates from 1082–1135, but is based on an even older work by Chang Hsuan, a court painter active from 713–742. *(Museum of Fine Arts, Boston.)*

either as thread or made up into cloth, was seen outside China unti[l] the rise of the Han dynasty in 206 B.C. During the rule of the Hans the boundaries of China were pushed back until China was as larg[e] as the entire Roman Empire. The emperor Wu Ti, who reigne[d] from 141 B.C.–87 B.C., trebled the size of the Chinese Empire. H[e] sent embassies to lands beyond his new frontiers, and this led t[o] the export of silk on a large scale.

In his endless wars against the northern Huns, Wu Ti wanted t[o] make an alliance with the Yue-Chi, a people living a fugitiv[e] existence in central Asia. They had been driven west of the Chines[e] borders, and the emperor probably hoped that they would help th[e] Chinese to establish trade routes. The man he sent on this missio[n] was an officer named Chang Ch'ien, a popular, generous-hearte[d] soldier described as having "strong physique." He needed it. He wa[s] to be away from Changan, Wu Ti's capital, for 12 years. He was t[o] travel thousands of miles through unknown lands, and endure gre[at] hardships.

Chang's expedition started disastrously. On the enemy's borde[r] he and his party of some 100 men were captured by the Huns. Chan[g] remained a prisoner for 10 years, and then, in about 128 B.C., [he] escaped with some of his followers and the barbarian woman [he] had married during his captivity. Chang continued westward a[nd] finally found the Yue-Chi, who had settled in Bactria beyond t[he] Pamirs and south of the Oxus River. He stayed with them for so[me]

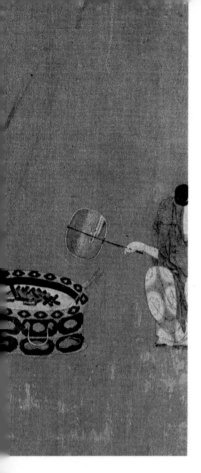

ime, but he could not persuade them to become China's allies in the fight against the Huns.

On his return journey to China by way of Tibet, Chang was once again taken prisoner by the enemy, but this time he escaped after only a short time in captivity. Despite the apparent failure of his mission, Chang's arrival home with his wife and the survivors of the expedition was greeted as a triumph by the emperor. Wu Ti considered that Chang had brought back something even more valuable than a military alliance. He had acquired unique information about other tribes and unknown territories. He could advise on the best and safest routes to carry China's trade into Asia Minor and Europe. After a further reconnaissance expedition made by Chang in 105 B.C., the Silk Road to the West was opened.

Within a few years, caravans of mules and camels were following the Silk Road 6,000 miles from northwest China to the Mediterranean Sea. With their cargoes of thread and bales of patterned damasks and taffetas, they set out from Changan westward along the valley of the Hwang Ho (Yellow River). They took the tracks that led north of the mountains of Tibet to Kashgar (near the present-day frontier between western China and southeastern Russia). On this part of the journey they had to choose whether to travel north or south of the burning desert of Taklamakan. The more usual way was to the south, where there was a chain of oases to provide water for men and animals.

Above: the Chinese emperor Wu Ti of the Han dynasty, who sent Chang Ch'ien on a mission to make an alliance with the Yue-Chi. Chang was away from Wu Ti's capital for 12 years. *(Museum of Fine Arts, Boston.)* Below: a pottery figure of a warrior, which dates from the Han dynasty.

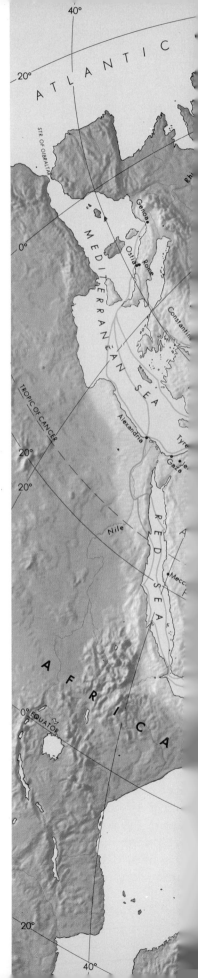

Above: the ramparts of Bactra, capital of the ancient land of Bactria in what is now Afghanistan. The city, which was later renamed Wazirabad, was one of the main centers for the silk trade, and a stopping place on the road between the Pamirs and Merv. In Chang Ch'ien's time, this part of the Silk Road was controlled by the Yue-Chi people.

Right: this map of Asia, Europe, and Africa shows the journeys of both Chang Ch'ien and Hsuan-tsang. It also shows the most important trade routes to China by both sea and land. The Great Wall of China and the boundaries of the early (Western) and later (Eastern) Han dynasties are also shown.

As far as Kashgar, the route lay in Chinese-dominated territory. The next stage of the journey took the caravans over the Pamirs and on, by way of Samarkand or Bactria, to the oasis city of Merv (near the present-day city of Mary on the border between Russia and Iran). Merv was regarded by central Asiatic people as the cradle of mankind. This part of the Silk Road was controlled by the Yue-Chi, the people to whom Chang had been sent by the emperor.

The route was divided into four stages: from Changan to Kashgar; from Kashgar to Merv; from Merv to Ctesiphon (south of what is now Baghdad in Iraq); and from Ctesiphon to the ports of the Mediterranean. Each of these stages was under the control of a different people, and it appears that caravan drivers traveled only a certain distance and then transferred their merchandise to the next driver. Whether these drivers were acting as agents for the original Chinese merchant, or were just carriers, is uncertain. Possibly the Chinese financial interest ended with the first change of hands, and the silk was sold, resold, and sold again in the thriving markets of the key cities along the route.

Whatever the method, it created a series of middlemen, each of whom took a large profit. This forced up the cost of silk, so that by

N

ARCTIC CIRCLE

ARCTIC CIRCLE

80°

80°

60°

SHETLAND IS

18

16

Scandinavia

URAL MOUNTAINS

Volga

Volga

14

CASPIAN SEA

Kyzyl Kum

Tashkent

Samarkand

TIEN SHAN

Turfan 2

M o n g o l i a

Gobi Desert

Manchuria

built c.300 B.C.

built c.290 B.C.

Merv

Oxus 2

Balkh

Bactria

PAMIRS

Kashgar

Taklamakan Desert

Khotan

built ?1/3

1/2 B.C.

Shang (An-Yang)

Hwang Ho

EAST CHINA SEA

HINDU KUSH

Peshawar

Kashmir

Indus

2 Khotan

1

Changan

PARTHIA

Multan

Indus 2

Benares

Ganges

Yangtze R.

TROPIC OF CANCER

ARABIAN SEA

BAY OF BENGAL

Madras

Malabar Coast

C. Comorin

CEYLON

G. OF SIAM

STR. OF MALACCA

Canton

PACIFIC OCEAN

2

SOUTH CHINA SEA

INDIAN OCEAN

Malay Pena.

EQUATOR

.... Chang Ch'ien 1 138-126 B.C.

——— Hsuan-tsang 2 A.D. 629-645

——— Trade routes

▪▪▪ Great Wall of China

——— Boundary ot early (Western) Han dynasty c.100 B.C.

– – – Boundary of later (Eastern) Han dynasty c.A.D.100

0 250 500 750 1000 1250 1500
Miles

© Geographical Projects

80°

100°

120°

Above: the ruins of Palmyra, lying under the hot desert sun. Palmyra was a meeting place for several caravan routes, and the splendor of what remains shows what a wealthy city it once was. It was built at an oasis in the Syrian Desert and became so important that the Romans developed an elaborate system to guard the routes leading to and from the city.

the time it reached Rome the price was exorbitant. The most serious increase occurred in the third stage of the Silk Road immediately west of Merv in Parthian territory. The Parthians were strong enough to exercise absolute control on all goods passing through their empire. They probably imposed a heavy tax on the caravans which added still further to the eventual price of the silk.

From Merv, it was about 1,300 miles' journey over mountainous territory to the Parthian royal city of Ctesiphon. The final journey to the Mediterranean ports began there. The most direct route would have been due west, reaching the coast at, say, Tyre. The

was, however, impossible as it would have meant a trek of 400 miles through the waterless Syrian Desert which even camels could not manage. Instead, the caravans went northwest, following the fertile valley of the Euphrates River.

Those on the main Silk Road, whose objective was Rome, continued up the river to Zeugma, in present-day Syria. Those whose destinations were the more southerly coastal towns of Syria, Palestine, and Egypt branched off at Hit on the Euphrates River. They then headed northwest for Palmyra in Syria, skirting the north of the Syrian Desert.

Palmyra, which lies about 130 miles northeast of Damascus, was an oasis village which Rome and the caravan trade transformed into a magnificent and thriving city. Isolated in the middle of the desert, its ruins still testify to its former glory. From Palmyra, the silk went to Damascus and on to textile-manufacturing and dyeing cities such as Tyre and Gaza. Palmyra was also the starting point for a southerly route through Petra (in the southwest of present-day Jordan) to Alexandria, Arabia, and the Red Sea ports. So important was this caravan city that the Romans developed and guarded routes to and from it by building forts and sinking wells every 24 miles along the way. They established an armed camel corps to patrol the route, and the caravans traveled in convoy under its protection. These caravans consisted of as many as 3,000 camels, and the geographer Strabo likened them to armies on the march.

Silk bound for Rome itself had reached the western limit of the Parthian Empire at Zeugma. At this frontier town of the Roman Empire, there was a bridge across the Euphrates. At Antioch (Antakya in southern Turkey), 150 miles farther on, merchandise

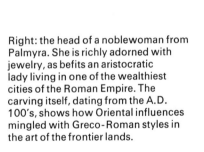

Right: the head of a noblewoman from Palmyra. She is richly adorned with jewelry, as befits an aristocratic lady living in one of the wealthiest cities of the Roman Empire. The carving itself, dating from the A.D. 100's, shows how Oriental influences mingled with Greco-Roman styles in the art of the frontier lands.

was loaded on ships for the voyage that completed the journey. By the time the material was on sale in the Vicus Tuscus, Rome's chief silk market, a year had passed since it had left China.

The effort involved in these expeditions might seem excessive, but supply was answering demand. Silk had become the rage of Rome, the symbol of wealth and position, and a necessity for all noblewomen. They delighted in wearing gauzy, semitransparent silk dresses. "I see silken clothes," wrote Seneca, "that in no degree afford protection either to the body or modesty of the wearer, and clad in which no woman could honestly swear she is not naked." Pliny was scandalized at the practice (which grew into an industry on the Aegean island of Kós) of unraveling and reweaving silk yarn into see-through material.

So great a drain was the cost of silk on the Roman treasury that attempts were made first to fix prices and then to restrict the import of silk along with other expensive and exotic goods. This official attitude was probably one of the main reasons why Rome was slow in opening up her own trade routes to China. It was not until the reign of Marcus Aurelius in the A.D. 100's, when war with Parthia caused a complete breakdown in the overland Silk Road, that Roman merchants showed any enterprise. In A.D. 166, some private adventurers succeeded in reaching China by sea, thus establishing the first direct contact between the great empires of East and West. But the sea route to China was long, dangerous, and infested with pirates, and few sailors dared to repeat the voyage. From time to time over the next few centuries Rome sent what are described as "embassies" to China by the sea route. But these visits did nothing to bring down the price of silk, or to establish a regular sea trade with China.

Right: the Vicus Tuscus, the silk market near the Forum at Rome. It was here that the silk imported from China was eventually sold. By that time its price was enormous, forced up by the number of middlemen who had taken their profits as it was brought west.

Marcus Aurelius tried to set an example by not wearing silk, and would not let his wife wear it. But it was the Byzantine Emperor Justinian—ruler of the eastern half of what had been the Roman Empire—who caused the worst crisis by fixing prices in A.D. 540. By this time the Persians (who had overthrown the Parthians) had a virtual monopoly of the silk trade. They refused to sell at the Roman figure. Faced with the possibility of being cut off from all supplies of silk, the Romans resorted to what must be the earliest example of industrial espionage. They decided to smuggle the

secret of silk cultivation out of China and to start producing silk themselves.

The accounts of this audacious undertaking are colorful but may not be true. It is said that, twelve years after Justinian's edict, two monks presented themselves to the emperor in Constantinople capital of the Byzantine Empire. They belonged to the Nestorian order, long exiled for their heresy in denying Mary as the mother o God. Their proposition to Justinian was also unorthodox.

The monks had traveled from India, where they had lived nea the Chinese border. They were able to cross the frontier into China without exciting suspicion and were prepared, they said, to penetrate into the closely guarded silk-producing area, steal some silkworms eggs, and smuggle them out. It was a dangerous mission. Deatl was their certain fate if they were caught. They would need to b well paid.

Cost was unimportant compared with the chance of starting sil

roduction in the Roman world. Justinian promised the monks a
uitable reward, and they traveled back to the East. Many months
vent by. Then, at last, the two Nestorians presented themselves
nce again to the emperor. They had with them the precious eggs,
vhich they had hidden in the hollow of bamboo canes. It is a
eculiar feature of such stories that, vague though they are in outline,
ney are surprisingly minute in odd details. The names and particulars
f the monks are completely unknown, and yet we are told the
xact number of stolen eggs—550.

From these eggs, hatched and reared on the mulberry trees of
onstantinople, grew the silkworms that freed the West from
liance on China. After more than 3,000 years, during which China
ad so carefully guarded its secret, silk could be produced in the
Vest. Syria became the center for silk production, and by the end
f the A.D. 500's was apparently able to meet all the demands for
lk in the Mediterranean world.

Above: Nestorian priests. It is
said that two Nestorian monks eventually solved the mystery of how silk
was made, smuggling silkworm eggs
out of China in bamboo canes. At last,
the Chinese monopoly was broken and
the Romans could make silk themselves.

The End of the Beginning

11

The fall of Rome in A.D. 476 left no nation to carry on voyages and land expeditions on a large scale. Barbarian invaders from the north and east swept into the western part of the Roman Empire, replacing the Roman provinces with a confusion of small, individual kingdoms which were constantly at war with one another. Although the eastern part of the empire, centered on Constantinople, survived, it was fully occupied with defending, rather than expanding, its frontiers. In China, the Han dynasty had fallen, and the Chinese Empire had split into a collection of small states. The known world was in a turmoil of wars, migrations, and violent political change. Trade, which had been one of the prime motives for exploration,

Left: a Roman road map. The Romans built magnificent roads, many of which have survived to this day. As mapmakers, however, they were less expert. This map, a copy made in the 1200's of a Roman map of the 200's, does not attempt to show the true size, shape, or position of the various features it depicts. All the rivers appear to run from east to west, regardless of their real course—the Rhine, for instance, actually flows south to north.

Above: a coin showing the head of Attila the Hun, leader of one of the barbarian tribes that invaded the Roman Empire in its dying years.

me to a halt as a series of small, self-sufficient communities devel-
ed where once great civilizations had flourished.

During this period of upheaval, the urge to travel was kept alive
some extent by a new force—religion. The missionaries of
hristianity—the religion adopted by the Roman Empire in its
st days of power—went forth to seek converts in new lands. And
early as the A.D. 300's, small parties of Christian pilgrims traveled
Jerusalem from the farthest corners of the known world. Al-
ough these pilgrims were not explorers, their journeys were very
abitious undertakings for their time.

In China, too, religion provided an incentive for travel. A number

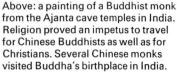
Above: a painting of a Buddhist monk from the Ajanta cave temples in India. Religion proved an impetus to travel for Chinese Buddhists as well as for Christians. Several Chinese monks visited Buddha's birthplace in India.

of Chinese converts to Buddhism, which had been brought t China by A.D. 100, made the journey to India to visit the birthplac of Buddha and seek greater understanding of the beliefs of th Buddhist religion. One such traveler was the Chinese monk F Hsien, who set out from Changan in about A.D. 400 with thre companions. After six years' journey, the four men reached centr India. There they spent a further six years studying and traveling i India and Ceylon before returning to China by sea.

In the A.D. 600's, another fervent Chinese Buddhist made vow to "travel in the countries of the west in order to questic the wise men on the points that were troubling his mind." H name was Hsuan-tsang, and he was one of the greatest travelers the ancient world. By the time of Hsuan-tsang, China had been r united under the Sui dynasty, which, in 618, had been succeeded the T'angs. Central Asia was still in a state of turmoil, and t emperor forbade Hsuan-tsang to leave China. Undeterred, t 19-year-old Hsuan set out to cross the desert wastes of the Go Abandoned by his guide and by his friends, he found his way following the tracks of camels and other pack animals. At one sta he went without water for five days after dropping his watersk But he finally reached Turfan in western China, where a local ru provided him with an escort of men to accompany him on the n stage of his journey, and pack animals to carry his belongings.

With his new companions, Hsuan fought his way across the icy Tien Shan mountains. In the course of this crossing, 13 men and many of the animals lost their lives. But still Hsuan traveled on. He reached Tashkent and pushed on to Samarkand. His journey took him over the Oxus River and into Bactria, where he visited a number of Buddhist monasteries. Then he crossed the Hindu Kush, traveled through the Khyber Pass to Peshāwar (in what is now the northern part of West Pakistan), and explored the Swat Valley. Before him lay the gorges of the Indus, where, he wrote, "the roads were very dangerous. . . . Sometimes one had to cross on rope bridges, sometimes by clinging to chains. Now there were gangways hanging in midair, now flying bridges flung across precipices." These hazards once behind him, Hsuan reached Kashmir, on the northern borders of India. He remained there for two years, studying under the guidance of a learned Buddhist monk.

In 633, Hsuan traveled to the sacred Ganges River and spent several years visiting cities, monasteries, and libraries. He then journeyed southward across the Deccan and northward along the west coast of the Bay of Bengal. After exploring the region of Assam in northeastern India, he at last decided to set out for home. He made his way back across the Punjab and traveled up the valley of the Oxus River. In the face of biting winds, he journeyed over the Pamirs and made his way down to Kashgar. He then followed the route of the silk caravans to Khotan and across the desert of Taklamakan. In 645, 16 years after leaving China against the emperor's orders, he returned in triumph to his native land. At the emperor's request, he wrote a detailed account of his long and arduous journey, which included a great deal of valuable information about the lands he had passed through. Hsuan then spent the rest of his life translating the 740 religious manuscripts he had brought back with him from India.

Apart from the peaceful journeys of Hsuan-tsang and pilgrims like him, religion also inspired wars of conquest. The end of the Roman Empire left the Mediterranean world divided and vulnerable. Swiftly, ruthlessly, and with astonishing efficiency, the Arabs swept to power. Inspired by the teachings of the prophet Mohammed (born in Mecca in about A.D. 570), they surged north into Syria and made Damascus their capital. Then they spread east and west.

Above: Hsuan-tsang, the young Chinese Buddhist who traveled to India in the 600's to learn more about his faith. His arduous journey lasted 16 years. Some of this time he spent in India studying in various monasteries.

In Persia, they won immediate victory, and they proceeded to carry their religious beliefs as far as the Indus. A new capital was set up at Baghdad. The forces of Islam—the religion of Mohammed's followers—also drove westward to conquer Egypt and Libya. The Moslem Arabs, superbly mounted and armed with deadly bows and arrows, streamed along the north coast of Africa to the Pillars of Hercules, which they named Gebel-at-Tarik—Gibraltar. The capture of Alexandria gave them a great port from which to attack and capture Crete and Cyprus. Spain fell to them, and they established a frontier along the Pyrenees. Within 100 years, the Moslem Empire stretched from northern Spain to India. Trade was revived, and the Arabs made regular voyages to the East.

But while the travelers of the Far East and the conquerors of the Moslem world kept the spirit of exploration alive, most of the inhabitants of Europe felt little urge to challenge the unknown. Hardly any journeys of exploration were made from the Western world during the first 700 years after the birth of Christ. The Europeans of the time lived in an enclosed world, bounded by the Atlantic Ocean to the west and the vast plains of Asia to the east. Fear and superstition prevented them from venturing beyond the world they knew. An immense change in the attitudes and beliefs of the peoples of Europe was needed to generate the excitement and overwhelming curiosity that inspired the great explorers.

Is it true that no sailor had been out into the Atlantic farther

Left: one of the lakes in Kashmir, with the mountains in the background. Hsuan-tsang spent two years in Kashmir—a region on the northern borders of India—studying with a learned Buddhist monk there.

Below: a manuscript illustration of two Moors in Spain, playing a form of chess. The tide of Islam swept north throughout what is now Spain, and the Moorish rule was maintained in parts of the peninsula for over 700 years.

west than the Canary Islands by A.D. 700? There is speculation
notably promoted by the Norwegian ethnologist Thor Heyerdahl
that by this time the Egyptians may have reached the New World—
the Americas—in boats made of papyrus, a type of water reed
Heyerdahl does not, however, venture a definite date. It has also been
suggested that the Phoenicians and the Chinese may have sailed to
the shores of America in early times. There is even an idea (based
on an inscription found on a stone in Tennessee in 1885) that Jews
reached North America sometime before 500 B.C. But little real
evidence in support of these suggestions has ever been found.

Above: Thor Heyerdahl's primitive craft, *Ra II*, in which he crossed the Atlantic in an effort to prove that it would have been possible for the Egyptians to reach America in papyrus boats. He speculates that they may have built the pyramids found in Mexico.

Disunity, warfare, and the decline in trade, all played their part discouraging exploration in the West during the Dark Ages—the period between the A.D. 400's and 900's. But there was yet another force behind this prolonged lack of interest in foreign lands—the church. Although the rise of Christianity led to a limited amount of travel, the church also played a decisive part in blocking the progress of geographical knowledge. Hostile to pagan learning and achievement, the Christianized Roman Empire, centered in Constantinople, was satisfied with the limits set on the world by the Bible. The scientific theories of the great Greek philosophers, astronomers, and geographers were denounced as heretical—contrary to accepted belief.

The church enclosed the world in blinkers. It even rejected the knowledge, by then fully accepted by all men of learning, that the world was a sphere. God had created the universe, the churchmen believed, and it was undesirable to pursue knowledge that added to, and might run contrary to, Holy Scripture. This attitude is exemplified in a book called *Christian Topography*, written by Cosmas, a monk who was born in Alexandria in the A.D. 500's. Cosmas attempted to disprove the ideas of men such as the Greek geographer and astronomer Eratosthenes, who believed the world to be a sphere, and who, as early as 200 B.C., had calculated its circumference with remarkable accuracy. Turning to the Bible for guidance, Cosmas found a phrase comparing the world to the Tabernacle of Moses. The Tabernacle, a place of worship built by Moses and the Israelites at the command of God, was a large, rectangular tent. Cosmas therefore represented the universe as a rectangular box with the sky as its curved "lid." In the box, he believed, lay the inhabited part of the world, which was surrounded by ocean. Beyond the lid of the box lay heaven.

As well as stifling exploration, this lopsided theology had a

Below: a drawing from Cosmas' *Christian Topography*, showing Cosmas' view of the world. Basing his idea on a phrase in the Bible, he pictured it in the form of the Tabernacle of Moses. The walls and lid form the heavens and the sun rises and sets over the center mountain, while from above the Creator surveys his handiwork.

serious effect on geography. In the place of maps with scientific value, monks began to produce *wheel maps*. These showed Jerusalem as the center of a flattened, circular world. The chief divisions of land and sea radiated from the hub of Jerusalem like spokes. Piety also demanded that the sacred east, and not north, should be placed at the top of the map. As a result, no map of any geographical value was produced for nearly a thousand years. So great was the effect of the church's determination to ignore scientific fact that as the centuries passed many of the discoveries of the ancient world were forgotten. Europeans began to regard the church's theories as fact, and a web of fear and superstition grew up about the world beyond Europe. Nowhere was this more apparent than in the prevailing belief during the Dark Ages that the world was indeed flat, and that, if a sailor voyaged too far, he would fall off the edge.

Throughout the Middle Ages, the only real map of the world to which men could refer was the one devised by Claudius Ptolemy in about A.D. 150. Ptolemy, a Greek, was the greatest geographer and astronomer of ancient times. Although his idea of the world was limited and not strictly accurate, it was the most complete view available, and comparatively little information was added to it until the end of the 1400's. Ptolemy's map may therefore be regarded as a

Below: in his book, written between 535 and 547, Cosmas rejected the idea that the earth was round. He found the idea of a world facing downward, and men walking about beneath our feet, ridiculous, and argued that, according to the Bible, there was only one "face of the earth" which God gave to man for him to dwell upon.

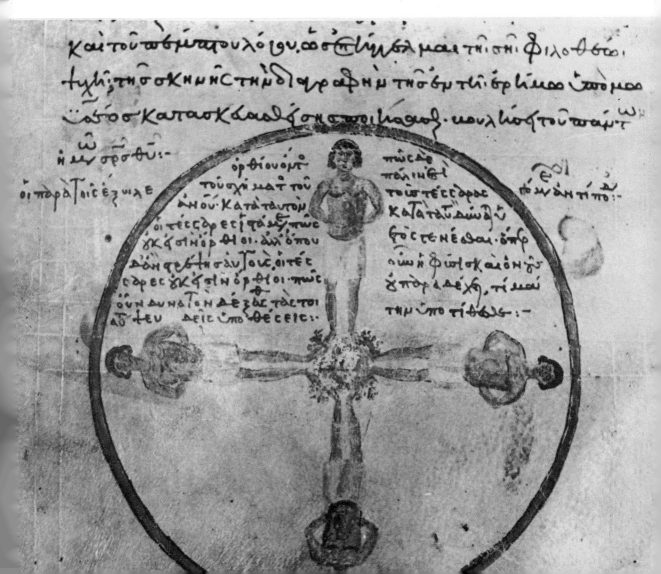

Above: a doorway of the cathedral in Florence, Italy, depicting the great geographer Ptolemy, who lived and worked in Alexandria in the A.D. 100's.

fair representation of the world as it was known in A.D. 700.

The curious thing about Ptolemy's map is that, strictly speaking, it does not exist. Ptolemy himself may never have drawn more than rough sketches of his ideas for his own use. But he did prepare a volume of instruction in mapmaking which was used as a guide by later cartographers. The representations which are today referred to as "Ptolemy's map" are based directly on these instructions, or are copied from earlier versions of Ptolemy's ideas. The oldest of these still in existence dates only from the A.D. 1200's, more than a thousand years after Ptolemy wrote his book.

Fortunately, Ptolemy's *Geography*—also called *Instruction in Mapdrawing*—contained the sum total of all geographical knowledge up to his time. He provided the names of 8,000 places, and the lines of latitude on which they were to be found. For 180 of these places he also gave the lines of longitude. Like every geographer of ancient times, Ptolemy had to be content to show only half the world extending from China in the east to Africa in the west through 180

154

Left: one of the world maps based on the theories of Ptolemy, the greatest geographer of the ancient world. This map was drawn in the 1400's, when Ptolemy's *Geography* (written in about A.D. 150) was still the chief source of reference for geographers. Like the Greek philosopher Aristotle, Ptolemy believed the Indian Ocean to be an inland sea, and thought that an unknown land in the south linked Africa with eastern Asia. He represented Asia as stretching indefinitely away to the east—a view which later influenced Columbus in the belief that he could reach Asia after only a short voyage across the Atlantic.

f longitude. His latitude extended to 67° north of the equator, nd to 16° south of it. The lines of longitude and latitude are curved s they should be, and Ptolemy's world has the appearance of n inverted fan with the lines of longitude as ribs. The ribs do ot converge at the North Pole, for Ptolemy did not know of the rctic or attempt to map it. To the south of the equator his *projection* –the depiction on a flat surface of what is really a sphere—turns harply downward at the edge of the fan. This was a conventional evice, and saved putting in the lower part of the globe about which e was also ignorant.

The one serious mistake made by Ptolemy lies in enclosing the ndian Ocean by a southern land mass. This means that Ptolemy did ot accept Herodotus' account of the Phoenicians' journey around frica. He joined East Africa just south of the equator to China, nowing the Indian Ocean as a vast inland sea. This was a mis- onception that was to persist until Bartholomeu Dias rounded the ape of Good Hope in the 1400's.

Another strange feature of the map is the way in which the Indian Peninsula is shrunk and Ceylon increased to 14 times its real size. This is particularly surprising because a Greek doctor of the 500's B.C. had written a book on India, and the Romans had visited Ceylon. In addition, a travel manual called the *Periplus of the Erythrean Sea,* written by an unknown Greek seaman in about 30 B.C., gave a detailed description of the Indian coastline, as well as describing the Red Sea ports and the East African coast. However, both the Indus and the Ganges rivers are correctly placed on Ptolemy's map, the first thanks to the information brought back by Alexander, the second probably from data in the *Periplus.*

The Malay Peninsula and Indochina—or possibly Burma—are indicated a trifle sketchily. Until Nero's time, the Greeks and Romans thought of Burma as an island. Then they discovered it to be a great headland which they called Chryse. Ptolemy turns his land mass south after what he calls the "Great Gulf," which may be the Gulf of Siam, or possibly the South China Sea, of which he would have heard from returning traders.

The eastern limit of the map fades out into *Terra Incognita*—unknown land—as it was to remain until the expedition of Marco Polo late in the A.D. 1200's. But because of the Silk Road, central Asia could be mapped with some accuracy. The Caspian Sea had been explored by the Greeks as a result of expeditions they had made into the Ural Mountains in search of gold and fur. Scythia, too, was known through Greek traders who had gone north of the

Left: an example of Byzantine silk. Even after the collapse of the Roman Empire, Eastern goods were still trade along the traditional Silk Road.

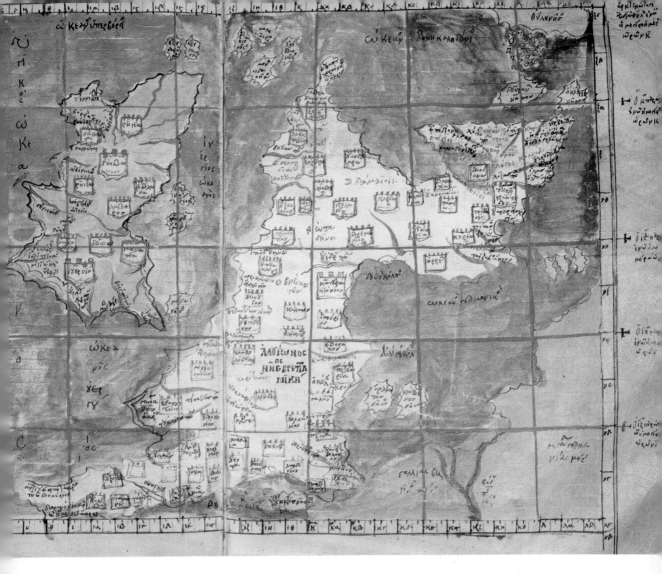

Above: the map of the British Isles
from the manuscript of Agathodaemon.
It is odd that Ptolemy did not have
more accurate information on the shape
of the islands, for they must have
been surveyed during the years
of Roman occupation.

lack Sea into southern Russia for metals, ceramics, wheat, and gold.
nformation about the Ukraine was plentiful. Herodotus had visited
)lbia, a colony near the Dnepr estuary in western Russia. Strabo,
)o, had traveled to the Dnepr River and reported that it was
avigable for 70 miles. Under the Emperor Hadrian, a trade route
ad been established by the Romans as far north as Kiev.

Neither Norway nor the Baltic Sea appear on Ptolemy's map.
or the far north there was only Pytheas' description of Thule
) go on, and, when the Romans recalled their northern armies
om the Rhine in A.D. 16, Scandinavia had still not been explored.
he oddly shaped British Isles must have been far better known
aan the map suggests. After over 100 years of Roman occupation,
ritain must have been fully surveyed. The Orkney Islands, the
hetland Islands, and the Hebrides off the coast of Scotland were
n maps before the time of Agricola, the Roman general whose fleet
ad explored the coasts of Scotland and may even have sailed around
ritain in about A.D. 80. Ireland, too, should have been more
ccurately depicted by Ptolemy. Although the interior was not

explored for many centuries, the coast, including the town of Eblana (on the site of present-day Dublin), had been described by the Roman geographer Pomponius Mela in A.D. 43.

Continuing south past Spain to the west coast of Africa, little more is shown on the map than had been revealed by Hanno's colonizing expedition more than 400 years before the birth of Christ. South of the equator, Ptolemy lets the continent trail away vaguely. But the east coast of Africa must have been better known than the map indicates, for information about it had been included in the *Periplus*. However, the reluctance of Arab sailors to venture much below the equator accounts for many misconceptions, not all of

Above: Pico de Teide, Tenerife, in the Canary Islands. The Phoenicians and the Greeks certainly knew of the islands' existence. The Greeks said that this mountain, which they called Mount Atlas, supported the sky.

Right: pottery from Las Palmas, in the Canaries. It has been suggested that the original inhabitants of the islands might have been of Egyptian origin.

them geographical. The Arabs are said to have thought that the southern seas boiled, just as the Portuguese later believed a similar legend about the sea to the south of Cape Bojador on the coast of present-day Spanish Sahara.

The Azores were not mapped in A.D. 700, even though they may have been visited by the Carthaginian sailor Himilco. But Hanno had probably visited Madeira, and the Canary Islands were also known at this time. The Roman historian Pliny, who was writing in the A.D. 100's, knew of five islands and described Tenerife and La Palma. Ptolemy mentions six and names three, though he sites them too far out in the Atlantic.

Most of the rivers which caused so much curiosity among early peoples had been explored by Ptolemy's time. He knew of the Volga and described it as flowing into the Caspian Sea. Tiberius (who became Roman emperor at the time of Christ) had followed the Danube to its source, and Roman explorers had navigated most of the main rivers of middle Europe to open up southern Germany. Sources of rivers were of the greatest fascination, and, presumably trusting the story of Diogenes, Ptolemy shows the Nile rising in the Mountains of the Moon.

As the ancient world came to an end and Europe entered the Middle Ages, not all of the ideas and achievements of the early civilizations were forgotten. But it was in the Moslem Empire, above all, that the great heritage of classical learning was preserved. The Moslems collected many texts in Damascus, and later in Baghdad, where a scientific academy was opened for translation into Arabic. Ptolemy's *Geography* was just one of the numerous works that appeared in an Arabic version and served an Arab author as a model for his own book on geography. Hundreds of years later, at the time of the Renaissance (the great revival of learning which began in Europe in the 1300's), the Arabic versions of the ancient classical works were discovered in the universities the Moslems had founded in Spain, and the libraries of the Arab world. Now they could be translated into Latin—the language of most educated

Below: an Arab map of Ceylon. Drawn in the 1000's, it accompanies a manuscript by the Arab geographer Musa al-Khawarizmi, who was strongly influenced by Ptolemy.

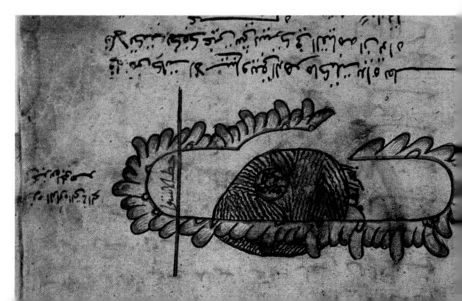

Below: the world map of al-Idrisi, 1154. Arab maps of this period were drawn with the south at the top, and the Indian Ocean is therefore shown above the Mediterranean Sea. According to al-Idrisi, the world was flat and measured 22,900 miles around the edge. He believed that it was encircled by water which held it "stable in space like the yolk of an egg." (*Bodleian Library, Oxford. MS. Pococke. 375, fols. 3v–4r.*)

Europeans in the Middle Ages and of most books of the time.

When the work of Ptolemy was translated into Latin soon after its rediscovery in A.D. 1407, it became a major influence in the renewal of interest in geography and on plans for the voyages that were to launch the great age of discovery in the 1400's. But hundreds of years before these voyages had even been dreamed of, two peoples were to take up the challenge of the unknown. From Ireland, and from the misty regions of the north, the Irish and Vikings would strike out across the Atlantic for new lands beyond the horizon.

Acknowledgments

Aldus Archives 55(B), 74, 109(T), 109(B); Photo Ashmolean Museum, Oxford 69(T), 72; Barnaby's Picture Library 20, 54(R); Photo Roloff Beny 79; Courtesy of the Biblioteca Ambrosiana, Milan 80; Biblioteca Mediceo Laurenziana, Florence/Photo Guido Sansoni © Aldus Books 152, 153; Bibliothèque de l'Arsenal, Paris/Photo R. Lalance © Aldus Books 115; Photo Bibliothèque Nationale, Paris 89; Bibliothèque Nationale et Universitaire, Strasbourg/Photo © Aldus Books 159(R); Courtesy of the Curators of the Bodleian Library 160; Photo Denise Bourbonnais © Aldus Books 46, 90(L), 94; Reproduced by courtesy of the Trustees of the British Museum 19(B), 45, 48, 54(L), 65(T), 75, 76, 77, 85, 88, 91 99(BR), 123(B), 129, 131, 155, 157; British Museum/Photo John Freeman © Aldus Books 24; British Museum/Photo Michael Jaanus © Aldus Books 65(B), 95, 99(BL), 106, 107(T), 108; Courtesy of The Brooklyn Museum, Charles Edwin Wilbour Fund 26; J. Augusta and Z. Burian, *Prehistoric Man,* Prague 6; Photo by J. Allan Cash 11(T), 14, 43, 50(B), 84; Photo Anthony W. Chaffe © Aldus Books 158, 159(L): Photo Peter Clayton 35(L); H. Albrecht/Bruce Coleman Ltd. 63; Simon Trevor/Bruce Coleman Ltd. 59(B); Courtauld Institute of Art, courtesy Lord Leicester 112; Photo J. E. Dayton 19(T); Courtesy Director General of Antiquities, République Libanaise, Beirut 35(R); C. M. Dixon, London 21, 68; Photo W. Forman 10, 15, 31, 32(L), 49; Geographical Projects Limited, London 11(B), 18, 23, 56–7, 92, 97, 102, 118–9, 137; Painting by Peter Sullivan © Geographical Projects Limited, London, courtesy Mansell Collection 147; Giraudon, Paris 36, 38(T); Photo George W. Goddard © Aldus Books 126(B), 132(R), 133, 141, 154(L): Photo P. Gotch 138; Government of Hyderabad, Pakistan 146(L); Reproduced by gracious permission of Her Majesty Queen Elizabeth II/Photo A. C. Cooper, Ltd. 114; Photo Michael Holford © Aldus Books 100; Michael Holford Library 8, 9, 16, 30, 32(R), 34, 37, 52(T), 52(B), 70, 73, 93, 103, 140, 149; Photo André Jodin, Paris 58; Keystone 71; Kunsthistorisches Museum, Wien 116; Redrawing © Aldus Books from Paul Aucler, *Carthage,* Librairie Delagrave, Paris 50(T); Mansell Collection 145; The Metropolitan Museum of Art, New York 28; Musée Cernuschi, Paris/Photo Jean-Abel Lavaud © Aldus Books 135(B); Musée du Louvre, Paris/Photo Denise Bourbonnais © Aldus Books 27(L), 29, 38(B), 41; Musée du Louvre, Paris/Photo Service Documentations Photographiques © Aldus Books 78; Museo, Paestum/Photo Scala 66; Museo delle Terme, Roma/Photo Scala 123(T); Museo Nazionale, Napoli/Photo Scala 42, 82, 113, 122; Museum für Indische Kunst, Staatliche Museen, Preufsischer Kulturbesitz, Berlin-Dahlem 143; Staatliche Museen Stiftung Preussischer Kulturbesitz, Museum für Ostasiatische Kunst, Berlin 132(T): Museum of Archaeology, Madrid/Photo Mas © Aldus Books 53, 60(B), 61, 104; Chinese and Japanese Special Fund, Courtesy, Museum of Fine Arts, Boston 134; Ross Collection, Museum of Fine Arts, Boston 135(T); Ny Carlsberg Glypotek, Copenhagen 83, 96(R); Bild-Archiv der Österreichischen Nationalbibliothek, Wien 144; Piazza Armerina/Photo Scala 121(B); Picturepoint, London 13(T), 39, 96(L), 107(B) 124, 126(T), 128, 148; The Pierpont Morgan Library, M.917 (folio 109) 120; Josephine Powell, Rome 86, 87, 90(R), 136, 146(R); Ravenna, S. Vitale/Photo Scala 142; Photo Ann Reading 47, 69(B) 81; Photo Marshall Cavendish Ltd. reproduced by permission of The Master and Fellows, St. John's College, Cambridge, 40(L); British Crown Copyright, Science Museum, London 33(T), 101; Secretariat d'Etat aux Affaires Culturelles et a l'Information, République Tunisienne, Le Bardo 67, 110; Charles Swithinbank 99(T); The Tate Gallery, London 111; Sally Anne Thompson 60(T); U.P.I. 150–151; From collections of the University Museum of the University of Pennsylvania 40(T): Courtesy Daniël Van Der Meulen 121(T); Victoria & Albert Museum, London/Photo John Freeman © Aldus Books 156; Villa Giulia, Roma 127; Photo C. Woolf © Aldus Books 55T; ZEFA 17.

PART TWO

Beyond the
Horizon

Below: a lake near Hangchow in China. During the years Marco Polo spent in China in the 1200's, he traveled all over the vast country. He was particularly impressed with Hangchow, and in *The Book of Marco Polo,* he describes the city in detail. He also reports on the beautiful lakes nearby.

Beyond the Horizon

BY MALCOLM ROSS-MACDONALD

Right: a wooden Viking figurehead from the bow of the Oseberg ship, discovered in 1904. Carved heads of dragons or serpents were typical features of the bows and sterns of Viking ships. The Vikings believed that they would guard the ship from evil spirits.

Foreword

The painfully gathered geographical reports of the ancient world, translated into Arabic, lay in the Moslem academies. The turmoil and shattering economic breakdown that followed the collapse of the Roman Empire left her former colonies turned inward. China writhed in discord as the Han dynasty crumpled and the Mongols stirred in the steppes to the north. Everywhere, men who might otherwise have ventured abroad chose the familiar hazards of home over the desperate uncertainty of travel in a chaotic setting.

Only the edges of the civilized world still seethed with men restless enough to explore new country. In general, these restless men were also ruthless and violent, with no thought of increasing the sum of geographical knowledge. They made their swift, darting journeys for gold and jewels, for rich goods and fine land snatched from the wealthy communities of Britain, Ireland, and Europe. They kept accurate enough accounts to be able to return to plunder still further; but that was all. Even the men in the narrow long ships crossing the Atlantic seem to have had no interest in whether the world was round or flat: they were simply continuing to press on from one island to another further west.

In this part of the story, the chronological progression of ancient exploration—one powerful people being succeeded by the next and building on the accumulated knowledge—breaks down into a series of unconnected forays. The Irish carrying the gospel abroad, the fierce Vikings from the north making their raids, Marco Polo trading in the heart of China, the Christian friars following the roads to the East—none of them were able to use the knowledge of their predecessors. For each of them, the way ahead was completely unknown, and the outcome unpredictable.

The Great Atlantic Ocean

1

bove: a stone carving of Saint
atrick, patron saint of Ireland. He
ent most of his life converting the
ish to the Christian faith.

eft: in this world map of the A.D.
00's Britain (Brittannia) and Ireland
Hibernia) appear at bottom left, while
e Scandinavian lands are shown
s islands separate from Europe.

More than 400 years after the birth of Christ, the European world still centered on the Mediterranean Sea. To the west, the European horizon was bounded by the Atlantic Ocean, a great mass of water stretching away into the unknown. To the east lay the vast lands of Asia with their fierce barbarian inhabitants. The peoples of Europe feared what might lie in these distant regions, and were content to stay within the world they knew. No one had yet crossed the horizon. When, in the A.D. 400's, the Europeans did eventually break down the barrier of fear which had prevented them from venturing into the unknown, it was the Atlantic Ocean that they first explored. Eight hundred more years were to pass before they turned their attention to the East.

In the A.D. 400's, the peoples living on the fringes of the Atlantic Ocean had no idea of what might lie farther to the west. Ancient classical writers had described mysterious and beautiful lands called the "Fortunate Islands" or "Islands of the Blessed" a long way out into the Atlantic. These islands have since been associated by different scholars with the Azores, the Canaries, or even the West Indies. But, at that time, no living person had ever seen them. No one knew of the existence of America, nor even of the islands of Iceland and Greenland much nearer home. As far as the people of Europe were concerned, the vast sea might stretch for ever.

The fears and superstitions that hedged around the lives of Europeans of the time made exploration difficult. People thought that the world might be flat, and that, if they sailed too far west, they would fall off the edge. Moreover, they believed that the sea was the home of fierce monsters, and that its waters were ruled by powerful gods. Sailors were able to set a rough course at sea by the stars, but there were no proper navigational instruments, and certainly no charts. The first steps toward discovering the secrets of the Atlantic were taken by two peoples of northern Europe, and for very different reasons. The Irish braved the ocean to convert to Christianity any pagans that they might find. The Viking peoples of Scandinavia, on the other hand, regarded it simply as the route to rich countries where they could raid, or settle.

The Irish and the Vikings were not the first people to sail the waters of the Atlantic. The fishermen of western Europe and the British Isles had long been familiar with the coastal waters. And as long ago as 800 B.C., mariners from Phoenicia—a country in the eastern Mediterranean on the coasts of present-day Syria, Lebanon, and Israel—had sailed through the Pillars of Hercules (the Strait of Gibraltar) into the Atlantic. By the 300's B.C., Phoenician sailors had reached the shores of the British Isles and carried on a regular trade in tin with the British people. Greek sailors, too, braved the vast ocean. In about 325 B.C., Pytheas, a Greek explorer from Massalia (present-day Marseille), sailed past Britain and probably as far north as the frozen seas of the Arctic. However, mariners still did not dare to venture far out of sight of land. Seamen driven out to sea by storms seldom survived, and the few sailors lucky enough to find their way back could tell only of vast, empty waters. The Europeans believed that Europe's western shores were the ultimate edge of civilization. They thought that nothing of value could lie beyond.

It was the missionary work of the Irish that was responsible for filling in the first blank spaces on the map of the Atlantic. For more than 400 years, Irish priests and monks sailed their frail boats over its perilous waters in their efforts to spread the word of God among the pagans. They made many converts to Christianity in the islands of the North Atlantic. Even more important, for the first time they broke beyond the confines of the European world.

Before the 400's, Ireland had been almost entirely pagan. It was a land of scattered homesteads and small individual communities

Above: hermit cells at the Skelligs, County Kerry, Ireland. Irish hermits seeking converts to Christianity were among the first people to travel in frail boats across the unknown seas. Left: a page from the Book of Kells. Probably produced by the Irish monks of Kells in the 700's or 800's, this illuminated copy of the Gospels is a fine example of early Christian art.

Right: the Irish abbot Saint Brendan with his companions aboard ship on one of his missionary voyages. The book describing his travels tells how his rudderless boat, steered by one oar and with one sail, was encircled by a huge fish with its tail in its mouth.

under the rule of local noblemen. Most of the population lived by fishing, or near-subsistence farming, or by raiding the property of neighbors more wealthy than themselves. Early in the 400's, one such raiding party returned from the west coast of Wales carrying among its booty a 16-year-old boy called Patrick, who had been captured as a slave. Patrick was later to become the patron saint of Ireland. After six years in captivity, Patrick escaped and fled to France, where he became a monk. In 432, he returned to Ireland and spent the rest of his life on missionary tours throughout the country. In some places he converted the pagan inhabitants to Christianity. In others he organized the tiny pockets of Christianity which already existed, and brought Ireland in closer touch with Rome and the church of western Europe.

Because there were no large towns, nor even any very large villages, there were in Patrick's time no natural centers of political power in Ireland. Accordingly, there was no one obvious geographical center for the church. The noblemen converted by Patrick, or by other wandering priests, set up local monasteries, each independent of the others. Into these monasteries they gathered their relations and lay followers—that is, those followers who were not members of the clergy. When a monastery throve, it followed the example set by Patrick and sent out missionary groups in its turn. Many of the missionaries traveled long distances within Ireland itself. Many made much longer journeys far beyond the Irish shores.

The Irish brand of Christianity was a passionate one, and Irish Christians were particularly zealous in doing what they considered to be their duty. Armed with this zeal, the Irish set out to convert their neighbors. Their first subjects were other people of Celtic origin like themselves. They began with the inhabitants of Cornwall, in southwest England, some of whom had already been Christian for over 300 years. Then they turned their attention to the Welsh,

171

who had also known Christianity. The Irish established Christia[n] foundations in France and Germany, and as far away as norther[n] Italy. Many of these monasteries kept records from which we deri[ve] much of our knowledge of the earliest Irish travelers overseas.

In 563, Saint Columba, a monk from the north of Ireland, esta[b]lished a monastery on Iona, a tiny island off the west coast of what [is] now Scotland. From Iona, monks began the conversion of t[he] Pictish people on the mainland. Iona rapidly became the hea[d]quarters of the church in Scotland, and served to keep the Irishm[en] who later came to settle the country in touch with their homelan[d].

From the 500's onward, Irish monks and hermits began to tu[rn] their attention away from the known world. Sometimes alo[ne,] sometimes accompanied by experienced sailors and supporting [lay] communities, they traveled and settled in little-known lands. T[he] earliest travelers sailed in *coracles,* the simple boats used by all Cel[tic]

peoples of the time. Coracles had wicker frames covered with cowhide. Normally they were shaped like broad, round-bottomed, keelless bowls. Although frail, the coracles had important advantages. They were unlikely to sink because they were light, rode with the waves, and did not easily ship water or capsize. Coracles could be rowed or, if the wind were in the right direction, sailed. Coracle-making has been preserved as a craft in Ireland and in Wales, and coracles are still used by some Irish and Welsh fishermen. Today, however, the frames are of wood and the covering of canvas or tarred cloth. Nowadays only very small coracles are built, but in missionary times they were large enough to transport men, goods, and livestock.

Individual Irish hermits and small bands of holy men seem to have treated sea-voyaging as a pious venture. They saw it as their own version of the sojourn in desert and wilderness through which Jesus and the early saints sought closer communion with God. In the process they traveled farther and farther from home.

Most of the stories about the exploits of the first brave voyagers have survived only in legends. In these tales, ancient Celtic heroes and later Christian heroes are confused, and mythology conflicts with fact. Some of the stories, however, do have a firm basis of fact, as we know from existing historical records. The most famous of these stories concerns Saint Brendan, one of the first generation of

missionaries, and, according to the legend, one of the first Irishmen to travel beyond the shores of Europe to the islands of the Atlantic.

Saint Brendan (484–577) was an Irish abbot born at the Bay of Tralee, in the southwestern part of Ireland. Brendan became a missionary. Determined to spread the word of God among the pagans, he sailed out into the Atlantic in search of converts. Among the places he visited were the Sheep Islands—perhaps identifiable with the modern Faeroes, a group of islands in the North Atlantic Ocean north of the Shetlands—and the Paradise of Birds—perhaps the Shetlands or Outer Hebrides. He also reached what he thought were the Islands of the Blessed described by the ancient classical writers. Many of the stories of Brendan's activities carry a strong moral and allegorical content, but there is enough sober description in them to convince us that they tell of real voyages rather than imaginary ones. We know from records kept in monasteries that Brendan certainly visited Scotland, Wales, and Brittany.

The Irish-Scots, too, began to travel beyond the confines of their own land. It is a matter of historical fact that they reached the Faeroes in about 700. In about 825, an Irish monk named Dicuil, who studied and taught in Europe, wrote an account of his country-men's colony in the Faeroes in a work called *Concerning the Dimensions of the World*. He wrote: "There are many other islands to the north of Britain which can be reached from the northernmost isles by sailing directly for two days and nights under full sail with a favorable wind. A religious man told me he sailed to them in quite a small boat. Some of the islands are fairly small; most are separated by narrow straits. Hermits from out [of] Scotia [Scotland] had lived there for about a hundred years, but they have now abandoned the place

to the Norse brigands. Only their sheep remain. We have never
found mention of these islands in the books of other authors." The
fact that this is the first record of a colony settled 125 years previously
shows the loose structure of Irish Christianity then.

From the Faeroes, it was only two days' sailing to the southeastern
waters of Iceland. The way lay across the uncharted seas of the
North Atlantic but this cannot have deterred the Irish-Scots for we
know that, in about 770, they arrived in Iceland. In the same book
in which he mentions the Faeroes, Dicuil also says that he had heard

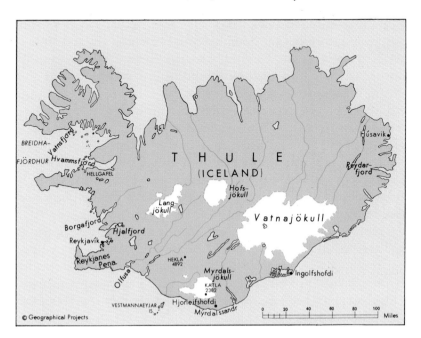

of Irish monks reaching Iceland, which he refers to as Thyle or
Thule. "It is now 30 years since certain priests who had been on
that island [Iceland] from the first of February to the first of August,
told that not only at the time of the summer solstice [midsummer]
but also before and after, the setting sun hides as it might be hidden
by a small mound, so that there is not even the shortest period of
darkness. It is so light that a man could even pick lice out of a shirt,
just as though the sun were up. And had they been on a high mountain perhaps the sun would have been visible all night.

"At the season of greatest cold they always had alternation of day
and night, except around the summer solstice. But at a day's sail
northward they found the sea frozen."

From other sources, it is clear that in Dicuil's time Irish monks
were regularly traveling to and from the Iceland communities,
probably using the Faeroes as a station on the way.

During the 700's, the people who were to continue the Irish
explorations of the North Atlantic first appeared on the European
scene. They were the Vikings, sometimes called the Norsemen—the
men from the north. Sweeping down from the harsh countries of
Scandinavia, the Norsemen made for the fertile lands of Europe,

where they burned and looted, taking gold, cattle, and slaves. In 795, they reached Ireland. Soon the Norsemen began to raid farther afield. By way of the Hebrides and the Faeroes they eventually reached Iceland. It was these Norse raiders who were responsible for driving the Irish settler still farther west.

The descendants of the early Norsemen mention in their writings the Irish of Iceland: "Christians lived here [Reykjavik] whom the Norsemen call 'papa.' Later they went away because they did not wish to live here together with heathen men. They left behind Irish books, bells, and crosiers [ceremonial staves carried by bishops]." It is probably something of an understatement for the writer of this description to say that the Irish left simply because they "did not wish to live with heathen men." By the 870's, the Irish at home and abroad had experienced nearly a century of Norse ferocity. It is much more likely that the little band of Irishmen had sighted the Norse ships and had left in a hurry, abandoning all their possessions.

As Norsemen had reached Iceland via the Faeroes and Hebrides, the Iceland Irish probably judged it unwise to make for home through those same waters. They had heard how the Norsemen treated the inhabitants of lands they wanted to settle. The Irish had been in Iceland long enough not just to have sailed around it, but also to have learned of the larger island of Greenland, two days' to the west. We know that they had arrived in Greenland by about 870. When the Norsemen came, the westward route was the only safe way out, and, the story says, the Irish took it. This voyage from Iceland to Greenland was possibly the first crossing of the North Atlantic by European sailors.

The Norse writings contain indirect evidence of the Irish occupation of Greenland. Shortly before 980, for instance, some storm-driven Norsemen, forced to winter on the Greenland coast, fell to squabbling over a purse of Celtic gold they found in a burial mound. And on his first reconnaissance of Greenland in 982, Eric the Red found deserted houses and boats similar to the coracles used by the Irish.

There is a theory, not yet fully substantiated, that the Irish may have been the first Europeans to reach the shores of North America. Norse writings contain tales of white Christian men in a land called either Hvitramannaland or Ireland the Great. The stories, often highly fanciful in detail, refer quite casually to Norsemen,

Right: a beautifully carved crosier (bishop's stave) from Lismore, a town in Ireland sacked by the Norsemen. The ritual objects which the Irish left in Iceland, when they were driven out by the ferocious Norsemen, included things such as this crosier.

176

blown off course on their way to Greenland, having reached a country where white men "went about in white robes, carrying poles and banners and singing loudly." They mention this with no further explanation, as though it were common knowledge.

The earliest French missionaries to Canada in the 1500's and 1600's, came across rites which could just possibly have been the last vestiges of Irish Christianity. In their efforts to convert the Iroquois (Indians of the locality), the French often encountered strange and perverted reminiscences of Christian ritual quite out

of character with other aspects of Iroquois religion. Crosses were widely used in tattoos and craft decorations. During a week of festivities a dog was crucified. Except that it took place in winter not spring, the ceremony in many ways resembled the Christian Holy Week.

As yet, however, no concrete evidence has been found to prove that the Irish missionaries really did reach North America. Stories of their settlement of the country are still based only on speculation, and nothing has been proved beyond reasonable doubt.

Left: a modern Greenland landscape— the village of Kap Dan, Kulusuk Island, on the east coast. This is one of the islands reached by the Vikings, and possibly the Irish as well, on their voyages to the west from Iceland.

Below: a drawing of a North American Indian holding a strip of *wampum* (beadwork) decorated with small crosses. Such designs have led scholars to believe that the Christian Irish may have reached North America before the Vikings set foot there.

179

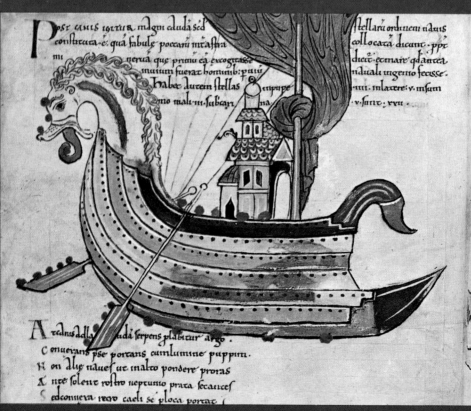

Post canis igitur magni cauda sed
constitua e: qua fabule poetam miastra
mi   nerua que primu ea excogitasse
          maium fuerat hominib: patu
          Habet autem stellas puppe
          mo mali in subeant   na

stellaru ordinem radius
collocata dicant . ppt
dicit eemain qdantea
nduali ingenio fecisse
iiii. inlatere: v. insam
v. sunt. xvii .

A redmis della cauda serpens plabitur argo.
C onuehens ipse portans cumlumine puppim.
N on alie naues ut malto pondere proras
A nte solent rostro neptuno prata secantes
S edconuersa recro caeli se ploca portac.

The Viking Raiders

2

eft: a stone carving in the museum f Holy Island (Lindisfarne), off the oast of Northumberland. It shows a olumn of Viking warriors, armed with xes. In 793, Danish Vikings sacked nd burned the Lindisfarne monastery.

The Irish went to far-distant lands in order to convert more people to Christianity. Theirs was a missionary motive. The next group of travelers, the Vikings, ventured abroad for quite different reasons. They migrated not to spread the word of God, nor yet to trade, but to plunder, wage war, and win themselves first glory and later land.

The Vikings came from the north, from the modern Scandinavian countries of Norway, Sweden, and Denmark. In the old Norse language, the word *Viking* described a man who came from a *fiord*— an inlet or a creek. To go *i viking* came to mean to leave one's inlet home and go raiding and marauding. A Viking, therefore, came to mean, particularly to the peoples of other parts of Europe, a ferocious merciless pirate.

The plundering raids of the Vikings were not just the whim and pleasure of a blood-loving race. They were a solution to many problems in the Viking homelands. In the so-called Dark Ages, overpopulation and land shortage were extreme in Scandinavia. The limitations of farming around the fiords of the Atlantic coastline, with its scant soil and cold winter weather, were severe. At first, the Vikings sowed crops before setting out on their raids, and returned later to harvest them. As time passed, however, periods of violent internal dispute in Denmark and long family power struggles in the many small kingdoms in Norway, forced numbers of dispossessed Norsemen to look elsewhere for a living. Forced into exile by hunger or by new overlords, the Vikings took to the seas. Fortunately for those who wanted, or were compelled, to get away, the Viking ships were the best-developed sailing vessels of their time. They were to remain so for several centuries. Viking warships became a familiar and hated sight to the inhabitants of the European countries to the south, east, and west of Scandinavia. They prayed for storms and rough seas, and welcomed harsh winters when the raiders could not travel far. "From the fury of the Northmen, good Lord deliver us!" was a frequent prayer among the frightened people along the coasts of northern Europe.

The prospect of a violent end in some skirmish in a foreign land was no deterrent to the Vikings. Death in battle was to them the most glorious end to life on earth. Odin, chief of the gods they believed in, particularly admired valor in fighting. He knew of everything that happened on earth, and in time of battle sent warlike goddesses, known as Valkyries, to collect dead heroes from the

t: a painting from an Anglo-Saxon nuscript of the 900's, showing a se dragon ship. These warships, h their high decorated prows and are sails, terrorized the inhabitants estern Europe for over 200 years.

181

Above: a painting from an Icelandic manuscript, depicting Valhalla, (in Norse mythology the hall of slain warriors). On the left is the great palace, with 540 doors, each so wide that 800 warriors could pass through side by side. On the right is the serpent of Midgard (Middle Earth, the home of mankind), which lay coiled around the world. The god Thor tried unsuccessfully to capture the serpent with an ox's head as bait.

battlefield to transport them to the heavenly Valhalla, the hall of dea[d] heroes. There the warriors fought again each day outside th[e] heavenly palace, those who were killed in the fighting being late[r] restored to life. Afterward, they feasted and drank wine. Befor[e] wounded human warriors died in battle, they chanted the record [of] their past victories and moments of bravery so that Odin, reminde[d] of how valiant they had been, would send his Valkyries for them.

The success of the Viking attacks on other peoples depended to [a] large extent on the element of surprise. The swiftness of their ship[s] and their ability to come close inshore or penetrate shallow rive[rs] made this possible. The warships used by the Vikings for makin[g] sudden raids on their neighbors' lands were called long ships, fro[m] their long, narrow shape. The Vikings' victims came to know th[e] boats as dragon ships because they often had a fearsome dragon[-] head carved on the prow. The long ships were very fast but n[ot]

lways very seaworthy, and they often broke their backs in rough
weather. They had oars, sometimes a square sail as well, carried
etween 30 and 40 oarsmen, and could achieve impressive speeds.

The ships used by Vikings for longer voyages were bigger and
much more solidly built, but still long and narrow. Like the long
hips, they were made of wooden slats, usually of oak, joined by
oundheaded iron rivets and caulked with tarred animal hair or
ool. Oars were of pine wood and varied in length along the ship's
de so that they struck the water together. The mast was also of pine,
ith a square woolen sail. The larger ships frequently had a small
ip's boat stored on board or towed behind.

The Vikings launched their first attack on their neighbors, the
habitants of the British Isles, in the A.D. 780's. At the time the
ritish Isles were subdivided into many kingdoms that were
onstantly at war with one another. England was made up of

Above: the Oseberg ship dates from
around A.D. 800, and was found, well-
preserved in clay, more than a thousand years later. Together with the
Gokstad ship, unearthed some years
earlier, it is the most important surviving example of a Viking long ship.
Clinker-built (with overlapping planks
fastened with nails), and carrying a
single square sail, with up to 10
rows of oars on either side, it was
probably used as a ceremonial ship.

three major kingdoms—Northumbria, Mercia, and Wessex—and four smaller kingdoms—East Anglia, Essex, Kent, and Sussex. Scotland was divided into Dalriada, Strathclyde, and the kingdom of the Picts, but, by the mid-700's, the Picts had become overlords of the other two kingdoms. In Ireland, the High King in Tara was paid homage by the leaders of a number of small kingdoms. Wales was similarly partitioned.

In 789, three Viking ships landed on the coast of Dorset in southwest England. The invaders killed the local chief, collected booty,

Left: in 875, the monks fled from Lindisfarne, in fear of a second Viking attack. They took with them the famous Lindisfarne Gospels, now in the British Museum. Later, monks did return to the island, and these ruins date from Henry VIII's reign.

Right: a fanciful medieval painting of a fleet of Viking ships on its way to invade England. The Danes stepped up their attacks in the 800's, and some settled permanently in England.

and then returned to their homeland. Four years later, the rich monastery on Lindisfarne, also called Holy Island, off Northumbria in the north of England, was sacked and burned. "In this year terrible portents appeared over Northumbria and sadly affrighted the inhabitants; these were exceptional flashes of lightning, and fiery dragons were seen flying in the air. A great famine followed soon upon these signs, and a little after that in the same year . . . the harrying of the heathen miserably destroyed God's church in Lindisfarne by rapine and slaughter." For several years thereafter, the Vikings were busy raiding throughout the continent of Europe.

In the 830's, they again resumed their attacks on England. It became necessary for a permanent watch to be kept along the coasts of England for Viking ships ready for the attack. When they were sighted on the horizon, church bells would be tolled, men would hurry to arms, and priests would rush to bury their treasure. At first, the Vikings were content to attack, pick up as much booty as they could carry, and retreat to their ships. After 851, they came to

settle, attracted by a land rich and pleasant compared with their own.

A few years later, the Vikings felt strong and practiced enough in warfare to conquer England. In the late 800's, a strong force of Vikings set up a base in York. By 869, they had defeated the armies of East Anglia and Northumbria and had forced the neighboring kingdom of Mercia to pay tribute. Then Alfred, king of Wessex, defeated the attacking Danes, who suffered so many casualties that they at length agreed to a truce. In 878, the Danes, led by Guthrum, overran Wessex but were finally routed at the Battle of Ethandun in Wiltshire. Guthrum had no choice but to make peace, and in 886, agreed to a pact dividing England between himself and Alfred. Land in the north and east came under the rule of the Danes, the *Danelaw* as it was called.

Another wave of Viking invasions began in 980, when Vikings raided the east and south coasts. The English king of the time, a feeble-hearted man, was known as Ethelred the Unready. Instead of leading his people into battle, he tried to buy the enemy off with gold. The tax he collected from his people for the purpose was known as *Danegeld* (Dane gold). The Vikings returned again and again to collect their easy winnings. In 1013, a king of Denmark named Sweyn Forkbeard invaded England, but died before its conquest was complete. The final conquest was completed by his son Canute, who was crowned King of England in 1016.

Scotland also suffered at the hands of the Vikings. The blow first fell on the islands of the Orkneys, Shetlands, and Hebrides. In 795, Vikings pillaged the island of Iona, and in the 800's, they began raiding the mainland. A great host stormed Dumbarton, capital of Strathclyde, in 870. In 904, they ravaged Dunkeld, farther to the east. The Scottish king eventually regained the Hebrides some

Above: King Canute placing a cross on an altar. Canute was king of Denmark and Norway and ruled England for 19 years, after the death of Ethelred's son Edmund Ironside.

Left: the Danes took home valuable plunder from their raids. The Gundestrup bowl, believed to have been made by Celtic craftsmen, was probably taken in northern France. The base of the bowl shows a hunting scene, with dogs attacking a bull and the hunter poised to kill it with a sword.

undreds of years later in 1266. The Orkneys and Shetlands, how-
ver, remained under Norwegian rule until the 1470's.

The first raid on Ireland took place in 795, when the monastery on
ambay Island, off the eastern Irish coast north of Dublin, was
cked. The people of Ireland did not wear armor and were easy
ctims for the Vikings, who carried two-edged swords, bows and
rows, and daggers. To protect themselves, the Vikings carried
und, hide-covered wooden shields with iron bosses. Chieftains
ore corselets of iron rings, other Vikings had corselets of leather
thick cloth. All wore round or conical helmets.

A fleet from Norway arrived in about 830 and captured Armagh,
e chief town in the north. Some 10 years later, the Vikings founded
ublin and established bases at Wexford, Cork, and Limerick.
The sea spewed forth floods of foreigners over Erin [Ireland] so
at no haven, no landing place, no stronghold, no fort, no castle
ght be found, but it was submerged by waves of Vikings and
ates." During the late 900's, Norsemen settled along the south
ast of Wales.

As far as the rest of Europe was concerned during this period,

Above: the coronation in A.D. 800,
of Charles the Great (Charlemagne)
as Emperor of the Romans. Viking
attacks during Charlemagne's lifetime were thrown back, but after his
death the empire was disrupted and
the raiders' task was much easier.

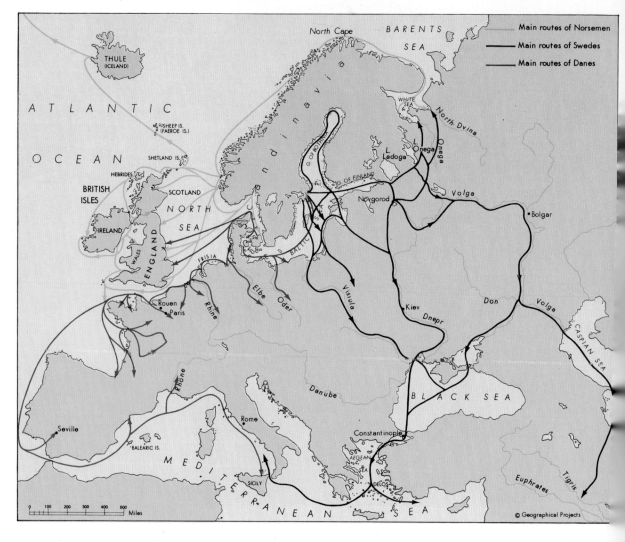

Above: the Vikings from Scandinavia traveled far and wide in their long ships between the 700's and the 1100's. Their main routes for raiding and later for settlement were across the North Sea to the British Isles, and across the Atlantic to Iceland and later to Greenland. Some Danish Vikings, however, raided the Atlantic coast of Europe and, passing through the Strait of Gibraltar, attacked the coasts of Spain, France, and Italy. Vikings from Sweden sailed and rowed many hundreds of miles along the rivers Volga, Dnepr, and Vistula to raid as far south as the eastern Mediterranean and even the Tigris Valley.

the Vikings were causing equal havoc. After the death of the Emperor Charlemagne in 814 and the disintegration of his vast empire, western Europe was in a state of great unrest. The large areas of France, Germany, and northern Italy which had been united under the emperor were now divided out among squabbling leaders. The countries were obviously weak and vulnerable, and this gave the Vikings a chance to attack and subdue individual nations.

The Danes invaded Frisia (the northern part of The Netherlands) in 834. In 864, they diverted the course of the Rhine River and thereby caused the decline of the important hunting town of Dorestadt, which was on the river. Rouen in France was sacked in 841. Vikings entered Paris on Easter Sunday in 845, and later sacked the city. In 885, they returned to Paris, and the Frankish king paid 7,000 pounds of silver to persuade them to depart peacefully. The French kings tried many times to buy the Vikings off with Danegeld, but this only brought more Vikings eager for such easy spoils.

In the 800's, a Viking group invaded northern France. In 911, the French king bribed their leader by granting him a large slice land which became Normandy—the land of the Norsemen. It was a descendant of the Vikings of Normandy, William the Conqueror, who defeated Harold of England at the Battle of Hastings in 1066.

During this time, Spain was ruled by the Moors. When Vikings raided Seville in 844, they took on more than they had bargained for. The well-disciplined Arabs finally routed the rough Norsemen and forced them to return most of the booty. The Arab leader, the emir, sent 200 severed Viking heads to his allies in Tangier, in northern Africa, as evidence of his triumph.

But the Vikings were determined men and were not easily put off. Sixty-two ships under Bjorn Ironside and Hastein sailed from Brittany for Spain in 899. When Arab forces proved too strong, the Vikings gave up and instead raided the north African coasts in the region of Cap des Trois Fourches, on the north coast of what is now Morocco. The warriors returned by way of the Balearic Islands to islands at the mouth of the Rhône River, where they spent the winter. In the spring of 900, they sailed south along the Italian coast with the intention of capturing Rome. Arriving at a magnificent city on the coast, which they imagined to be Rome, the Vikings tricked the inhabitants into allowing them into the city. There they found, to their dismay, that they had captured the little, relatively unimportant, seaport of Luna.

While the Danes and Norwegians were pillaging western Europe, Swedish Vikings were making raids on Russia. The Slavs and Finns who then lived there came to look on the Swedes as protectors and paid them tribute. The Varangians, one of the tribes of Swedish Vikings, were called *Rus* by the Finns, and some experts think this is how Russia got its name.

The Rus, unlike the Danish and Norwegian Vikings, were interested in trade. In 862, their chieftain Rurik arrived in Novgorod, north of Lake Ilmen, and established a center of commerce there. Rurik was succeeded by Oleg, who in 882, captured the city of Kiev on the Dnepr River. He also fortified the surrounding towns against the Khazars of the east and the savage Patzinaks who lived at the mouth of the Volga River. Merchants from Novgorod sailed down the Msta and the Volga rivers to the Caspian Sea, where they exchanged slaves and furs for silver. From Kiev they sailed down the

Above: a woodcut from the book by Olaus Magnus, showing Rus Vikings carrying a boat overland on a trading mission. The Rus were traders as well as warriors, and they took furs, skins, honey, and other goods to sell to the inhabitants of the land which became known as Russia.

Right: the Rus were not welcomed peacefully everywhere. Here a group of Byzantine (Middle Eastern) cavalrymen are overwhelming some Vikings.

Dnepr River to the Black Sea and Constantinople (now Istanbul), then capital of the Byzantine Empire. Early in the 900's, they attacked Constantinople, and the Byzantine emperor had to pay to save the city. Often the Patzinaks would try to ambush the convoy of boats as they came down the river. This was made possible because, at places where there were rapids or sandbanks, the boats had to be carried or hauled overland.

In 910, 16 Rus ships sailed down the Volga, through the territory of the Khazars, and ravaged the Persian coast of the Caspian Sea. At the mouth of the Volga they were defeated. The very few survivors were finally exterminated by the Khazars. In 941, another Rus expedition tried to capture Constantinople, but failed. On a voyage across the Aegean Sea, a band of Rus may have made a journey to the sacred island of Delos. The proof of their visit is a rhyme, carved in their script on a stone lion.

One Viking who was not interested in killing and booty was Ottar of Norway, a merchant shipowner who traded with the Finns for bearskins, walrus tusks, and hides. Ottar sailed north along the coast of Norway until he reached North Cape, the northernmost point of Europe. He then followed the coast around, first to the east, and then to the south, until he reached the mouth of a river. This was probably the North Dvina, or the Onega, in northern Russia. Ottar was the first European to round North Cape and sail through

Left: this stone lion, which sits outside the Royal Arsenal in Venice, was taken from the Greek port of Piraeus and may have originated on the island of Delos. The Swedish runic inscription carved on its flanks and legs suggests that the Vikings may have sailed as far south as the Aegean.

he Barents Sea, which lies north of Norway and European Russia.
His voyage took place 700 years before the sea was "discovered"
y the Dutch navigator Willem Barents.

The period known as the Dark Ages (A.D. 400's to 900's) gets its
ame because it was once thought that during that time learning died
ut in Europe. It has since been discovered that this is not so, but,
evertheless, little is known about what was happening in the world
uring this time. How do we know, therefore, what the Vikings
d and where they went?

Three main sources of information are available. Sometimes they
pport one another, sometimes they provide apparently conflicting
eces of evidence. The first source is the wealth of archaeological
mains dating from Viking times. For centuries, and as a result of
er-improving modern techniques, particularly in the last century,
ofessional and amateur archaeologists have been discovering
king ruins, tools, and weapons all over Europe and beyond. Often
eir finds confirm, or put into perspective, details of the picture of
king activity we get from two other principal sources. These are
e Norse sagas (prose narratives) of the 1100's–1300's, and the
ntemporary accounts of historians and chroniclers of the countries
Vikings invaded.

Scholars hold conflicting views about the origin of the Norse
as. Some now think that they are the result of a conscious
ort at storytelling, rather than simply legends passed by word
mouth from generation to generation and then written down.

Above: North Cape, a rocky island
off the northernmost tip of Norway.
The Viking merchant Ottar sailed
around this island on his epic voyage
around northern Norway to the
Barents Sea and the White Sea.
Ottar gave a firsthand account of
his voyage to King Alfred of England.

The latter theory is, however, still current. During the Viking age there were no books or other ready-made pastimes for the long dark winter evenings. The sagas probably began as tales of heroism and adventure told around the fireside and handed down from father to son. Repetition by word of mouth is a notoriously bad means for the accurate transmission of information. And good storytellers then as now, prefer not to be too closely restricted to the facts. Inevitably, with the passing of time, stories which were originally true were changed and romanticized to make them more exciting.

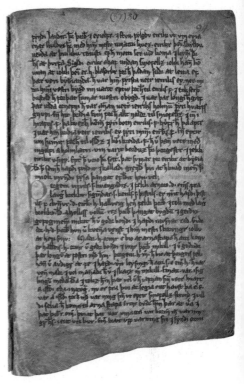

Above: a page from *Eric the Red's Saga*. This folio tells the story of how and why Eric named the new-found country of Greenland.

Left: an Icelandic painting of a colonist's family gathered to listen to the reading of a saga—a story describing the voyages and adventures of the early Norse heroes.

Some tales must doubtless have been lost for ever, and with them individual heroes and their journeys. But during the classical age of saga writing, the 1200's, about 120 sagas and many short stories were written down. The most important sources of our knowledge are the *Landnamabók*, first written down in the 1200's, and the *Flateyjarbók*, a collection of sagas written down by two priests between 1387 and 1394. From this material, scholars have been able to piece together what would otherwise have been a very confused period of history.

Iceland and Greenland
3

In the 800's, despite the booty they were carrying back to Scandinavia from raids on the British Isles and the rest of Europe, the Vikings' needs constantly outstripped the meager resources of their fiordlands. Instead of depending on short marauding voyages, they began to look for places where they might settle permanently.

During the period between 860 and 870, three Viking voyagers are believed to have reached the country known today as Iceland. It is possible, however, that there were earlier, unrecorded voyages.

According to the *Landnamabók*—other sources make no mention of it—the first landfall was made, purely accidentally, by a Swede called Gardar Svarsson. He sailed from his home in Scandinavia to claim a family inheritance in the Hebrides, but was driven off course by a fearful storm which swept him northwest across the Atlantic to the southeastern coast of Iceland. In calmer weather, Gardar sailed north and spent the winter at Húsavik—house bay. Continuing around Iceland the following summer, he proved beyond doubt that it was an island. Gardar named the island Gardarsholm, after himself. On his return home he praised it very highly, making it sound an appealing alternative to Sweden.

Naddod, a Norwegian Viking, was the next explorer to come across Iceland, also accidentally. He too was storm-tossed across the sea, and landed at Reydarfjord in the Austfirthir. In the hope of seeing signs of human habitation, Naddod climbed a mountain, Reydarfjall, but could see no evidence that people lived on the island. As he and his men sailed for home, a heavy snowstorm enveloped the land behind them, and so Naddod named it Snaeland—land of snow.

The first Viking to go to Iceland with the intention of settling there was a Norwegian called Floki Vilgerdasson. Taking his family and livestock with him, Floki offered up sacrifices to the gods and set sail. His party stopped off at the Shetlands and the Faeroes, and then made for Iceland. When they were well on their way, Floki set free one of three ravens he had taken with him. The raven flew straight back to the land they had left. Some time later, Floki released a second raven. This one flew up into the air and then returned

Left: the lava-covered landscape near Thingvellir in Iceland. Thingvellir was the site of the *Althing,* (Icelandic national assembly), for over 900 years. It is today preserved as a place of special historic interest.

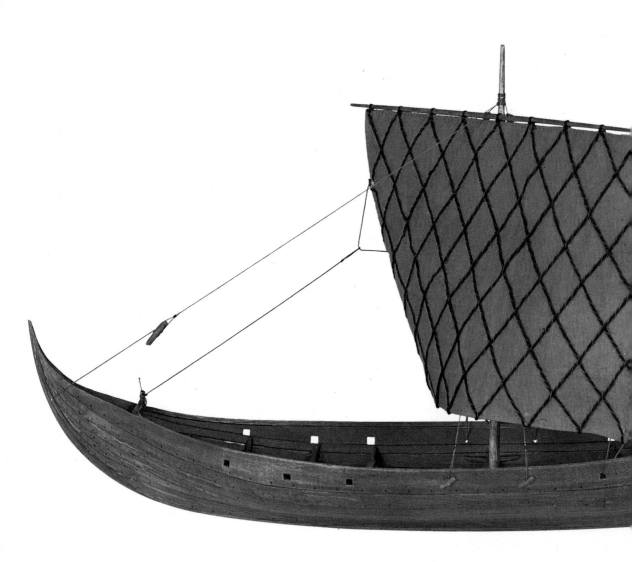

and perched on the rigging, so he knew they were still many mi...
from land. Then Floki loosed the third raven. It flew on ahead a...
gave him a bearing for land.

The ship sailed along the south coast of Iceland and then north
Breidhafjördhur, where the company stopped at a place call...
Vatnsfjord. They found its waters full of fish, and it was because th...
spent so much time fishing and sailing that they failed to ma...
provision for winter. When the cold weather set in, the livesto...
perished for lack of hay.

In the spring, Floki climbed a mountain from which he could s...
the pack ice in the fiords, and so he called the land Iceland. Aft...
their experience of winter conditions, the settlers thought the lar...
too hard for living in and prepared to sail home. Because of hig...
winds, the ship failed to clear the Reykjanes Peninsula and w...
forced to turn back. Floki and his family therefore had to spend th...
following winter at Borgafjord. When he eventually got back ...
Norway, Floki, now nicknamed Raven Floki, had nothing good ...
say of his adventures. But a companion, Herjolf, not wishing, we a...

told, either to condemn or to condone Iceland, "spoke well of some things and ill of others." A second, named Thorolf, was very enthusiastic about the country he had visited and told avid listeners of his adventures.

Around 870, two foster brothers, Ingólfur Arnason and Leif Hrodmarsson, were forced to give up their land in Norway after being involved in some vicious killings. A drunken young man had sworn that he would marry Ingólfur's sister and no other woman. Because Ingólfur's sister was already betrothed to Leif, this vow cost the young man his life. Within a year the young man's brother had also been killed. Forced to flee the country, Ingólfur and Leif decided to go to see the land Raven Floki talked about. They fitted out a big ship, probably in this case not a warship but a *knärr*. (A knärr was a merchant ship in common use at the time, longer and broader in the beam than a warship.) They explored the Alptafjord area of Austfirthir. After wintering in Iceland, they went home, planning to return to settle in the land they thought so promising.

The country they had chosen to colonize was one of harsh contrasts. Only the land around the coast was fertile and habitable. The interior of Iceland consists of deserts of lava—the molten rock that

pours out of volcanoes—and glaciers. Iceland lies in the North
Atlantic Ocean and its northernmost point nearly touches the Arctic
Circle. An eighth of it is covered with glaciers. Iceland is set across
the Mid-Atlantic Ridge, a great fault in the earth's crust which runs
from Jan Mayen Island in the Arctic through Iceland, the Azores,
Tristan da Cunha, and on into Antarctica. Because of the volcanic
activity along this fault, Iceland is constructed largely of volcanic
material. Many volcanoes, notably Hekla and Katla, have erupted

Right: Iceland's interior contains
many volcanoes, some of which were
active when the Vikings arrived.
This woodcut of the 1500's includes
the most famous, Mount Hekla. Mount
Hekla has erupted on many occasions,
the last time being in May, 1970.

several times since the country was first occupied. Volcanoes occasionally erupt underneath the glaciers. In various places all over Iceland the earth's crust is very thin, and hot springs are found.

Ingólfur and Leif did not have time to discover or realize all these disadvantages before they returned to Norway full of enthusiasm for his new land. Ingólfur stayed to raise money and to interest people in going with him to Iceland. Leif went off on another Viking expedition to Ireland to capture booty and slaves. During this visit, Leif became known as Hjörleif or Sword Leif. He got this name because he is supposed to have entered an underground house or chamber which became filled with light from a sword held in a man's hand. He killed the man and, taking the sword and other riches, continued to plunder far and wide in Ireland. Taking back 10 thralls (slaves) he rejoined his foster brother in Norway.

Three or four years after their first voyage to Iceland, probably around 874, the two men were ready to sail back. Each had a ship and took his family, retainers, and slaves with him. On sighting the coast of Iceland, Ingólfur cast overboard the high-seat pillars (ornately carved poles) from his homestead in Norway. These were richly carved with sacred images and dedicated to the god Thor. Ingólfur vowed that wherever they drifted ashore, there he would take his home. In the meantime, as winter was drawing near, he spent the cold months at a place still called Ingolfshofdi, on the south coast below Vatnajökull.

Above: in 1963, an undersea volcano
started to erupt south of the Vestmannaeyjar. Its eruption formed a
new island, which is called Surtsey.

Hjörleif traveled another 60 miles west and landed at Mýrdals-
sandr, a coastal stretch of marsh and sand. He built two great
houses at a site known as Hjörleifshofdi.

In the spring, Hjörleif decided to sow corn. Having only one ox, he
also hitched his thralls to the plow. While Hjörleif was in his house,
one of the Irish thralls suggested to the other that they should kill
the ox and say that a bear had slain it. Presumably, neither they nor
Hjörleif knew that there are no bears in Iceland. As Hjörleif and his
men scattered in search of the bear, the thralls attacked and killed
them. Then the thralls collected all the small belongings, seized the
women, stole one of the boats, and made their way to some islands to
the southwest of Iceland.

Meanwhile, Ingólfur had sent two of his thralls westward along
the shore to look for his pillars. When they came to Hjörleifshofdi
and saw what had happened, they returned to Ingólfur and told him
about it. Ingólfur sought out the killers, slew them, and reclaimed the
women. He then returned to Hjörleifshofdi, where his party spent
the second winter. The islands the thralls had fled to became known
as Vestmannaeyjar—the isles of the west men, which is what the
Vikings called the Irish.

Ingólfur's third winter in Iceland was spent on the Olfusa River,
and it was during this time that he found his high-seat pillars again.
He settled there and called the place Reykjavík (smoky bay) because
of the steam from the hot springs in the area. Ingólfur's party settled
the land between the Olfusa River and Hjalfjord, north of

Above: an illustration from the *Flateyjarbók,* one of the most famous Norse saga collections, showing Harold Fairhair, the king who united Norway. Here he greets Guthrum, the Viking chief who overran Wessex in A.D. 878.

Reykjavík—the first permanent community in Iceland. Later they came to be revered in Icelandic lore as Iceland's founding fathers.

During the late 800's, Harold Fairhair became Norway's first king. Norway had previously been divided into districts governed by *jarls* (petty chiefs). Harold was a local chieftain who warred against the jarls both on the land and from the sea. He vowed he would not cut his hair or bathe until he had conquered all his enemies. When at last he trimmed his hair and washed it, having presumably achieved his aim, his followers were amazed at his appearance and gave him the name Fairhair.

Many once-powerful men whose lands Harold usurped, saw him as a tyrant and fled the country. Iceland now became an obvious place of refuge, and "there began a great emigration out of Norway until Harold placed a ban upon it because he feared that the country would be abandoned."

Breidhafjördhur, where Floki had landed, was settled by a man called Thorolf Mostrarskogg. On Hellgafel (holy mountain) he built a temple dedicated to Thor, and the mountain was made sacred, a place where no harm should befall man or beast.

Aud, the Deep Minded, widow of a Viking killed in battle in Ireland shortly after he had proclaimed himself king of Dublin, settled around Hvammsfjord at the head of Breidhafjördhur. He

son Thorstein made his home in the Hebrides, and her grand-daughters founded a noble lineage on the Faeroe Islands. Being a baptized Christian, Aud set up crosses and an altar on her land. When she died, however, her followers·reverted to paganism and made sacrifices on her altar.

The early pioneers found good grazing for their cattle and also grew a modest supply of grain. Lakes and rivers were full of trout and salmon and the seas were rich in herring and seal. Sometimes whales were washed ashore, providing the islanders with food and

Right: a silver amulet, in the shape of a cross but with a monster's head, found in southern Iceland. The first Viking settlers in Iceland were pagans, but in the year 1000, the Althing decreed that Christianity should be the new state religion.

il. Eider ducks and many other types of birds bred on the island.

We know from the sagas that within 60 years of its discovery, by the 930's, Iceland was fully occupied. The *Landnamabók* notes the names of 400 families, the elite of the settlers, many of whom had been Vikings or were of noble blood. Roughly one-seventh of the settlers had Irish origins or connections. The majority came from southwest Norway, the others by way of Scotland, the Orkneys, the Shetlands, and the Faeroes.

The Iceland communities took their law, language, and religion from Norway. Some of the settlers were already Christians, but to begin with others were less committed to Christianity. For example, Helgi the Lean "believed in Christ, and yet made vows to Thor for sea-voyages and in tight corners, for everything which struck him as of real importance!" By the end of the 900's, Iceland was officially Christian under the jurisdiction of the pope.

After Iceland had been fully colonized, its new inhabitants gave up seafaring for a time and settled down to become farmers. But, as in Scandinavia, the amount of fertile farmland was insufficient for the number of people who wanted to live there, and pressure on the available land became intense. By 975, every habitable area was filled to overflowing. Human and animal populations overstepped the subsistence limit and there was a great famine.

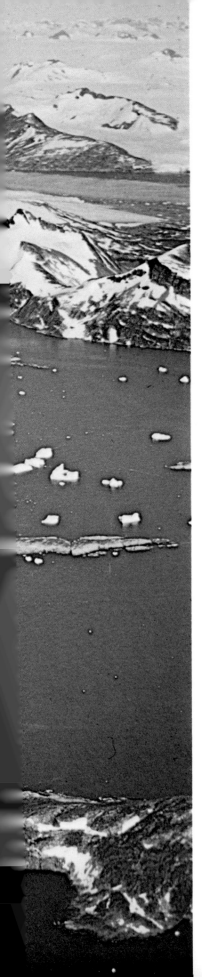

Left: an aerial view of the east coast of Greenland. This was the type of bleak scenery sighted by the first Vikings from Iceland. These settlers continued southward and set up their first bases on the more fertile and friendly western coast.

Right: Eric the Red, rather fancifully depicted by an artist of the 1600's. He is wearing medieval armor belonging to a period some 500 years later than his own. Eric and his companions were the first Vikings to explore the coast of Greenland and later to settle there.

Some 100 years earlier, in 875, reports of land farther to the west began to filter back to the Vikings in Iceland. Then in 900, a Viking named Gunnbjørn was driven off course while sailing from Norway to Iceland. Blown to the west, he saw a new, bleak, and rocky coast. Gunnbjørn made no attempt to land, but when he eventually arrived in Iceland he made it known that he had seen unexplored territory. When the famine came, therefore, in 975, Icelanders began to think seriously about the possibilities of moving west.

The first of the Norsemen, so far as is known, to do anything more than talk about the unknown land, was a young settler named Eric the Red. Eric had come to Iceland with his father, who had been exiled from Norway for killing a man. In 982, Eric was outlawed from Iceland for a period of three years as the result of a serious feud. He determined to concentrate on looking for Gunnbjørn's land in the unexplored west.

Eric set off with a band of followers in 982. The company sailed west. After only a few days they sighted land. The country looked barren and uninviting, so Eric and his men turned south. Soon, they rounded a cape, and found that the land turned north. The travelers found this coast more pleasant than the one where they had first landed, and decided to pass the winter there. They called the place where they wintered Eriksey—Eric's island—in the entrance to Eriksfjord. With the arrival of spring, Eric and his men started up the coast again, naming many places on their way. They returned to their base for the second winter, and made another reconnaissance

Above: the eider duck is one of the numerous arctic and subarctic sea birds. Even in Viking times, the fluffy plumage—eider down—was an important commodity, and the birds were afforded special protection.

trip the following summer. After spending yet another winter i Eriksfjord, the party finally returned to Iceland, their period c banishment over.

Back in Iceland, Eric talked at length and with great enthusiasm c the land he had spent the last three years exploring. Then, becomir involved in new quarrels with old enemies, he decided finally to s back to his new land and colonize it. Eric called his discove Greenland, because of its green coasts. The sagas tell us he thoug the fine name would tempt people to go there with him and see it f themselves.

The name Eric had chosen was a good description of the ne country. The land around the Greenland fiords was indeed gree Driftwood, a most important commodity to settlers in northe lands, was in far better supply than in Iceland. Eric could truthfu report fishing and hunting as being excellent. There were also pler

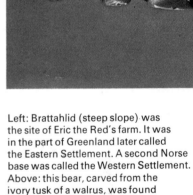

Left: Brattahlid (steep slope) was
the site of Eric the Red's farm. It was
in the part of Greenland later called
the Eastern Settlement. A second Norse
base was called the Western Settlement.
Above: this bear, carved from the
ivory tusk of a walrus, was found
at a farm on the Western Settlement.
It is apparently a child's toy.

of eider ducks, whose down was so highly valued by all Norsemen.

When, therefore, Eric led his party of would-be colonists to
Greenland in the summer of 985, those who reached it were not
disappointed by what they found. The sagas disagree about the
number of ships that set out on the venture from Iceland—one says
5 ships, another 25. But they agree that only 14 of them got safely to
Greenland. The ships were very heavily laden, and some probably
had to return to Iceland, unable to finish the journey. Others presumably were lost in the stormy, icy waters off the southern tip of
Greenland.

The number of pioneer settlers has been estimated at between 400
and 500. As Eric had been before and knew the country, he was able
to advise on the best places to settle. The majority pushed some 40
miles inland from the rocky coast and made their homes around the
heads of the fiords. The main center of habitation came to be known

as the Eastern Settlement—in the region of the modern port of Julianehåb. We know from the wealth of archaeological remains in the area and from the sagas that, at its height, the Eastern Settlement consisted of 190 farms, 12 churches, a cathedral, a monastery, and a convent. Because of his previous visit, Eric was recognized as head of the colony. He built himself a large house called Brattahlid at the head of the fiord he had named after himself. Modern visitors to the site of his farm at Brattahlid have remarked on the beauty of its setting and the richness of the land surrounding it.

Others among the first immigrants moved north up the coast to found the Western Settlement, around Godthåb Fiord. Summer after summer, encouraged by glowing reports from friends or relations who had gone ahead, more families arrived, and both settlements expanded and throve. A Norwegian, writing in the first half of the 1200's, gives the following account of Greenland in his time: "The people in that country are few, for only a small part is sufficiently free from ice to be habitable, but the people are all Christians and have churches and priests. If the land lay near to some other country it might be reckoned a third of a bishopric, but the Greenlanders now have their own bishop, as no other arrangement is possible on account of the great distance from other people. You ask what the inhabitants live on in that country since they sow no grain, but men can live on other food than bread. It is reported that the pasturage is

Above: ruins of the Norse cathedral built at Gardar, Eastern Settlement, in the 1100's. Today it is called Igaliko (great cooking place), the name given it by the Eskimos after the Vikings had departed.

Left: this amusing woodcut shows a fight between a Greenlander and an Eskimo. Eskimos arrived in Greenland more than a thousand years ago, and Eskimo attacks may have been responsible for the demise of the Norse settlements in that country.

ood and that there are large and fine farms in Greenland. The
rmers raise cattle and sheep in large numbers and make butter and
heese in great quantities. The people subsist chiefly on these foods
d on beef, but they also eat the flesh of various kinds of game such
reindeer, whales, seals, and bears."

The Greenland colony survived for more than 400 years. In 1261,
reenland became the farthest outpost of the Norwegian empire.
orwegian ships made annual journeys between the two countries
inging the supplies of grain the Greenlanders needed. The colon-
s handed over walrus tusks, bearskins, and sealskins in exchange.
en, sometime in the early 1400's, the ships stopped coming and
e Greenland colony died out. Perhaps it disappeared as a result of
epidemic, or fell to an Eskimo attack, or perhaps the end came
out because of a worsening of the always harsh climate. There is no
y of knowing.

Vikings reach North America

4

For more than 700 years, saga accounts of how Vikings reached North America, written down around 1200, were considered the products of imagination. However, with the general growth of scholarly and archaeological study and interest in the past, which took place in the 1800's and first half of the 1900's, there developed an increasingly large school of experts who believed strongly in the Viking achievements but who could produce no real evidence to support their theories. Then, in the early 1960's, a Norwegian archaeologist named Helge Ingstad discovered a site in northern Newfoundland that almost exactly fits a saga description of a

Above left: a Danish map of the North Atlantic, dated 1570, showing—more or less accurately—the British Isles, Shetlands, Orkneys, Faeroes, and Iceland. Greenland is linked to the American mainland, which includes Vinland, Markland, and Helluland, although they had long been deserted.

Above: dawn in Newfoundland. Reli[cs] of Viking settlements have been foun[d] here, indicating that the Norsemen reached America many centuries bef[ore] Christopher Columbus 'discovered' [it]

Viking settlement. Examination of the remains of buildings, tools, weapons, and other objects found on the site, verified Ingstad's contention that it dates from the 900's and 1000's, the period of Viking exploration westward. It now seems certain that the Vikings did indeed reach North America some 500 years before Columbus.

There are two versions of the story about discoveries of the land beyond Greenland, one in the *Greenlander's Saga,* and one in *Eric the Red's Saga.* The *Greenlander's Saga* is accepted by most authorities as the more reliable account. It must, however, be regarded as a sort of historical novel rather than an accurate record of facts.

According to the *Greenlander's Saga*, Bjarni Herjulfsson discovered the shores of North America quite by chance. Bjarni was a merchant shipowner who plied a regular route between Norway and Iceland. In the summer of 986, Bjarni set out from Norway with goods destined for his father in Iceland. Arriving there, he found that his father had gone with Eric the Red to Greenland. Bjarni and his men agreed to go in search of his father and they set off at once.

All went well for three days, until the wind dropped and a dense fog came down. The foul weather persisted for a further three days, and the sailors had no idea where they were. Then the fog lifted and the sun came out. Sails were hoisted and within a day the ship came in sight of land. Bjarni sailed in close to the coast and caught sight of low, forest-covered hills. Turning northward, he sailed on, and two days later reached another land. Bjarni had never seen Greenland, but he had heard about it, and he knew this could not possibly be it, since there were no glaciers. The boat drew closer to the shore and the voyagers saw that the land was flat and wooded. The wind dropped and the crew suggested going ashore for wood and water, but Bjarni forbade them, saying sharply, "You lack for neither." Once again they hoisted sail, and a southwest wind took them three days' distance before they saw land for the third time.

This time they saw a mountainous and glaciered land. Again, in spite of the entreaties of his crew, Bjarni refused to land. Consequently he lost his chance to become the first European to set foot on North American soil. Both Bjarni and his crew traveled back until they reached Herjulfsness in Greenland, where Bjarni's father lived. Here Bjarni settled down.

Some 14 years later, probably in the year 1000, Bjarni visited a jarl, called Eric, in Norway and told him of the three lands he had seen on his travels. Many who heard Bjarni's story were confounded by his lack of enterprise. Why had he not landed and explored the unknown countries? His words fired the imagination of many of the land-hungry Norsemen.

In Greenland, Leif, son of Eric the Red, heard Bjarni's account and determined to see the new lands for himself. He traveled to Herjulfsness, bought Bjarni's ship from him, and gathered together a willing crew of 34. Leif wanted his father to lead the expedition. Eric was reluctant, but agreed to go. On the way to the ship, however, Eric was injured in a fall from his horse and, considering the injury a bad omen, returned to his home, leaving Leif to lead the voyage.

Leif's expedition first reached land at the third of the countries Bjarni had sighted. They anchored the ship and rowed ashore in the ship's boat. The land was utterly barren, with glaciers in every direction. Leif named the area Helluland (flatstone land). Most authorities agree that this was the southern part of Baffin Island though some believe it to have been Labrador or Newfoundland. Leif and his crew went back on board and sailed to the second land Bjarni had talked of. This was low and wooded, and white sand beaches ran down to the sea. Leif called this region Markland (wood

Above: blacksmith's tools, dating from the time of the Vikings' Atlantic voyages. The tools include pincers, a file, cutters, and a hammer head. The Greenland smithies turned out farming implements as well as weapons.

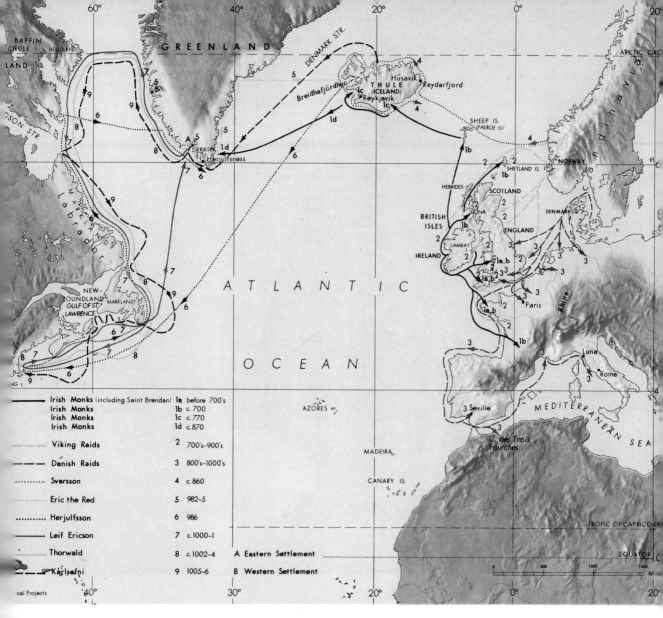

Map legend:

Line style	Label	Number	Date
———	Irish Monks (including Saint Brendan)	1a	before 700's
	Irish Monks	1b	c. 700
	Irish Monks	1c	c. 770
	Irish Monks	1d	c. 870
– – –	Viking Raids	2	700's–900's
— – —	Danish Raids	3	800's–1000's
· · · · ·	Svarsson	4	c. 860
– · · –	Eric the Red	5	982–5
· · · · · · ·	Herjulfsson	6	986
———	Leif Ericson	7	c. 1000–1
· · · · · ·	Thorwald	8	c. 1002–4
– · – ·	Karlsefni	9	1005–6

A Eastern Settlement
B Western Settlement

cal Projects

Above: this map of the North Atlantic Ocean gives a clear idea of the enormous distances covered by the mariners of the Middle Ages, from the Irish monks in their flimsy keelless coracles to the Vikings in their long ships. The green areas indicate the regions explored by the Irish and the Vikings during this period, though many of the actual landing places in North America are still uncertain.

Left: a painting from a church roof, dating from the 1300's, showing a boatload of Vikings. This double-ended vessel, with sail, is similar to that used by Bjarni Herjulfsson on the voyage when he accidentally discovered the coast of North America.

Above: a statue of the Viking Leif Ericson, in Iceland's capital of Reykjavík. Leif, son of Eric the Red, was probably the first European ever to set foot on American soil, shortly after the year 1000.

land)—it may have been Labrador, Newfoundland, or even Nova Scotia. Once again underway, Leif and his crew sailed with a north-east wind for two days before sighting land. They went ashore on an island which lay just north of a cape, and found lush grass. Returning to the ship, they sailed through the channel west around the cape and up a river. They moored in a lake and built temporary shelters. Later they built a more solid house and decided to winter there.

The salmon in the river were plentiful and larger than any the explorers had seen. The climate of the land was so mild that they had no need to prepare cattle fodder for the winter. During the winter daylight lasted longer than in Iceland or Greenland. On the shortest day of winter, the sun was still visible in the middle of the afternoon as well as at breakfast time—a story detail which is one of the clues to mapping the settlement.

Once the house was built, Leif decided to divide his company into two groups, one to stay behind at the house while the other went out exploring the countryside. One evening when both groups were together in the house, they realized that one of their number, Tyrkir, a German, was missing. Leif was most upset because Tyrkir was his foster father. Before an organized search party had set out, however, Tyrkir returned, babbling with excitement.

Tyrkir had apparently found vines and grapes. Leif, however, was unwilling to believe him. Tyrkir assured him that he knew what he was talking about—he did, after all, come from a wine-making country. The mystery of what these "grapes" were has not been satisfactorily solved. Many explanations have been put forward. Some scholars say that "grapes" is a mistranslation for "grasses," others that global climate changes since Leif's time make it quite feasible that at one time grapes grew farther north than they now do. There are countless other suggestions, and no general agreement has been reached.

Leif set his men to cutting the vines, whatever they were, and to collecting the so-called grapes. These were stored in the ship's boat. Next spring the men made ready to sail, and they all returned to Greenland. Leif gave the new land the name of Vinland (wineland). It is now thought that Vinland was situated somewhere between Newfoundland to the north and Long Island to the south. Much discussion and argument has arisen as to exactly where it was, but, although many claims are made, there is no undeniable proof of Vinland's exact position.

In about 1002, Leif's brother Thorwald borrowed a ship and set out for Vinland. Leif was kept at home by affairs in the Greenland colony. Nothing of Thorwald's journey is recorded before the arrival at Leifsbudir—Leif's house—where the party encamped for the winter. In the spring, a group set out westward by boat and explored several islands. Except for a beehive or helmet-shaped wooden grain store, they saw no signs of human habitation. These may have been built by the Algonkian Indians, who had granaries of this shape.

bove: clusters of wild grapes of e type known to have abounded on e Northeastern coast of America hen Leif Ericson landed on the rtile land he named Vinland.

ht: Olaus Magnus' woodcut of 1555, ws the Vikings catching salmon. e fish caught by Leif and his nrades in Vinland were, according to sagas, the largest they had ever seen.

Thorwald and his men returned to Leifsbudir in the autumn.

The following summer, Thorwald set off eastward and then north along the coast. His ship was caught in a gale which broke the keel and drove it onto a cape. Calling the spot Kjalarnes (keel cape), the sailors remained there to repair the ship.

From the cape, they then sailed due east into the mouth of a fiord, a place Thorwald thought very beautiful—so beautiful that he told his men he would like to make his home there. On a stretch of sand inside the headland the travelers came across three boats made from

Above: Olaus Magnus' book contains many scenes of everyday life, like this one of Vikings repairing a boat.

Above right: an assortment of Viking weapons (swords and a spearhead), and a stirrup, all showing the solid quality of their ironwork.

animal skins. Underneath each boat were three sleeping men. Th men from the sea killed all but one of the sleepers, whom the described as *Skraelings,* a word used in the sagas to describe th natives of different countries. These may have been Algonkia Indians—Jacques Cartier, a later French explorer, noted the habit c American Indians to sleep under overturned boats when traveling

Thorwald's party walked up onto the headland and saw man mounds which they took to be human habitations. Then, the sag says, overtaken by a great drowsiness, the Norsemen fell asleep. A at once they were wakened by a loud noise and looking about the saw Skraeling canoes putting out from the opposite shore. Th Skraelings fired arrows at the Norsemen and then withdrew. But or of their arrows mortally wounded Thorwald. As he died, he er treated his men to bury him at the headland he had selected for h home, and to call the place thenceforth Krossanes—cross cape.

An arrowhead of the type used by the Indians was found in tl 1950's by a Danish archaeologist on a farm in Greenland. Some e experts think it the very weapon which slew Thorwald, perhaj carried back by his shocked followers.

When Thorwald's brother Thorstein heard about Thorwald death, he decided to go to Vinland to fetch the body. But th expedition was storm-tossed all summer and never left Greenlar waters. During a winter spent at the Western Settlement, man including Thorstein, died of sickness. Thorstein's widow Gudrid took his body back to Eriksfjord for burial.

In the summer of 1005, a ship from Iceland brought Thorfinn Karlsefni, an Icelandic merchant, to Greenland. He stayed with Leif at Brattahlid and married the widow Gudrid that winter. Gudrid urged Karlsefni to go to Vinland, and when he agreed they sailed off with 65 men, 5 women, and some livestock. When they arrived safely at Leifsbudir they found a stranded whale, which kept them well supplied with food. Fishing and hunting generally were good.

Left: this Indian arrowhead made of Labrador quartzite was found at a farm in the Western Settlement of Greenland, and is claimed to be from the very arrow that killed Leif Ericson's brother Thorwald in Vinland.

Below: a statue of Thorfinn Karlsefni, who tried to establish a permanent colony in North America. The statue stands in Fairmount Park, Philadelphia.

Next summer, the settlers made contact with the Skraelings, who were much frightened by a bull the Norsemen had brought with them. The Skraelings gave the Norsemen furs in exchange for food, and then went away.

Karlsefni built a stockade around his house in preparation for the Skraelings' next visit. His wife Gudrid gave birth to a son, Snorri, who can lay claim to being the first European born on American soil. On their next visit to the encampment, the Skraelings tried to steal the Greenlanders' weapons and a skirmish ensued. The third encounter between Indians and settlers led to more serious fighting. This time Karlsefni, deciding that the new country's disadvantages outweighed its advantages, ordered his men to load up the ship, and the party returned to Greenland.

The next initiator of a Vinland voyage was a woman. Freydis, a daughter of Eric the Red, persuaded two brothers from Norway to

Above: this toy Viking ship, seen alongside a real one, was found in the ruins of a bathhouse in Greenland's Western Settlement.

Right: some fine examples of Viking jewelry—two gold brooches, a twisted gold wire ring, and (at top) a silver ring and necklace, with a pendant in the shape of Thor's hammer.

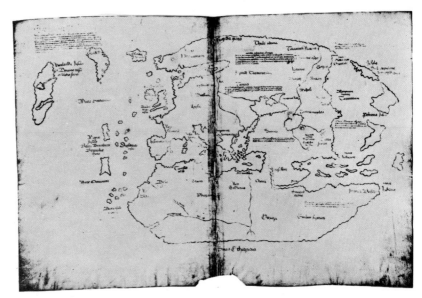

sail to Leifsbudir with her and her husband. Each party took with them 60 men and their womenfolk. They arrived at Leifsbudir, where Freydis built one house by the lakeside and the brothers built another. A quarrel broke out between the two houses, and Freydis goaded her husband into killing the two brothers and their men. Then Freydis took an ax and dealt with the women herself. Early in the spring she and her husband loaded the ships and sailed back to Greenland.

According to *Eric the Red's Saga,* it was Leif Ericson, not Bjarni Herjulfsson, who first discovered Vinland. *Eric the Red's Saga* was written down much later than the *Greenlander's Saga.* It is more fanciful, and most scholars take it as a variation on the theme, arising out of the many stories that circulated about the Vinland voyages between 980 and 1020.

One episode of *Eric the Red's Saga* describes Thorfinn Karlsefni's voyage. In this version his party followed the by now traditional route to Leifsbudir, and on the way found the keel of a ship at a place they called Keel Cape. To the south they could see the Atlantic shoreline's seemingly endless beaches, which they named Furdustrandir—wonder beaches.

The party rested at Leifsbudir for a while, then moved on by sea to find unclaimed territory. They put ashore a Scottish couple, named Hake and Hekja, to explore the land. In three days the couple came back bringing with them ears of wild wheat. The whole expedition set off again and sailed into a fiord indented with bays and streams which they named Straumsey (island of streams). Landing to explore the terrain, Karlsefni's men found it mountainous and very beautiful.

The winter which followed their landfall was harsh. The Norsemen had done nothing to prepare for it. Hunting and fishing were impossible. Ten of the would-be colonists resolved to return to Vinland. But their voyage ended badly. They were caught in a storm and driven across the Atlantic to Iceland. There they were captured by the inhabitants of the island and forced into slavery.

Above: a painting by an unknown artist of the 1600's of two American Indians. The Indians, who were called *Skraelings* (foreigners) by the Vikings, attacked the Norse settlements. After the Vikings left, no white man set foot on Indian territory until the 1500's.

Thorhall, the leader of the group, died while still a slave.

The rest of the colonists, except for a maintenance party which stayed behind, went on south with Karlsefni. They established a base at a place they called Hop (landlocked bay). Early one morning nine skin canoes arrived. Their crews carried staves which they whirled in the air with a threshing noise. The canoeists landed, surveyed the Norsemen with astonishment, stayed a while, and then paddled away.

The Norsemen spent the winter at Hop, where the weather was very mild. One spring morning, another fleet of canoes arrived and the strangers came ashore and bartered skins and fur for red cloth which they seemed to prize. A bull belonging to one of Karlsefni's men bellowed at them so loudly that the terrified Skraelings left in great hurry. Some days later, a vast horde of Skraeling canoes arrived and there was a fierce battle. In Eric the Red's version of the story, Freydis saved the day by sharpening her sword on her breast which frightened the Skraelings away.

In ever-diminishing prosperity and numbers, the Greenland

settlements hung on, the Western Settlement for 350 years, the Eastern a little longer. During that time it is very likely that traders and other sailors were blown off course to America just as Bjarni Herjulfsson had been. The Greenlanders themselves must often have crossed to Markland for timber, as they used up their own supplies of driftwood. Around 1290, there was a short-lived colonization of Newfoundland backed by Eric the Priesthater, King of Norway.

Archaeologists have unearthed various objects suggesting that Scandinavian settlement in North America may have penetrated some way inland. A theory enthusiastically supported by a small number of scholars—that a young Welsh prince named Madoc reached American shores in 1170—must remain only a story, as there is no conclusive proof.

At present, all that can be said is that, with the exception of the attempt to settle in Newfoundland, Freydis' expedition was the last journey of discovery and exploration by the Norsemen in North America. Nearly 500 years were to pass before Christopher Columbus' voyage again aroused European interest in the New World.

221

Right: the Mongolian steppes. These vast expanses of grassland are inhabited by nomads who move constantly from place to place, with their horses, sheep, and cattle, in search of fresh pastures.

Below: a modern Mongol, descendant of the fierce warriors of Genghis Khan. Like his ancestors, he rides a pony.

Genghis Khan and the Mongols

5

The Irish and Viking voyages in the North Atlantic Ocean made the peoples of Europe aware for the first time that the world did not end at Europe's western shores. They now knew that there were lands farther to the west that could be reached in a few days' sailing, and which had all the necessities to support life. But, even in the 1200's, the Eastern lands remained a mystery to Europeans. However, events were taking place in the East that forced the Europeans to look outward, and effectively ended their isolation from the rest of the world for ever.

The nomadic Mongol tribes of central Asia, the Tartars, Merkids, Kereyids, and others, had never been of any particular importance even in local Asian history. When drought struck their sparse, ill-watered grasslands north of the great Gobi Desert, or when winters were severe, the nomads had to raid their more civilized neighbors in order to survive. Sometimes the raiders would settle and be absorbed in the civilization they attacked. More often they withdrew to the grassy plains of their homeland—until the next famine came.

The only major civilization within Mongol reach was that of China. The Chinese, protected from attack by the Great Wall they had built in the northern part of their empire to stop the marauding Tartars, were usually safe. The Mongol tribes were weakened and divided by constant skirmishes and blood feuds. Long-time masters of political manipulation, the Chinese had also worked out a successful technique for keeping the Mongols at bay. "Set a barbarian to control a barbarian," was their motto. They would make alliances with some tribes, supporting them in their wars and blood feuds, in return for service in defense of the Chinese Empire.

Sometimes the Chinese were too clever and the allied tribes grew powerful enough to turn and sweep down on the empire itself, ousting and supplanting the ruling dynasty. This happened in A.D. 937, when the Khitan tribes took northern China and established the Liao (iron) dynasty. Khitan is the origin of the word *Cathay,* the ancient name for China. Between A.D. 1115 and 1125, the Juchen ousted the Liao from northern China and established the Chin dynasty there. From this comes the name *China.*

That might have been the pattern for centuries to come but for the birth, in 1167, of one of the most remarkable men in history—a man whose conquests were to make so deep a mark on the story of Asia

and Russia that the worst scars are only now being effaced. That man was Genghis Khan.

In 1167, Yesugai Baghutur, chief of the obscure Kiyad tribe of northeastern Mongolia, was returning from a battle against his neighbors, a Tartar tribe. Thirty years earlier, the Tartars had betrayed to the Chinese the chief of a tribe allied by blood to the Kiyads. Now, by way of revenge, Yesugai had taken a Tartar chief, Temujin. On his return home, Yesugai found that his wife had borne him a son. According to custom, he called the boy Temujin, to give him the valor and courage of the captured chief. This was the boy who was to grow up to become Genghis Khan.

Every young chieftain intended to be successful, or at least valiant, in war, and so to sustain the honor of his tribe. But from very early days, Temujin was determined to do much more. He never deviated from his aim to unite all the Mongol tribes, to weld them into a massive, loyal, invincible army, and then to force easy and regular tribute from every surrounding civilization—China, Arabia, Hsi Hsia (now northwest China), Khorezm (now Iran), and Russia.

To medieval Westerners, Genghis Khan was an ignorant, brutal savage. Opinion has only slightly mellowed with time, and it was not until the 1900's that scholars began to reveal the full extent of his political and military genius.

From the start, Temujin realized that he would have to break up the existing petty clan loyalties and feuds of his countrymen and replace them with a greater all-Mongol loyalty. He saw that the best way to do this was not militarily, by defeating other tribes and enforcing their obedience, but politically. He would use existing customs that helped his aims and he would devalue and destroy customs that ran counter to them. Warfare, much as he loved a good battle, was always subordinate to political craftsmanship.

There were two tribal institutions that Temujin seized upon and encouraged in every possible way. The first was the Mongol custom of one warrior (*nukur*) freely binding himself to the service of another. The binding oath took precedence over all other claims of loyalty, even those of tribe and marriage. The other institution was that of the protected or subordinate tribe—a system whereby a tribe voluntarily put itself under the protection of a powerful neighbor, performing vassal-like services in return for that protection. Often the superior tribe took advantage of the arrangement and oppressed

Above: a portrait of Genghis Khan in later life, from a Chinese album of emperors, dating from the 1200's.

its vassals. It was then no dishonor if the protected tribe deserted its guardians, even at the height of battle. Temujin owed several early victories to such desertions in his favor.

Though Temujin had as yet no way of knowing it, these institutions were very similar to those of chivalry and feudalism in Europe at that time. Because of the similarity, the earliest travelers from Europe felt surprisingly at home among the Mongols, despite the many strange, wonderful, and terrible things they saw and heard.

In fostering these institutions, Temujin inevitably destroyed the

Above: this Mongol painting, dating from the 1400's, shows scenes in a nomad camp. Both men and animals are skillfully, if not realistically, drawn.

older tribal and blood brother loyalties of the nomads. He als destroyed the system whereby all the more powerful tribes ha "left-hand" and "right-hand" branches, and power passed, b custom, from one branch to the other at each generation.

In three decades of such political maneuvering, using wh institutions he could, and destroying, with remarkably little bloo shed, what he could not, Temujin turned the divided and scatter Mongol tribes into some of the most efficient, loyal, and fearson warriors the world has ever known. He was no mere opportuni: The rigid code of loyalty he was trying to instil into his peop always came first, and no one stuck to it more strictly than he.

Again and again contemporary records tell how Temujin prais men who deserted to him but refused to betray their former maste If a deserter did betray his master, Temujin accepted the betra but always executed the betrayer. At a more political level, never turned against an ally merely because the time to do so v ripe and the chance at hand. He would maneuver and scheme ur

e could accuse the unwanted ally, man, or tribe, of disloyalty. That
ay he could justify his action in terms of the common good,
erhaps win over some of his opponent's supporters—and above all
ach everyone a lesson in building up the new all-Mongol spirit
nd forgetting old quarrels.

In 1206, Temujin, already *khan* (chief) of the Mongols, was
rmally proclaimed *Genghis* Khan. The word comes from Turkish
ngiz, meaning *ocean*. The Mongols thought the world was flat and
rrounded by water—hence Genghis Khan meant universal ruler
king of kings. It was at this time that Genghis Khan began in
rnest his career of world conquest.

Genghis Khan soon showed how brilliantly he could create new
cial forms to fit his new needs. He hastened the total breakup of
e old society by creating an elite bodyguard whose private soldiers
t-ranked officers of the regular army. Many of the guards were
ns of generals and military governors and as such were hostages
their parents' good behavior. Like any feudal chief, Genghis

227

Khan rewarded service and victory with grants of land and villages. The people thus given to a warlord soon learned that their loyalty belonged to him, not to earlier allies and kinsfolk, who now might "belong" to another lord.

In little over 30 years, Genghis Khan had created one efficient political unit. Such a system had taken European countries centuries to achieve. Moreover, he had done it without benefit of writing or of a single, organizing religion. Nevertheless, even this achievement was nothing compared with what was to follow during his *khanate*.

Above left: this large stone tortoise once supported a column, on which w probably inscribed helpful informatio for travelers. Such aids were of great use to travelers journeying through the vast Mongol Empire.

Europe, as yet, knew nothing of the changes that were taking place in the East. But among the merchants of the Moslem world—Persians, Turks, and Arabs—the knowledge was widespread. Moslem merchants traveled in Asia—to northern China, then ruled by the Chin dynasty, and southern China, under the rule of the Sung dynasty; to Hsi Hsia; India; Khorezm; and southern Russia. From them Genghis Khan learned of the wealthy civilizations to the west. He also learned of the powerful Uigur and other Turkish nomads living in the areas between his lands and the source of the great wealth. He saw that to exploit the westward possibilities for booty and tribute, he would have to make use of these nomads. Traveling merchants played a vital part in the expansion of Genghis Khan's empire, first as his spies, then as informal and formal ambassadors, and finally as administrators and governors of the enlarged empire.

Genghis Khan developed his military technology, too. The traditional nomad army had a limited, though terrifying, arsenal. Tactics centered on the cavalry and their tough little ponies. Each rider had four to six ponies, any one of which could carry him up to 100 miles in a day. By rotating his choice of mount, the rider could ensure that each animal carried only light equipment, food, and tents for three

five days between each man-carrying ride. In this way, the cavalry ould cover huge distances at unprecedented speeds, and strike, onquer, and loot, before either pressing on or vanishing back into e apparently endless steppes (the vast plains of Asia). The foot oldiers of the khan's armies, too, were used to long marches and uick strikes.

For those small, self-reliant units, a favorite tactic was to feign treat and draw the enemy after them, then to wheel about, re-form, d annihilate the astonished pursuers. These were adequate tactics r hit-and-run border raiders, but they were hardly world-beating. enghis Khan, realizing this, recruited the best Hsia and Chinese ilitary engineers, and, as his empire grew, called upon Persian and horezmian engineers as well. Within the space of just over 10 years, had transformed Mongol military tactics as thoroughly as he had e structure of their society.

Above: Genghis Khan (with scepter) pictured outside his tent. Like all feudal lords, he gave his subjects gifts of land and property, but in return he demanded willing service and absolute loyalty to the empire.

Armies in the field fell before Genghis Khan's cavalry and foot soldiers. Fortified towns were no more secure. His forces battered them with catapults and other devices, tunneled under their walls, and blew them down with gunpowder.

With these armies and tactics, Genghis Khan mastered most of northern Asia by about 1225. As early in his career as 1215, Genghis' forces had captured Cambaluc (modern Peking), and extended their rule over most of northern China and Manchuria. After taking Cambaluc, Genghis Khan turned his attention to the west, and between 1215 and 1222, subdued first Turkestan and then the Khorezm state. (This was the greatest Moslem power in central Asia.) Then he sent one band of troops to pursue the defeated Khorezmians across the Hindu Kush down into northwest India, and another band around the south of the Caspian Sea through Georgia and the Caucasus into southern Russia.

Genghis Khan died in 1227, a year in which his forces, or hordes as they came to be called, were laying waste and terrorizing much of southern Russia and the Volga Valley. Hardly a whisper of their activities filtered through to western Europe, though. Perhaps that is why the effects of these terrible atrocities have always been underestimated in Europe.

Southern Russia at that time was as economically advanced as the other countries of eastern Europe. It had well-developed towns with skilled workers and a growing middle class of merchants and tradesmen. In their century of occupation the Mongols destroyed it all. They replaced it with their own system of absolute rule, by which tax-gathering princes lived off crushed and obedient serfs. It was more than 200 years before Russia became even as prosperous as it

Above: Genghis Khan's cavalry had no equal in its time, and his men delighted in showing off their individual skills, circus-fashion, as depicted in this copy of a Chinese painting.

Right: modern Mongolians are still proud of their horsemanship. Here contestants assemble for the start of a horse race. Their mounts, similar to those that carried the Mongols across Asia and into Europe over 700 years ago, are stocky and tough.

Above: the death of Genghis Khan. Mourners gather around the bier of their great chief, who died during a campaign against the neighboring kingdom of Tanggut. His death was hastened by the effect of a fall from horseback while out hunting.

had been in 1220, by which time western Europe had moved well ahead.

Until after the death of Genghis Khan, western Europe heard nothing of the Mongols and their empire, save news of a great Mongol victory over the Russians on the banks of the Dnepr in 1222. The empire had by then stabilized south of the Caucasus Mountains and east of the Caspian Sea and the Urals. When Genghis Khan died, one of his four sons, Ogotai, continued the expansion of Mongol rule farther into China, into Arabia, and through Russia into eastern Europe.

Europe could hardly fail now to hear about the ferocious Mongols —the Tartars, as the Europeans called them. In 1239, Ogotai's armies crossed southern Russia and by 1240, they had penetrated as far as what is now East Germany, Czechoslovakia, and Yugoslavia. Nothing could stop them. Even the heavily armed Teutonic Knights, much feared by infidels (unbelievers) in the Crusades, were ignominiously defeated by Mongol troops at the Battle of Liegnitz in 1242.

The Mongols' reputation raced on before them. As early as 1238 while the hordes had still only reached southern Russia, the English chronicler Matthew Paris recorded that fear of the Mongols prevented the people of Gotland (in the Baltic Sea off southern Sweden), and Friesland (part of The Netherlands) from coming to England for the herring catch. As a result, herrings were so plentiful that year that they could be bought very cheaply, even far inland. Even today the memory of the Mongol hordes lingers on in eastern Europe, where "Tartars" are still the bogeymen of many favorite children's stories. The years between 1238 and 1241 must have been terrible times to print themselves so indelibly on people's memories.

In the West, one or two of the more astute rulers got the first glimmerings of the dangers that hung over them. A mission from Syria, which had suffered Mongol attacks, came to the English and French courts with proposals for a Moslem-Christian alliance against the Mongols. Nothing came of the request, but it helped to spread accounts of the awful devastation the Mongols left in their wake. The other nations of western Europe were divided by a quarrel between the pope of the time and the Holy Roman Emperor Frederick II, and they were also involved in the Crusades. In the event, western Europe was saved from a concentrated Mongol onslaught, which it was probably in no condition to resist, by the fortuitous death of Ogotai and the quarrels this caused among the other Mongol chieftains. After Ogotai's death in 1241, all the Mongol leaders, including the generals in charge of the European campaign, hurried back to Karakoram, their capital in Mongolia. They were all anxious to take part in the election of the next Great Khan—a process that could take years.

Giving up their campaign in Europe meant little to the generals. They had met no serious opposition and felt they could resume and swiftly conclude their conquest of Europe at any time. Europe, knowing nothing of the death of Ogotai, or its significance, could not understand why the Mongols had suddenly withdrawn. But they made no use of the respite they had so unexpectedly been granted. Instead, they continued to devote their attention to their internal affairs and to the papal-imperial quarrel, until a new pope, Innocent IV, was elected in 1243. This pope did two things about the Mongol problem. At a meeting of the papal general council he supported a decision to advise Christians to "block every road or passage" by which the enemy could pass ". . . by means of ditches, walls, build-

Above: Souboutai, the war general of Genghis Khan, seen here in fighting regalia. Souboutai led the Great Khan's armies into southern Russia, paving the way for Batu, Genghis Khan's grandson, to set up the Golden Horde there around 1240.

Above: Western fears of the 'yellow peril' from the Orient date from the years of the Mongol conquests. Cruel though they could be, the Mongols' bloodthirsty tendencies were often exaggerated, as in Matthew Paris' *Chronica Maiora,* where they are depicted as brutal torturers and killers.

Left: a realistic picture of two nomad travelers in conversation. It was only after Genghis Khan's death that Europeans saw for themselves what the Mongols were really like, and discovered the rich, advanced civilization of the Eastern lands.

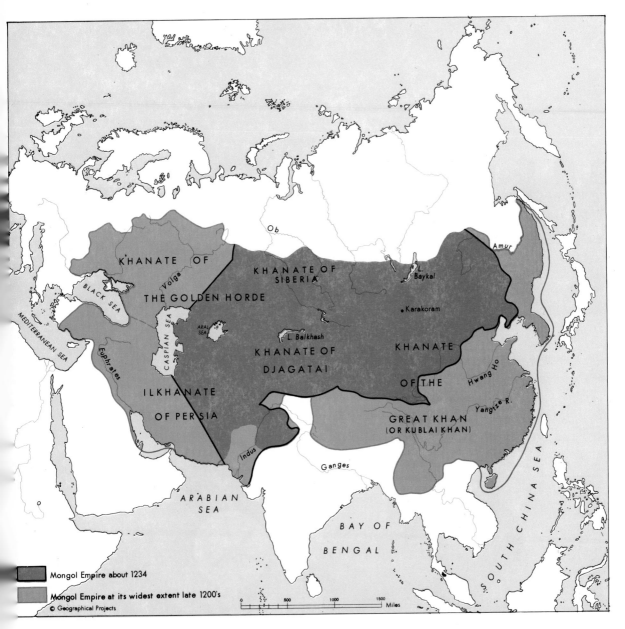

The map, with labels:

KHANATE OF
THE GOLDEN HORDE

KHANATE OF
SIBERIA

KHANATE OF
DJAGATAI

KHANATE
OF THE
GREAT KHAN
(OR KUBLAI KHAN)

ILKHANATE
OF PERSIA

MEDITERRANEAN SEA
BLACK SEA
CASPIAN SEA
ARAL SEA
L. Balkhash
L. Baykal
Karakoram
Volga
Euphrates
Indus
Ganges
Hwang Ho
Yangtze R.
Ob
Amur
ARABIAN SEA
BAY OF BENGAL
SOUTH CHINA SEA

Mongol Empire about 1234

Mongol Empire at its widest extent late 1200's
© Geographical Projects

0   500   1000   1500
Miles

gs, or other contrivances," and agreed that the church would help
foot the bills. More significantly, Innocent sent two parties of
issionaries to the Mongol chiefs with letters exhorting them to
give over their bloody slaughter of mankind and to receive the
hristian faith." As well as delivering the letters, the missionaries
ere to find out as much as possible about the strength and character
the Mongol Empire and bring the information back to the West.
One party, led by Friar Lawrence of Portugal, has left no record
its journey. Of the other, under Giovanni de Piano Carpini, we
ve his own firsthand account. His party not only reached the
ongol capital, Karakoram, a journey of some 3,000 miles overland,
t had the good fortune to arrive during the final ceremonies for
oosing the new Great Khan.

Above: this map of Asia shows the
Mongol Empire in about 1234—a few
years before Giovanni de Piano Carpini
set out on his amazing journey to
Karakoram. The map also shows the
empire at its greatest extent in the late
1200's, when the Polos visited Kublai
Khan at the new Mongol capital of
Cambaluc. By this time, Kublai Khan
had subdivided his western possessions
into four subordinate khanates, while he
himself ruled in the eastern khanate of
the Great Khan.

235

Envoys to the Great Khan

Friar Carpini seems to have been a most unlikely explorer. To begin with, he was more than 60 years old when he left Lyon at the start of his daunting journey. He was also an exceedingly fat man, and would have found the discomforts of the journey particularly severe. And Carpini had no knowledge at all of Asian languages. He acquired an interpreter, Benedict of Poland, but Benedict turned out to be a very poor linguist. Communication with the strangers they met on the way was very difficult.

Carpini must have had buoyant courage and faith to be able to set off barefoot into the heart of the unknown barbarian world. Starting out with little more than the clothes they wore, he and his party traveled through every country the Mongols had laid waste between Europe and Mongolia itself. They spent 16 months among fierce nomads, and survived periods of great deprivation and hardship. They brought back a most detailed account of Mongol society, law, costume, habits, diet, and, most important, military tactics and discipline. They also produced an accurate family tree of leading Mongols from Genghis Khan onward, and a list of all the important foreign ambassadors who brought presents to the new khan.

The letter Carpini was to take to the Great Khan was signed by the pope on March 9, 1245. On April 16, Easter Day, Carpini's party set off from Lyon in France where the pope was then living. As begging friars—they were Franciscans—Carpini, Benedict, and

Left: Mongol warriors besieging a city. The Mongol Empire, under the successors of Genghis Khan, stretched from China westward into Asia Minor and the eastern countries of Europe.

Right: Friar Carpini, the Franciscan monk, who, as an elderly man, traveled from France across Asia to the court of Kuyuk Khan. The epic journey took him more than two years, and made him the first European to cross Asia.

Above: Pope Innocent IV, in 1245, summoned a general council of the church to debate measures to be taken against the continuing Mongol threat. Carpini's journey was made with the pope's blessing, to learn more of Mongol plans, and in the hope of converting the Mongols to Christianity. *(Bodleian Library, Oxford. MS. Canon. Pat. Lat. 144, fol. 1.)*

their five servants traveled mainly on the charity of people they encountered. Fortunately for them, to begin with they mainly encountered rich men—the kings, dukes, and bishops of Silesia, Bohemia, and other eastern European countries—who gave alms in generous quantities. The friars were, after all, the ambassadors of the pope himself.

At the start, for the 1200's, their journey was comfortable enough, and they learned a great deal about the Mongols from people they visited on the way. Everyone they met stressed that the envoys would get nowhere with the Mongols unless they were prepared to make ample use of gifts and bribes, so Carpini and his companions spent some of the alms they received on buying furs. These would be gifts luxurious enough to please the Mongols, but light enough to carry easily on horseback.

At the beginning of February, 1246, Carpini and the others reached the Dnepr River and the city of Kiev, which had been the chief city of Russia until a few years earlier. Now, "traveling through that country we found an innumerable multitude of dead men's skulls and bones lying upon the earth. For it was a very large and populous city, but it is now in a manner brought to nothing: For there do scarce remain 200 houses, the inhabitants whereof are kept in extreme bondage." Kiev and the district around the city had become part of the Mongol Empire in 1240, and had very soon dis-

Right: a farmhouse in Perugia, Italy. Carpini was born in 1182, in a village near Perugia, but spent most of his life teaching in northern Europe.

overed the harsh penalties involved in being ruled by the Mongols.

Carpini learned at this point that the large European horses his arty had brought were quite unsuited to the journey across the teppes and deserts of Asia. From Kiev they would have to use the ardier Mongol ponies. Then Carpini and his followers set out into he vast Mongol-occupied Asian steppes, not knowing whether they ere going to life or death. Soon they had their first encounter with he Mongols—Tartars, as the Europeans called them: ". . . armed artars came rushing upon us in uncivil and horrible manner . . . hen we had [told] them that we were the pope's legates, receiving ome victuals at our hands they immediately departed."

Although, according to Carpini, they were generally "uncivil," he Mongols of these first outposts gave the party Christian guides to cort them through the realms of a succession of lesser warlords to e court of Batu, a grandson of Genghis Khan. Batu was one of the

Above: an illustration from a book of journeys to the Orient, dating from the 1600's. This section deals with Carpini's mission and shows Mongols with their horses, fording a river.

Left: Batu, grandson of Genghis Khan, conquered almost the whole of Russia and formed the Golden Horde, the name given to the part of the Mongol Empire in Russia and Kazakhstan.

Above: this hunting scene of the 1400's shows four Mongol noblemen with dogs and hawks, riding along the crest of a hill, while two leopards hide from them in the foreground

greatest Mongol chiefs, and founder of the Golden Horde, which comprised southern Russia and Kazakhstan. Batu's encampment was on the lower Volga River. To get there, Carpini and his party traveled through the Golden Horde, passing four mighty rivers on the way. Carpini was the first European to identify these rivers by their Russian names as the Dnepr, the Don, the Volga, and the Iaec (Ural). He was wrong, however, in thinking that they all ran into the Black Sea. Having journeyed down the Dnepr (which was frozen over) for several days, the Christian party reached Batu's encampment. He received them with reasonable graciousness, but forced them to take part in a ceremony which they must have found humiliating—purification by fire. No pain or danger was involved because they had only to pass between two widely spaced fires, but to medieval Christians fire was a purge for heretics and witches. It was, therefore, a strange ritual for the pope's own emissaries to have to perform.

With the help of Batu's most learned men, Carpini and Benedict translated the contents of the pope's letter into the Russian, Tartarian, and Saracen languages. Batu, Carpini says, "attentively noted" the contents. Although they had traveled long and hard to reach his camp, Batu then decided that the missionaries must go on almost at once to the court of Kuyuk, another grandson of Genghis and son of Ogotai, who was about to be elected the next Great Khan. Batu detained two of Carpini's servants, saying that he would send them straight back to the pope with letters from Carpini

...ing of the good treatment Batu had given his party. In fact, as ...rpini found on his return journey, the servants were kept inside ...ongol borders.

...On Easter Day, 1246, having said their prayers and taken a ...ender" breakfast, Carpini's party set out on the most trying stage ...their long journey. Carpini carefully noted the name of each ...d or governor through whose territory they rode, but gives little ...cription of the landscape. Perhaps there was not much to describe:

Above: a sensitive and highly stylized Chinese painting of two Mongols grooming their horses. The delicate treatment is typical of Chinese art throughout the centuries.

"Conditions were very wretched, and [we] found many skulls ar bones of dead men lying upon the earth like a dunghill . . . found innumerable cities with castles and many towns left desolate

Crossing central Asia north of the Caspian Sea and the Aral So the party reached the camp of Batu's elder brother, northeast Lake Balkhash, toward the end of June. Then, with only one da rest, they started off again on June 28, southeastward through t Syr-Darya Valley to the Altai Mountains and Mongolia. Their spe was impressive—all through the Asian part of the journey Carp and his men had to withstand the exhaustion of five or six changes mount in a day.

The Mongol post-horse system was obviously already w

Above: a nomad taking his horse to graze. The different viewing angles convey a sense of movement—a contrast to the Chinese handling of a similar subject seen opposite.

stablished at the time of Carpini's journey, although it had not yet eached its peak of efficiency. Toward the end of the 1200's, there vere 10,000 way stations, some with only a few ponies, some with p to 400, all kept in constant readiness for couriers, ambassadors, nd imperial officials. Using this system, riders could get from one nd of the empire to the other in a couple of months. On major outes there would be way stations every three miles. Relays of ouriers galloping from station to station could cover as much as oo miles in 24 hours. The system was an ingenious extension of ne nomad warrior's old system of traveling with a string of horses, nd changing frequently from one to another.

Riding as rapidly as their ponies could trot, Carpini's mission

traveled all day and often most of the night, "without eating anything and often we came so late to our lodgings that we had not
time to eat that night." During Lent and other periods of fasting,
the whole of their diet had been "nothing but millet with water and
salt . . . and we had nothing except snow melted in a kettle to
drink." Even when they were not observing religious fasts, Carpini's
party ate only enough to keep them alive. To travel so far on so
little food was a remarkable feat of endurance.

For many days, the mission followed the once-fertile valley of the
Syr-Darya, now devastated by Mongol attacks. Leaving the valley,
they continued eastward and at last entered Mongolia itself. They
rode on, still at top speed, for about three weeks, and "on the day of
Mary Magdalene [July 22], arrived at the court of the Emperor
Elect [Kuyuk]." They had not actually reached Karakoram but were
at the summer court of Syra Orda, half a day's ride from the capital.
Kuyuk did not let them see Karakoram, which, as later European
visitors were to find, was a most unimpressive place.

The emperor elect kept the pope's envoys waiting a long time and
allowed them only a near-starvation diet. In the context of the
huge empire of which Kuyuk had just gained control, the Christians

Above: travelers at a wayside inn.
This Chinese painting is full of action and indicates that, although on
many occasions the early travelers
had to sleep in the open, they sometimes found lodgings for the night.

Right: an illustration of Carpini's
journey, showing the tent of the khan,
surrounded by a wooden stockade.

and their pope were very small fry and he saw no need to give the envoys a lavish welcome. He did, however, eventually allow the travelers the rare privilege of entering his tent—anyone who stepped into it uninvited was immediately put to death.

Carpini spent some of the time in the four months his company stayed at Syra Orda listening to court gossip. He succeeded in working out the relationships and intermarriages of all the descendants of Genghis Khan. The family tree he brought back to the West was so accurate that it has been improved on only during the past 150 years, and then only in minor details. Carpini learned, too, how busy Kuyuk was destroying all the subjects of his empire who had grown too powerful during Ogotai's more lenient rule. While he was at Kuyuk's court, the coronation of the khan took place. In his reports of the journey, Carpini describes the ceremony, which, with its splendid Oriental trappings, must have seemed strange and wonderful to the European travelers.

Just before Carpini and his two companions were to leave the court, Kuyuk Khan decided that he wanted to send Mongol ambassadors back with the Christians to the pope. Carpini was particularly anxious to avoid this. He did not want the khan's personal envoys to realize how weakened Europe was by internal strife, or to spy out Europe's limited resources. Carpini also realized that if the Mongol messengers should happen to be killed by Christians, the consequences for Europe could be appalling. Fortunately the question was dropped, and, in November, Carpini and his companions set out for home alone.

This journey was no less hard than the outward one. They traveled all winter long and the weather made the going very slow. At night the elderly friar and his companions lay "in the deserts oftentimes upon the snow, except with our feet we made a piece of ground bare to lie upon. For there were no trees but the plain champion [hedgeless] field. And oftentimes in the morning we found ourselves all covered with snow driven over us by the wind."

It was May 9, 1247, before they arrived back at Batu's camp on the Volga. From there they were given safe conduct to the Mongol borders, collecting their servants and year-old letters to Pope Innocent on the way. When they reached Kiev on June 8, the citizens rushed out to meet them with great joy "as over men who had been risen from death to life."

Carpini and Benedict reached the pope's court at Lyon in the autumn of 1247, and presented Kuyuk Khan's letter. This letter has been preserved in the Vatican vaults. The travelers told the story of their amazing pioneer journey, but their report contained little to relieve Europeans of their fears of the Mongols. Carpini's detailed and accurate review of Mongol life, politics, and military organization would have been of immense value to a more united people. But the crises and alarms that divided Europe prevented the pope, or anyone else, from making preparations to face a fresh Mongol invasion. The only action that the pope thought necessary

Above: Kuyuk Khan, who was crowned during Carpini's visit. The khan declined the monk's invitation to become a Christian and gave him a letter for the pope, requesting him to journey east and pay Kuyuk homage.

was to send a further mission to the court of the Great Khan.

This party, under a Dominican friar called Ascelin, or Anselm, virtually retraced Carpini's footsteps and relived many of his experiences—nightmare travel, scant food, insults, delays. Ascelin had been ordered to visit the camp of the westernmost Mongol army and demand cessation of hostilities against Christendom. He seems to have been a poor diplomat. After a harsh reception, probably justified by his own rudeness, at the camp to the west of the Caspian

Right: the seal of Kuyuk Khan. The inscription reads: 'In the power of Eternal Heaven, the order of the oceanic Khan of the people of the Great Mongols. The conquered people must respect it and fear them.'

ea, he was saved from execution only by an envoy of the Great Khan himself. In 1248, Ascelin was sent home with a letter to the pope, similar to the one Carpini had carried. But Kuyuk had died, and the letter was written by the empress regent. Ascelin was accompanied on the homeward path by two Mongol envoys who were received at the papal court.

Pope Innocent's missions to the Mongol court all failed in their aim of persuading the khan to give up the idea of making further conquests in the West. But, apart from the easternmost countries, Europe was never invaded by the Mongols. There can be little doubt that only the imperial Mongol deaths and the resulting struggle for succession saved Europe from Mongol rampages during these critical years.

The Travels of William of Rubruck

7

In the mid-1200's, Europe waited, trembling, in fear of a Mongol attack. Meanwhile, King Louis IX of France, later canonized (made a saint) because of his devout and saintly life, was preparing a Crusade to Palestine. Among Louis' following was a certain Franciscan friar called William. He was born in 1215, in the village of Rubruck in Flanders, and is generally referred to simply as Rubruck. He would almost certainly have heard from Carpini's own lips a full account of that epoch-making journey to Mongolia and back. Perhaps it was Carpini's story that first fired Rubruck with the idea of making the journey himself.

If so, this ambition must have been boosted in 1248, when Louis' party, including Rubruck as envoy, arrived in Cyprus and was met by a messenger from Djagatai, the Mongol commander in the area of what is now Iran and southern Russia. The message he carried was highly complimentary to Louis, and it offered an alliance against the Moslems in Palestine. The timely arrival of this well-informed envoy shows how very competent the Mongol intelligence network in Europe was at that time. Louis sent a favorable reply to Djagatai and he also sent a mission to the Great Khan. He did not yet know that Kuyuk was dead.

This mission, under Friar Andrew of Longumel, who had been Louis' interpreter, set out in February, 1249, with letters and a rich assortment of gifts. Unfortunately, only second-hand accounts of their journey survive, and their route is known only from passing references in Rubruck's later account. In the meantime, Louis'

Left: King Louis IX (Saint Louis) setting out in 1248, on the first of his two Crusades. Louis was taken prisoner on his first Crusade and died of plague during the second.

Right: William of Rubruck, the Franciscan friar and envoy of King Louis, who trekked by covered wagon and on horseback to Karakoram, the court of Mangu Khan, and back to Europe—a round trip of about 11,000 miles.

Crusade was going disastrously. He had been defeated in Egypt, captured, and ransomed, when Friar Andrew returned with this message from the empress regent: "A good thing is peace; for in a land of peace those that go upon four legs eat grass peaceably. Those that go on two legs work the earth whose fruits come laboriously . . . these things we admonish you for your best advice; for you can have no peace except from us; the same could be told you by such and such kings . . . and all whom we have put to the sword. We advise you that if you will send us some of your gold and your silver, you will retain our friendship and if you do not do it, we will destroy you and your race as we have destroyed those mentioned above."

Andrew, though he penetrated only to the western edge of the Mongol heartland, brought back a wealth of information about the Mongols—and some misinformation, including rumors that the Mongol chief Sartach, son of the great Batu of the Golden Horde, had been converted to Christianity. If Rubruck had had no ambition to go east before, this must surely have aroused his interest. The chance of converting, as he thought, more of the Mongols to Christianity, was one that no devout Christian could neglect.

The next European envoy to the Mongols was Philip de Toucy, a French knight, who, together with some brother knights, had been sent on a mission to the Golden Horde by Baldwin of Flanders, emperor of one of the many small states formed from what had been the Byzantine Empire. One of De Toucy's party not only married a Russian princess, but also visited the imperial Mongol camp near Karakoram. Rubruck, with the other members of Louis' court,

Above: one of the five existing manuscripts of the journey of William of Rubruck, dating from the 1300's. As a record of Mongolian life and customs, it is as important as the later narrative of Marco Polo.

would have met and talked to all these travelers. From their account a great deal was learned about the Mongols.

De Toucy's party stayed with Louis for about a year, so Rubruck had ample time to ask advice and plan his route. De Toucy's advice determined him to travel by way of Russia instead of by the Middle East and Iran, as Andrew had done. Louis, still smarting from the empress regent's high-handed letter, would not give the mission his official seal, but he gave individual members of the party some money, a few gifts for the rulers they would meet on their journey, and letters of reference and commendation.

In the spring of 1252, Rubruck's party, accompanying De Toucy's men part of their way back to Baldwin, reached Constantinople. There Rubruck stayed until May 7, 1253, when he and his companions started on their 27-month round trip to Karakorum. In contrast to the other missions from the West, this one was purely religious in character. The members of the party were careful always to insist that they were not ambassadors but men of religion.

Left: a book illustration of the
1600's, showing the Volga camp of
Batu, which Rubruck visited both on his
outward journey and on his return.

nd that their sole concern was to teach and spread the word of God.
In some ways Rubruck's journey was easier than Carpini's. The
nknown was not quite as unknown as it had been eight years before.
arpini had blazed the trail, and other envoys had endorsed his
ccount of the conditions and peoples the traveler could expect to
eet. Rubruck was able to profit by their experiences and equip his
arty with regard to their advice. Moreover, he was starting his
urney from eastern, not western, Europe, and so, before leaving,
could have the letters he took with him translated into various
ntral Asian languages. He too was a fat and heavy man, but he
as younger and healthier than Carpini had been. Nonetheless
ubruck's achievements were highly creditable. Fortunately, the
ory of his adventures, written by his own hand, has come down to
intact. A much more personal account than Carpini's business-
e dossier of events, it is full of anecdotes and intimate observations.
From Constantinople, Rubruck and his companions traveled by
a to Sudak (now Soldaia), then a great merchant port in the

Above: Mangu Khan, like Batu a grandson of Genghis, was Great Khan—ruler
of the entire Mongol Empire—at the
time of Rubruck's journey. In 1253, he
received Rubruck's party at his camp.

Above: a monastery near the site of the khan's ancient palace at Kara-koram. Founded by Genghis Khan in 1220, the Mongol capital was not impressive by European standards. In 1264, Kublai Khan moved his capital to Cambaluc (later known as Peking).

Crimea, and terminus of the land route to Russia and Asia. Takin to the land, they set off with four oxcarts and made contact with th first Mongols within three days. Making much slower progress tha Carpini had done due to the cumbersome covered wagons, the par followed a more northerly route through central Asia than th taken by the Franciscans eight years before. Rubruck correcte Carpini's mistake about the true mouths of the Don and Volg rivers. He also realized that the Caspian is an inland sea, not, Carpini had thought, a gulf connected to the Mediterranean ai Black seas.

Like Carpini, Rubruck visited Batu at his camp on the Volga, ar was there directed to make for the court of the Great Khan. Touchir on Carpini's route again, Rubruck and his party underwent the sar kinds of hardships as the earlier mission had had to withstan But even throughout this taxing spell, Rubruck took the time

write full details of the journey, the countryside, and the different tribes and animals he saw on the way. A skilled linguist, he used his knowledge and observation to sort out the origins of a number of races and tribes. For instance, Rubruck noted the affinity among Russians, Poles, Slavs, and Bohemians, and he traced their descent back to a common origin. He also gave the first description, and it is nearly accurate, of Chinese writing—comparing it with Tibetan, Turkish, and other scripts. Then he described the scattered Christian communities he came across. Most of these had been converted to the Nestorian belief by Turkish merchants. Nestorians were members of a heretical sect which had been prominent in the A.D. 400's. They did not recognize Mary as the mother of God, and believed Jesus was an instrument of divinity not divinity itself. Rubruck also gave an account of Buddhism, and was the first European to identify Cathay as the home of silk traders known to Europe as "Seres, from whom are brought most excellent stuffes of silk."

On December 27, 1253, the traveling friars reached the encampment of the new Great Khan, Mangu, another grandson of Genghis Khan. Singing a Latin hymn, Rubruck and his men entered Mangu's dwelling. "The house was all covered inside with a cloth of gold . . . Mangu was seated on a couch and was dressed in a skin spotted and glossy, like a seal's skin. He is a little man, of medium height, aged 45 years . . . he appeared to me to be intoxicated." The friars' interpreter soon also began to suffer from the effects of too much

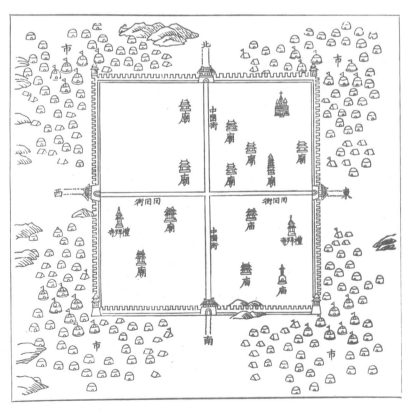

ght: plan of Karakoram, showing royal palace, mosques, shrines, d, improbably, churches. The outer lls are surrounded by nomad tents.

Below: the Mongols storming and capturing Baghdad. The city was taken in 1258 by Mangu Khan's brother Hulagu, and the caliph was cruelly executed. Hulagu's advance westward was halted by the Egyptians. He served as vassal to his brother Kublai Khan, who succeeded Mangu as Great Khan in 1259.

wine, and so after giving formal greetings, the Europeans retired. A miserable hut was assigned for their use, but the khan graciously invited the priests to stay at his camp for two months, until the end of the great cold. During these months, it was so cold that Rubruck says the tips of his toes froze, and he could no longer go barefoot as was his custom. Later, when they got to Karakoram, there was another spell of very cold weather, and the Mongols presented the other friar in Rubruck's party, and the interpreter, with cloaks, trousers, and shoes, all made of sheepskin. But Rubruck refused them, saying a fur cloak Batu had given him was enough.

When the two months were up, Rubruck accompanied Mangu to his capital and gave Europe its first account of that city: "You must know that, exclusive of the palace of the Khan, Karakoram is not as big as the village of Saint Denis [a small French provincial village], and the monastery of Saint Denis is 10 times larger than the palace."

Men of almost every race and religion met at the Great Khan's capital, and Rubruck recorded descriptions of many of them in his journal. He also wrote some highly colorful accounts of the endless drinking parties, which were a common form of entertainment among all nationalities.

One year after leaving Batu's camp, Rubruck and his companions passed through it again on their way home. They carried with them a letter from Mangu to King Louis. "The commandments of the eternal God are what we impart to you . . . if you understand it and shall not give heed to it nor believe it, saying: 'Our country is far off, our mountains are strong, our sea is wide' and in this belief you make war against us, you shall find out what we can do."

In 1255, they reached Christian soil again and Rubruck returned to the monastery of his order to send a report of his travels, and the not very encouraging message from the khan, to King Louis at 'Akko. Religious missions to Mongolia then ceased for more than 30 years.

Happily for Christendom, the Mongols now turned their attentions again to the Islamic countries. At the very time when Rubruck was in Karakoram, the Great Khan and his brother had been planning attacks on the two leaders of the Moslem world, the Caliph of Baghdad and the Grand Master of the Ismailis, and these they proceeded to put into action. In 1259, Mangu died, and power passed to his brother Kublai.

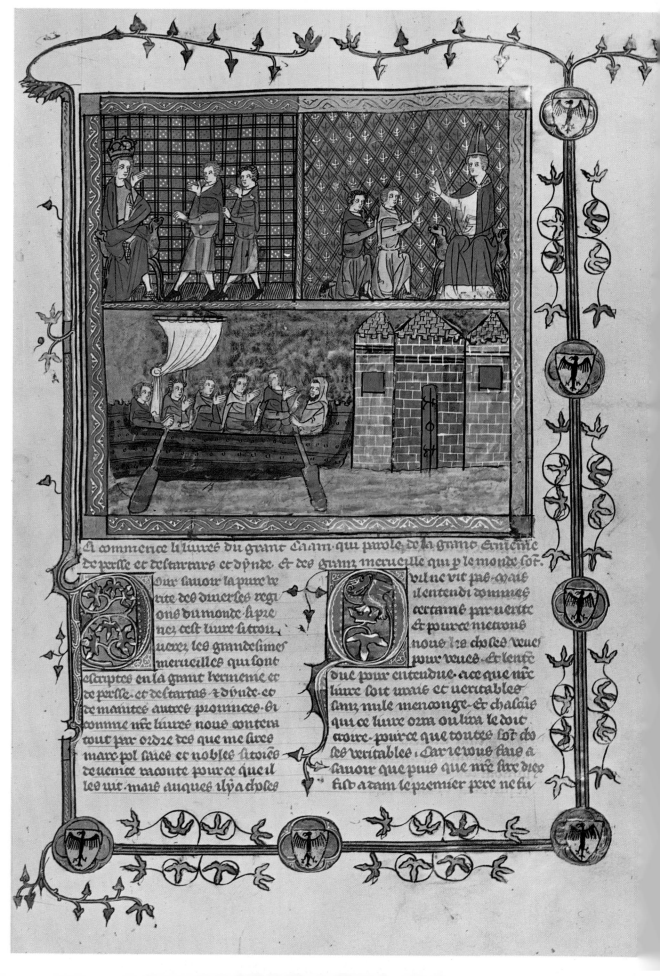

Ci commence li liures du grant caan qui parole de la grant seigneirie
de perse er destartaes et dynde et des granz merueilles qui p le monde soit.

Pour sauoir la pure ve-
rite des diuerses regi
ons du monde lipre
nez cest liure si trou
uerez les grandesimes
merueilles qui sont
escriptes en la grant bermenie er
de perse er destartas z dynde er
de maintes autres prouinces. Si
comme nre liures nous conterm
tout par ordre des que me sires
marc pol si les er nobles si toies
de uenice raconte pour ce que il
les uit mais auques il y a choses

vil ne uit pas mais
il entendi dommes
certains par uerite
er pour ce merrons
nous les choses ueues
pour ueues. er lente
due pour entendue. a ce que nre
liure soit urais er ueritables
sanz nule mensonge. er chasais
qui ce liure orra ou lira le doit
croire. pour ce que toutes sot cho
ses ueritables. Car ie uous fais a
sauoir que puis que nre sire dieu
fist adam le premier pere ne fu

Merchant Travelers

8

Left: a beautiful illumination, from
a medieval manuscript, of Nicolò and
Maffeo Polo setting out on their journey to the Orient. At top left, they
are seen arriving in Constantinople.
On the right, they are received there
by the Byzantine emperor Baldwin.
Below: they and their companions
row into a Black Sea port.

Most of the early European journeys to Asia were undertaken by men of God—missionaries seeking converts among the heathen, or envoys from the Christian pope. In the late 1200's, they were succeeded by merchants, who became the first non-Asians to cross Asia from the Mediterranean Sea to the Pacific Ocean. The first detailed account of Europeans visiting the Far East concerns two jewelers from Venice—Nicolò and Maffeo Polo.

The Venetian republic was at that time the richest and most powerful of the city-states into which the north of Italy was divided. Its merchants specialized in the valuable trade between Europe and the Middle East. Their ships sailed regularly to the ports of the eastern Mediterranean, and even as far as the Black Sea, carrying European products such as cloth on the outward journey and Oriental luxury goods and spices on the homeward trip. To secure and protect these profitable trade routes, Venice had gained posses-sion of a number of islands, including Crete, and of part of the Italian mainland. Venetian merchants were accustomed to dealing with Eastern traders, and many of them could speak the principal languages of the Middle East.

In 1259, Kublai, the brother of Mangu Khan, became Great Khan of the vast Mongol Empire. A man of immense vision, with an

Right: this Venetian ship, worked
jewels and enamels, is part of the
priceless *Pala d'Oro*, the great altar
screen in Venice's St. Mark's basilica.
In the Polos' time, sailing ships
carried Venetian traders to all parts of
the Mediterranean and the Black Sea.

Right: a silk moth. Silk was first made in China and was an important export commodity from the beginning of the Christian era. It was taken to Europe by the overland caravan route and by sea, but the trade had declined before Kublai Khan revived it.

outstanding talent for administration, Kublai was in many ways as rare a person as his grandfather, Genghis, had been. He extended the Mongol Empire to include the whole of China (then generally known as Cathay), Korea, and Tibet, as well as parts of Indochina and Burma. Other states outside this area, except Japan which he was never able to conquer, sent him tribute every year. Kublai ran the administrative machine of his empire with energy, compassion, and a sense of purpose. Because huge distances separated the parts of his empire, he appointed four subordinate khans in the west and then moved his capital from Karakoram to a city he called Cambaluc. This city in China was later called Peking.

During the reign of Kublai Khan, the Mongols gave up their destructive warlike activities, and a period of prosperity and tolerance began throughout their empire. The road system, with its

Below: when the Polos set out on their first journey across Asia in 1255, their home city-state of Venice had built up an important eastward-looking commercial empire in the Mediterranean. This map shows the extent of that empire and its trading routes in 1250. By 1450, this complex would make Venice the strongest sea power in the Christian world.

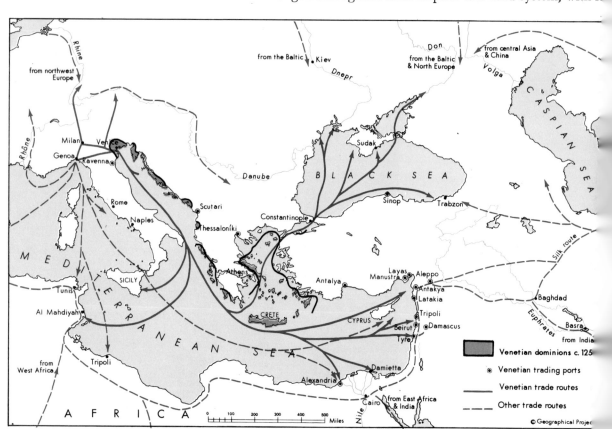

nns and post horses, was already efficient in the time of Carpini and
Rubruck. Now it was so well organized that anyone, Mongol or
foreigner, could travel easily from Europe to the empire's easternmost outpost. The roads were good. In most places they were
covered with earth, suitable for riders, elsewhere they were paved
for wheeled traffic. Trees marked the borders of the roads in fertile
areas, and in desert regions there was a line of white stones along each
side. The roads were also safe. "A maiden bearing a nugget of gold,"
it was said, "could walk these roads alone and unmolested." Merchants of many nations began to use the roads, and trade prospered
between West and East for the first time since the Roman Empire.
Then, there had been regular comings and goings along the Silk
Roads, the original caravan routes from eastern China to the West.
But communications had been severed after the Mohammedan
conquests in Asia in the 600's. Trade had come to a total standstill
and the roads had been forgotten. Six-and-a-half centuries later,
Kublai Khan received and welcomed merchants from the West
along his new wide roads. For a short time the East was accessible
again to Europeans.

In, or shortly after, 1255, while Rubruck was hastening back to
Europe, Nicolò and Maffeo Polo set out for Constantinople on a
trading trip. They remained in Constantinople for six years and then
sailed on to the port of Sudak in the Crimea where their brother,
Marco Polo the elder, was a leading member of the resident Venetian

Above: under the Great Khan, most
Mongols were pagans, worshiping the
spirit forces in winds, forests, and
mountains. These figures are demons,
part-human, part-animal. Despite the
later arrival of Buddhism and, in more
recent times, Communism, many
Mongolian peasants remain faithful to
the old pagan beliefs and customs.

261

Above: the ancient city of Bukhara, in Uzbekistan, Russia, was sacked by the warriors of Genghis Khan. By the time the Polo brothers visited the city, it had been rebuilt. They were so impressed with Bukhara that they stayed there for three years.

trading community. The Polos carried jewels with them instead of money or goods, because jewels were lighter, easier to carry, and easier to conceal. In Sudak, business seems to have been slack and the brothers had the idea of opening up a trading route to Russia— to Sarai (then a city on the lower Volga, northwest of Astrakhan) where Barka, brother of the now-dead Batu and new Khan of the Golden Horde, had set up his capital. For centuries Christian merchants from Italy had been trading profitably with their spiritual enemies—Moslems, Jews, and other *infidels* (unbelievers). Trade with the "Tartar devils," so recently the terror of the West, came just as naturally.

Leaving Marco in Sudak, Nicolò and Maffeo went to Sarai, where their venture was a great success. The Polos presented all their valuable jewels to Barka, and he gave them goods of twice the value in return. The Polos stayed at his court for a year, a period about which very little is known. Then, just as they intended to start back to the Crimea, Barka went to war with the khan whose lands lay to the south and west of Sarai. Bitter fighting made the route by which the Polos had come too dangerous to travel.

Nicolò and Maffeo decided to try to find a roundabout way home, and set off eastward. From Bolgar, at the northern limit of Mongol dominions, they crossed the Volga and then traveled to Bukhara, chief city of another of the subsidiary khans, Djagatai. The Polos remained for three years at his court, and thought Bukhara the "finest city in the whole of Persia" and very good for business. Then, one day in 1265, Mongol envoys from the west of Iran came through Bukhara on their way to Cambaluc. The envoys said that Kublai was most anxious to meet Westerners, and invited the Polos to make the long journey to China with them.

Perhaps in the spirit of adventure, perhaps in the hope of increasing trade, the two Polos took up the invitation, and joined the Mongol caravan. They traveled eastward for about a year, with none of the haste but some of the discomfort the religious travelers had put up with. On the way, they stopped at Samarkand, now in Uzbekistan, which they later described as "a very great and noble city . . . it has splendid gardens and a plain full of all the fruits one could possibly desire." Then they progressed along the northern branch of the Silk Road to join the southern branch at Tunhwang in north central China. From Tunhwang the Polos and their escorts went eastward to the Yellow River (now the Hwang Ho) and then on to Peking, once the center of ancient China, at that time (under the name of Cambaluc) capital of the Mongol Empire.

Kublai Khan received the Venetians with courtesy. He was interested in these foreigners and questioned them closely on Western customs and affairs. The brothers had by now lived in Mongol states for several years, long enough to become fluent in Asian languages. Their answers impressed and pleased the Great Khan. He determined to send them, with one of his own noblemen,

elow: a detail from the Catalan tlas of 1375, showing the brothers olo traveling by camel caravan.

as his envoys to the pope. They were to request the pope to send Kublai 100 men "skilled in the seven arts," and having a deep knowledge of Christianity, to argue and demonstrate the superiority of their religion before the court in Cambaluc. Kublai also asked for some of the oil from the lamp over Christ's sepulcher in Jerusalem. Then he presented the Venetians with a golden tablet, a kind of passport to comfort on their journey back. The tablet was a 15-inch gold strip with an inscription on it to the glory of the khan of khans. At any point within the Mongol Empire the tablet guaranteed the traveler food, lodgings, fresh horses, and an escort.

The Mongol nobleman fell ill early on the journey back and returned to Cambaluc. Nicolò and Maffeo continued on their own, not reaching 'Akko in northern Palestine until three years later. Little is known of their route, and why they took so long. Presumably they stopped for long intervals to trade at places on the way. From 'Akko, the Polos embarked directly for Venice. There Nicolò learned that the wife he had left behind some 14 years earlier had long since died. His son Marco, who had been a baby when he left, was now a bright and strapping 15-year-old.

It was a bad time to bring Kublai's request back to Europe. Pope Clement IV had died in 1268, and a long quarrel was going on about his successor. The Polos waited impatiently for more than two years, daily hoping for the appointment of a pope who would grant Kublai's request. By 1271, their patience had run out. Fearing that the trading trail they had blazed would close up if they delayed any longer, the brothers left for 'Akko again, this time taking young Marco with them. At 'Akko they met the papal legate, Tebaldo Visconti, and explained the situation to him. Visconti saw at once the golden chance their contact with China presented to Christendom and agreed that the Polos ought to keep open the line to Cambaluc. But he could give them no official papal reply until there was a pope to authorize it.

Left: Kublai Khan handing the golden seal to the Polo brothers at his new capital of Cambaluc. The Polos left no written record of their time there.

264

The Polos went to Jerusalem to get the holy oil that Kublai had asked for. Then they set off again for Cambaluc. They had only reached Laya, a port in the northeast corner of the Mediterranean, when they heard that a new pope had been elected and they were to return to 'Akko. The new pope was none other than Tebaldo Visconti, who assumed the title of Pope Gregory X. He was still at 'Akko. He gave the Polos full ambassadorial status and many fine presents, including valuable crystals, for the khan. The church could neither muster nor spare the 100 learned theologians Kublai Khan had asked for—especially at such short notice. Instead, the pope sent along two Dominican friars, Friar Nicholas of Vicenza and Friar William of Tripoli, to help convert the Chinese and Mongols. The two friars got no farther than Laya. There, scared by the fighting then going on between Egyptians and Armenians, they handed all their privileges, papers, and letters over to the Polos and made for home. At a time when Kublai and the Mongols were open to conversion, who knows what a lost opportunity their defection may have caused to the Christian church?

Tebaldo Visconti had traveled out to 'Akko in the suite of Prince Edward, later Edward I of England. In the English prince's retinue at that time was a young romance writer called Rusticello. He had certainly heard of, and probably met, the three Venetians whose most exciting adventures were then beginning. Their tale, entitled

Above: the port of 'Akko, in Israel. Akko dates back 3,500 years. In the Middle Ages, it was the gateway to the East. Nicolò and Maffeo Polo sailed from there to Venice in 1269, and returned two years later with young Marco Polo, at the beginning of their second journey to the East.

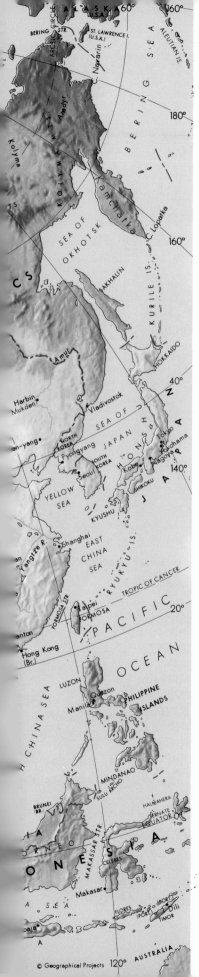

Right: title page of the first printed edition in 1477, of *The Book of Marco Polo.* There are over 140 known manuscripts of the book, including handwritten versions of the 1300's.

Left: Asia and eastern Europe, showing the vast distances and formidable terrain that the early European travelers, missionaries, and merchants braved in their amazing journeys to the East.

Below: an illustration from a medieval French manuscript of Marco Polo's *Book,* showing travelers in Armenia, a region in southwestern Asia.

The Book of Marco Polo, he was to set down in a Genoese prison which he shared with Marco Polo the younger over 25 years later.

In a way, Rusticello's collaboration mars the early part of Marco's story, which reads much more like a romantic fable than a real journey. Marco Polo's main contribution to the joint work was probably the rather dull commercial geography which is typical of long sections of the book. For instance: "Southwest of the Black Sea, the region of Mount Ararat [Greater Armenia] is a large province. Near the entrance to it stands a city called Erzincan, in which is made the best buckram in the world and countless other crafts are practiced." Rusticello, like the princes, bishops, knights, and merchants who read his words or listened to his tales, already knew the Middle East fairly well, and so he included at this stage a series of lengthy passages repeating well-known Middle East legends, no doubt intended to make the work more exciting.

For the later and greater parts of this amazing journey, when the Polos had passed out of the reasonably familiar Middle East into lands he knew nothing about, Rusticello had to rely on Marco Polo's memories. From that point the story is richer, more detailed, and more interestingly told.

Cy apres commence le liure de marc pol teus meruailles duse la grant et om
nium pour ceminer. Et des diuerses regions du monde
Pur sauoir la puie ierite te omerses regions du mon
te. Si prenes ce liure cy et le lautres liur. si y trouuerez les
grandismes meruailles qui y sont esciiptes. De la grit
amienie. et te perse. et tes tartars. et dinte et te main
tes autres prouinces. si comme nir liure comptera y
ordres apertement. te quoy mestre marc pol. sages et
nobles ciuois te ueusse racompte pour ce que il le

The Venetians Return

9

Left: a page from an illuminated medieval manuscript, showing the Polos leaving on their second journey to the court of the Great Khan.

The three Polos, having taken their leave of the timid friars, set off again from Laya in 1271, to make their way to Hormuz at the southeastern corner of the Persian Gulf. Traveling about 20 miles a day along a wide, fertile plain set between arid mountains, the Polos reached Kermān in southeast Iran without undue incident. Here the caravan roads ran north and south. The Venetians took the south road to Hormuz, about 200 miles away. As soon as they left Kermān, there was a sharp climb up into a 10,000-foot-high pass where they were exposed to extreme cold and the possibility of being maimed by frostbite. Surviving the dangers without harm, the travelers then had to make their way down the long descent to a hot, densely populated plain, infested with marauding bandits. A group of these raiders attacked the Polos, who had a very narrow escape, doubtless one of many on the early part of their journey. Three days' march took them on to the well-watered, fruitful plain leading to Hormuz itself.

Hormuz was the terminus of the sea routes from India and China. It was then centered on an island just off the coast, although within the next 200 years it was moved to the mainland. Each week, ships brought in spices, precious stones, pearls, gold, silks, elephants' tusks, and other exotic wares. In spite of the richness of its trade, Marco found Hormuz an extremely unattractive place. He hated

Right: the Polos planned to travel by sea from Hormuz, a port on the Persian Gulf. They changed their minds when they saw the rickety ships intended to transport them across the Indian Ocean. In this picture, travelers are trying to board a boat already carrying a camel, a horse, and an elephant!

Above: a nomad family in Iran (Persia). The Polos' traveled through Iran and across the central plateau to what is today Afghanistan. The country they passed through was probably very like that seen here.

its hot, dry climate, so different from the plains behind it, and re counts the terrifying tale of how a whole army was once destroye there by the burning heat and the suffocating dust-laden wind fro the desert.

At this stage of their journey, Maffeo, Nicolò, and Marco decide to go the whole way to the court of the khan by land. They ha thought of going by sea from Hormuz, but changed their min after their first sight of the flimsy, unseaworthy-looking boats th would have sailed in.

With their retinue, the Polos went north again from the coast Kermān, along a more easterly route up a path studded with ma "hot baths"—sulphur springs. Kermān was at the southeastern edge of a great desert land, 100 miles of huge gravel slopes and sand hills with only occasional salt lakes to relieve the dryness. Grim reminders of the perils the desert held for the unlucky traveler were ever present in the animal skulls and skeletons which lay scattered all over the ground. Marco's own description of this part of the journey gives a very clear picture: "On leaving the city of Kermān one has seven days of most wearisome riding and I will tell you why. During the first three days one finds no water, or practically none, and what one does find is brackish and as green as meadow grass, and so bitter that no one could possibly drink it . . . On the fourth day one reaches a fresh-water river flowing underground . . . at the end of these seven days one finds the city of Cobinah [possibly now Zarand in south central Iran]."

After several days more of arduous desert travel, the Venetians reached the welcome, temperate climate of Tabas, on Iran's northern border. The townsmen of Tabas told Marco many tales about a person known as the "Old Man of the Mountains," one of the most amazing of legendary Asian rulers. The Old Man lived in a great castle south of the Caspian Sea. He was head of a heretical Islamic sect founded in the 1000's, and his subjects believed him to be the vice-regent of God. The Old Man had constructed near his castle a garden, representing paradise, "running with conduits of wine and milk and honey and water, and full of lovely women for the delectation of its inmates."

The Old Man drugged young men among his followers with hashish—from which comes their title of *hash-shāshīn* (hemp-eaters) or Assassins—and had them conveyed to the garden to enjoy its pleasures. They were then drugged again and taken out of it.

Above: a village in modern Afghanistan, near the Silk Road, with typical dome-shaped houses. Merchant caravans passed regularly through this rugged country, as did the Mongol warriors from the East. The Polos traveled through the Hindu Kush and the Pamirs – the so-called "roof of the world."

Believing that they had been in paradise itself, the Assassins woul[d] do anything the Old Man ordered them to do, exposing themselve[s] recklessly to any danger, even loss of life, in order to get back int[o] "paradise." As a result, the Old Man was able to get rid of h[is] enemies by commanding the Assassins to murder anyone he wante[d]. When the Mongols conquered the Persian area of central Asia, the[y] came up against the Old Man, and, after a long struggle, final[ly] eradicated him and his sect in 1256, 16 years before Marco's visit t[o] Tabas. Though some of the stories about the Old Man are on[ly] legends, they had a basis of truth. Such murders—*assassinations*—ha[d] taken place during the reigns of certain Moslem rulers in the ar[ea] from the 1000's on. And the uses of hashish had certainly bee[n] exploited by these leaders.

Leaving Tabas, the Polos journeyed eastward along the fert[ile] valley of the Harī River. In his story of this part of the trave[ls] Marco mentions the city of Balkh, farther to the north and east [of] his route, although he probably did not visit it. This city, still gr[eat] and noble in the late 1200's, had, he says, been even more magn[i]ficent in earlier times but "the Tartars and other peoples ha[ve] ravaged and destroyed it." In the classical age, Balkh had bee[n a] symbol of the power and extent of Alexander the Great's empi[re]

d the farthest point that the Macedonian conqueror was supposed
have reached. In the Polos' time it still marked a well-known
nction of trade routes. From Balkh, roads ran due north to
.markand, northwest to Bukhara, southeast to Kabul (today the
pital of Afghanistan), and the mountain province of Peshāwar,
d east to Kashgar and Yarkand. On their previous visit to Cathay,
e elder Polos had gone east from Bukhara. This time, with Marco,
ey decided to take a different route. South of Balkh they joined
e more direct and shorter but more difficult southerly route.

This path lay east through the mountain ranges of the Hindu
ush and the Pamirs, known as the *roof of the world*. It was the
eatest undertaking the travelers had yet attempted. The first
ctions of the march were taxing but not too difficult. In the plateau
the Pamirs, "after a hard day's work to get to the top," the Polos
ched a wide grassy plain with flowering trees and trout-filled
eams. This "tableland" was regarded by valley dwellers in the
ality almost as a health resort. Marco had been ill for about a year,
t recovered "at once" on the plateau. It is not clear from his
itings how long had elapsed since the start of the Polos' journey,
t at about this time, perhaps because of Marco's ill-health, the
velers stopped and rested for several months.

Above: an execution in Afghanistan.
This illumination comes from *Les
Livres Merveilles,* a medieval French
manuscript containing Polo's *Book*.

Below: a magnificently horned
wild sheep of the Pamir plateau,
named *Ovis poli* after Marco Polo.

273

From the plateau, the Polos went up into higher mountains, traveling for 12 days northeastward along the great Oxus River (the Amu-Darya). Still going northeast, they climbed steeply for three more days to reach "the highest place in the world." On this plateau, between 13,000 and 15,000 feet above sea level with peaks of 19,000 feet or more in view, Marco Polo saw the wild sheep with curved horns 4½ feet long which are today called *Ovis poli* after him. Here, too, Marco comments on the bitter coldness of the weather and the difficulty that he and his companions experienced in cooking their food. "No birds fly here because of the height and the cold. And I assure you that, because of this great cold, fire here is not so bright nor of the same color as elsewhere, and food does not cook well." He did not know that with increased altitude and decreased atmospheric pressure, water boils at a lower temperature, and the food in it does not cook as quickly as when water boils at 100°C.

Leaving the Pamirs thankfully behind, the Polos went down by the side of the Gez River to the pleasant city of Kashgar, chief town of the vast plain of east Turkestan, now the region of Sinkiang, part of the People's Republic of China. Kashgar, an oasis indeed after the barren treeless mountains, had "splendid gardens and vineyards and fine farms," and its people lived "contentedly by trade and handicrafts."

To the east of Kashgar lies the vast, impassable desert of Takla-makan, 125,000 square miles in area. Annual rainfall over the whole area is negligible and the oases around the edges depend on the few rivers and water holes. Here is Marco's view of the region: "All this province is a tract of sand . . . when it happens that an army passes through the country, if it is a hostile one, the people take flight with their wives and children and their beasts, two or three days into the sandy wastes, to places where they know that there is water and they can live with their beasts. And I assure you that no one can tell which way they have gone because the wind covers their tracks with sand so that there is nothing to show where they have been, but the country looks as if it had never been traversed by man or beast." When what Marco calls "friendly" armies passed by, the inhabitants would merely drive their animals into the wastes so that the soldiers could not seize and eat them. When the locals harvested their meager supplies of grain, they stored them in caves in the desert, far from human habitation and the passing armies, and then

Left: a drawing from a book on early Chinese exploration, showing a camel caravan, the only safe means of traveling across the vast Gobi Desert.

took back home whatever rations they required month by month

The Polos skirted the desert's western edges to Yarkand, in present-day Sinkiang, where, Marco Polo notes, "they mostly have goiters [a swelling of the thyroid gland in the neck, usually caused by lack of iodine in the diet]." Travelers in the present century have confirmed that this is still the case, one indication that many thing in these remote regions have changed very little since Marc Polo's time.

For each of the principal oases on the caravan route through the sands of Sinkiang, Marco Polo gives a condensed guide to merchant concerning its size, trade, local products, and customs. All the cities he mentions at this stage of the journey had once been famou as stopping places on the southern branch of the Silk Road. For gotten and neglected for centuries, they were no longer prosperou As can be seen from Marco's account, most had been attacked an overrun several times by successive nomad bands before th Mongols came to power. Nonetheless, although the roads had n been reopened long enough to regain very much of their past prosperity, certain prized commodities were still to be found in the towns along this part of the road. Among these were coveted precious stones, including jade, and various unusual products, such as asbestos.

When the Polos reached the oasis called Lop, near Lake Lop Nor, after five days' exhausting trek across the sand, they were nearing the edge of the great Gobi, the most terrifying desert of all. Here "travelers take a week's rest in order to refresh themselves and their

animals, they take food for a month for man and beast . . . this desert is reported to be so long that it would take a year to go from end to end and at the narrowest point it takes a month to cross it. It consists entirely of mountains and sand and valleys. There is nothing to eat . . . but after traveling a day and a night in winter you find drinking water . . . all the way through the desert you must go for a day and a night before you find water . . . beasts and birds there are none, because they find nothing to eat." Marco then goes on to tell of the strange tricks the desert can play upon lonely travelers— mirages, phantom sounds, ghostly marauders, and spirit voices that terrify or lure men to their destruction in the empty wastes.

About this point in the journey, the youngest Polo may more than once have doubted his elders' wisdom in embarking on such a route. Not counting detours, the three men and their attendants had traveled some 2,500 miles since setting out from Hormuz—almost the whole way through deserts and high mountains. What wares could possibly justify trade along so difficult and hazardous a route?

Above: camels in the Gobi Desert. The total area of the desert is about 500,000 square miles, but despite Marco Polo's daunting description, only certain parts consist solely of sand. Much of it is rocky, with sparse vegetation and occasional grass-land, watered by seasonal streams.

Left: sets of Chinese gold earrings of the Mongol period. Such ornaments would have been brought back to Europe by the merchants who traveled by the Asian caravan routes or by sea.

Right: shipping on the River Karakoram, fortified castles, and a traveler and packhorse approaching an inn. Marco Polo did not go through the old Mongol capital on his journey, but probably visited it at a later date. (*Bodleian Library, Oxford. MS. Bodley 264, fol. 245 v.*)

If Marco Polo ever did entertain such doubts, he was quite right to do so. We have no record that any European trader ever trod this part of the Polos' path to Cathay again by way of regular business, although such goods as silk, cotton, iron, leather, and gems did pass from merchant to merchant all the way along it from Cathay without duty or hindrance. Some of the goods also found their way to the Middle East and so to Europe. Certainly, after the Polos eventually returned to Venice, they sent no caravans back along the route they had taken, nor did they encourage others to do so. The route favored by later traders was always the more northerly one taken by the two elder Polos on their first visit.

Any hope of easy trade must have dwindled further in Marco's mind as he and his companions made their way from water hole to water hole along the fringes of the great Gobi. Nevertheless, Marco must have had cause to return to this region at least once during his years in the service of Kublai Khan, because he describes places well away from the route the Polos took through Sinkiang at this time. Among those he writes of are Karakoram, 40 days' march away (in the late 1200's, no longer the Mongol capital), and the Turfan Depression, where one can stand in a plain that dips to 505 feet below sea level and look north to where the Bogdo Ola Mountains rise to almost 18,000 feet above it.

On this first journey, after 30 days' march from the last oasis, Marco, Nicolò, and Maffeo Polo reached the city called Tunhwang in Cathay, near the junction of the north and south branches of the Silk Road. Nicolò and Maffeo had already been there on their previous journey. In the 1900's, a scholar and archaeologist working at

Above: the Siberian Mekriti tribe was described by Marco Polo as a savage people who hunted and rode on reindeer. Strange though they may have appeared to Europeans, they can hardly have been quite as grotesque as this painting suggests.

the site of the Caves of the Thousand Buddhas, about eight mile from Tunhwang itself, found a huge hoard of manuscripts, paintings embroideries, and figurines dating from the A.D. 400's to 900's. It i not known whether Marco visited these caves, but he describe Tunhwang as having "abbeys and monasteries all of which are fu of all kinds of idols, to which they [the inhabitants of the region offer great sacrifices and pay great honor and worship." He als describes the Buddhist practice of cremating the dead, and explain how paper models of men, camels, and horses were burned besic the corpse, in the hope that they would be of use to the decease person in the life after death.

From Tunhwang, the Polos' caravan traveled for "10 day between north and northeast to Suchow [Kiuchüan] and thence t Kanchow [present-day Changyen. The Polos stayed there for sever months], and Lanchow." This journey gives rise to a curiou feature of this section of *The Book of Marco Polo*. In the Polos' da the Great Wall of China ran unbroken from the southern fringe the Gobi Desert to the sea east of Cambaluc. But although the caravan must have followed beside, if not actually ridden upon, the wall for most of the way from Kanchow, which is on its extremit Marco never once mentions its existence.

Leaving Lanchow, the Venetians pushed north again, going the Yellow River and away from the usual caravan route. They ma "eight more stages to the east. . . ." Marco says the route then through the "principal sea of Prester John . . . whose descendar still live there . . . in that part that in our country is known as G and Magog, [according to the New Testament, two nations th make war on the kingdom of Christ]." This mistaken reference *The Book of Marco Polo* to the kingdom of the legendary Christi

Prester John in central Asia perpetuated the myths about him for many years.

It was at this stage of their journey that the Polos were met by messengers from Kublai Khan. The messengers had been instructed to welcome the Polos warmly and to escort them in comfort to the khan's favorite summer palace at Shangtu, about 180 miles northwest of Cambaluc and outside the Great Wall of China.

The last stage of their journey took some 40 days. The whole journey, from Hormuz, on the Persian Gulf, to the khan's summer palace had taken, according to Marco Polo's account, $3\frac{1}{2}$ years.

Below: an imaginary portrayal of the battle between Genghis Khan and Prester John. Despite Marco Polo's assurances, Prester John was a legendary character. *(Bodleian Library, Oxford. MS. Bodley 264, fol. 231v.)*

The Polos
in China
10

Kublai Khan was delighted with the arrival of the Venetian traveler at his court. At a public audience, he received the Polos and the honored him in the Mongol way by prostrating themselves sever: times at his feet. The khan was greatly pleased with the letters an presents from the pope, particularly with the bottle of holy oil from Jerusalem. Noticing the young Marco, the Khan inquired who h was. "Sire," said Nicolò, "He is my son and your liege man."

Marco Polo was at once enrolled among the khan's attendants of honor, and became a favorite and close friend. Marco was anxiou to learn as much as he could about Mongol ways. Soon he wa:

Above: the Polos hand their letter from the pope to the Great Khan at the end of their 3½-year journey. (*Bodleian Library, Oxford. MS. Bodley 264, fol. 220.*)

Left: the fabulous palace of the Great Khan at Cambaluc. Marco Polo said it was the largest ever seen, with priceless treasures, and set in beautiful parkland, full of game.

luent in speaking, reading, and writing three Asian languages—Mongol, Turkish, and Persian—and had acquired a smattering of Chinese. He never, however, mastered Chinese script.

Influenced by Marco's charm and his obvious willingness to learn, Kublai determined to try out the young Venetian as his personal ambassador. He sent him on important and confidential tate business to a place some six months' journey from Cambaluc, nd, when Marco carried out this commission to the khan's satisaction, Kublai employed him as a full-time civil servant. He sent im on secret missions to almost every part of the Mongol Empire.

From time to time Marco traveled on his own initiative, but always with the consent and sanction of the khan. During his 17 years in the khan's service, Marco covered great distances and saw more of the world than any European had ever done. As he says in the preface to *The Book of Marco Polo,* "to this day there has been no man, Christian or Pagan, Tartar or Italian, or of any race . . . who has explored so many of the various parts of the world and of its great wonders as this same . . . Marco Polo."

As far as we know, Marco's claim is perfectly valid. Certainly

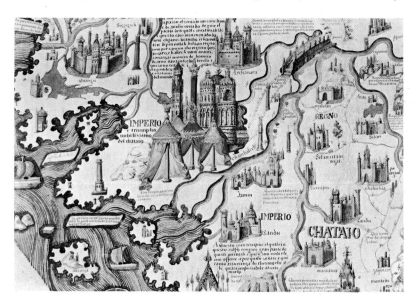

Left: part of a map of 1459, based on Marco Polo's description of Cambaluc. The artist has drawn a Western-style Renaissance city, with Kublai Khan's palace in the center.

some of the places he visited were not seen or written about again by Europeans until the middle of the 1800's. There must have been a number of Europeans—merchants, craftsmen, mercenaries, preachers—who made the long journey across the northern steppes and central deserts during Polo's time. Some of them must have penetrated to Mongolia and the borders of China. But none has left a record like Marco Polo's, and possibly no one saw as many wonders.

To Marco, reminiscing at the end of his long years in China, one of the most beautiful of all the sights he ever saw was the very first, the summer palace at Shangtu—the magical Xanadu of Coleridge's poem "Kubla Khan." When the Polos arrived in China, Kublai Khan was the most powerful man alive. The style in which he lived was far more lavish than that of any European monarch. The luxury and grandeur, which reached their peak during Kublai Khan's reign, were eventually to decline into a decadence and indulgence which proved disastrous for the Mongol empire. But in the 1260's and 1270's, the splendor of the Mongol court was at its height.

Shangtu was beautiful, but Cambaluc itself, the true capital, was amazing. After a summer spent in hunting and feasting at Shangtu, the whole court returned to Cambaluc around November. The first time Marco saw it, Cambaluc had recently been partly evacuated by Kublai because his astrologers had told him that an internal rebellion

Above: the Great Khan out hunting. Marco Polo wrote about the royal hunting parties, which took place during the three months Kublai spent each year in Cambaluc. According to him, besides dogs, the khan hunted with leopards, lynxes, and even lions. (Bodleian Library, Oxford. MS. Bodley 264, fol. 240v.)

was imminent. He had built an extension to the city at Tai-du, or ʹa-du, northeast of the old town. The new city was built in a ʹerfect square, six miles by six, and enclosed by a rampart 20 paces ʹpproximately 50 feet) high. Polo's readers, who lived in cramped, ʹvisting, medieval alleys, must have been startled to read of the ʹty's spaciousness. It was full of fine mansions, with booths and ʹops edging each main street. Every block of buildings was ʹrrounded by good, wide roads, and the whole interior of the city ʹas laid out in squares like a chessboard "with such precision that ʹo description can do justice to it."

Beyond the city walls were huge suburbs where there were ʹlaces and hostels for the thousands of visiting merchants. To ʹnphasize the size of this vast city, Polo adds that 1,000 cartloads of ʹk yarn were brought to the Cambaluc weavers every day.

Within the old city itself, stood the khan's palace—a city within ʹity. Inside the great fortress of the outer marble walls, stood the ʹgh-roofed main building, its interior "all gold and silver and ʹcorated with pictures . . . the ceilings similarly adorned. . . ." The ʹin hall was so vast that 60,000 men could be served there. "No ʹn" Marco says, "could imagine any improvement in design and ʹecution. The roof is all ablaze with scarlet and green and blue ʹd yellow and all the colors . . . are so brilliantly varnished that

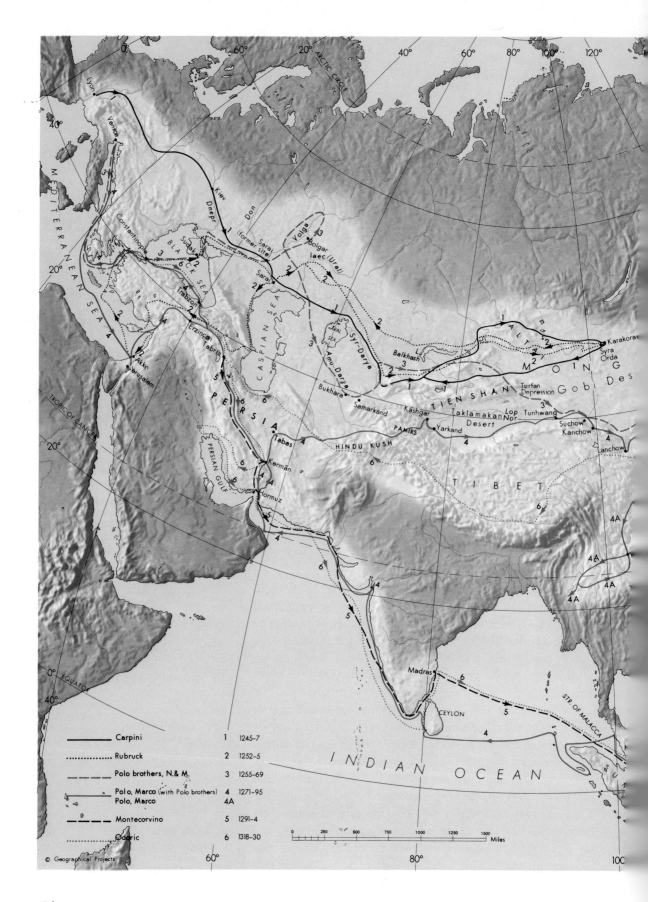

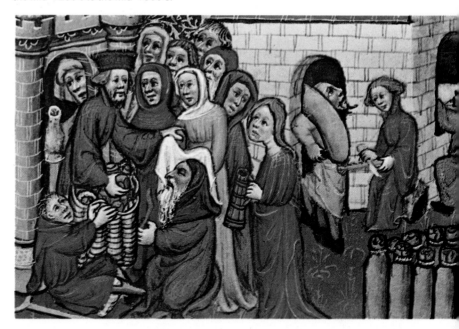

Left: Asia and eastern Europe, showing the routes of European travelers from Carpini to Odoric of Pordenone, from the mid-1200's to the mid-1300's.

Above: Marco Polo reported the Great Khan to be a charitable man. He is seen here handing alms to the poor. *(Bodleian Library, Oxford. MS. Bodley 264, fol. 244.)*

it glitters like crystal . . . the sparkle can be seen from far away." Around the park was a well-stocked game park with an artificial hill in it, planted with samples of the finest trees in the world. In 1275, Kublai was engaged in building another palace, equally vast and well equipped, for his son Timur.

Marco Polo often remarks on the khan's "stupendous munificence," and contemporary Asian writers also commend Kublai as brave, just, and generous. Living in great luxury himself, the khan was also aware of the problems of the poor people in his realm, and helped them "like a kind of father" as often as he could. At harvest time he sent inspectors throughout the land to inquire if any of his subjects had suffered a crop failure. For those who had, Kublai exempted them for that year from paying the statutory annual tax, and often gave them some of his own grain. In winter, he checked on the cattle of his subjects. If he heard that a man had lost cattle, he gave him some of his own. If he learned of an honest respectable family impoverished by misfortune or unfit for work through illness, the khan saw to it that the family was given money enough for a whole year's expenses. Officials appointed to superintend the khan's expenditure presided over the issuing to the needy of sums for subsistence. When a poor man could produce a certificate for the sum paid the previous year, they made provision for him to receive the same rate again. As a result, all the people held Kublai in such esteem that they revered him as a god.

Despite such bounty, the khan was still very rich. Marco's lists

287

of his possessions are almost endless: 12,000 costly robes of cloth of gold given by the khan to his leading knights; 156,000 robes studded with gems and pearls for the same knights for the 13 great feasts of the year; 100,000 white horses; 100,000 personal servants; 5,000 elephants, each bearing 2 giant chests of precious gems, gold plate, and rich apparel; camels beyond number; 10,000 falconers; tents lined with thousands of sable furs, each fur costing over $5,000 by today's prices . . . and so on, and so on.

To many of Marco Polo's European readers these lists seemed

unbelievable. People were unable to grasp how vast was the empire Kublai governed and from which he took tribute. Even Marco, who eventually traveled the length and most of the breadth of Kublai Khan's domain, misunderstood the source of most of his wealth. Marco thought the secret lay in the emperor's ability to print paper money—something then unknown anywhere in the world outside China. Marco also thought that Kublai had invented paper money, not knowing it had been common in China since at least the 1000's and that Friar William of Rubruck had mentioned its existence in the 1250's. Marco did not realize that the gold and silver which merchants deposited against the issue of paper money was the real strength behind it. To be fair, Kublai did not quite grasp the fact either, and at one stage almost bankrupted his administration by printing far more money than could be backed in gold and silver.

One of Marco's first official missions was a visit of inspection to the province of Yunnan, in southern China, and beyond. On this, and on trips he made in eastern China, Marco was given a chance to exercise his powers of observation and his interest in alien customs and beliefs. In the usual manner, he lists all the towns, cities, villages, and rivers he saw—their size, trade, manufacture, wealth, and importance to the khan. He also describes the long journeys between towns through remote rural areas or through mountain districts where the road was often little more than a plank walk shored up with timbers along precipitous bluffs.

In "Tibet," probably not the Tibet we know today but the western edges of Szechwan and Yunnan, Marco saw how travelers frightened off marauding lions and bears by burning giant canes. The explosions from these freshly cut and still sap-filled canes echoed for miles around and terrified anyone who was not used to them.

In some sections, Polo's account reads like a modern anthropological survey. He has a fair claim indeed to be called the father of modern anthropology (the study of man). For instance, he noted one tribe with a very strange birth custom. On the birth of a baby the husband took the child and went to rest in bed while the woman went straight back to her household work. This practice, called *couvade,* was new to medieval Europeans. Anthropologists have since found it in places as far apart as Africa and the Amazon forests.

Another custom noted by Polo among the tribes in remote places and by later observers among other primitive peoples, was their habit of eating any person of rank or quality—anyone with a "good shadow"—who happened to stay the night. This was not done in order to rob the visitor, it was rather because they believed "his 'good shadow' and the good grace with which he was blessed and his intelligence and soul would remain in the house." According to Marco, this belief caused many deaths before the Mongol conquest, but the practice had later been forbidden by the khan.

The men of one tribe had gold-capped teeth. Another tribe used cowrie shells for money. Here they prevented their horses from swishing their tails by removing two or three of the tail bones.

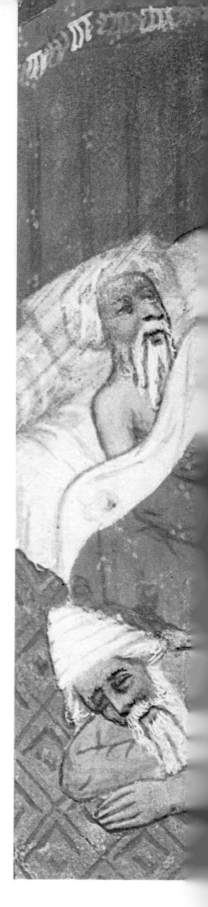

Right: the custom of *couvade,* in which a wife got up immediately after giving birth, while her husband took to his bed with the baby, was reported by Marco Polo to occur in Burma. It still takes place today among some primitive communities. *(Bodleian Library, Oxford. MS. Bodley 264, fol. 249v.)*

Above: the gold and silver towers which Marco Polo reported seeing when he visited the Burmese city of Mien. (Bodleian Library, Oxford. MS. Bodley 264, fol. 251v.)

There they rode with their stirrups long "as the Latins do." Ever oddity caught Marco's attentive eye.

In a Burmese city, Marco saw one of the wonders of Southeas Asia—a local king's tomb with two towers, one of gold, one o silver. Both towers were fully 10 paces (25 feet) high and circular and were set with gilded bells which tinkled every time the win blew. Kublai refused to have these unique towers dismantled an taken to Cambaluc because Mongols would never disturb the pro perty of the dead.

On his return from Burma, Polo seems to have made a number o detours to Cochin China (now Laos and South Vietnam), Tonki (North Vietnam), and other regions, all of which he painstaking describes. Some time later, Marco made a similar journey dow through eastern China. For a number of years he was Kublai personal representative in the city of Yang-chou on the Yangt River. He probably covered the ground between Cambaluc an central China many times. The *Book* declares that Marco Polo w governor of Yang-chou but there is no evidence to support th claim. Polo may also have made the rest of the journey south, dow as far as Amoy, Mandarin Hsia-men, on the mainland opposite Formosa, during his years of service with the khan. He certainly did so when he left China toward the close of the century.

While Marco was traveling, the elder Polos stayed in or near the court of the khan. Little is known of their activities, but they were engaged in some kind of commerce, and most profitably. Like Marco, they became extremely rich.

Despite their many privileges as Kublai's friends, the Polos longed to see Venice again. The yearning grew stronger and stronger

Right: a painting of Marco Polo dressed in Mongolian-style clothes. Being young, he was able to travel widely, while his father and uncle stayed nearer to the khan's court.

Above: this illumination from a copy of Marco Polo's *Book* shows the weird creatures he thought lived in India. *(Bodleian Library, Oxford. MS. Bodley 264, fol. 260.)*

Right: Arghun, ruler of Persia, in his garden. The Polos finally left Kublai Khan's court in the retinue of Arghun's Mongolian bride, whom they escorted to Persia.

as the years passed. Time and again they asked the khan to let them go home, but Kublai was fond of them, and they had become useful to him. Nothing would persuade him to let them go. The Polos were concerned by the fact that Kublai was now in his 70's and could not be expected to live much longer. There was no guarantee that his successor, or the regent, would grant the Polos the same favors and privileges. Like all courts, the one at Cambaluc was full of intrigue and broken bargains, and the Polos had acquired enemies as well as friends in their years in China.

Then chance gave them the perfect excuse for returning home. Queen Bulagan, wife of the Persian khan Arghun, died in 1286. She had stipulated in her will that her successor should come from her own tribe in Mongolia. So Arghun sent envoys overland, probably following the route the Polos had taken nearly 15 years earlier, to ask for a young, unmarried noblewoman of Bulagan's lineage for his next wife. Kublai granted his request and envoys set out on the return journey with the princess.

A year or so later they were back again in Cambaluc. Their route had been blocked by an outbreak of intertribal wars like those common among the Mongols before the days of Genghis Khan.

Marco Polo returned in about 1290 from an official mission to India, of which he gives no details except to say that part of the voyage had been by ship. He reported that the sea passage to India was open and safe. Hearing this, the envoys begged Kublai to let

the Polos, known to be experienced sea travelers, escort them alon
the sea route to Persia. Kublai reluctantly agreed. He gave th
Polos passports stamped on gold, letters and gifts for the pope an
princes of Christendom, and presents for themselves. He fitted out
fleet of 14 ships, 5 of them large enough to need crews of 260 mer
All the vessels were divided into watertight sections. This mear
that if the ship were holed, the flooding could be confined to th
section of the hull.

With mingled joy and sorrow, the four old friends parted for th
last time in 1292—Kublai, then 76, Marco still only 38, and Nicol
and Maffeo now elderly men. The Polos set out on the famili
road southwest from Cambaluc, the great highway along whic
Marco had begun most of his travels in the khan's service. A lar
section of the route ran down the Grand Canal, the giant man-ma
river that is still China's second most important waterway, aft

Left: a group of merchants returning two girls to their fathers and offering them jewels. According to Marco Polo, it was an accepted custom in some parts of China for girls to live with men before being married.

he Yangtze River. Marco Polo thought that Kublai had built this
canal and the broad, stone-paved avenues that flanked it. In fact it
had been created by the Chinese much earlier, as long ago as A.D.
605–610. They had joined up existing rivers and lakes and cut new
channels. Kublai had only restored the canal and extended it to the
outskirts of Cambaluc.

Marco's unflagging eye and memory were as busy as ever throughout the journey home. At Ts'ang-chou, pure, white, fine-grained salt
was produced and he describes the method. The province around
T'sin-nan-fu produced "silk past all reckoning" and the city itself
had "many delightful gardens full of excellent fruit."

Marco the anthropologist adds notes on the appearance and
demeanor of the young ladies of Cathay, whose modesty and decorum he much admired. He praises, too, their custom of never
speaking to an older person unless first spoken to. He fills several

more pages with observations of marriage customs, beliefs, oracles, and the like.

At Chi-ning the Polos saw one of the wonders of the Grand Canal. The Wen River was partially diverted so that while some of its waters joined the generally northward flow of the canal, the rest went on south alongside the canal. Because of these contrary flows, the Polos witnessed the seemingly miraculous sight of river traffic free-floating in both directions between the towns along the course of the canal and river. Many Europeans would not believe this tale

Right: Chinese women pulling a barge along the Grand Canal, near Suchow. This vital waterway was constructed in the 600's and was later restored and extended by Kublai Khan.

until it was later confirmed by visitors to China during the 1800's.

Polo tells us that the Yellow River then ran between Haui-an and Ching-chiang—the only clue he gives us to its course at that date. In 1852, as many times earlier, the river burst its banks and changed course to run along a more northerly channel than in the 1200's. Polo says that the Yellow River was only a mile wide and the cities on its banks held 15,000 of the khan's military ships, each kept ready with a crew of 20 to carry up to 15 troopers, their mounts and provisions. It was such an armada that the khan sent on an

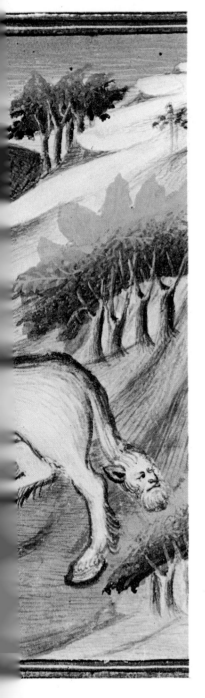

ill-fated expedition to conquer Japan in 1281, when the army was
routed by the Japanese and the khan's fleet destroyed by a typhoon.
Polo gives the full history of the ill-fated and mismanaged campaign,
including the terrible punishment handed out to the two commanders. One was beheaded, the other marooned on an island with his
hands bound in freshly flayed buffalo hide, tightly sewn. As it dried,
it tightened further and he died either of gangrene or starvation.

Curiously enough, Polo tells us next to nothing of Yang-chou, the
city he says he governed. But he gives a fascinating picture of the
Yangtze River at Icheng, farther south:

"... in the amount of shipping it carries and the total volume
of traffic it exceeds all the rivers of the Christians put together and
their seas into the bargain. I give you my word that I have seen in
this city [Icheng] fully 5,000 ships at once, all afloat in this river ... I
assure you that the river flows through more than 16 provinces,
and there are on its banks more than 200 cities, all having more
ships than this ... fully 200,000 craft pass upstream every year and
a like number return." Marco also explains how the ships were
hauled upstream by teams of horses hitched to the bows by long
towropes.

The highlight of the Chinese part of this journey was a visit to
the mighty city of Hangchow. The Polos had arrived in China
shortly before Kublai extended his rule to the whole country. For
the Chinese, his was the last of a whole series of nomad conquests
extending over the centuries. Kublai's rule finally broke the back of
China's ancient high civilization. For though Kublai was a wise
and far-seeing ruler, the Chinese under him were still a conquered

Within the image, map labels include:
HAVA · ORIENS · asitera · acàbis · aspicia · tagurus · mons taxurus · brama · casali · Sacratte · magnifico porto de Zaiton · Regno de Zaiton · civitas Caiton · Smaelia · cas · isula be Zimpa gu · Inquesto porto de zaiton el granchan tien nave assai a bi sogno del suo stabo ed ancho li capita assai nave dall'india e de diverse parte e isole con diverse mercatanzie cue sperie zioe etc. per lequal esso scuode nota dei datij · ungue · Regno de zaiton · Caiton · Regno cong · zucharo e cose molte · Eogin · gengero galanga seda · Inquesto mar oriental sono molte isole grandee famose che non ho · Regno de fuguy

people and their old spirit never revived. This decline was just beginning in Marco's time, and he—the first European to study China in any depth—was also the last to witness its cultural greatness. For this reason alone, his picture of Hangchow, one of China's foremost cities, gives a unique and priceless insight into that vanished greatness.

Hangchow was about 100 miles in circumference and housed 1,600,000 families. Marco says that there were 12,000 bridges in Hangchow, some so high-arched that tall-masted ships could navigate beneath them. But they were also gently pitched so that wheeled traffic could easily pass over them. All streets were paved in stone and the main roads had storm drainage.

There were 10 main squares, each holding thrice-weekly markets visited by up to 50,000 people in search of everything from rare pearls to such staple foods as meat, fish, game, fruit, and herbs.

Marco says five tons of pepper were sold there daily. There were hundreds of smaller local markets, too.

The city's industry was managed by a dozen craft guilds each with about 12,000 workshops employing between 12 and 40 craftsmen. For the very wealthy workshop owners and their richly dressed wives and children, the pleasures of life centered on the sumptuous pavilions around the islands of the city lake. These were fully furnished for parties and banquets. Over 100 banquets could be held there simultaneously. On the lake and through the canals plied innumerable pleasure boats with ornate and comfortable cabins.

The city was a leading center of education, art, and culture, with more library books than any other Chinese city. But the shadow of the Great Khan was everywhere. Each of the bridges housed at least five guards to check insurrection. Every hotelkeeper was obliged to record the names of each visitor, where he came from, and where he was bound. "A useful piece of knowledge," Marco says, "to prudent statesmen."

Marco, who was present at many reckonings, puts the total tax

Below: Indian ships, described in some detail by Marco Polo. *(Bodleian Library, Oxford. MS. Bodley 264, fol. 259v.)*

revenue from Hangchow at over 3,250,000 ounces of gold, of which the salt duty alone contributed almost 1,000,000.

From Hangchow the Polos continued south to Zaitun, in medieval times the great port of southern China near Amoy. Details of this stage of the journey are skimpy and it is impossible to plot their route with certainty.

The Book of Marco Polo describes the long voyage home by sea. The Venetians stopped in Indochina, Ceylon, India, and Persia, but the visits were short and there is little of the detailed observation found in the main section of the book. Marco's geography is accurate, as usual. So, too, is the information he gives on the trade and produce of each country. He has a lot to say, for instance, of the gems mined in Ceylon and of the pearl-diving industry in the nearby Indian waters. But the highlight of the homeward section is Marco's penetrating and sympathetic observation of Indian religions. He gives a fairly accurate paraphrase of the life story of the Indian who became the Buddha. Like Rubruck, Polo acquired a deep respect for the gentle Buddhist faith. He wrote sympathetically, too, of the Hindus and their yogis.

The wealth of India impressed Marco greatly and he described it all in glowing terms. This detailed account of the vast subcontinent proved of great interest in Europe, and for nearly 200 years formed the sum of European knowledge about India.

But it is Marco's love of—and obvious nostalgia for—China that is the lasting impression in the reader's mind at the end of *The Book of Marco Polo*. When he left, Marco knew that he would probably never return to the lands of the Great Khan. Even before he and his father and uncle got back to Venice—when they landed in Persia to deliver the Mongol princess to the khan—they heard of Kublai's death.

In 1298, Polo was captured by the Genoese in the course of a war against Venice and thrown into the same jail as the writer Rusticello. To while away the days, he told of his adventures in far-off Cathay with such a wealth of detail that those who started listening in disbelief soon knew he was telling the truth. His cellmate Rusticello, seeing his great chance, persuaded Polo to collaborate in setting down the whole story. Polo agreed and sent to Venice for his notes and diaries. Later published as *The Book of Marco Polo,* Marco's story was for a long time disbelieved as being too fantastic to be true. Nevertheless, it had a resounding popular success. And, more than 150 years after it had been written, it provided inspiration for the great explorers of the 1400's.

In 1299, Venice and Genoa signed a truce and all prisoners of war were freed. Marco Polo went back to Venice and, after the death of his father and uncles, started trading as his forefathers had always done. He settled down, married, had a large family, and never traveled again. When he was dying, in 1324, friends asked Marco whether he would not correct the exaggerations of his story. He answered, "I did not write half of what I saw."

Right: the courtyard and gateway, part of a more recent building, are all that remain today of Marco Polo's house in Venice. It was called Millionaire's Court because Marco became a rich man as a result of his travels.

304

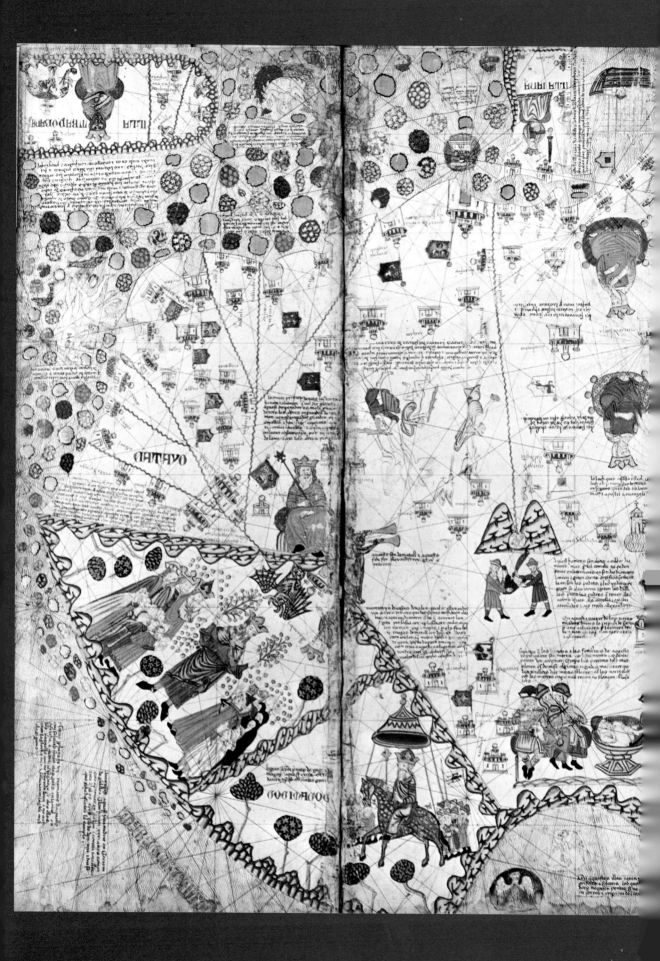

Missionaries to Cambaluc

11

Above: Pope Nicholas IV, like his
predecessor Innocent IV, had hopes
of converting the eastern khans to
Christianity. In 1291, he sent out
the missionary John of Montecorvino
to try to achieve this aim.

For about 50 years after the Polos' return to Venice, the trade routes through Asia to Cathay remained open and safe, and trade with the Far East prospered. China and the East were visited by so many merchants that, in 1355, one merchant called Pegolotti set down his favorite route for the use of other travelers. A welcome was extended to religious travelers as well. The ambassadors of the four main religions, Buddhism, Christianity, Confucianism, and Islam, were entertained and given a hearing in the khan's capital at Cambaluc. The khan and his leading citizens entertained representatives of all religions at court, and attended ceremonies in each of the religious centers established by the foreigners in Cambaluc. Possibly the Mongol open-mindedness was the result of a desire to be on the right side, religiously speaking, by being on all sides. They may have thought that by listening to the prayers of holy men of all religions they were ensuring themselves some sort of passport to a happy afterlife. Whatever the reason, there was unprecedented and unique liberal-mindedness and freedom of speech and thought in China during the period of Mongol occupation.

Christian missionaries took the road east by land and by sea. They were determined to seize the chance of converting the Mongols which had been lost by the two Dominican friars who had deserted the Polos at Laya. One of the most notable of the missionaries was a Franciscan friar called John of Montecorvino. Montecorvino was born in a village in southern Italy in 1247. As a young man, he took part in missions to Armenia and Persia, and spent a period of about 14 years traveling in the Middle East. Afterward, he returned to Europe and reported to Pope Nicholas IV his high hopes of being able to convert the Khan of Persia, Arghun. If Arghun were con-verted to the Catholic faith, all of his subjects would follow suit. Pope Nicholas was highly pleased by this news, and decided to send Montecorvino back to Asia carrying letters to all patriarchs and princes of the East, including Kublai Khan and Kaidu, the khan of the house of Ogotai in central Asia, who was Kublai's subject but his bitterest enemy.

In 1291, as the Polos were at last about to leave China, John of Montecorvino left from Tabriz in Persia on the first stage of his journey, in the company of a rich and friendly Italian merchant named Pietro of Lucolongo. Pietro was familiar with trade routes in the Middle East and central Asia, and was, therefore, a valuable

Above: John of Montecorvino succeeded in founding Catholic communities in both India and China, although reports that he had baptized the Great Khan himself were not verified. In 1305, the pope made him Archbishop of Cambaluc and Patriarch of the Orient.

companion. They made their way to Hormuz and sailed from there to southern India.

The party spent a period of about a year in India, their stay occasioned by the outbreak of a violent war between Kublai and Kaidu. During his time there, Montecorvino visited the sacred place called Saint Thomas' Shrine, near Madras, where the bodies of four Christian martyrs were buried. He also baptized, as he claims in a later report to the pope, about a hundred persons. In 1294, Kublai died and was succeeded by his grandson Timir. Shortly afterward, Montecorvino reached China.

In the same letter to the pope, dated 1305, Montecorvino tells of the near 12 years he had spent working diligently in Cathay, helped occasionally by the merchant Pietro and joined "only recently" by a friar, Arnold of Cologne. Timir appeared sympathetic to the Christian's endeavors, but gave him little practical help. Montecorvino's main success in those first dozen years seems to have been his conversion of a follower of the Nestorian sect, a nobleman called George "of the family of Prester John."

George was son-in-law of the Great Khan, and ruler of the Ongut Turks of northwest China. George supplied the money for the building of a beautiful Catholic church 20 days' journey from Cambaluc, possibly in Tenduc. Unfortunately for Montecorvino, and for the growth of Chinese Christianity, George soon died. Montecorvino had to report to the pope with much regret that the Ongut Turks had reverted to the Nestorian version of the faith.

Montecorvino had some other successes in his long hard-working years away from home. He worked diligently in the capital and succeeded in establishing an active center of Mongol Catholicism. Six years before writing his letter, he had been given permission and assistance by Timir Khan to build a church in Cambaluc. The priest had assembled the rudiments of a choir and had "gradually brought [into the faith] 150 boys, the children of pagan parents ... 11 of the boys already know the service and form a choir. His majesty the emperor delights to hear them chanting."

The pope was so impressed by Montecorvino's optimistic report of conditions in China that he officially appointed Montecorvino Archbishop of Cambaluc and sent seven Franciscans out to China to help him. Three of them died on the way, unable to withstand their first experience of the Indian climate. The others reached

Right: a form of Christianity—the Nestorian church—which originated in the Middle East, had made converts in central Asia, and even reached Mongolia and China, some centuries before the Catholic missions arrived. Its clergy became increasingly Oriental in outlook, and the religion soon lost its impetus. The woman depicted in this Nestorian religious painting has typically Chinese features.

China where they worked under the leadership of Montecorvino. Three of them served in succession as bishops of Zaitun.

For more than 20 years, the Christian mission in China flourished under Archbishop John. After he died, having been the first and last effective Archbishop of Cambaluc, the mission lost much of its vigor. A French friar called Nicholas was appointed as Montecorvino's successor, and set out with a party of 20 friars and 6 laymen. Nothing is known of their fate, but they did not reach the court of Cathay. The movement struggled on for 40 years, ever weakening, before dying out almost completely. The last medieval Catholic bishop in China was martyred in 1362, and in 1369, the Christians were expelled from Cambaluc, not to return until the French missionaries of the late 1600's.

An account of the missionary activities in China toward the end of John of Montecorvino's life is given in the contemporary *Journal of Friar Odoric*. Odoric of Pordenone, in Italy, was a Franciscan friar. As a young man he was renowned among the members of his order for his asceticism. He always went barefoot, and always wore either haircloth or ironmail shirts as a denial of luxury and comfort. He lived mainly on a diet of water and a very little bread.

Around 1318, Friar Odoric was sent to the East as part of an extension of the Catholic missionary movement into Asia. From then on he became addicted to travel. First he visited India, where he arrived in 1321.

As Montecorvino had done, Odoric visited Saint Thomas' Shrine near Madras. Taking with him the bones of the martyrs as sacred relics, Odoric then sailed to Sumatra, where he recorded that he saw islanders using deadly blowpipes, the first mention of these in European writings. Then he traveled on by way of Java and the coast of Borneo before going overland through China to Cambaluc.

Odoric was the first traveler after Marco Polo to leave a full written account of all the places he had visited and seen. He gives details of the customs and peoples he observed in many countries. He also vividly describes the scenery and buildings in places he passed through.

Like Marco Polo, Odoric describes Cambaluc as a beautiful, enviable place, superior to even a major city in Europe in its luxury and attractiveness. He describes its beautiful buildings and spacious roads, and gives a detailed account of the khan's palace and court, and of the lavish ceremonies which took place there. The Great Khan celebrated four major feast days in the year. On these occasions all the khan's barons, his musicians, his stage-players and "everyone of his kindred" were invited to eat at the palace. Friar Odoric was not favorably impressed by some of the ceremonies which took place on those occasions. Often he disapproved of what seemed to him a foolish exercise of the khan's absolute rule over his people. He writes of one such occasion: "When the time is come . . . a certain crier calls out with a loud voice saying 'Bow yourselves before your emperor.' With that all the barons fall flat upon the earth. Then

Right: the court of Tamerlane, a descendant of Genghis Khan. In its riches and splendor, the court of Tamerlane equaled that of the earlier Mongol emperors, and this picture gives a good idea of the magnificence of that court.

Above: John of Montecorvino's success in China was short-lived. So[me] forty years after his death, Peking expelled its Christian community. So[?] little remained to show that it had eve[r] existed, apart from sober reminders such as this drawing of a missionary'[s] last resting place.

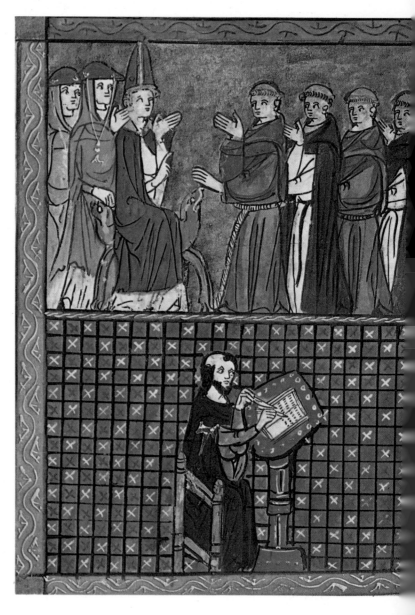

Right: Friar Odoric leaving on his travels to Asia. His journey took him overland to Hormuz, by sea to India, and then on to China. Odoric's account of his three-year stay in China, during which he visited Cambaluc and Hangchow, was the most informative after that of Marco Polo.

he cries 'Arise all.' And immediately they all arise. Likewise . . . h cries 'Put your fingers in your ears.' And again . . . 'Pluck ther out'. . . . At the third point he calls: 'Bolt this meal'. . . . And whe the musicians' hour is come, then the philosophers say 'Solemniz a feast unto your Lord.' With that all sound their instruments. . . And immediately another cries 'Peace, peace.' and they all cease.

But, in general, Odoric appreciated the treatment he himse received from the khan. "I, Friar Odoric, was present in person [the khan's] palace. For we minor friars have a place of abo appointed out for us in the emperor's court and are enjoined to g and bestow our blessing upon him."

At the time of Odoric's visit there were eight Christian missio aries and one Saracen (a representative of Islam) in permane residence in the court. They were all supplied by the khan wi

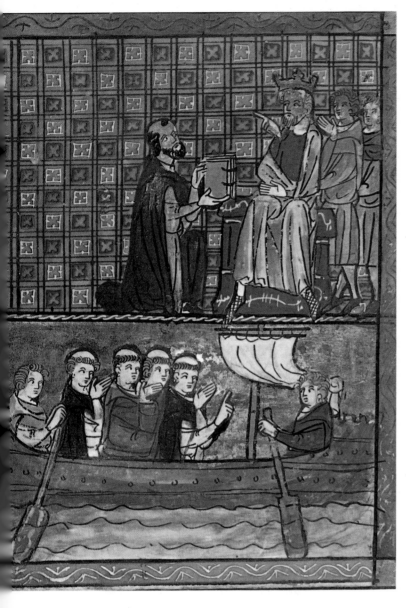

everything that they required in the way of food and clothing.

Like Marco Polo before him, Odoric tells of the marvelous road and communications system that prevailed right across the empire. 'The emperor so that travelers may have all things necessary throughout his whole empire has caused certain inns to be provided upon the highways where all things pertaining to victuals are in a continual readiness. And when any news happens in any part of his empire, if he chance to be far absent from that part his messengers upon horses or dromedaries ride post to him, and when they and their beasts are weary, they blow their horn, and at the noise of it the next inn likewise provides a horse and a man who takes the letter of him that is weary, and runs to another inn. And so by many inns, and many posts, the report which ordinarily could scarcely come in two days, is in one natural day brought to the emperor. Therefore no

Above: a fragment from a manuscript of 1444 describing Odoric's journey to the lands of the infidel (Mongols). Odoric traveled in the Middle East before setting out for China.

Left: the Mongol city gate in Peking.
The Mongols ruled in Cambaluc until
1368, when the Chinese rebelled and
drove them out, together with the
last khan, Timur. The Chinese then
established the Ming dynasty and
renamed the city Peiping (later Peking)

happening of any moment can be done in his empire but straightwa
he has intelligence thereof."

After three years in Cathay, Odoric set off overland across Asi
through Sinkiang and Persia, and home to Italy. On this journey, to
he was the first traveler after Marco Polo to write an accou
of the places he had passed through, and was the last to do so f
hundreds of years.

A letter to Pope Benedict in Rome, in 1338, from Timur Khan le
to the last important medieval mission to China. Timur asked for t
pope's benediction, and included in his letter a commendation
the Christian Alans, inhabitants of the far western part of his empi

He asked for horses and other souvenirs of the West—"land of the sunset." In answer to his request the pope sent out an embassy headed by a man called John Marignolli. The mission left Avignon (where the papal court had been held since 1309) in 1338, and traveled by land to Cambaluc, which was reached in 1342. The ambassadors enjoyed royal hospitality for a period of about four years, and then returned to Europe by the sea route Marco Polo had taken. Very little is known about the Marignolli mission, but it is recorded that the Christians presented the Mongol emperor with a war horse 11½ feet long and 6 feet 8 inches high. More Chinese writings survive about the horse, which was a great wonder to them,

Above: Odoric met the people as well as the nobility during his travels. In Mongolia, local trade depended much on itinerant peddlers. One is seen here with his family.

儒林華國古今同
行詠飛觴醒醉中
為士作新知入彀
此圖猶喜見文雄

日承謹依
韻和進

以特不與百官同
表人歸大道中
笑當年十八士

than about the priests who presented it, in whom they showed little interest.

With this mission, Christianity in China virtually died out until the early 1800's. After Kublai Khan's death, the Mongols declined in power and prestige. Their leaders dedicated themselves more and more to personal luxury and comfort rather than to the development and care of the existing empire, and were so weakened that, in 1368, a Chinese leader came to power. Two years later, the Mongols were driven out of China and back to their homeland, and the gates to the Far East closed behind them.

European travelers had achieved a great deal during the 10 centuries between 400 and 1400. Irish missionaries had ventured out into the Atlantic Ocean. The Vikings had sailed far to the west to Iceland, Greenland, and the northeast shores of the American continent. The Polos and a handful of dedicated priests and friars had traveled amazing distances overland across Asia, to trade with the Mongols and Chinese, and convert them to Christianity. But none of these achievements had any real lasting value. The Viking attempt to settle on the coast of Greenland was a failure. During the 1400's, disease, a worsening of the harsh climate, or Eskimo attacks wiped out all the little colonies. The settlements established in Vinland by Karlsefni and Freydis had been shortlived. Only Iceland remained, a colony first of the Norwegian and then of the Danish kings, until it became an independent republic in 1944.

The European travelers in the Far East also achieved little in the long term. Europeans in the 1400's knew less about China and

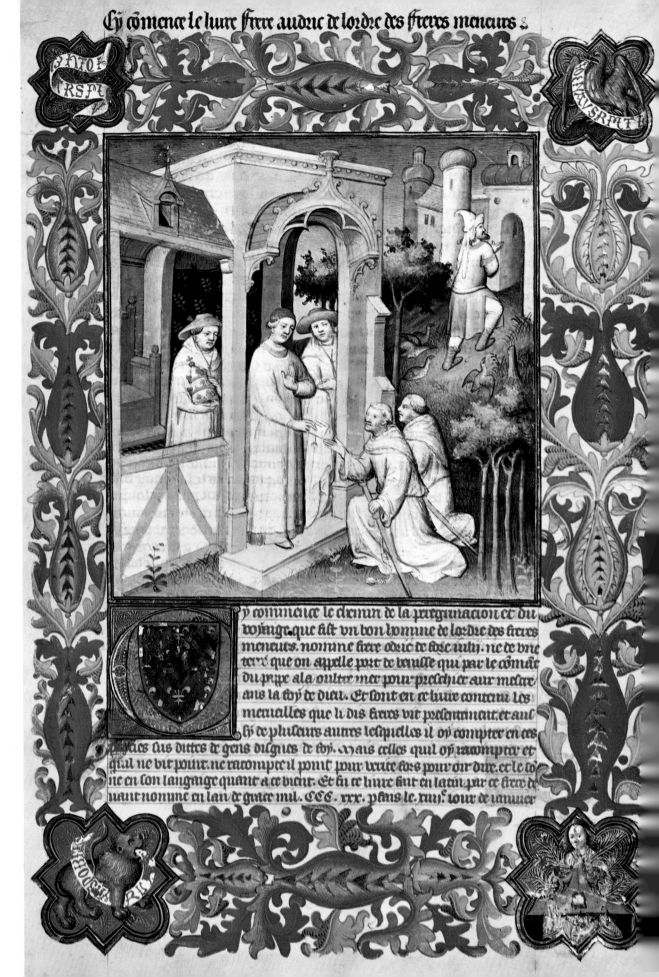

y commence le chemin de la pregrinacion et du
voyage. que fist vn bon homme de lordre des freres
meneurs. nomme frere odric de soye iuly. ne de vne
terre que on appelle port de venisse qui par le comant
du pepe ala oultre mer pour preschier aux mesare
ans la foy de dieu. Et sont en ce liure contenu les
merueilles que li dis freres vit presentement. et au
ssy de plusieurs autres lesquelles il oy compter en ces
places sus dittes de gens dignes de foy. Mais celles quil oy racompter et
quil ne vit point. ne racompte il point pour verite fors pour oir dire. et le co
ne en son langaige quant a ce vient. Et fu ce liure fait en latin par ce frere de
uant nomme en lan de grace mil. CCC. xxx. puis le xiiij. iour de ianuier

had less contact with its people than they had in the 1200's. There were two main reasons for this. In 1370, the Chinese drove out the Mongols from China, back to the windswept plains of central Asia from which they had originally come. The collapse of the Mongol Empire, with its superb system of roads and way stations across Asia, and the readiness of its rulers to receive traders and Christian missionaries from Europe, was a disaster for East-West relations. All contact between China and the West came to an end. Never again would China be as open to Western travelers, trade, and ideas as it

ove: this ancient bridge near king is named after Marco Polo, the veler who successfully forged a k between East and West 700 years o. Peking today consists of two es. The Inner City in the rth lies more or less on the site of old Mongol capital of Cambaluc.

had been under the khans. Historians have even suggested that people in the West in the 1200's knew more about China than we do today.

There was another serious obstacle to European contact and trade with the Far East after the mid-1300's. In 1345, an army of Ottoman Turks—at the time unequaled in military skill and organization—crossed the narrow straits, now called the Dardanelles, that separate Europe and Asia, and attacked the southeast corner of Christendom. In May, 1453, after just over a hundred years of intermittent warfare against the armies of Christian Europe, Sultan Mohammed led a triumphant army into the city of Constantinople. For three days the Turkish soldiers plundered, terrorized, and destroyed the city, which for centuries had been the capital of eastern Christianity. The fall of Constantinople and the rise of an aggressive Islamic empire in the eastern Mediterranean meant that the main gateway of the overland route to China and the Far East was closed. Turkish and Arab middlemen controlled the Far Eastern trade routes, and the European end of the trade was handled almost solely by the Italian city-states of Venice and Genoa. From now on, Europeans had to look for new routes to the fabulous wealth of the Orient.

Above: by the 1400's, thanks to
the reports of missionaries and merchants, mapmakers were able to fill
in important features, previously
missing, on their atlases. In Venice,
the monk Fra Mauro completed his
world map in 1459. Africa and Asia,
though still inaccurate in many respects,
are drawn with a wealth of detail.
Like most maps of the middle ages,
it shows the world as a flat disk
surrounded by sea, with south at
the top and north at the bottom.

But in spite of this abrupt shutting out of European travele
from Asia and the Far East, the achievements of Marco Polo and t
missionaries were not entirely wasted. A small Christian communi
survived in China until the next wave of European missionari
arrived by sea in the 1600's. And it seems almost certain th
Christopher Columbus was inspired by *The Book of Marco Polo*
attempt to reach the Orient by sailing the other way around t
world—to the west. So it was that an account of a Venetian mercha
about the East led Columbus to rediscover, quite by accident, t
continent in the West that the Vikings had found, colonized a
subsequently abandoned.

Acknowledgments

Aldus Archives 233, 237, 240, 246, 247, 249, 253, 255, 276, 308, 310; Photo Almasy 272; Courtesy of the Arnamagnaen Collection, Denmark 182, 193, 205; Hannes Betzler/Bavaria-Verlag 274; Kurt Hoerold/Bavaria-Verlag 251; Afred Strobel/Bavaria-Verlag 277; Photo Bibliothèque Nationale, Paris 229, 232, 236, 257, 264, 267(B), 268, 269, 273(T), 280, 282, 289, 295, 296, 300, 306, 318; Bodleian Library, Oxford 238(T), 271, 277, 281, 283, 285, 287, 291, 292, 294, 301, 303; Reproduced by permission of the Trustees of the British Museum 169, 179, 180(B), 199, 220, 221, 252(L), 258, 278, 284, 302, 311, 313(T), 313(B); British Museum/Photo John Drake © Aldus Books 173, 189(T), 197(B); British Museum/Photo John Freeman © Aldus Books 263; British Museum/Photo Michael Jaanus © Aldus Books 174(B), 198, 208, 216(L), 239, 245(B), 252(R); Canadian Government Travel Bureau 211; J. Allan Cash 262; W. Harstrick/Bruce Coleman Ltd. 260(T); James Hyett/Bruce Coleman Ltd. 206(L); Leonard Lee Rue/Bruce Coleman Ltd. 214(R); Columbia University Libraries 267(T); By courtesy of the Master and Fellows of Corpus Christi College, Cambridge 234(T), 250; Published by permission of the Danish National Museum 186(B), 207(R), 212, 216(R), 217(L), 218(B); Harrison Forman World Photos 222(T); Geographical Projects Limited, London 175(R), 188, 213(T), 235, 260(B), 266, 286; Photo George W. Goddard © Aldus Books 190, 259; Irish Tourist Office, London 170(R); Mats Wibe Lund, Jr., Reykjavik 178, 194, 204, 206(R), 209, 214(L), 217(R); The Mansell Collection 186(T), 224, 307; Photo Mas, Barcelona 189(B); The Metropolitan Museum of Art, Gift of A. W. Bahr, 1947 230–31; Monitor, London, 265; Musée du Louvre, Paris/Photo Giraudon © S.P.A.D.E.M. 248; Musée Goya, Castres/Photo Giraudon © S.P.A.D.E.M. 187; Musée Guimet, Paris 242; Ross Collection, Courtesy, Museum of Fine Arts, Boston 244; National Museum of Iceland/Photo Myndiön © Aldus Books 192, 200, 203; National Museum of Ireland 169, 177 Collection of the National Palace Museum, Taipei, Taiwan, Republic of China 225, 315, 316; Picturepoint, London 238(B), 270; The Pierpont Morgan Library 200; Axel Poignant 180(T); Asmundur Poulsen 172; Photo Mauro Pucciarelli, Rome 293, 305; © Rhodos, Copenhagen 213(B); The Royal Library, Copenhagen 202, 210; Scala, Florence 320; © Christopher Scarlett 314, 319; Sea and Airborne Education 191; Sólarfilma s.f., Reykjavik 174–5, 197(T), 201(L), 201(R); Staatliche Museen, Berlin-Dahlem 309; John Massey Stewart 228, 231(B), 254; Wolf Suschitzky 273(B); Topkapi Saray Museum, Istanbul 226, 227, 234(B), 241, 243, 261, 317; Emil Schulthess, Black Star/Transworld Features 165, 288, 298–99; Courtesy the Board of Trinity College, Dublin 170; Universitätsbibliothek Heidelberg. Cod. Pal. Germ. 60, fol. 179v 171(R); The University Museum of Antiquities, Oslo. Branch: The Viking Ships Hall, Bygdoy 183; The Viking Ship Museum, Roskilde, Denmark 196; The Viking Ship Museum, Roskilde, Denmark/Photo Carrebye © Aldus Books 218(L): Reproduced by permission of Yale University Press from R. A. Skelton, Thomas E. Marston and George D. Painter, *The Vinland Map and the Tartar Relation* © 1965 by Yale University 219; ZEFA/J. Bitsch 222(B).

PART THREE

The Great Age of Exploration

The Great Age of Exploration

BY DUNCAN CASTLEREAGH

Left : a battle on land and sea between the
Portuguese and Arabs at Surat, in India.
After successful battles against the Arabs,
the Portuguese controlled Eastern trade.

Right: Portuguese ships like those that made up the fleet of Francisco de Almeida, in which Magellan sailed to India in 1505.

Foreword

At the dawning of the new century in 1400, it might have seemed that the vine of European exploration was finally perishing. The fall of the Mongol empire closed the door to China. Constantinople was about to surrender to the Moslems, who would tighten their grip on the rich overland trade of Eastern luxuries. The last bits of Viking settlement in Greenland were fading away. The Atlantic Ocean was as vast and as unknown as ever, an apparently impenetrable barrier to the men of the Mediterranean.

A little over one hundred years later there was an established trading route around the tip of Africa to India, Columbus had landed in America, and Magellan's men brought the first ship home after sailing around the world. In a glorious explosion of exploration, the Great Age of Discovery had swept aside the curtain of the unknown.

This is the story of that Great Age. It began with one man's determination. It developed as his mapmakers and navigators joined the newly-rediscovered knowledge of the ancient world to the skills of the Arabs, and created instruments that finally moved toward a solution of the crucial problem of knowing where you were on a ship at sea. The instruments and maps of the 1400's were accurate enough to guide a ship's captain to the farthest point reached by his predecessor and beyond—and then to bring him home again, to make his report in turn.

The stories of these men, and the men who sailed with them, surpassed the wildest travelers' tales of the Middle Ages—and they were true. As the ships returned with the luxuries of India and reports of an unbelievably vast New World, the kingdoms of Europe turned outward. Never again would the Mediterranean be the center of the known world. Never again would the world be so small.

The Historical Challenge

1

One day, late in the summer of 1522, a small and sorry-looking vessel limped into the harbor of Sanlucar de Barrameda in southern Spain. Her foretopmast, damaged in a storm, creaked painfully under the pressure of the light wind in her sails. Her timbers were worm-eaten and heavy with barnacles. Her seams were leaking so badly that for weeks past only round-the-clock pumping had kept her afloat.

The 17 men aboard the tiny vessel presented a heart-rending sight. Of the ship's original complement of 50 officers and sailors, they alone had survived the rigors of their voyage, and even they were half-dead from starvation, scurvy, and sheer exhaustion.

Yet to all who saw them, the battered *Victoria* and the ragged men aboard her appeared wreathed in glory. They had made history's first voyage round the world.

The *Victoria's* achievement was a remarkable one by any standards. But perhaps the most significant thing about it was that it occurred less than a century after European sailors had first begun venturing beyond the confines of their own coastal waters. Before 1422, none but the Vikings had ever sailed more than 800 miles into the vast oceans beyond Europe's shores. Yet by 1522, when the *Victoria* made her famous voyage, Christopher Columbus had already discovered the New World and Portuguese mariners were making regular trips to the Far East.

What had happened in the short span of 100 years to transform Europe's coast-hugging seamen into world-ranging explorers? What combination of factors had conspired to launch the brilliant period of exploration we now call "the great age of discovery"?

The best way to answer these questions is, perhaps, to consider the historical forces which, in preceding centuries, had made far-flung exploration not only unthinkable but impossible. It is necessary, therefore, to go back in history as far as the 400's, when the western half of the great Roman Empire fell to barbarian invaders from the north and east.

When Rome fell, her conquerors carved out for themselves numerous small kingdoms in the provinces she had once ruled. But rivalry for more land and power led to constant conflict among them. And,

Left: it was in ships such as this that the early navigators sailed from Portugal on their voyages of exploration and conquest. Buffeted by storms and hampered by contrary winds, these sturdy vessels enabled the gallant seamen to penetrate unknown regions. The Portuguese established colonies and trading stations and tried to spread Christianity throughout Africa.

after two centuries of warfare and upheaval, little of the old Roman culture remained in western Europe except Christianity, the religion adopted by the Roman Empire in her last days of power.

During this period of turmoil, the system of mutual protection and support that we call feudalism developed. Rulers of small kingdoms granted land and privileges to lesser lords in exchange for their allegiance and military support. In turn, these lesser lords gave peasants the right to live under their protection in exchange for working their land.

World map, based on Gall's projection, showing the main geographical features.

Because continual warfare made travel unsafe, and because each
feudal estate produced all that its inhabitants needed, trade—and with
it, towns—declined during the early Middle Ages. And, as trade and
city life ground to a halt, so too did the exchange of ideas upon which
the advancement of learning depended. The one great civilizing force
in Europe at this time was the Church, whose doctrines dominated
medieval thought, and in whose monasteries such classical learning
as still existed was kept alive.

It was to be several centuries before trade, towns, and learning

reawakened in western Europe, and even longer before powerful nation-states emerged.

In the meantime, one important sector of the Roman Empire had not succumbed to the barbarian invaders. This was the eastern half of the empire, which included Asia Minor, Greece and its islands, and the lands now occupied by Lebanon, Syria, Israel, and Egypt. While the last vestiges of the old Roman order were disappearing in the West, this eastern region—which came to be called the Byzantine Empire— was flourishing. In fact, its capital, Byzantium (later called Constantinople, and later still Istanbul), was experiencing a golden age of power, prosperity, culture, and learning.

Not surprisingly, the Byzantine Empire's wealth and power made it the frequent target of would-be conquerors. From the north and west it was assailed by the barbarians; from the east by the Persians; and from the south by a new and dangerous enemy, the Arabs.

The Arabs of northern Africa were Moslems, followers of the new religion called Islam, founded by the prophet Mohammed in the early 600's. They embarked on a determined effort to spread their religion by conquest. Between the late 600's and the early 800's, they succeeded in wresting from Byzantium the territories that now make up Syria,

Left: Rumeli Hissar Fort, Istanbul, Turkey, is typical of the fortifications built around Constantinople (later Istanbul). The city was founded by Constantine the Great in A. D. 328 from the ancient city of Byzantium. Walls were built around the city, giving complete protection on all sides. The western wall was damaged by earthquake in 447 and was replaced by three walls 20 yards apart, each flanked by 96 towers. These formed a barricade about 200 feet thick and 100 feet high, in which were housed troops and equipment to meet any foe. These walls, which were restored from time to time, defied barbarous assaults for more than a thousand years.

banon, Israel, and Egypt. And, by the middle of the 900's the Moslem
mpire stretched unbroken from western India to the Atlantic shores
northern Africa. During this great period of conquest, Moslem
oors—a people originating in northwestern Africa—even reached
rope. They established themselves in the Iberian Peninsula, site
present-day Spain and Portugal.

For a time, it seemed that the Byzantine Empire would succumb
the Moslems. Ultimately, however, the Byzantines staged a come-
ck, and managed to drive the Moslems back on several fronts. In
t, by about A.D. 1000, the Byzantine Empire was once more strong
ough to begin expanding again. But just at this point, an aggres-
e and powerful new enemy, the Moslem Turks, invaded from the
t. Within a short space of time, the Turks had made such inroads
Byzantine defenses that the security of the entire empire was
eatened.

number of powerful kingdoms—among them England, France,
the Holy Roman Empire—had, by this time, begun to emerge in
stern Europe. And, on the Mediterranean coast, the republics of
nice and Genoa were already showing signs of becoming great sea
vers. It was to Christendom, then, that the beleaguered Byzantine
pire turned for help against the Moslem Turks in the 1000's. (Ironi-
y, the empire was ultimately to suffer as much, if not more, at the

Above: Islam, the Moslem religion,
was founded by Mohammed in the late
500's or early 600's. It is based on
the word of the Koran (through which
God is said to have revealed himself
to Mohammed) and the sayings and way
of life of the prophet himself.
Followers of the creed are required,
among other things, to worship
God five times a day, with the worship-
er facing Mecca. Early Moslem
conquests spread the Islamic doctrine
far and wide and by the mid-900's the
empire reached from North Africa to
eastern India. This picture shows
Mohammed taking part in a siege.

hands of its Christian allies than in the struggles against the Moslems.)

The men of western Christendom were only too glad to take up the cudgels against the Moslems. Sporadic fighting between Christians and Moslems in the Iberian Peninsula and in the islands of the Mediterranean had been going on since the 800's. But the time had now come for a concerted Christian effort against the infidels.

Thus began the series of "Holy Wars" known as the Crusades, which continued for almost two centuries (1096–1270). But however much they tried, the crusaders never succeeded in gaining more than a few temporary advantages over the Moslems. Indeed, the Crusades merely served to prove beyond a doubt that Christendom had neither the unity nor the strength of arms to push the Moslems back from the eastern and southern shores of the Mediterranean.

The Crusades produced a further source of frustration in revealing to the men of Christendom what riches lay beyond their reach. At the eastern end of the Mediterranean, they had seen the profusion of rich commodities which poured into the Moslem Empire from the Orient: silks, spices, tapestries, porcelain, and precious stones. Once seen, such goods were earnestly desired. Unfortunately, they could be had only on terms dictated by the Moslems, whose strategic geographical position gave them control over all East-West trade. In fact, the Mos-

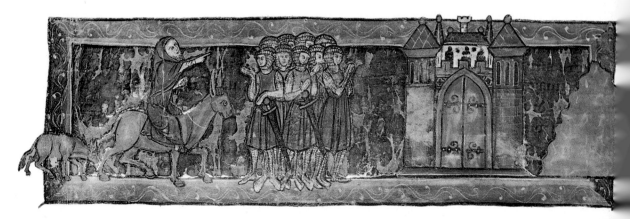

Above: Peter the Hermit, priest of Amiens, whose oratory attracted many pilgrims to the first crusade. Their journey to Constantinople was one of the preliminary acts of the first crusade. Peter reached Constantinople in July, 1096, but the crusaders were routed by the Turks (whom they attacked against Peter's wishes), leaving him to await the princes in May, 1097. Photo by Denise Bourbonnais, from Bibliotheque de l'Arsenal, Paris.

Above: view of Venice from a manuscript of 1338 showing St. Marks and the Doge's Palace. The former was originally the private chapel of the Doge, richly decorated with materials from the East. The latter is the head of state's official residence. After the crusades, Venice was a thriving center of trade, her merchants buying from the Moors coveted goods from the Orient, for resale elsewhere in Europe at higher prices. MS. Bodley 264. Fol. 218.

lem barrier to Western commerce with the East was so formidab that it had been penetrated only by a few rare travelers such as Mar Polo in the second half of the 1200's.

The Moslems had firmly established themselves at the crossroa between East and West when Christendom was weak and disorg nized. Now, when towns and commerce were beginning to flourish on more in western Europe, Christendom found itself cut off from t richest sources of world trade. Only the city-states of Venice and Ger profited from this situation, for they possessed a trade monopoly w

the Moslems. Eastern goods reached the shores of the Mediterranean via caravan routes, the Indian Ocean, the Red Sea, and Egypt. Once in Mediterranean ports, they were sold by Moslem traders to Venetian and Genoese merchants, who then proceeded to sell them elsewhere in Europe at exorbitant prices.

After Christendom's repeated efforts to weaken the Moslem Empire had failed, the trade barrier stood firmer than ever. The remaining possibility was to seek an alternative route to the East—an ocean route that would completely bypass the Mediterranean and its Moslem-held shores. But the search for such a route would entail voyaging far out into unknown Atlantic waters, and it was to be almost two centuries before any European mariners would attempt a feat so daring.

In the meantime, Europe had to content itself with obtaining the Eastern luxuries it wanted from Venice and Genoa. In any case, most of the western kingdoms had, by the 1300's, grown weary of fighting the Moslems, and were preoccupied with other matters. The Holy

nt: the Palacio de Generalife
ace of the Architect) in Granada,
of the outlying buildings con-
ed with the Alhambra, the ancient
ce and fortress originally built
e Moorish Kings between 1284
1354. Considered to be one of the
t examples of Moorish art in
pe, it has been restored many
s. Granada, a maritime province
uthern Spain, became the leading
of Moorish Spain when Córdoba
Ferdinand of Castile in 1236.

Above: quayside of the Portuguese
capital of Lisbon. Portugal was dominated by the Moors from A.D. 711, but
in 1147, Alfonso I incorporated Lisbon
into his kingdom. For centuries the
city suffered earthquakes and in 1755
was reduced to ruin by a simultaneous
devastating earthquake and tidal wave.

Roman Empire was pursuing a policy of expansion; France and England were at war with each other; and the Italian city-states were experiencing the dawn of the Renaissance.

Only in the Iberian Peninsula was the crusading spirit still very much alive. There the struggle to oust the Moslem Moors had continued for centuries. And by the late 1200's this unceasing effort had succeeded in driving the Moors out of every part of the peninsula except the south, where the Moslem kingdom of Granada still remained strong.

The three Christian kingdoms in Iberia were Aragon, Castile, and Portugal. All three were coastal seafaring nations. All three were determined enemies of the Moslems. As it was becoming clear that the Moslems would never release their hold on East-West trade, all three might have been expected to seek an alternative sea route to the East. But Aragon's sole coast was on the Mediterranean, and it was content to confine its maritime interests to that sea. Castile, possessing both an Atlantic and a Mediterranean coastline, was kept busy defending its southern border with Granada.

Of the three Iberian kingdoms, Portugal alone possessed both the political and the geographical advantages necessary for the development of interest in ocean exploration. Portugal's only land frontier was with Castile. More important still, its only coastline was along the Atlantic.

t: political map of Europe, with governments of approximately 1400.

339

Because the Atlantic offered Portugal its only highway to the o
side world, it was, from the beginning, a nation of seafarers. Soon a
the little kingdom emerged from Moorish domination in 1143,
tugal founded its own fighting navy. According to legend this in
navy succeeded in capturing an entire Moorish fleet off Lisbon,
tugal's capital, as early as 1150. By 1300, the Portuguese navy ha
own admiral and a score of Genoese pilots to captain its ships and t
its crews. Meanwhile, growing numbers of Portuguese merc
vessels were plying the sea routes to France, England, and Flan
with goods for trade.

The largest of the Portuguese trading ships, the *naves,* were st
decked sailing ships of 200 tons and more. And Portuguese sea

...ere not content to confine their maritime activities to the familiar ...aters of their own and neighboring coasts. As early as 1341 they ...ade the first recorded Portuguese visit to the Canary Islands, 800 ...iles southwest of the Iberian Peninsula.

But fear of the unknown kept the Portuguese from venturing far- ...er into the Atlantic. They not only had no idea of what lay beyond ...e Canaries, but were unfamiliar with astronomy and mathematics, ...e two chief handmaidens of navigation. Like men everywhere in ...urope at that time, the Portuguese knew less about these subjects— ...d about geography—than the ancient Greeks had known.

As far back as the 300's B.C., Greek philosophers had believed that ...e earth is round. By the 200's B.C., the principles of geometry had ...en worked out by Euclid, and the astronomer Eratosthenes had ...ade a remarkably accurate estimate of the earth's circumference. ...nd, in the A.D. 100's, a Greek mathematician, astronomer, and ge- ...grapher named Ptolemy had written two great works summarizing ...l that was then known about astronomy and geography.

The Roman Empire had preserved this heritage of Greek learning. ...ut, in the upheaval that followed the fall of the empire, most of it had ...en lost. In the monasteries of western Europe, some classical writ- ...gs had survived, but they were by and large purely philosophical, ...ther than scientific works.

The ancients' contributions to mathematics, astronomy, and geog- ...phy did, however, eventually find their way back to Europe—by ...extremely roundabout route. One place where the learning of the ...ssical scientists had been preserved was the Byzantine Empire. ...d one of the Moslems' first conquests was the Byzantine territory ...Syria. Here the conquerors came into contact with the writings of ...e ancient Greeks. They translated these important works into Arabic ...their own use, and later took copies of them to the great universities ...ich they established in the Iberian Peninsula.

...or many years, the Moslem universities in Iberia were open only ...Moslems and to Jews (who had begun settling in the Iberian Penin- ...a long before the Moslem conquest). But as the Christian recon- ...st of Iberia proceeded, the Moslem universities fell one by one into ...ristian hands. Not all the Moslem and Jewish scholars who taught ...hem were banished. Many stayed on, some after undergoing a real ...nominal conversion to Christianity. They continued to work, trans- ...ng the classical scientific works from Arabic into Latin, the lan-

Above: the Patio de las Escuelas at Salamanca University. Salamanca, capital city of the Spanish province of Salamanca, stands on the river Tormes. The university was founded in 1233 by Alfonso IX of Léon, but it was under Alfonso X that it became widely known. Columbus gave lectures there on his discoveries.

Below: northern carrack of about 1470. Northern galleys, about 45 feet long, possibly developed from simple dugouts, the two ends being carved from solid blocks and the sides formed of overlapping planks, in clinkerbuilt fashion. The steering gear on the northern vessels was superior to that of their Mediterranean counterparts.

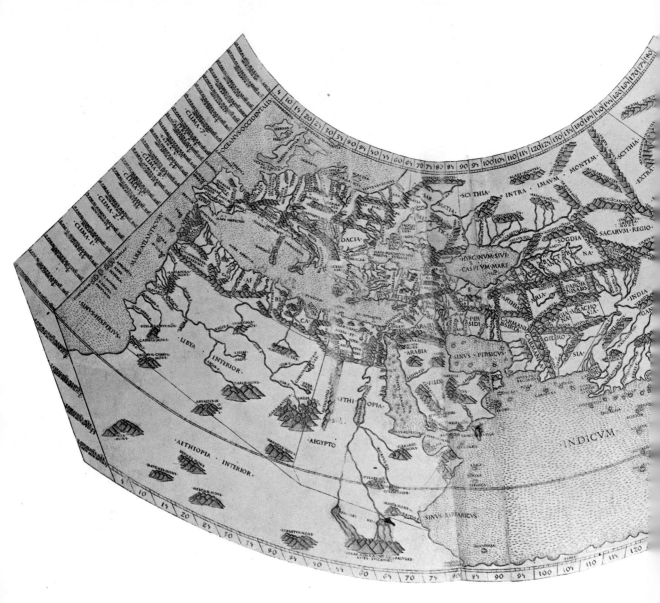

Above: world map from Ptolemy's *Geography*, Rome Edition of 1508. In this work Ptolemy tried to make geography a scientific study and a convenient and easy form of reference. As an astronomer he was able to explain the mathematical relationship of the earth and the celestial bodies. He divided the equatorial circle into parallels of latitude and meridians of longitude and within the framework thus created he outlined the then-known regions of the world.

guage which was then used by all educated European Christians.

Not long after this source of ancient learning had been opened European scholars, another source also began to provide long-lo classical works. During the Holy Wars against the Moslems, the cr saders had established a so-called "Latin Empire" in Byzantium. Fro that center of culture and learning, at this time called Constantinop ancient works now began flowing directly back to Christendom. high-water mark of this flow was achieved in 1407, when a copy Ptolemy's *Geography* reached the West. Within two years, Latin tra lations of it were available to European scholars.

As yet, however, the great works of classical learning had been s only by scholars. Printing was still to be invented, and the use manuscripts becoming available were rare and costly. Furthermo only educated men well versed in Latin could read them. So, des the recovery of Ptolemy's *Geography* and other scientific works of past, most people remained in ignorance of astronomy, mathema

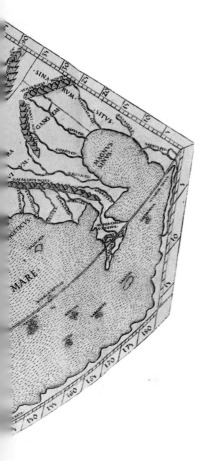

Right: Henry the Navigator (1394—1460).With his two elder brothers he took part in the conquest of Ceuta, during which he realized the importance of seapower against the Moslem enemies. Third son of King John I of Portugal, Prince Henry spent a great part of his life encouraging Portuguese exploration, spending most of his personal fortune in the process. He founded a school of navigation and mapmaking, where he employed experts not only to train captains and pilots, but also to interpret the information they brought back from their voyages. His encouragement led, after his death, to the circumnavigation of Africa and the discovery of an ocean route to the Orient from Europe.

...d geography. It was, for example, still widely believed that the earth ...as flat.

Ocean exploration could not possibly be undertaken by mariners ...norant of the basic principles of navigation. What was needed was ...man who could bridge the gap between the scholars and the sailors, ...man who possessed both learning and a vital interest in pushing back ...e frontiers of navigation. He would have to be a man of daring and ...etermination, for any plan to explore the unknown would be met ...th strong opposition by mariners and landsmen alike. He would ...so have to be a man of great persuasion, for any serious attempt to ...plore the unknown would take masterly organization and tremen-...us financial backing.

Fortunately for the history of exploration, just such a man came ...:ward at this time. And perhaps it is no coincidence that he was born ...orince of Portugal, the little nation of seafarers whose only highway ...the world was the broad Atlantic.

Response
2

In August, 1385, Castile suddenly launched a full-scale invasion against Portugal. The Portuguese Army was heavily outnumbered, but aided by a small force of English troops, they won a resounding victory. The resultant strengthening of existing Portuguese-English ties led to the marriage of King John (João) of Portugal to Philippa, the daughter of John of Gaunt. The royal match was to have historic consequences—not only for Portugal, but for the whole of Europe—for it produced the remarkable prince who was to set in motion the great age of discovery: Henry the Navigator.

Prince Henry was the third son born to the royal couple, and so third in order of succession to the throne. Ordinarily, such a position in the royal hierarchy would have left the prince with a lifetime of court and ministerial duties. Circumstances decreed otherwise. When Henry was 21 a dramatic event changed the whole course of his life.

As a boy, Henry and his elder brothers, Edward (Duarte) and Peter (Pedro), received their religious training and general education from their devout and learned mother. And their father, the king, instructed them in the arts of war and the code of chivalry.

By the time the princes had reached their late teens, all three were eager to win knighthood, proof of a young man's personal honor and courage. Traditionally, however, knighthood could be won only in battle, and Portugal was now at peace with Castile. Nevertheless, King John sympathized with his sons' ambition, and offered them an alternative path to the title they coveted. He would hold a year-long series of jousts and tourneys, during which they would have ample opportunity to distinguish themselves.

But the king's plan did not satisfy the young princes. They wanted to make their reputations in battle as their father had done. One day, while they were wishing aloud for a real war in which to prove themselves, they were overheard by the king's treasurer. This thrifty gentleman might have shuddered at the thought of having to raise money for a war to gratify the romantic ambitions of three royal youths. How-

Left: in 1387, the marriage between King John I of Portugal and Philippa, eldest daughter of England's John of Gaunt, helped to strengthen the ties between the two countries. This royal union is best remembered for one of its remarkable offspring, Prince Henry, the Navigator.

345

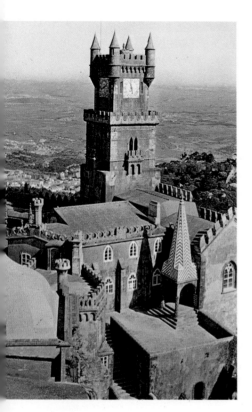

Right: jousting was a chivalric exercise in which young knights could practice for battle, experienced ones demonstrate their superior skills, and all exhibit their tremendous bravery to their ladies. This is thought to be a tournament in the Constantinople Hippodrome, from a manuscript illustrating Sir John Mandeville's travels.

Above: the Portuguese royal family maintained a fortress at Pena Palace, Sintra, from the 1100's to the 1300's. Later the fortress was rebuilt, partly in deliberate imitation of a medieval fortress and partly using a monastery that had replaced the original fortress.

ever, at that particular time, he happened to have been turning ove in his mind a certain military expedition. This project, he calculated would not only satisfy the yearnings of the three princes, but also if successful, bring great financial advantages to Portugal. What h could not know, however, was that it would set Henry on his momer tous path of exploration and discovery.

The treasurer had been told by a servant (who had once been a Moslem prisoner) about the wealth of the northern African port of Ceuta According to the servant, the city was wide open to attack from the se

While mulling over the benefits to Portugal of a successful attac against Ceuta, the treasurer had also been considering the cost of a yea of lavish feasts and tourneys. Surely an expedition against the port Ceuta was a more profitable way of spending the king's money. S the royal money-keeper commended the young men for their nob ambitions, and suggested that they try to persuade their father to mal war on Ceuta.

At first, the king refused to take their proposal seriously. In the who history of the struggle to retake the Iberian Peninsula from the Mo lems, no serious blow had ever been leveled at Moslem-held norther Africa. In fact, it was from Ceuta itself that the Moslems launched mar invasions against Christendom. So it was hard to believe that this Mo lem stronghold could actually be as vulnerable as the treasurer repor ed it to be. King John pointed out to his sons the immense dange and difficulties of the expedition they proposed, and urged them think again. They were determined, however, and Prince Henry, t spokesman for the three brothers, gradually overcame his father objections.

A main concern of King John was the possible military repercu sions of the venture. If Portugal succeeded in taking Ceuta, he argue then the Moslem kingdom of Granada, which depended heavily help and supplies from that port, would fall prey to the milita might of Castile. And with Granada out of the way, Castile would certain to turn her forces against her old enemy, Portugal.

In dealing with this objection, Henry revealed the strong crusadi spirit that was later to be a driving force behind his campaign of disc ery. To take Moslem Ceuta, he argued, would be to render a servi to God. By the same token, to withhold that service, for fear it mig help Castile, would be a sin against God. "Even if the king of Cas were our greatest enemy," he concluded, "he would be so only by ac

Above: the port of Ceuta at the southeastern end of the Strait of Gibraltar which the Portuguese captured from the Moors in the 1400's. Right: the Strait of Gibraltar is 31 miles long, and between the Rock of Gibraltar and Mount Atho, just east of Ceuta, the width is a mere 14 miles. These two forts controlled the passage between the known world of the Mediterranean and the almost unknown world of the Atlantic.

dent, for he is a Christian, as we are. The Moslems, on the other han are our enemies by nature." It was almost certainly this argument th persuaded the king to undertake the venture.

The first step was to scout out Ceuta's defenses without arousir suspicion. This was done by sending two galleys on a trumped-up di lomatic mission to Sicily. The two captains were instructed to dro anchor along the way (as if to rest their crews) as near as possible Ceuta, and take careful note of all they saw.

One man, on his return from this scouting mission, built a moc of Ceuta's defense works and sea approaches out of sand, ribbons, a beans. On this evidence, King John decided that a well-organiz attack from the sea stood a very good chance of success, and began prepare an expedition.

All three princes were given important responsibilities. To Her fell the task of organizing the building and outfitting of ships and t assembling of crews in the northern part of the country, with Opo serving as his headquarters. Peter had a similar task in the south, w

eadquarters in Lisbon. Edward, meanwhile, was put in charge of
ortugal's financial affairs and given responsibility for the adminis-
ation of justice in the kingdom. The king was thus left free to con-
ntrate on the diplomatic problems that would inevitably arise, and
organize the supply of artillery and other armaments for the fleet.
For many months no one talked of anything but ships and munitions,
rticularly in Oporto and Lisbon. In these cities, there was hardly
soul not engaged in making ropes, fashioning casks, slaughtering
ttle, and salting down beef, baking biscuits, catching and drying
h, caulking seams in hulls and decks, or packing bombards and can-
ns.

News of this build-up of arms and supplies could hardly be kept
m the outside world. But, apart from the royal household, no one
ew exactly where the great fleet was intended to strike. Both Castile
d Granada took fright. But King John allayed their fears by sending
ultimatum to the Duke of Holland, and took care that everyone
ard of it. At the same time, he notified the duke in secret that the ulti-

natum had been sent solely to deceive the real victims of the forthcoming attack. Even the Portuguese government was kept in the dark about the real target of the operation until the entire fleet was assembled near Lisbon and ready to sail. At that crucial point, Queen Philippa fell sick of the plague. She called her sons to her bedside and gave them each a sword and her blessing for the proposed expedition. She died a few days before the fleet sailed.

The citizens of Ceuta had no inkling of what was in store for them until the second week of August, 1414. Then they were confronted by more than 200 Portuguese vessels suddenly appearing off the coast of the tiny peninsula. The battle was short and decisive. The Portuguese landed at daybreak on August 15, and, after a single day of fierce hand-to-hand combat, the port fell.

During the fighting, the three princes proved their daring and bravery. As they had wished, they were tested—and found worthy—on the field of battle. With the swords given to them by their mother, they were now knighted by their father in the city they had helped to conquer.

Below: this illustration from the Nuremburg Chronicles shows boat-building in the 1400's, which was common to any seaport of the period. The typical Portuguese and Spanish ship was the caravel, the largest being the 50-ton ocean-going caravel for long voyages.

ft: an altarpiece by Nuno Gonçalves, inted about 1450, showing St. ncent, patron saint of Lisbon, in center. On his left, wearing a large , stands Henry the Navigator, with future King John II, the boy in the nical hat. Kneeling in the foreground Alfonso V, called "the African" cause of his successes against the ors in Africa, and his queen.

The conquest of Ceuta played a significant role in shaping Prince Henry's future, and with it, the future of the world. In helping to create the fighting fleet, he had come into contact with many experienced seamen and had learned that a well-provisioned ship could remain at sea for a long time. The capture of the port had also taught him how effective sea power could be against the Moslems. Moreover, while at Ceuta, he learned that the Moslem Empire extended far down the west coast of Africa—farther than any European had yet traveled. And he picked up valuable geographical information about Africa from the merchants of Ceuta who regularly plied the caravan routes that led south and west to the Guinea coast.

Back in Portugal, Prince Henry began to fit these and other bits of information together. How could they be used to further his most cherished ambition—to strike a crushing blow against the Moslem Empire?

Henry was Grand Master of the Order of Christ, a religious order sworn to fight the infidels. But he knew that, throughout most of Christendom, men had lost interest in waging crusades. He also knew the futility of mounting a Portuguese campaign against the Moslem Empire. For the little kingdom could not hope, on its own, to do more than it already had done against Moslems in the Mediterranean. But now appeared that their empire stretched southward along Africa's west coast. If Portuguese ships could stay at sea long enough to explore the coast, Henry could learn just how strong Moslem defenses were in that quarter. If, as he strongly suspected, the Moslem Empire was weak at its farthest limits, it could be successfully attacked from the rear.

To undertake such a venture, Portugal would need allies. Here a medieval myth offered some hope. When the Moslem Empire had first begun to expand, a few pockets of Christianity had been trapped within its confines. Over the centuries a belief in the continued existence of such outposts of Christianity had combined with a little optimism to give rise to the legend of a powerful Christian kingdom. Ruled by one "Prester John," this kingdom was said to flourish somewhere deep inside Asia or Africa. This idea was universal in Europe from about the middle of the 1100's to the beginning of the 1300's. The Asia story then faded away but the name of the "priest king" remained and in the 1400's the legend was renewed, especially by Portuguese explorers. This time Prester John was specifically thought to be the

Above: Fez, capital of northern Morocco, where life for ordinary people has changed little over the centuries. Below: frontispiece from a book of 1540 showing Prester John, the legendary Christian priest-king of Moslem Asia.

Emperor of Ethiopia. Henry believed that if Portugal could make contact with Prester John, his aid could be enlisted against the Moslems. Although this contact never materialized, the belief at the time provided a further incentive to seek a way to the East.

To take up the "holy war" against Islam, from a new and as yet untried direction, was thus Prince Henry's chief motivation in beginning— as he was soon to do—his great campaign of exploration. However, he had further motives for wanting to explore the unknown. One was simply a craving to know more about the world. A chronicler of Portuguese history during this period, Gomes Eannes de Azurara, tells us that Prince Henry "wanted to know what lands were beyond the Canary Islands and Cape Bojador, for up to that time no one knew." Another strong incentive to exploration was a desire to increase Portugal's trading opportunities. According to Azurara, Henry believed "that if in these territories there should be any harbors where men could enter without peril, they could bring back much merchandise at little cost, because there would be no other persons to compete with them."

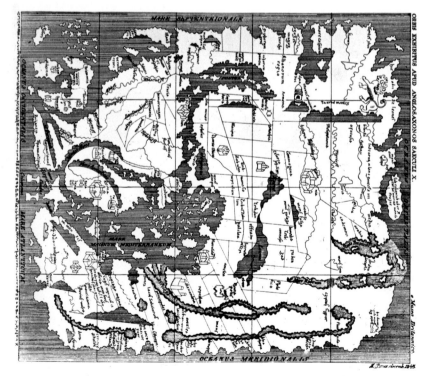

Left: the Latin inscription bordering this map attributes it to the 900's, but by modern reckoning it was probably drawn during the 1000's. It possible that this map was seen by Henry the Navigator and encourage his quest for a direct route to the ea

Right: this section of a Catalan ma using lines radiating from compass points as a form of grid, is attributed to Abraham de Gresque Lavishly ornamented and on fine parchment, it was probably made f Charles V of France, but it could have been put to practical use.

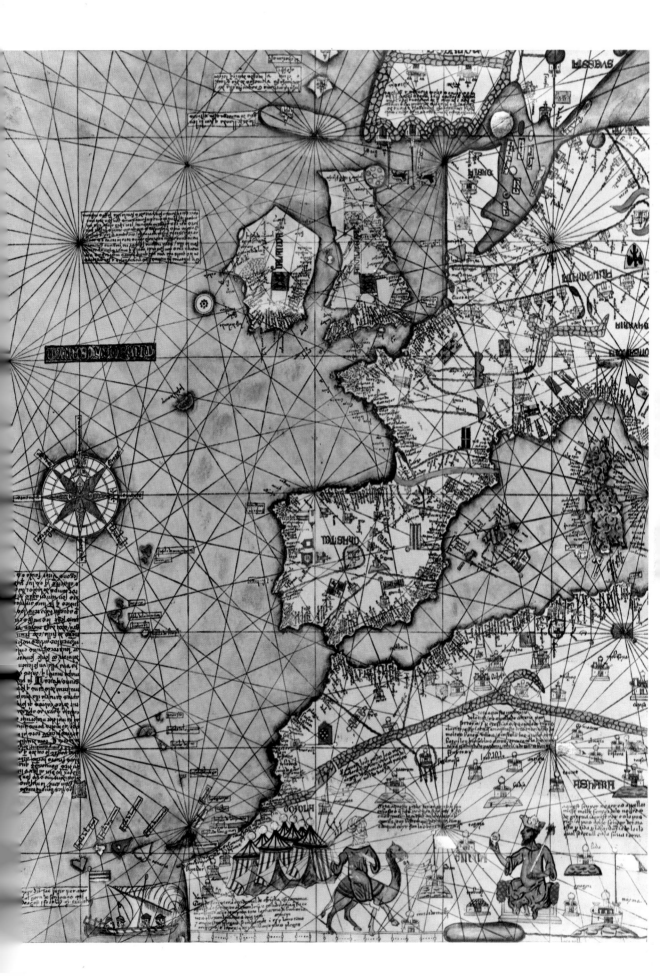

There is some evidence, though no certainty, that even at this time, Henry envisaged a direct sea route to the East.

It was soon after returning from a second stay in Ceuta, in 1418, that Henry resolved to begin a program of systematic and purposeful exploration. He did not intend to become an explorer himself. As he saw it, his role was to plan and supervise the program—to choose, train, and encourage promising sea captains and pilots, and to analyze and interpret the results of their expeditions. With this plan in mind, Henry gave up court life—though he always remained ready to serve as statesman or soldier when his country so required. He took up residence near the port of Lagos, and prepared himself for what was to be his life's work by a diligent study of mathematics, astronomy, and geography.

A few miles from Lagos, at the extreme southwestern tip of Portugal, stood Sagres, a small, bleak promontory pointing toward the African coast. There, in time, Henry built an observatory, a fortress, a naval arsenal, and a small town. There too, he established what we have come to call his "school of navigation."

Little is known about this institution, for the Portuguese were almost as secretive about their ocean voyages as the Phoenicians had been before them. All that is certain is that at Sagres pilots were chosen, given their instructions and some form of training, and sent on their way. It has also been established that Henry had the services of an expert on nautical instruments and mapmaking, a certain Master Jacome of Majorca. Master Jacome was employed by Henry to update charts

Above: Henry the Navigator's connection with Sagres began when he was made governor of Algarve, Portugal's southernmost province, and his private chapel can still be seen. On the site now occupied by a lighthouse, he built a navigational school and observatory.

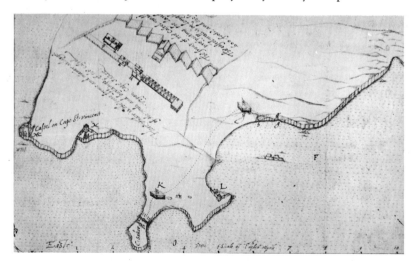

Left: this drawing from the 1500's shows about 11 miles around Sagres where Prince Henry built a naval arsenal and fortress as well as his famous school of navigation.

the African coast and the Atlantic islands as each voyage of discovery
ought back new information.

But even so accomplished a cartographer as Master Jacome must
ve been very limited in the help he could give to Henry's pilots. For
that time mapmaking was anything but an exact science, and the
w navigational instruments were still very primitive.

There were no accurate instruments for determining a ship's posi-
n and direction. Much of the time the early mariners had to sail out
sight of land to avoid the danger of being blown onto the coast by
ong on-shore winds. Although the north-seeking properties of mag-
ts had been known for centuries, nothing was yet known about
gnetic variation and deviation. As a result, the most advanced in-
ument in use—the mariner's compass—could be very misleading.
t of sight of land, therefore, Henry's pilots had to rely heavily on

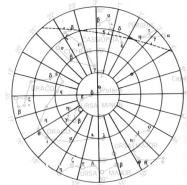

Above: Henry's pilots' most accurate aid to navigation was a knowledge of the stars. North of the equator they judged direction from the Pole Star. Below: the astrolabe was used to measure the positions of the stars.

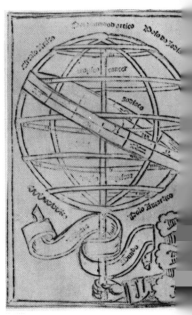

Left: this compass in an ivory box dates from about 1500. There is no definite record as to who first used a compass, but pieces of magnetic iron had been used since the 1000's to guide ships within sight of land.

their knowledge of the heavens to determine their changing position and direction.

By night, so long as they remained north of the equator, pilots could see the Pole Star, which they knew always lay very close to true north. By day, so long as they remained north of the Tropic of Cancer, the sun would always be due south at noon. And it would be 15° farther to the east for each hour nearer to sunrise, and 15° farther to the west for each hour nearer to sunset. To tell the hour during the day, mariners depended on the sun. The shadow of a stick set upright on deck grew shorter as morning wore on, longer again as afternoon moved toward sunset. The moment when the shadow was at its shortest marked true noon. By night, pilots could tell the time from the changing position of the stars in the constellation Ursa Minor.

To determine the ship's position was even more difficult than establishing the ship's direction. And it was, of course, just as difficult to determine the exact position of newly-discovered capes, islands, and river mouths. The discovery of Ptolemy's *Geography* a few years before Henry's program of exploration began, led to fresh thinking. As a result of this work, learned mapmakers such as Master Jacome had begun to realize that the ideal way of fixing a ship's position was in terms of latitude and longitude. But this was no easy matter in the 1400's.

To determine longitude at sea it is necessary to know, precisely and simultaneously, both local time and the time at some other fixed point, such as the home port. There was no simple method of ascertaining these two times at once until the 1700's when the marine chronometer was invented. In the meantime, pilots attempting to fix longitude had to use Ptolemy's rough estimate of the east-west distance represented by one degree of longitude along each parallel of latitude. This meant that they had to keep track of how far east or west they traveled on each stage of their voyage. To do this, they noted the direction in which they were sailing, how long they had sailed in that direction, and the speed at which they had traveled. Speed could be assessed by throwing some floating object overboard from the ship's prow and timing how long the vessel (whose length was known) took to pass it. Latitude could be determined (in theory at least) by measuring the angular distance of the Pole Star above the horizon. Land-based astronomers had long been able to take such measurements quite accurately with the aid of a sophisticated instrument of Arab invention called the astrolabe. But the astronomer's astrolabe was useless on the heaving

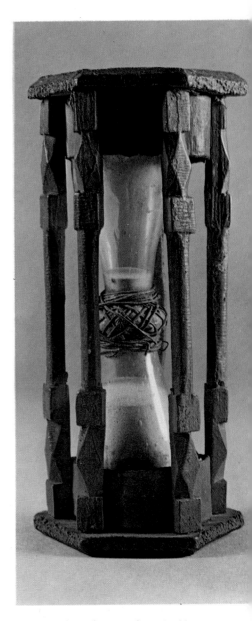

Above: an hourglass was important to early mariners, as mechanical clocks were unreliable at sea. Time measurement was an important element in "dead reckoning," by which the early pilot worked out the ship's position.

359

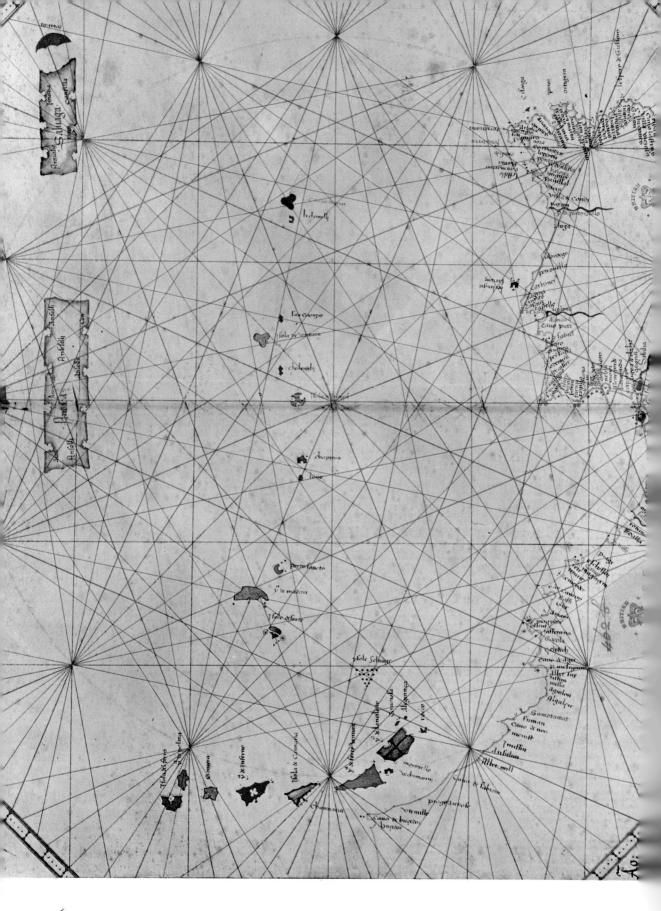

deck of a ship at sea. The quadrant was a simpler instrument that could
also be used for angular measurement. But it was not, so far as is known,
employed by Portuguese pilots until a year or two before Prince Henry's
death. Instead, an even simpler "instrument" was used—the pilot's
hand! When attempting to fix latitude, most pilots measured the height
of the Pole Star above the horizon simply by stretching out a hand at
arm's length. If the space between horizon and star was blocked out
by the thickness of a finger, the star's angle above the horizon was about
2°; if blocked out by the thickness of the wrist, about 8°; if blocked
out by the full span of the hand, about 18°.

The rough and ready results obtained by these methods made it impossible for cartographers to indicate exact location by reference to
latitude and longitude. Indeed, until well into the 1500's, maps of the
African coast were usually plotted on the same kind of complicated
chart that had been used by Mediterranean mariners since the last of
the Crusades. Such charts were drawn on a grid consisting of many
criss-crossing lines. These radiated from two or more compass points
near the edges of the chart and indicated compass bearings. With the
help of a ruler and a pair of dividers, the pilot could determine which
grid line was most nearly parallel to the course between his present
position and the harbor he was seeking. Then, by tracing that line to
the compass point from which it radiated, he could discover which
compass bearing he would need to follow.

Thus, when Prince Henry sent forth his first ships, navigational
instruments were barely adequate to the needs of ocean explorers. And
maps and cartographic devices were only slightly better at recording
their discoveries. But Prince Henry had at his command two very important assets—good ships and competent men.

Coincidentally, it was just about the time of Henry's first explor-
ative mission that a new type of ship, the caravel, was coming into use.
Though light, the caravel was broad of beam and capable of carrying
a good supply of water and provisions. In addition, these seaworthy
vessels often had two types of sails: triangular lateen sails for tacking
and making full use of light and side winds, and square sails for moving
fast before a following wind.

More important still to Henry's program was the availability of
many brave and experienced seamen. The prince was to make wise use
of these resourceful men in the great campaign of discovery and exploration he now undertook.

Above: typical of the Portuguese ships
which Henry sent out, this ship has
square-rigged sails and normal
lateen construction, by which a long
yard suspends the sails from the mast.

Sea of Darkness

3

ince Henry began his campaign of exploration with high hopes.
fully expected his mariners would soon be sailing down the coast
Africa and returning with the news he longed to hear: that the
ast had been thoroughly explored and charted; that a substantial
mber of non-Christians had been converted to the true faith; and
at valuable new trading contacts had been established. But the prince
s to be kept waiting many years for even a partial fulfillment of his
ams, mainly because of the fearsome stories then prevailing about
e "Sea of Darkness." This became particularly evident when the
loration involved sailing into the unknown seas beyond the Ca-

Above: in the 1400's and 1500's,
Portuguese navigators explored up and
down the coast of Africa, establishing
colonies and trading stations. At first
fear of the unknown was stronger than
their obedience to Prince Henry and all
his exhortations to sail south of Cape
Bojador failed. However, this bulge
(which now appears to us quite
insignificant) was eventually rounded
and the myth of boiling seas and
waterless land exploded. Portuguese
exploration flourished, leading
eventually to circumnavigation of
the African continent.

Above: in this day and age dress had not yet become specialized and uniform was unknown. This ship's captain is wearing the same type of clothes as any reasonably well-to-do gentleman of the period and he would wear the same whether on his ship or on land.

nary Islands, which lay 800 miles southwest of Portugal. And Henry's mariners were still less eager to venture past Cape Bojador, a small bulge of land on the coast of the present-day Spanish Sahara, some 15 miles south of the Canaries. No one, to their knowledge, had ever sailed past Bojador and returned to tell the tale. Keen and well-trained as Henry's mariners were, they were loath to risk their necks for the sake of mere exploration.

The stories that abounded about the seas beyond Cape Bojador were enough to make even the stoutest hearts quail. Some had it that beyond Bojador the ocean boiled and steamed. Others stated flatly that "beyond this cape there is no population, no water, neither trees nor green herbs; and the sea is so shallow that a league [a unit of distance varying between three and four miles] from the shore its depth is hardly a fathom. The tides are so strong that any ship which passes the cape will never be able to return." It is small wonder then that Henry's seamen asked themselves, "How shall we pass beyond the limits established by our elders? What profit can the prince win from the loss of our souls and our bodies?"

So, for some 15 years, instead of following Henry's instructions to pursue a steady course south beyond Cape Bojador, his mariners would veer off in other directions and go crusading or trading. Some sailed east into the Mediterranean to raid Moslem-held Granada on the southern coast of the Iberian Peninsula. Others sailed even farther east to the lands at the other end of the Mediterranean, where they devoted themselves to the capture of infidels.

How did the prince react to the news that his orders had been completely disregarded? Henry was a patient man—perhaps too patient. Instead of reprimanding his reluctant explorers, he rewarded them for their crusading efforts.

Meanwhile, some of Henry's mariners—either acting on instructions, or seeking yet another way to avoid going past Cape Bojador—were making more useful excursions. These captains sailed westward into the Atlantic. They took their ships and crews to the Canary Islands, the Madeira Islands, and the Azores. As a result of their journeys, Portugal became the first nation to use these islands for the purposes of regular trade and colonization. Eventually the Canaries and Madeira became ports of call for ships en route to more distant lands.

All three archipelagos had been known to Europeans for centuries. As far back as the A.D. 100's, Ptolemy had mentioned the Canaries

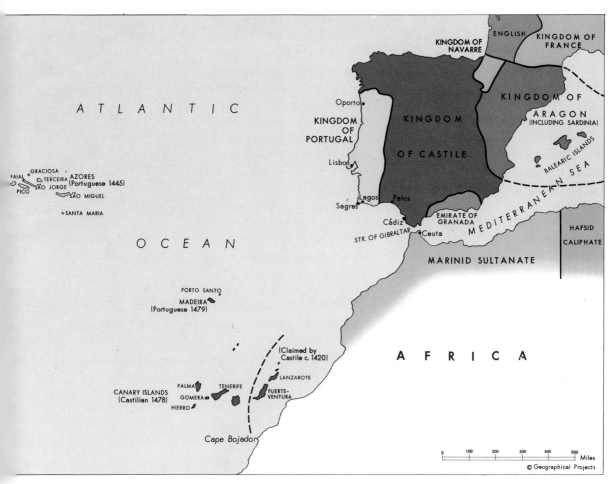

 shows map labels: ATLANTIC OCEAN, KINGDOM OF NAVARRE, ENGLISH, KINGDOM OF FRANCE, Oporto, KINGDOM OF PORTUGAL, KINGDOM OF CASTILE, KINGDOM OF ARAGON (INCLUDING SARDINIA), BALEARIC ISLANDS, Lisbon, GRACIOSA, TERCEIRA, AZORES (Portuguese 1445), FAIAL, SÃO JORGE, PICO, SÃO MIGUEL, SANTA MARIA, Lagos, Palos, Sagres, MEDITERRANEAN SEA, Cádiz, EMIRATE OF GRANADA, HAFSID CALIPHATE, STR. OF GIBRALTAR, Ceuta, MARINID SULTANATE, PORTO SANTO, MADEIRA (Portuguese 1479), (Claimed by Castile c. 1420), AFRICA, LANZAROTE, CANARY ISLANDS (Castilian 1478), PALMA, TENERIFE, GOMERA, FUERTE-VENTURA, HIERRO, Cape Bojador, 0 100 200 300 400 500 Miles, © Geographical Projects

Above: Portugal and Castile, just before Ferdinand and Isabella expelled the Moors from Granada, showing the Azores, Madeira, and the Canary Islands.

...ling them the Fortunate Isles. Since then, the Canary Islands had ...en visited from time to time by sailors from the Moslem Empire, ...noa, Normandy, Castile, and Portugal. By the time Prince Henry's ...plorations began, Castile had already staked a claim to the two islands ...arest the African coast, Lanzarote and Fuerteventura. The outer ...nds, however, remained virtually unexplored. Realizing their ...tential as springboards for future African exploration, Henry de-...mined to take possession of these islands.

...n 1425, he sent a fleet carrying more than 2,000 men and 100 horses ...conquer the outer island of Gran Canaria, and in 1427, he sent another ...t on the same mission. Both expeditions, hampered by inadequate

provisions, failed to overcome the stubborn resistance of the natives. But efforts to take the outer islands were renewed from time to time, and Portugal soon made enough headway to worry the Castilians.

In 1435, Castile and Portugal asked the pope to settle the question of possession of the Canaries. His decision, given in 1436, was that Castile should retain Lanzarote and Fuerteventura, while Portugal should have a free hand in the outer islands of Gran Canaria, Tenerife, Palma, and Gomera. Much later, in 1479, Spanish sovereignty over the Canaries was finally established by the treaty of Alcacova between Portugal and Castile. However, while Portugal retained her right to the outer isles, her sailors made good use of them as bases for replenishing their drinking water and food supplies on long voyages.

Oddly enough, the sister islands of Madeira and Porto Santo had never yet been claimed, despite the fact that they lay closer to Europe than the Canaries. During the first years of Henry's exploration program they became Portuguese possessions almost by accident.

As early at 1418, Henry had fitted out a ship for two of his young squires, João Gonçalves Zarco and Tristan Vaz Teixeira, and instructed them to sail south along the African coast beyond Cape Bojador, until they came to Guinea. Zarco and Teixeira had not sailed far before

Left: Gran Canaria, the most fertile of the Canary Islands (known to Ptolemy as the Fortunate Islands) in the Atlantic 60 miles northwest of the African coast. It was to Gran Canaria that Prince Henry turned his attention in the early 1400's when two expeditions sent by him tried to gain control of the island. A decree by the pope in 1436 gave Portugal control of the outer islands, among them Gran Canaria, and they made good use of bases set up there. The control lasted until Spain took over all the islands in the late 1400's.

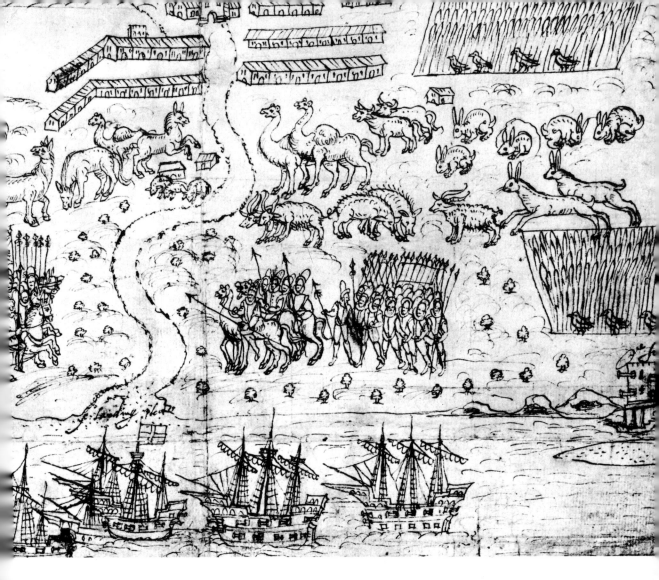

ey met with contrary winds. They had to do a good deal of tacking
make any headway, and in the course of their maneuvers, sighted
rto Santo. Landing there, they decided that the island was well suited
r colonization, and sailed back to Sagres immediately to report the
od news.

Henry was pleased with their report and at once sent some colonists
Porto Santo. Unfortunately, however, one of them took along a
egnant rabbit. Its first offspring multiplied many times very quickly,
d soon multitudes of hungry rabbits were eating up everything the
lonists planted. In the end, the settlers had to abandon Porto Santo
d transfer to Madeira some 12 leagues distant—this time without
bits! Madeira's abundant sunshine and water made crops flourish,
rticularly sugar cane and grapes, and the islanders soon prospered
exporters of wine and sugar.

The Azores, like the Canaries, had been discovered centuries before,
hough no one knows exactly when or by whom. Certainly their po-
ons had been plotted (albeit inaccurately) on the Laurentian Por-
an, a map made in 1381. However, like Madeira and Porto Santo,

Above: the island of Lanzarote, the
most easterly of the Canary Islands,
from an old manuscript drawing of
about 1590. Lanzarote and Fuerteventura remained under Castilian rule by
the pope's decree of 1436. Mountainous and barren, and of volcanic
origin, the island is about 31 miles
long and 5 to 10 miles in width.

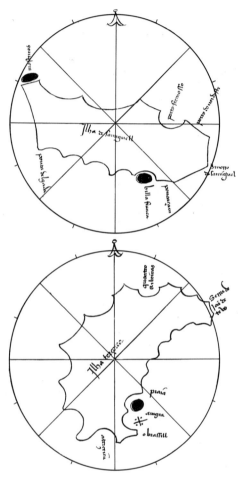

the Azores were first colonized by the Portuguese. In 1431, Henry sent Gonçalo Cabral to sail westward in search of islands he believed must exist. Cabral was unsuccessful, but the following year he reached an island which he named St. Mary. Twelve years later, Henry, upon hearing reports of a larger island, commissioned Cabral to set out again. As a result of this voyage the island of St. Michael was discovered in 1444, and the first Portuguese settlers arrived there about 1445. The Azores never achieved the same economic importance as Madeira. They were, however, very useful havens for Portuguese vessels returning from South Africa, because the trade winds made the detour to the Azores the easiest way home.

On the credit side, then, the first years of Henry's exploration program had produced some satisfactory results. His men had struck a number of minor blows against Moslem power in the Mediterranean. They had colonized Madeira and staked a claim to the Azores. They were close to taking several of the Canary Islands. *But they had not yet ventured beyond Cape Bojador.* In this, the first step in Henry's exploration program, his mariners had produced no results at all. Henry's patience, like his money, was fast running out.

In the year 1433, the prince placed one of his squires, Gil Eannes, in command of a barca, and once again gave the order to proceed as far as possible down the African coast. The squire set out bravely, but in the end, he "made the same voyage as the others had made and, overcome by the same dread, did not pass beyond the Canary Islands." On his return, Eannes unwisely excused his failure by detailing the extreme perils he had been warned about by other seamen. At this Henry's patience finally gave out. "In truth, I marvel at these imaginings which have possessed you all," he said. "If these things possessed an authority, however small, I might still find excuse for you. But I am astonished that you accept them from the opinion of mariners who know only the navigation of Flanders, and cannot handle a compass or a chart of the seas."

With this, Henry sent Eannes out to try again, and the good squire "promised himself resolutely that he would never again appear before his lord without having accomplished the mission charged upon him."

This resolution must have stood him in good stead. For in 1434 Eannes returned with the joyful news that he had succeeded in rounding Cape Bojador. He had landed just beyond it and gathered a few plants—St. Mary's roses—to show the prince what grew there.

Above: an early map of the Azores, showing the islands of Terciera and Samiguell, from Cartas de Valentim Fernandes 1506—1508. While the rough shape of the islands is correct, the mapmaker has made no attempt to make a detailed outline of the coast. The Azores, which were colonized by Portugal in the mid-1400's, are the remotest group of any of the Atlantic islands, the nearest continental land—800 miles east of Samiguell—being Cape da Roca in Portugal. The islands became a rendezvous for fleets on their voyages from the Indies.

Above: Gabo Girão, a lofty headland
stretching out into the sea from
Madeira, the larger of the two inhabited islands in the Funchal group in
the North Atlantic, about 360 miles
from the African coast. Madeira was
colonized by Henry the Navigator
and much of the island brought under
cultivation. A thriving trade in
Madeiran sugar was soon started.

Below: Hull evolution 1400—1600.
On the left is a carrack with
consolidated forecastle and raking
guns in round open ports. This later
developed, as on the right, with two
counters aft, a heavy forecastle with
boomkins (spurs on either side of
the bow holding the foresail foretack)
beneath. Its guns are in rectangular
ports furnished with lids.

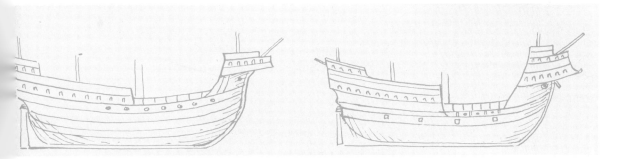

Right: Resurrection plant (Anastatica hierochuntina), the "St. Mary's rose" found by Gil Eannes when he landed after succeeding in rounding the dreaded Cape Bojador in 1433. A member of the mustard family, during the dry season the mature plant loses its leaves and the stem curls into a ball with the seed pod inside. This is blown about by the wind, like a tumbleweed, until the rainy season. When wet the plants unfold and the branches spread out and turn green.

In general, his voyage had been calm and uneventful, and "he had fo matters very different from what he and others had imagined."

If we think only in terms of geography, Eannes' voyage had acc plished little, for Cape Bojador is only 150 miles south of the Cana The value of his voyage, however, lay not in passing a particular c but in surmounting a barrier of fear. For centuries, sailors had thou of the seas south of Bojador as a waste of waters fraught with ho and disaster. To them, the sea there was aptly described by the A term for it— "the Sea of Darkness."

Eannes, whose voyage had done so much to dispel man's fears ceived a knighthood. Now many other seamen came forward and clared they were ready to go farther than Eannes.

Left: monk seals found along the northwest coast of Africa. Baldaya took seals back to Portugal from an expedition 500 miles south of Cape Bojador. He had previously seen footprints in the area, so Prince Henry sent him back to speak with, and possibly to capture, some of the inhabitants. Baldaya failed to make contact with a group of people that he saw, so he killed and collected the seals to make up for his failure.

Prince Henry knew that Eannes' success marked the long awaited turning point in his campaign. This opinion was supported by his elder brother Edward, who had become king on the death of their father in the summer of 1433. As proof of his faith in the future of his brother's program, Edward improved Henry's financial position by making over to him the "royal fifth" of all profits accruing from Madeira's fast-growing export trade.

In 1435 Henry dispatched another expedition, consisting of a barinel captained by Alfonso Gonçalves Baldaya, and a caravel captained by Gil Eannes. The two ships sailed 200 miles beyond Cape Bojador, and brought back the news that, on landing, the crew had seen the tracks of men and camels.

When Baldaya reported this to the prince, Henry said, "Since you have found these footprints, it seems to me that there must be some population not far off, or perchance there are people who go there with merchandise for some seaport. Thus I intend to send you again in the same barinel; and I charge you to do your best to contrive to speak with these people, or capture some of them so that I may receive intelligence of their land."

It was probably in 1436 that Baldaya and his small crew set out again. This time Baldaya sailed almost 100 miles beyond Bojador before landing near an inlet which he mistook for a river mouth. Here he dispatched two youths, mounted on the horses they had brought with them, and armed, to look for local inhabitants or traders. They had ridden several miles along the shore when they suddenly spotted a group of 19 men armed with spears. Thinking that the men would be at a disadvantage because they were not on horseback, the two youths fell upon the group in an attempt to take prisoners. In the fray that followed, they not only failed to take captives, but barely escaped with their lives. They managed to get away and reach the coast, where they reported to Baldaya. The next day, he and a few others returned to the place where the armed men had been seen, but the natives had disappeared.

Baldaya had failed in his mission to "speak with these people or capture some of them," or to discover "whether they were Moors or Gentiles or what was their manner of living." But before returning, he did what he could to make up for it. On a sandbank near where his barinel lay at anchor there were thousands of large seals. He and his men killed as many as they could and loaded their ship with the skins. This

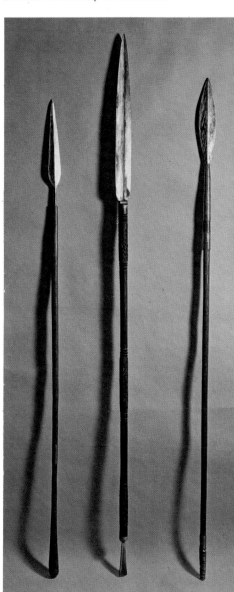

Above: three short stabbing spears of the type used by African tribes. The center one was merely for ceremonial use, but the others were actual weapons used against the Portuguese invaders.

Right: richly decorated Portuguese map of about 1558 by Bastiam Lopez. It has flags of nationality of the various countries shown, and in the African continent are pictures of Portuguese horsemen chasing Moors, above a range of mountains. On the southwest coast is a castle surrounded by palm trees and guarded by a rampant lion.

Above: Prince Ferdinand of Portugal, Henry's youngest brother. When the Portuguese attack on Tangier in 1437 failed, Ferdinand had to be left behind as a hostage. He died six years later, still a Moslem prisoner.

was to be the first cargo of commercial value to reach Portugal from the bulge of Africa. Before returning home, Baldaya sailed another 100 miles southwest and reached the narrow bay that was later named Río de Oro—river of gold. Baldaya did not know it, but he was within striking distance of the gold-bearing area regularly visited by Arab caravans.

When Baldaya finally reached home with his cargo of sealskin, it seemed that the time had come at last for a full-scale program of exploration, and the realization of Henry's hopes. But just at this moment an ill-conceived attempt to repeat the success of the Ceuta episode played havoc with the fortunes of Portugal in general and of the royal family in particular.

Henry's younger brother Ferdinand (Fernando), now 34, was impatient to be knighted on the field of battle. He therefore urged King Edward to mount an attack on the northern African port of Tangier, a Moslem stronghold about 40 miles west of Ceuta. Somewhat reluctantly, Edward agreed and launched the attack in August, 1437, with Prince Henry leading the army.

The expedition failed disastrously and the Portuguese were allowed to escape with their lives only by promising to restore Ceuta to the Moslems. Furthermore, they were compelled to leave Prince Ferdinand behind as a guarantee of good faith. In the end, Ceuta was not returned to the Moslems. The Church maintained—as, of course, Henry did—that a Christian city (and Ceuta was now officially a Christian city) belonged to God and could not be handed over to infidels. As a result, the luckless Prince Ferdinand had to be left in Moslem hands. He died, still a Moslem prisoner, some six years later. In the meantime, King Edward, who had for a long time been in poor health and was now tortured by remorse over the fate of his brother, worried himself into an early grave.

In September, 1438, when Edward died, his son and heir, Alfonso, was still a child. The question of whether his mother or his eldest uncle, Peter, should be regent until Alfonso came of age brought Portugal to the verge of civil war. Prince Henry played a leading role in the delicate diplomatic maneuvers which eventually restored an atmosphere of calm under the regency of Prince Peter. But not until the matter was finally settled, in 1441, could Henry give his attention once more to exploration.

In that year he sent out a small vessel under the command of one An-

Os montes claros em a frica

Caste lodamina

Above: a thriving trade in human beings was set up in the mid-1400's when at last Prince Henry's explorers rounded the fearful Cape Bojador. Expeditions from 1441 on brought back captives, from whom Prince Henry tried to find out about their country, and whom he tried, with moderate success, to convert to Christianity. Others, however, saw the captives only as the basis of a lucrative slave trade, and more and more expeditions were undertaken for the sole purpose of bringing slaves to the Lagos markets.

Gonçalves, and an armed caravel under the command of a knight, Nu⸗ Tristão. Because Gonçalves was very young, he was simply ask⸗ to go as far as he could and return with a cargo of sealskins and seal o⸗ Tristão, accompanied by one of Henry's Moorish servants to act ⸗ interpreter, was instructed to bring back natives of the African co⸗ who might be able to provide useful geographical information. Gonç⸗ ves reached a point just south of the Río de Oro and quickly collect⸗ his cargo. Then, on his own initiative, he decided to take a few captiv⸗ With nine crew members he marched inland, and, after several sk⸗ mishes, managed to take two prisoners: a Berber of the Azenegue tri⸗ and a Negro slave who belonged to the Azenegues.

By then, Tristão's caravel had reached the same spot. The two cre⸗ joined forces in a second inland raid. This time, after surroundi⸗ two small camps of natives, they took 10 more captives, includi⸗ a chief named Adahu, who had traveled more than his fellows and co⸗ speak the Moorish tongue. We are told that, from Adahu, Prince He⸗

ter obtained "intelligence of a great measure of the affairs of the region
which he inhabited." Gonçalves now returned to Portugal, while
Tristão, in an unsuccessful attempt to take more captives, sailed farther
on to Cape Blanc, a point about 250 miles south of the Río de Oro.

Prince Henry regarded the 12 captives primarily as sources of information and as souls to be saved. But other men in Portugal saw them
in terms of potential profit. To such men, the capture of these people
heralded the opening of a lucrative slave trade. As a result, however
lofty Prince Henry's motives remained, more and more of his captains
took advantage of their sailing orders to raid the African coast for slaves
and cheap-bought cargoes. Some genuine exploration still went on,
but it usually took second place to these more mercenary objectives.
The regent, Prince Peter, certainly realized that African exploration
now appeared capable of paying dividends. Knowing how much Henry had already spent on fostering African exploration, Peter made over
to him the "royal fifth" of all profits it might bring in. He also decreed
that no ship was to sail beyond Cape Bojador without Henry's permission.

In 1442, Gonçalves made a second voyage. With him he took Chief
Adahu and two of the other Azenegue captives, hoping to exchange
them for a greater number of the Azenegues' Negro slaves. He succeeded,
and returned home with 10 slaves, as well as a little gold dust and many
ostrich eggs. But he had not advanced the cause of exploration at all,
having sailed no farther than the Río de Oro.

The following year, Nuno Tristão did sail about 100 miles beyond
Cape Blanc to a bay, in present-day Mauritania, in which he discovered
the island of Arguim. (Here the Portuguese soon afterward established
their first permanent trading station in tropical Africa.) At Arguim
he took 28 captives and promptly set sail for home, "more joyous than
the first time because the take was greater, and also because he was alone
and had no need to share it."

When Tristão returned, he landed at the port of Lagos. The report
of his success soon reached the ears of the city's treasurer, a man called
Lançarote. Seeing the chance for a profitable investment, Lançarote,
with Henry's permission, equipped and manned six caravels and set
out to duplicate Tristão's voyage. In and around Arguim and its adjacent islands—Tider and the Isle of Herons—he and his crew captured
more than 200 men, women, and children, who were brought back to
Lagos and sold at public auction. Azurara reports with pride that most

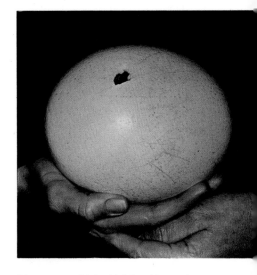

Above: an ostrich chick breaking out
of an egg. Ostriches are the largest
living birds—the male can be as tall
as 8 feet, and can weigh 345 pounds.
The female lays as many as 10 eggs
in a clutch and these are of equally
mammoth proportions. Nearly six
inches in diameter, weighing about
three pounds, they have a thick shell
and are a dull yellow color. Antão
Gonçalves took several ostrich eggs
back with him from Cape Blanc.

Left: a young Arab boy holding a goat. For many centuries before the arrival of the Portuguese invaders, nomadic Arab tribes had wandered through the African continent spreading the word of Islam by conquest.
Below: Lagos, seaport of southern Portugal. It was here that Prince Henry established the town of Sagres, near Cape St. Vincent. In the 1440's, Lagos became the center of the slave trade, where captives from the islands around Cape Blanc were auctioned.

of them were well treated and later became good Christians, but spares none of the grim details in describing the agonizing scene the auction as husbands were parted from their wives, and child from their mothers.

Despite the growing Portuguese interest in slaving, Henry him continued to press for exploration. He now equipped a caravel Gonçalo de Sintra, a man reared from childhood in his own househo and urged him to concentrate on discovery and on nothing else. N

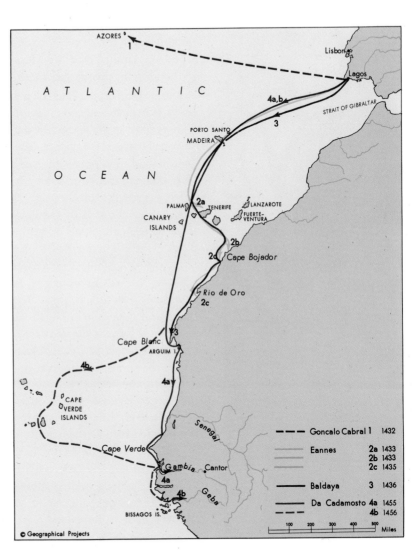

Above: the routes of the Portuguese explorers during the mid-1400's, west to the Azores, and southwest through the Canary Islands and down the west coast of Africa.

ape Blanc, however, De Sintra was tempted to try his hand at slaving. ut the people of this region had learned from the fate of their hapless eighbors to beware of white men. Turning on the would-be slavers, ey killed De Sintra and seven of his companions.

In the same year (1444), several vessels set out from Portugal with e laudable purpose of arranging a treaty of trade with the Azenegues. he attempt failed—again because previous Portuguese visits had ught the people to distrust white men. The expedition did have one

Above: the use of feathers and paint by the Africans led the Portuguese to conclude that these people, whose customs, behavior, and dress were so different from their own, were uncivilized, primitive, and childlike.

notable result, however. One of the crew, João Fernandes, who understood the language of the Moors, requested that he be left behind to live among the people and learn their ways. After staying with the Moors and their Berber and Tuareg neighbors for several months, he returned to Portugal and gave an informative report to the prince.

Thereafter, several expeditions did venture much farther south—if only because it was easier to capture slaves where the white man's reputation had not preceded him. But, in general, exploration for its own sake continued to take a back seat to slave trading.

In 1445, on his third voyage, Nuno Tristão sailed far beyond Arguin Island, past the end of the desert coast, and reached a shore "where there were many palms and other trees, and all the fields looked to be fertile." Here Tristão took 21 captives before he set sail for home. Some months later, an elderly man named Dinis Dias, who had turned explorer because "he was unwilling to let himself grow soft in the well-being of repose," set a new record by sailing some 500 miles south of Cape Blanc and reaching the most westerly point in all Africa. This point (the site of present-day Dakar, in Senegal), he named Cape Verde. Perhaps the success of Dias' voyage owed something to the fact that he contented himself with taking only four captives.

During the next three years, there were numerous other expeditions, one of which consisted of a great fleet of 26 vessels from Lagos, Lisbon, and Madeira. But few captains who set out from Portugal during this period sailed farther south than had old Dinis Dias. In 1446, however, Nuno Tristão succeeded in reaching a point about 200 miles south of Cape Verde. Here he met his death in a slave raid. But on this, his last voyage, he had reached the shores of Guinea. Later in 1446, a man named Álvaro Fernandes sailed some 500 miles beyond Cape Verde, reaching the area now occupied by Sierra Leone.

Although there were other voyages down the African coast during the next two years, no further progress had been made by the end of 1448 when Azurara brought his *Chronicle of the Discovery of Guinea* to a close. The *Chronicle* had been commissioned by King Alfonso V and scrutinized by Prince Henry himself, and in all probability its coming to stop in 1448 was because civil war broke out. This caused a second major pause in Portuguese exploration. In any event, Guinea had long last been reached, and possibly Azurara believed that "what came to pass afterward did not call for such effort and fatigue" as had been required in pioneering the first 1,500 miles of coastline beyond Bojador.

South to Hope
4

The cause of the civil war, which brought exploration to a halt, aro[se]
from a quarrel between the young Alfonso V and his uncle Peter, t[he]
former regent. Prince Peter was defeated and killed on the field of batt[le]
in May, 1449.

Prince Henry, torn between love for his brother and loyalty to [his]
nephew, the king, had taken no part in the fighting. Neverthele[ss]
it had been impossible for him to devote his energies to explorati[on]
until peace was restored.

Then another hindrance to Portuguese exploration presented itse[lf].
This was the continuing trouble (despite the pope's decision of 14[3?])
with Castile over possession of the Canaries. Between 1450 and 14[??]
the two nations were frequently on the brink of war over this issu[e].
During this time, many of Henry's ships were needed in the vicin[ity]

the Canaries to protect Portuguese interests there. As a result, he
⸱d few ships available for voyages of discovery.

With the conclusion of hostilities between Portugal and Castile,
⸱rtuguese exploration seems to have sprung to life once more—al-
⸱ough at first in a small way. Certainly, Portuguese ships began
⸱siting the African coast in ever-increasing numbers. Among the
⸱ariners of this period was Alvise da Cadamosto, a Venetian sea trader
⸱ho entered Prince Henry's service in 1455 and who later wrote a full
⸱count of his experiences. His narrative, although it records no great
⸱scoveries, tells us much about what had so far been achieved by Portugal
⸱ the way of exploration and colonization. It also gives us a vivid descrip-
⸱n at first-hand of what it was like to be one of Prince Henry's mariners.
⸱Cadamosto first took to sea trading in an effort to restore the lost

Above: ladies and gentlemen of the
Portuguese court, showing the
elaborate style of dress fashionable in
the 1500's. One of the difficulties that
explorers had to face was that their
orders came from a center of culture
and luxury and may not always have
been relevant to the rough and ready
conditions of the explorers. But
the captains under Henry the Navigator
were fortunate, as the prince
apparently kept himself aware of the
circumstances of his men and was
sympathetic to their needs.

Above: Alfonso V succeeded his
father, Edward, when only six years
old. He was under the regency of his
mother and then of his uncle, Peter,
whose daughter he married. After
assuming control in 1448, he was
misled into believing Peter to be a
rebel and Peter was killed at the
ensuing battle of Alfarrobeira.
Alfonso successfully invaded
Moorish Africa and became
known as "Alfonso the African."

fortunes of his family. He had already visited lands as far apart as Egypt
and the Netherlands when, in 1454, he set sail with a trading fleet bound
for Flanders which made a stop in southern Portugal. While there
Cadamosto learned of the profitable voyages being made by Portuguese
seamen, and saw some of the valuable cargoes they were bringing back
from Madeira and Guinea. He made inquiries, and found that a foreigner could participate in this trade if he obtained Henry's permission
and accepted his terms.

Having obtained the necessary permission, Cadamosto immediately
abandoned the Venetain fleet to enter Henry's service. The prince offered an adventurous man every chance of making money with no financial risk to himself. Henry would provide him with a caravel and goods
to trade free of charge. In return, he was to sail as far as he found reasonable and return with as much valuable cargo as possible. The profit
from the sale of the cargo would be divided equally between the prince
and himself. If there should be no profit—and even if there should be
no cargo to speak of—Henry had agreed to stand the loss.

Cadamosto set out on his first voyage for the prince on March 2,
1455. In three days he had reached Porto Santo, and in six, Madeira.
Although he did not stay long at either, he had much to report about
both. Porto Santo, he found, had by now been successfully colonized,
and the settlers there were prospering by raising cattle and exporting
quantities of honey and wax. In Madeira, there were now four settlements. Besides producing wine and sugar for export, they were growing wheat, cutting timber, manufacturing furniture, and raising
cattle.

Cadamosto then called in at Gomera and Ferro in the Canaries. Here
he learned that, as in the neighboring islands of Lanzarote and Fuerteventura, most of the natives had been converted to Christianity.

But it was about the African coast that Cadamosto had most to report.
At Cape Blanc, he learned of the caravan route between the north
coast of Africa and Timbuktu (a city in present-day Mali). Moslem
traders from northern Africa traveled south along this route carrying
articles of brass and silver which they traded at Timbuktu for gold,
pepper, and slaves. Cadamosto discovered, however, that already the
volume of trade along this overland route had been noticeably affected
by the Portuguese sea trade. Coastal goods that had once been available
only to overland merchants were now being bought by Portuguese
traders and shipped to Lisbon.

PRIMO

¶ In comenza el libro de la prima Nauigatione per loe ceano a le terre de Nigri de la Bassa Ethiopia per comandamento del Illust. Signor Infante Don Hurich fratello de Don Dourth Re de Portogallo.

¶ El primo che ha trouato la nauigation del mare oceano uerso el mezodi. c.i.

Ssendo lo Alouise da Cada mosto stato el primo: ch delanation de la nobel Cita de Venesia siadimosso anauigare el mare occeano di sori del stretto de zibeltera uerso le pte demezodi in leterre de Nigri dla bassa Ethiopia. doue i qsto mio itinerario hauendo uisto moke cose noue: & degne di qualche noto: acioche quelli che de mi haueráno adiscendere possino itendere qllo sia stato lo aio mio in hauer messo accerchare uarie cose in diuersi & noui lochi: che ueraméte & icostumi: & lilochi nri in cóparatió dela cosa per me ueduta & intesa: uno altro mondo se poteria chiamare: de qua e adunqua pcesso: che benemerito farne qualche nota. che come lamemoria me seruira: cusi cu la péna transcorero le cose pdicte: le quale se p mi nó seráno cusi ordinatamente messe: come lamateria richiede: almeno nó manchero de itegra uerita in ogni pte: & questo senza dubio piu psto de mancho dicendo: che ultra el uero alcuna cosa narrando. Adúqua e da sapere: che qlui che fu el primo Inuétore de far nauigar qsta pte del mare occeáo uer

a

Farther south, at the island of Arguim, Cadamosto saw the fort that had been erected on Henry's instructions to protect Portuguese trade. Here at Arguim, he learned, only licensed and resident Portuguese merchants were allowed to trade directly with the Arabs. In exchange for such goods as wheat and cloth, which were brought south from Portugal in Henry's ships, merchants obtained a considerable quantity of gold, and as many as 1,000 Negro slaves each year. Henry apparently hoped that slaves purchased from the Arabs would later convert to Christianity more readily than slaves that had been captured from their villages by raiders who were professed Christians. From Arguim, Cadamosto pushed on to the Senegal River, which meets the sea about 100 miles north of Cape Verde. The Portuguese had already established trade relations with the people of this area and, at a spot some 50 miles farther on, Cadamosto decided to do some trading

f his own. In negotiations with a chief named Budomel, he traded Spanish horses, woolen cloth, and Moorish silk for slaves.

From Cadamosto's account, it appears that relations between the Portuguese and the native peoples in this part of the coast were very cordial. Budomel saw to it that Cadamosto was royally entertained and invited his guest to enter the local mosque where he himself worshiped. Also, as it was now common practice for Henry's mariners to be accompanied by African slaves who spoke Portuguese, the African chief and the Venetian sea trader were able to talk about the Christian faith. From what Budomel said, Cadamosto was certain that only the fear of losing power among his own people prevented the chief from converting to Christianity.

The most distant point reached by Cadamosto on this, his first voyage for Prince Henry, was the mouth of the Gambia River. This river in 100 miles south of Cape Verde, in present-day Gambia. But, although he had made no notable discoveries, he had taken careful note of all he had seen. Years later, when he wrote an account of his travels, he recalled vividly his first sight of lions, elephants, and hippopotamuses, his first taste of ostrich eggs, and his first observations in the unfamiliar skies over Africa of constellations he had never seen before.

Above: the Senegal River. Known then as Senega, the mouth was entered by Dinis Dias in 1445. He thought it was the western arm of the Nile.

Left: trading has probably not changed very substantially in the last 500 years and the goods that the Portuguese brought back were probably acquired in markets not very different from this one at Abidjan on the Ivory Coast of West Africa. Built on a peninsula into a lagoon, Abidjan has become one of the best ports in West Africa.

Right: traditional designs of silverware made by Kabyle craftsmen from Algeria and northwestern Tunisia. These examples show a pendant, bracelets, a pair of brooches, and a casket box of the type that would have been fashionable in the 1500's.

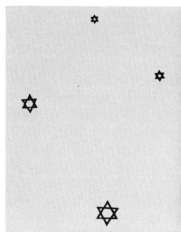

Left: the Southern Cross (Crux Australis) was probably the constellation that Cadamosto described in the account of his journeys. It is in the path of the Milky Way and its bright stars form a small, but well-defined cross, the upright of which points almost to the south celestial pole. The constellation was an entirely new one to the first Portuguese explorers, since it is not visible much north of the Equator.

Within a year of his return to Portugal, Cadamosto set out again, this time with three caravels. Leaving Lagos in early May, he sailed ast the Canaries without stopping, and made straight for Cape Blanc. ast off that cape, he tells us, his ships were overtaken by a fierce storm hich carried them off course in a southwesterly direction for several ys. In this way, Cadamosto says, his ships came upon two large undis-vered islands—part of a large group off Cape Verde. The truth of damosto's claim that he himself was the original discoverer of e islands is doubtful.

When the storm that had driven him off course subsided, Cadamosto ain followed the coast southward. He first revisited the area around the negal River, and then sailed on to the mouth of the Gambia River.

Above: hippopotamuses on the banks of a river in Africa. These animals are extremely large and ungainly, with thick bodies and short legs, but they are surprisingly agile. Their hairless skin is almost two inches thick in places. They spend much of their time in water and their eyes and nostrils protrude to enable the animal to see and breathe while floating. The exotic animals of Africa were a source of wonder to the explorers, who contin-ually commented upon them in the records of their voyages.

Below: an African woman selling
beads in the market at Cotonou,
Dahomey, in West Africa. Once
used as a currency for buying slaves,
beads have always been, and in fact
still are, an important article of trade
all over the African continent.

After traveling many miles up the river (along whose banks he saw numerous elephants and hippopotamuses), he encountered a native tribe. With the chief of this tribe, one Batti-Mansa, he traded some of his European goods for slaves and a little gold. In addition, Cadamosto was given many presents, including gold ornaments, fruit, and exotic animals. He then traveled some 100 miles farther south along the coast to the Bissagos Islands (opposite present-day Portuguese Guinea). But, finding trade impossible because none of his interpreters could speak the local language, he set sail for home.

In 1458 — that is about two years after Cadamosto had made his second voyage — another expedition was also engaged in exploring and trading along the African coastline. It consisted of three caravels under the command of Diogo Gomes, a man of Prince Henry's household. Apparently Gomes' vessels followed much the same course as Cadamosto's. Like Cadamosto, Gomes sailed up the Gambia River, where he also did some trading. He seems to have done rather better in this regard than Cadamosto, however, for he succeeded in obtaining some 180 pounds of gold for the cloth and beads he had brought with him. Existing accounts tell us little more about his expedition, apart from noting that Gomes was the first Portuguese navigator to use the quadrant.

By the time that Cadamosto and Gomes returned home, Henry was nearing 70 and far from well. He died in November, 1460, never having seen the distant lands to whose shores he had sent so many mariners. Yet, through the reports of his captains and correspondents, and through his careful study of all the known facts about West Africa, he had come to know more about this part of the world than any other man of his time.

For 40 years, Henry the Navigator had persevered, with infinite patience and unshakable determination, in forwarding the cause of Portuguese exploration. He, and he alone, had provided the initiative, guidance, and financial backing for this first history-making period of Portuguese exploration. Who would now take up his vital role as exploration's sponsor and director?

Henry's lifelong generosity to his pilots, together with his willingness to bear the loss of commercially unsuccessful voyages, had so impoverished him that he had died heavily in debt. Neither King Alfonso V nor his brother, Fernando, who was legally Henry's heir, wished to be placed in a similar financial position. What is more, both brothers were far more interested in crusading against the Moslems in

Above: an illuminated page from the Comentario do Apocalipse de Lorvao, showing Portuguese horsemen preparing for a crusade against the Moors at the time of Alfonso Henriques (1112—1185).

Right: the voyages which rounded the hump of Africa, eventually moving down across the Gulf of Guinea to the south.

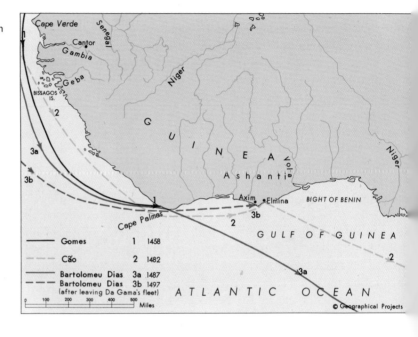

Below: old fort at Dahomey on the Slave Coast of West Africa. The part of the coast fronting onto the Bight of Benin, which includes Dahomey and Lagos, became known as the Slave Coast because, for 300 years, it was the main source of African slaves.

Morocco than in attempting to outflank Islam by exploration.

Nevertheless, Henry's work had made exploration part and parc of Portugal's way of life. And many strictly business-minded men the kingdom knew that voyages to Africa would become increasing profitable in terms of trade. Even King Alfonso, indifferent as he mig have been to exploration for its own sake, saw its value in furtheri trade. And, indeed, it was to be a hardheaded commercial contra that ultimately opened the way for the next great period of Portugue exploration.

For the first few years after Henry's death, however, very few sh sailed farther afield than before. Contemporary records speak of o one expedition—that of Pedro de Sintra—that achieved anything sigr icant during these years. In 1462, De Sintra surpassed Alvaro Fern des' 1446 voyage to Sierra Leone by sailing several hundred miles farth on to the coast of what is now Liberia. Meanwhile, trade with Gui continued, and Diogo Gomes and other captains completed the exp ration of all 10 of the Cape Verde Islands.

Then, in 1469, King Alfonso made a unique, five-year agreem with a wealthy Lisbon citizen named Fernão Gomes. In return exclusive trading rights along the Guinea coast, and all the profits

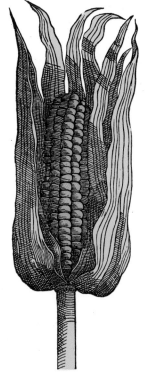

Above: African woman pounding corn and taro root. Both became staple foods for the African peoples. Taro is an herbaceous plant with bulbous underground tubers. It has a very high nutritional value and, when ground down, is mixed into a paste of varying thicknesses.

Above left: an early drawing of mealie corn, described by the Italian geographer, Ramusio, as "the miraculous and famous corn called maize in the India occidental, on which half the world nourishes itself...." Maize was introduced into Europe as a result of the voyages of Christopher Columbus.

ould make from them, Gomes undertook to sponsor the exploration f 400 miles of new coastline every year for five years. This contract, hich made it possible for Portuguese exploration to continue at no st whatsoever to the king, must be one of the most extraordinary history. Still more extraordinary is the fact that it worked. Gomes d not lose by it, since we know that he grew rich enough to contribute ndsomely toward the cost of King Alfonso's crusades in Morocco. nd Portuguese exploration certainly gained by it, for in five years e seamen in Gomes' employ explored 2,000 miles of previously known African coastline.

Unfortunately, none of Gomes' captains wrote of their adventures Cadamosto had written of his. Moreover, because exploration was w in private hands, there was no royal historian like Azurara to record eir deeds. All that contemporary records tell us of this momentous riod of exploration is a few names and a few facts.

We do know that one captain, named Da Costa, sailed beyond Li- ria to Axum, on the coast of present-day Ghana. Axum later became ortified center for Portugal's burgeoning gold trade. Then Pero Escolar and João de Santarem sailed 100 miles beyond Axum, to nina (also on the Ghana coast). These men, in contrast to their pre-

Above: John II (1455–1495), known as "the Perfect," succeeded his father, Alfonso V, in 1481. He was already much involved in Portuguese exploration and continued to take an interest as king. It was in his reign that Bartolomeu Dias discovered the Cape of Good Hope.

Right: the epic voyages down the coast of Africa searching for the way to the Indies. The brown areas are the vast expanses still unknown to the outside world during the period of the voyages.

decessors, found themselves following the African coast in an easterly, rather than a southerly direction, and probably thought that they were now in sight of a clear eastward passage to Asia. It was at this point that Captain Fernando Póo, having followed the coast to the delta of the Niger River and beyond, reached the Bight of Biafra, the great bay along the coasts of modern Togo, Dahomey, and Nigeria. Far out to sea he discovered the large island that still bears his name. But Póo also found that the mainland coast now ran from north to south once more. Another captain, Lopo Gonçalves, now sailed southward from the Nigerian coast and possibly became the first European to cross the equator, which runs through present-day Gabon.

In 1474, Fernão Gomes' contract expired and, strangely enough, was not renewed. Perhaps his very success had convinced the king that African trade and exploration should once more be the monopoly of the crown—and so it now became. But Alfonso's duties as king prevented him from giving his full attention to the task of supervising exploration. Consequently, he placed his 19-year-old son, John, in charge of it, conferring on him all the duties and privileges that had once belonged to Henry the Navigator.

John had all of Henry's enthusiasm for exploration, and all his determination to outflank Islam and capture a share of the Far East trade. He was an impatient man, bent on quick results, and was as ready to punish as to reward in his eagerness to achieve his goals. Nevertheless, he was unable to get on with his task for several years. From 1475 to 1479, Portugal was involved in a war with Castile, and John himself served as a soldier. Then, in 1481, his father died, and the whole responsibility for governing the country fell upon his shoulders.

Even so, King John II, as he then became, at once showed his interest in the cause of Portuguese exploration. Almost immediately after his accession to the throne, he ordered the rebuilding of the fortifications at Arguim, and the construction of a new fort at Elmina, on the Ghanaian coast. His orders made it clear that he expected these places to serve not only as trading posts, but also as future springboards for new voyages of discovery. The very next year he sent out Diogo Cão to make the first of those voyages.

That extraordinary marine contractor, Fernão Gomes, had set a record by pushing discovery forward at the rate of 400 miles a year. Now, in a single voyage, Diogo Cão pioneered some 850 miles of unexplored coastline. After leaving Elmina, where he stopped to take on provi-

Above: the Congo, largest river in Africa, second only to the Amazon in the world. The mouth was discovered by Diogo Cão in 1482 when he erected a marble pillar on what is now called Sharks Point, recording the discovery, and claiming the land for Portugal. At first the river was called Rio do Padroa (pillar river), or Zaire (native word meaning "big water") but it was finally named Congo, after the ancient kingdom called Kongo.

BLACK SEA

M E D I T E R R A N E A N   S E A

Azores
Terceira
Lisbon
Lagos
Porto Santo
Madeiras
Str. of Gibraltar
Ceuta
Canary Islands
Cape Bojador
Rio de Oro
Cape Blanc
Arguim I.
Senegal
Niger
Cape Verde
Cantor
Gambia
Bissagos Is.
Cape Palmas
Axim Elmina
Bight of Benin
B. of Biafra
Gulf of Guinea
Fernando Pó
Príncipe
São Tomé
Annobón
Cape St. Catherine
Congo
Mouth of the Congo

Tropic of Cancer
Cancer
Red Sea
Nile
Equator
Lake Victoria
Lake Tanganyika

A T L A N T I C

O C E A N

Ascension I.

St. Helena

Cape St. Mary
(Cape Lobo)
Monte Negro
Lake Malawi
Zambezi
Sofala

Tropic of Capricorn
Cabo da Volta
(Dias Pt.)
Cape Cross
Walvis Bay
Cape Corrientes
Natal

Orange
St. Helena Bay
Mossel Bay
Algoa Bay
Cape of Good Hope
Indian Ocean

Gonçalo Cabral	1	1432
Eannes	2a	1433
	2b	1433
	2c	1435
Baldaya	3	1436
Da Cadamosto	4a	1455
	4b	1456
Gomes	5	1458-60
Cão	6a	1482
	6b	1485
Bartolomeu Dias	7	1487
Da Gama	8	1497-9
(B. Dias after leaving Da Gama 8A)		
Pedro Cabral	9	1500
(with Diogo Dias 9A)		

200 400 600 800 1000
Miles

Tristan-de-Cunha

© Geographical Project

Right: the two caravels commanded by Bartolomeu Dias just before they discovered the Cape of Good Hope on the way back to Lisbon in 1488. Owing to a storm, the cape had not been visible to them on the outward journey. This expedition opened up 1,260 miles of hitherto unknown coast and proved the possibility of an ocean route around Africa.

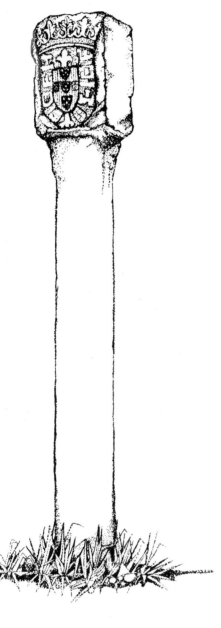

Above: drawing from a book by Diogo Cão which was published in Lisbon. It shows the "Padroa de Santo Agostinho," the pillar, bearing the arms of Portugal, which Cão erected at Cape St. Mary, or as it was then known, "Santo Agostinho."

sions, he pressed on to Cape St. Catherine, just south of the equator St. Catherine marked the very farthest limits of Portuguese navigation so far reached. After three landings made in search of drinking water. Cão came to an area where the ocean water itself was almost as fresh as waters of a lake. This could only mean that he was near the mouth of a mighty river. Sailing shoreward, Cão soon found himself between the banks of the great Congo River. Some way up the river he sighted a village, and, although none of his own interpreters could speak the inhabitants' language, he conversed with them by means of signs, and even managed to trade with them. Then, having set up on the south bank of the river a great stone pillar bearing the arms of Portugal, he continued southward along the coast. He erected a second pillar a Cape St. Mary, more than half the way down the coast of present-day Angola, before he returned home in the early spring of 1484.

King John II was delighted—as well he might have been—with the success of Cão's voyage. The king rewarded Cão generously, and then sent him off again to attempt an even longer voyage.

Little is known about Cão's second voyage. It may have begun in 1484 or in 1485; Cão himself may have arrived home again safely or he may have died on the return journey. On these points contemporary accounts differ. Nevertheless, it is certain that Cão far excelled his first effort, for he again erected two commemorative pillars. The first was put up on the high headland of Cape Negro, more than 100 miles farther south than Cape St. Mary; the second was erected at Cape Cross, less than 200 miles from the Tropic of Capricorn, in present-day South West Africa.

Ptolemy, the master geographer and astronomer of antiquity, had maintained that a huge bridge of land joined southern Africa to southeast Asia, making of the Indian Ocean an enormous land-locked sea. Portugal's hope of pioneering a sea route to East Asia rested on the optimistic premise that Ptolemy was wrong, and that beyond the southern limits of Africa, the Atlantic Ocean merged with the Indian Ocean.

King John felt that Cão must surely have come within reach of Africa's southernmost point, and he was impatient to put the matter to the test. Adding to his burning interest in this question was the fact that in 1486, he had learned (from a Portuguese trader who lived in Benin) of the existence of a powerful Christian king named Ogané who ruled in East Africa. This king, John thought, might well be the legendary Prester John or one of his descendants. John believed that if Portugal

394

uese seamen could pass beyond southern Africa and into the Indian
Ocean, they might accomplish two very important things in one stroke.
Not only might they secure for Portugal a share in the lucrative spice
ade with the East; they might also make the long hoped-for alliance
ith Prester John's kingdom and presumably powerful resources.

To make a start toward accomplishing this dual aim, King John now
spatched an expedition under the command of one Bartolomeu
ias. His mission was to travel southward along the coast of Africa
ntil he reached the southernmost tip of Africa, and then to sail north-
st into the Indian Ocean.

Dias set out from Lisbon in August, 1487, with two small caravels
d a slower, broader-beamed store ship to carry extra food supplies.
mong the items the fleet carried with them were three commemora-
ve stone pillars. Not one was to be erected until the expedition had
ssed Diogo Cão's last landing point.

As far as Cape Cross, Dias probably followed much the same course
Cão had taken. Not far beyond it, and now in unknown waters, he
me to Walvis Bay (halfway down the coast of present-day South West
frica) and there, it seems, he left his cumbersome supply ship. Then
sailed on for some 400 miles. Not until he reached a point close to
e mouth of the Orange River (now the boundary between South
est Africa and South Africa), did he erect his first pillar. After a few
ore days at sea, his ships were caught in a fierce storm, and were driven
adily southward, out of sight of land, for nearly two weeks.

Above: Benin sculpture in bronze of a
warrior-horseman. Negro sculpture
from Benin and other parts of Africa,
has had an increasing influence
on sculpture in other parts of the world.

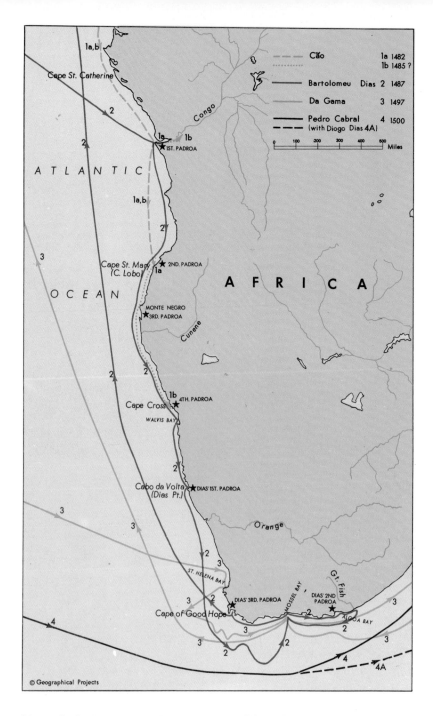

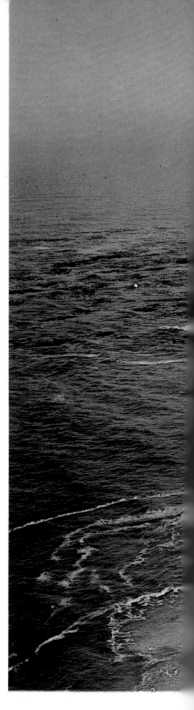

Above: the final stages of exploration down around the Cape of Good Hope.

When the storm abated, Dias naturally sailed eastward, as Portugue[se] sailors had done for the past 70 years when, in sailing along the Afric[an] coast, they had wished to put in to land. Yet, after several days of saili[ng] east, Dias saw no sight of land. Then, beginning to suspect the trut[h,] he turned northward, and soon afterward reached what is now call[ed] Mossel Bay. He was halfway along Africa's southern coast.

Realizing that he had, in fact, found the southern limits of the gre[at] continent, Dias now traveled farther east, and set up a second sto[ne] pillar near Algoa Bay, close to the point at which the south coast [of] Africa begins curving northward. By now, however, his crew believ[ed]

emselves to be dangerously far from their store ship, and insisted
turning back. On the return journey, they came to a great cape which—
ause of the storm that had prevented him from seeing it on the out-
rd voyage — Dias named the Cape of Storms. There he erected his
rd and last pillar before making sail for Portugal.

n December, 1488, when Dias returned, John II received his report
h relief and joy. But he did not approve of Dias' name for the great
e. John knew that this cape, which marked the southern extremity
Africa, held out the promise of a clear sea route to the Indies. For
reason he renamed it the Cape of Good Hope.

Above: the Cape of Good Hope, so
named by King John II of Portugal
after its discovery by Bartolomeu
Dias. Dias, who was blown round it
in a gale, had called it Cabo Tormen-
toso (Cape of Storms), but King John
thought his name more appropriate
for the promontory marking the
southernmost extremity of Africa,
discovery of which had opened up
an ocean route to the Indies.

Below: this sort of opulent picture of the East—here, the birthday party of the Kublai Khan from a manuscript of the travels of Marco Polo—presented an alluring prospect of riches for the country and men able to bypass the Arab middlemen. Bodleian Library MS. Bodley 264, fol. 239.

West to Revelation
5

For a number of years prior to Bartolomeu Dias' voyage, King John had been pestered by a strange young man who claimed to know a sea route to the Indies. In 1484, John had called a committee of experts to assess this plan. The committee finally dismissed it as impossible, and the young man, thoroughly discouraged, had left the country. The young man's name was Christopher Columbus.

Several months after Dias had left for Africa, however, King John had begun to have second thoughts about Christopher Columbus' idea, and had made it known that he would welcome him back. But Columbus did not choose to come back, and John was forced to content himself with the hope that Dias would be successful. The king was still not at all sure that the Indies could be reached by rounding southern Africa, and he feared that, by dismissing Columbus, he had also thrown away the only clue to a possible alternative route. He was vastly relieved, therefore, to hear Dias' promising report on his return from the Cape of Good Hope. Now, perhaps, John could forget the fanciful theories of young Columbus. Little did he know that one day those same fanciful theories would result in one of the world's most historic voyages.

Not much is known about the early life of the man who, at successive stages, styled himself Colombo, Colom, Colomo, and Colon, except that he almost certainly was born in Genoa in 1451, and was the son of a weaver. We also know that he had two brothers, one of whom, Bartholomew, became a highly skilled mapmaker. Columbus himself took to the sea at an early age to make what money he could by trading.

During his early years at sea, Columbus learned a great deal, not only about navigation. He was of a studious nature, and the slow sea passages of those days gave him time to read whatever came to hand. Although he had little formal education, he soon became proficient in Latin, and very knowledgeable about the cosmographical theories then prevalent in Europe. He also got to know the scriptures thoroughly, particularly the books of prophecy. It may have been this that gradually convinced the young seaman that God had destined him to perform great deeds—deeds connected with the sea.

In 1476, he sailed with a French corsair fleet which attacked some Italian ships off the tip of Portugal. In the ensuing battle Columbus' vessel caught fire, and, preferring immersion to incineration, he jumped overboard and struck out for land. The swim was a long one, but at last, completely exhausted, he found the solid ground of Portugal beneath his feet.

Columbus regarded the strange turn of events that had brought him to Portugal as a sign from God. Although a man of strong family feeling, he had never felt any sense of loyalty to his native city of Genoa. If God had now seen fit to cast him up on Portuguese shores, then he would look to Portugal for help in furthering his life's work. He could hardly have come to a more appropriate place than this land of explorers.

He quickly seized whatever opportunities for ocean travel Portugal could offer. Within a year of his arrival, as he himself wrote later, he had visited Thule (by which he meant Iceland) and sailed 100 leagues beyond it. This journey must have meant much to him as the first step in realizing his destiny, for we know that he had already translated the following prophetic passage from Seneca's *Medea*: "There will come a time when a great part of the earth will be opened up, and a new sailor . . . shall discover a new world, and Thule shall no longer be the last of lands."

Perhaps, too, while sailing the silent opal seas of the Arctic, Columbus heard tales of the ancient Vikings, who had voyaged westward to Greenland, and thence southwest to a land called Vinland. Whether or not such tales could be authenticated, Columbus would have believed them, for he was firmly convinced that there *were* lands that could be reached by sailing across the Atlantic. The fact that in the Viking

Right: details of the birth and early life of Christopher Columbus are uncertain, but he was probably born in Genoa in 1451. What is certain, however, is that at a very early age he became a sailor and that he made many voyages with the Portuguese fleet, after being shipwrecked off Lisbon in 1476. During his voyages, and because of his reading, he became convinced that it would be possible to reach Asia by sailing west.

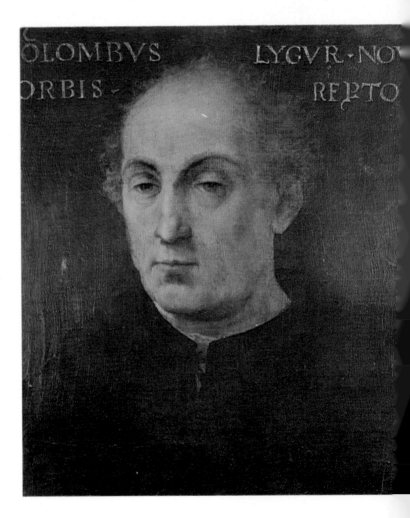

gas they were called "Vinland" was of no importance; he was cer-
in that they were none other than the lands of eastern Asia.

During the next few years, he took part in various Portuguese voy-
es to Porto Santo, Madeira, and the Guinea coast. From the men
met, he picked up more hints of lands across the Atlantic. Among
her things, he learned the curious fact that, on the coasts of Madeira,
e Canaries, and the Azores, carved wooden statuettes were occa-
nally washed ashore when the wind blew strongly and steadily from
e west. Once, he was told, the seas running before a strong west wind
d even washed up the body of a man whose features were neither
ropean nor of any known African race.

Above: this Catalan map of 1375 was
the sort of map available to Henry the
Navigator and his scholars. The areas
which were well-known were correctly
charted, but outside the well-traversed
ways the picture was very sketchy.

Other men had heard these tales with relative indifference. Maybe there *were* distant lands to the west, but what of it? Portuguese seamen had already found the Cape Verde Islands and the Azores. Possibly there were other islands still farther away. But to make a deliberate search for them would be as hopeless as looking for a needle in a haystack. Columbus, however, heard these tales with avid interest, for they offered substantiation for his own developing geographical theories.

Ironically, these theories—which were ultimately to lead Columbus to the New World—were based on a mass of misinformation and erroneous conclusions. He had read in the Apocrypha that "Upon the third day Thou didst command that the waters should be gathered in the seventh part of the earth: six parts hast Thou dried up...." On the basis of this text, he had concluded that six-sevenths of the globe was made up of dry land, the seventh of water.

Like most well-read men of this time, Columbus accepted the fact that the earth is round, and it seemed quite logical to him that the combined landmasses of Europe, Africa, and Asia should occupy the requi-

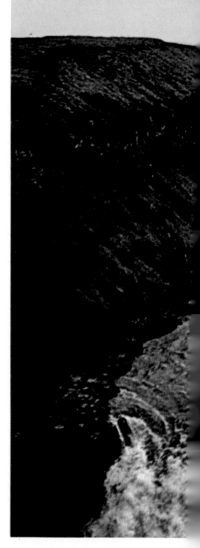

Above: waterfall at Gullfoss ("golden waterfall") in southwest Iceland. Waterfalls are a common sight on the island in the North Atlantic, the most northerly point of which is on the Arctic circle. Columbus claimed to have visited Iceland in the late 1400's. For many years it was considered the last land of the world.

Left: Genoa, port of Liguria, Italy, from the Nuremburg Chronicles of 1493. The prowess of Genoese sailors against the Saracens led to the growth of a powerful navy and it is therefore not surprising that, being born into such an atmosphere Columbus chose a maritime career.

te six-sevenths of the globe. If all the oceans together occupied the
remaining seventh, the Atlantic could not be so very large after all!
Indeed, from his study of the writings of Ptolemy and Marco Polo,
he had concluded that the land between West Africa and eastern Asia
stretched eastward through more than 280° out of the total 360° com-
prising the earth's circumference. Thus, he reasoned, the distance
westward from West Africa to eastern Asia could be traversed by voyaging through less than 80° of longitude.

It remained only to translate that figure into miles. Here Columbus
made still another error. Unaware that the Arab mile is longer than the
European, he used the Arab figure of $62\frac{1}{2}$ miles per degree of longitude at the equator. (There are actually 69 European miles per degree
of longitude at the equator). Then, deciding that the first transatlantic
voyage could best be made in the latitude of the Canaries, where
degree of longitude is smaller than at the equator, he whittled the
figure still further down to 50 miles per degree of longitude. Multiply-
ing 50 miles by 80° of longitude, he then came up with the figure of 4,000

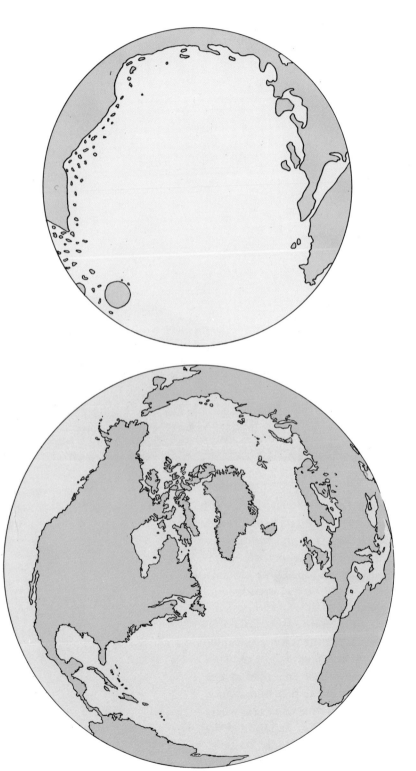

Left: the upper globe shows the worl[d]
as Columbus must have imagined it f[rom]
his inaccurate calculations. The lowe[r]
globe shows the actual proportions, [with]
the unsuspected New World squarel[y in]
the path from Europe to the Asian co[ast]

miles as a measurement of the distance from the Canaries to eastern Asia.

Columbus was somewhat vague about his ultimate destination, since he, like most other men in the Europe of 1492, had only a rough idea of Far Eastern geography. He therefore described his goal variously as Cathay (China), Cipango (Japan), India, the Indies, or the Empire of the Great Khan. Nevertheless, he knew roughly what he meant, and so did everyone he talked to about his great plan.

The man he most wanted to talk to, of course, was "the perfect king," John II of Portugal. How did Columbus, a foreigner of humble origin, gain an audience with the king? It happened (perhaps not entirely by accident) that whenever he was in Lisbon he chose to worship at a convent which was also a home for daughters of the nobility. Columbus was tall, red-haired, handsome, and not without charm. Before long, one of the high-born ladies at the convent had succumbed to his attractions and married him. Marriage into a noble family, of course, made only a matter of time before Columbus gained access to the royal family.

The young seaman began trying to persuade John of his theories in 1478 (three years before John became king), and kept on trying for four fruitless years. It is not known in precisely what way he unfolded his ideas, but, since he was both secretive and given to exaggeration, is reasonable to suppose that he presented them with certain significant omissions and fanciful additions. He doubtless left out what believed to be the main points of evidence for the new sea route, fearing that others might profit from the information and rob him of the glory of discovery. And, in order to gain John's support, he no doubt elaborated on the fabulous wealth of the Orient and stressed the ease with which Portugal might obtain it using his route.

King John, however, was not convinced by Columbus' presentation. Moreover, he was aghast at the high value which this upstart seaman placed on his services. Columbus was demanding nothing less than a knighthood, the title of admiral, the viceroyalty of all the lands he might discover, and a tenth of the value of "all profitable things" found in them. Nevertheless, John did not dismiss the scheme entirely until 1482, when a council of learned men pronounced it impossible.

Disappointed in Portugal, Columbus decided to offer his plan to other monarchs. In 1485, already widowed and with a small son to provide for, he went to Spain, the recently united kingdom of King Ferdinand of Aragon and Queen Isabella of Castile.

Below: it must have been such books that Columbus studied while seeking royal support in Portugal and Spain.

Above: view of Lisbon from the Castello de São Jorge, showing typical terraced houses built into the surrounding hills. The city is divided into five districts and the Castle of St. George is a notable feature of one of them, Lisboa Oriental. Once a Moorish citadel, it was later converted into a fort and barracks. Columbus met his wife, daughter of a noble family, at a convent in Lisbon, giving him his desired entrée to the court.

In Spain, Columbus found his first friends among the learned mon and wealthy seamen of the port of Palos. They were impressed by strange visionary scheme, and introduced him to certain noblem who had access to the king and queen. In this way, Columbus gain his second chance to present his theories before royalty. Again he unfol ed his great plan—mysteriously, guardedly, and with embellishmen again he demanded the same exorbitant price for his services; a again he persevered for six years without success. Indeed, in 1488, thought seriously of going back to King John, but although the P tuguese king expressed himself willing to see Columbus, he did not Probably he refrained from doing so because at this time his brot Bartholomew was—unsuccessfully—laying the plan before Englan King Henry VII.

In 1492, however, Columbus' long battle for royal support met w

den success. In January of that year, Ferdinand and Isabella's forces
tured the city of Granada, the last Moorish stronghold on Spanish
. Euphoric over this victory, they generously decided to sponsor
umbus' scheme and ensure that he had ships, men, and supplies.
ey even accepted his outrageous terms with scarcely a reservation.
y the beginning of August, 1492, three caravels, under the command
Admiral Christobal Colon (as he now called himself), lay ready in
harbor at Palos. His flagship, of which he was also captain, was the
ta María. It was about 115 feet long, with a deck length of over 60
. Her three masts, unlike those of most caravels, carried square sails.
Pinta, faster, but less than half the length of the flagship, was simi-
y rigged. The third ship, the Niña, was even smaller than the Pinta,
was conventionally lateen-rigged.

Although the ships sailed in those days were small, Columbus thought

Above: the refectory of the Franciscan
monastery of La Rábida, Palos, where
the despairing Columbus went in 1485
when yet another attempt to enlist aid
for his venture had failed. It was
through Juan Perez, of the monastery,
that Queen Isabella finally agreed to
his terms and it was from Palos that
he sailed on August 3, 1492.

407

them quite big enough to undertake the voyage across the Atlantic. In fact, for later voyages of discovery, he came to prefer vessels as small as the *Niña* to those as big as the *Santa María*.

Columbus was well pleased with his captains as well. Both Martin Pinzón, captain of the *Pinta*, and his brother Vincente, captain of the *Niña*, were experienced mariners. The brothers had also supplied much of the financial backing for the voyage, and could be depended on to do their utmost to ensure its success.

As to the sailors on board the three vessels, Columbus seems to have been confident that he had with him a sufficient number of "good and seasoned seamen." They were, however, a motley crew. Some 20 or 30 of the men were friends of Columbus, domestic servants, or officers of the king "who fancied to sail out of curiosity." The remaining 90 or so were sailors, shipboys, and pilots. About one fourth of their number were one-time convicts who had been granted pardon in return for their services on this voyage. The others were free men who had been persuaded to take part in the voyage by Martin Pinzón's promises of fame, riches, and the sight of "gold-roofed houses" across the ocean.

At daybreak on the morning of Friday, August 3, 1492, Columbus gave the signal to begin, and the little fleet put out to sea, every sail belling in the wind. Each ship carried cannon and was stocked with about six-months' supply of provisions. On board, too, were "slight wares fit for commerce with barbarous people." (Columbus apparently expected to come upon uncivilized off-shore islands before he reached the cultured and luxurious Orient.)

The fleet's short passage to the Canaries should have been routine and uneventful, but it was not. On the way, the *Pinta* twice broke her helm, causing irritating delays. Then there were three days of dead calm, during which all three ships had to lie motionless. When the fleet did reach port, it was kept waiting for a month while the necessary repairs to the *Pinta* were made. Columbus, feverish with impatience, was comforted only by the fact that the enforced delay had provided an opportunity for exchanging the *Niña's* lateen sails for square ones which would increase her speed.

Not until Thursday, September 6, was the fleet able to leave the Canaries and begin its task of sailing westward into the vast uncharted seas of the Atlantic. Ferro, most westerly of the Canary Islands, gave the sailors what many of them already feared might be their last sight of land. Unlike Columbus, they were not at all sure that their voyage would

Above: Ferdinand and Isabella became patrons of Spanish exploration. Here they are seen waving goodbye to an expedition setting off to the Indies.

end in success. Their concern was not surprising because, although most of them were familiar with the methods of navigating by sun, stars, and compass, few of them had ever done so for long out of sight of land. Now, with wholly unknown seas ahead, they had nothing but these ways of finding their way out and back home.

Columbus alone was firm in his belief that the voyage would bring them safely to their destination. His faith in his plan was unshakable; so was his confidence in his own powers; so, as a result, was his courage.

The fleet was sailing along latitude 28° N. Columbus had chosen this course after concluding, from a passage in Marco Polo's book, that in this latitude he would find Cipango (Japan), the great island that lay some 1,500 miles off the coast of Cathay (the traditional name for China). So Columbus and the Pinzóns kept firmly to that course. It proved to be a lucky choice, for it kept the fleet within the belt of favorable trade winds.

As the familiar shores of Europe dropped ever farther behind them, more and more of the sailors on board the three vessels became dubious and fearful. To keep them from panicking, Columbus gave the order that the fleet was to sail nonstop, day and night, for 700 leagues. After that, it was to sail only during daylight hours. He made no promises, but left the crew to draw the obvious conclusions. They did, and took heart. Their admiral clearly did not expect to sight land for 700 leagues, but after that, he was so sure of sighting it that he would risk no night sailing for fear of missing it.

Columbus calculated rightly that this order would keep his crew from worrying for many days. But what then? It was all very well to assure them that they would sight land after 700 leagues, but what if they did not? After all, Cipango was probably a good 1,000 leagues from the Canaries, and, although Columbus hoped to find islands in between, he could not be sure that his hopes would be rewarded. What would happen if there was no land sighted after 700 leagues? There was a frightening possibility the crew might mutiny. To forestall this, Columbus took to keeping two logbooks. One, meant for his eyes alone, recorded the actual distance covered by the fleet each day. The other, which he made available to the crew, gave a shortened version of the distance covered. It was Columbus' fervent hope that, using this second log, his men might still be waiting to complete the first 700 leagues when they had actually traveled 800 or more.

Meanwhile, another cause for anxiety had presented itself. Along

Above: a model of the *Santa Maria*.
It seems incredible now that anyone
would be bold enough to attempt —
let alone succeed in — crossing the
then-uncharted part of the Atlantic
Ocean in a vessel such as this, a
half-decked ship of 100 tons, with a
crew of only 40 men. Columbus had
faith in himself and in his ship — a
faith which was entirely justified.

Right: early voyages crossing the
Atlantic Ocean. The green edges of the
American continents show the areas
discovered by Europeans by about 1526.

Above: Columbus made entries in his
journal after leaving Palos and is
thought to have drawn sketches of
the ships in his fleet. A book
(belonging to Columbus' son, Ferdin-
and) in the Columbine library in Seville
shows a map decorated with
the outlines of three such ships.

Below: wooden traverse and wind rose
used in conjunction with an hourglass to record changes in direction
and speed during watches.

the Atlantic coast of Europe the compass needle always pointed slightl
east of north. But a mere four days after Ferro had disappeared from
view, Columbus had begun to find that the compass needle was point
ing considerably *west* of north. If ever mariners had needed to trus
the compass it was here, in mid-ocean. Now, without warning, it wa
proving inaccurate. The then-unknown problem of the earth's magnet
ic variation could not have made itself felt at a worse possible moment

Columbus must have been badly shaken by the discovery that h
could not trust his compass, and we can be sure that, from then on, h
relied heavily on the Pole Star for direction-finding. But the failur
of the compass offered yet another possible cause for alarm amon
the crew. Columbus knew well how disastrous it would be for the
morale to lose faith in the instrument. He therefore let it be known tha
the trouble lay not in the compass, but in some fault on the part c
the Pole Star. This sounded reasonable because it was at that time be
lieved (even by Columbus himself) that the compass needle wa
attracted by the Pole Star.

However dubious Columbus' methods may seem to us now, the
were the only means at his command for calming his crew. By the tim
they had reached the seaweed-covered waters of the vast Sargasso Se
in the western Atlantic, fear and despair had fixed their grip on almo
every man. The king's officers who had come along "out of curiosity
were devoutly wishing themselves back at court; the convicts we
longing for the security of their jails; and the honest seamen were yearn
ing for the humdrum routine of sea trading in coastal waters.

To boost their flagging spirits, Columbus told them to look close
at the tangled weeds floating all around them. Were they not, he aske
"very like green grass... recently drifted away from land?" The Pi
zóns were quick to add encouraging words of their own. It was th
in fact, who, some time later, drew attention to the significance of fligh
of birds and "showers without wind." Both phenomena, they point
out, were sure signs that land could not be far off.

On the evening of September 25, Martin Pinzón shouted from t

ARCTIC CIRCLE

GREENLAND
DENMARK STRAIT
ICELAND

BAFFIN ISLANDS
FOXE BASIN
DAVIS STRAIT
HUDSON STRAIT

HUDSON BAY

Labrador

NEWFOUNDLAND

St. Lawrence

APPALACHIAN MTS.

Mississippi

Florida

GULF OF MEXICO

BAHAMA IS.
CUBA
CARIBBEAN SEA

TRINIDAD
Orinoco

A m a z o n
Amazon Basin

A N D E S

Paraná

River Plate

STR. OF MAGELLAN
FALKLAND IS.
Cape Horn

PACIFIC OCEAN

CAPRICORN

SARGASSO SEA

AZORES

MADEIRA
CANARY IS.

CAPE VERDE ISLANDS
C. Verde

C. St. Roque

S O U T H

A T L A N T I C

O C E A N

NORTH SEA

Scandinavia

Bristol
Dieppe

Bayona
Lisbon
Palos
Cadiz

MEDITERRANEAN SEA

Cape Bojador
TROPIC OF CANCER
Cape Blanc
S a h a r a   D e s e r t

Niger

GULF OF GUINEA
EQUATOR

Congo

TROPIC OF CAPRICORN

Cape of Good Hope

80°   FOXE   60°   DAVIS   40°   20°   0°   20°

———	Columbus 1 1492–3 (with the Pinzón brothers)	
– – –	Columbus 2 1493–6	
–·–·–	Columbus 3 1498	
·········	Columbus 4 1502–3	
———	John Cabot 5 1497 (with young Sebastian Cabot)	
·········	John Cabot 6 1498	
·········	Vespucci 7 1499–1500	

·········	Vespucci 8 1501–	
–·–·–	Pedro Cabral 9 1500	
———	Gaspar Corte-Real 10 1500	
·········	Gaspar Corte-Real 11 1501 (with Miguel Corte-Real 11A)	
·········	Miguel Corte-Real 12 1502	
··–··–	Sebastian Cabot 13 1509	
– – –	Sebastian Cabot 14 1526	

0   500   1000   1500   2000   Miles Equatorial Scale

Right: the beach at San Salvador where Columbus landed on October 12, 1492. This island in the Bahamas, known as Guanahani to the native peoples inhabiting it, was renamed San Salvador by Columbus and his arrival marked the discovery of the New World.

Above: frigate bird, a large sea bird, one species of which is found in the Atlantic. They have extremely long, slender wings, a forked tail, and a long, hooked beak, with which they attack and rob other sea birds. Frigates do not alight on water, as they have no oil glands to waterproof their feathers, but they are extremely skillful in the air and dive to catch fish dropped by the birds they attack. Birds such as this have always been well-known to sailors as a sign they are nearing land.

castle of the *Pinta* that he had sighted land. The fleet changed cour immediately, and headed in the direction of the sighting. But the lig of the following sunrise revealed only an unbroken horizon of sea an sky. The crew's disappointment quickly turned to anger at their con mander, and some began to talk of mutiny. The Pinzóns, when the heard of this, were strongly in favor of hanging the ringleaders. C lumbus, however, was willing to overlook the conspirators' treacher provided they would agree to sail on for a few more days. Realizing th they would find no mercy at the hands of the Pinzóns if they did rel against Columbus, the would-be mutineers accepted his offer an the fleet sailed on.

On October 7, wisely taking his clue from the direction of a flig of birds, the admiral changed to a southwesterly course. Several da later, sticks and reeds were seen floating by. Land could not be far now! On the night of October 11, just before 12 P. M., Columbus thoug he saw the light of a fire shining dimly in the distance. But only one oth man on board the *Santa María* agreed with him. Then early the ne morning a cannon shot—the prearranged signal for a positi sighting of land—boomed out from the *Pinta's* bows.

This must have been Columbus' supreme moment. At long last efforts had been rewarded and his dream fulfilled; he had reached A by sailing west. He did not know—and would never know—tha continent and another ocean still separated him from the Orie

When land was sighted, the fleet was lying off the coast of Guanab (later called San Salvador) in the Bahamas, some 500 miles southe of Florida. On the morning of October 12, the Admiral of the Oc Sea went ashore, and formally took possession of the island for F dinand and Isabella. These proceedings were regarded with curio

the island's copper-skinned inhabitants, who had gathered to watch
the white man's arrival. Columbus soon made friends with them and
did some trading, exchanging various "slight wares" for parrots and
little ornaments of gold.

For the next few days, Columbus explored this island and others
in the Bahamas. He sought in vain for the source of the gold from which
the islanders' ornaments were made, but did ascertain that the island
possessed many other valuable raw materials: oak, pine, and what
he thought to be cinnamon and musk.

The natives had given him to understand that there was another
very large island (Cuba) to the southwest. And so, on October 23, after
writing in his journal that "it must be Cipango, according to what these
people tell me of its size and wealth," he set out to find it. With him he
took seven Guanahani islanders.

Inside a week he had reached Cuba and begun to explore it. Its northern
coast was so long that he decided that this was not, after all, the island
of Cipango, but rather the edge of the Asian mainland itself. Perhaps,
even now, he was at the outer limits of the Great Khan's empire. He
and his men were charmed by the country's beauty and by its gentle,
tobacco-smoking men and women. But Columbus was anxious to
move on. If this were indeed the mainland of Cathay, then Cipango
could not be far off, and he wanted to find it. Martin Pinzón seems to
have had the same object in mind, for one November day, while the
fleet was busy charting Cuba's north coast, he and his crew slipped
away in the *Pinta*.

Columbus, left with only the *Santa María* and the *Niña,* was prevented from leaving the shores of Cuba for some time by contrary winds.
Early in December, however, he managed to reach Haiti, the great

Above: illustration from the first
edition in 1493 of Columbus' letter
reporting his discovery. It shows the
Spanish idea of American Indians.
Observe the ship has oars, which of
course none of Columbus' ships had.

Above: an aerial view of Haiti, an island in the West Indies to which Columbus gave the name La Española (later corrupted to Hispaniola), when he discovered it in the early 1490's. He found an island inhabited by Indians who were obviously competent farmers and fishermen, for the island was well cultivated.

island southwest of San Salvador. This island, which he found ev[…] more pleasing than Cuba, must certainly be Cipango, for here g[…] was to be found in great quantity. Certainly the Haitian natives w[…] not at all hesitant about exchanging the precious metal for the "sli[…] wares" Columbus had brought with him.

During his stay in Haiti, Columbus noted with delight the islan[…] cultivated valleys, stands of valuable timber, and splendid clim[…] As a compliment to the European kingdom that had sponsored [...] voyage, he named the island La Española (later called Hispaniola).

But the island did not prove lucky for Columbus. On Christ[…] Eve, disaster befell the *Santa María* as she lay at anchor on the co[…] Every man on board was asleep save for a boy whose duty it was to k[…] watch. It was an exceptionally calm night and there seemed no rea[…] to have a more experienced man at the helm. This reasoning pro[…] fatal for the ship, however, for somehow she ran aground and wa[…] badly damaged that she could never be refloated.

Columbus was now left with two crews and only one ship. Bow[…] before what he took to be God's will, he decided to leave some 4[…]

s men on the island as settlers. He and the rest of the crew would sail
ack to Spain in the *Niña* to report the success of the voyage.

On January 16, 1493, when Columbus set sail for home, he had no
ualms about the welfare of the men he had left behind. The island
as fruitful, and the Haitian natives had shown themselves to be
endly and cooperative. Alas, when he returned to Haiti on his second
oyage the following year, he was to find to his horror that every single
ie of his men had been killed by the islanders.

On January 18, 1493, two days after Columbus had set off for Spain,
met up with the *Pinta*. He had a short, sharp quarrel with the truant
artin Pinzón, and then gave the order that the two ships were to sail
together. The eastward passage was made in a more northerly lati-
le than the outward voyage, and in the trip's later stages the two ves-
s encountered far worse weather. Both caravels were taking in a great
al of water, and when a storm hit them in February there was scarce-
a man on board who did not fear for his life. It seemed a miracle,
erefore, when, on February 18, they sighted Santa Maria, the southern-
st island of the Azores. Here the two vessels anchored, and Columbus
ve his men permission to go ashore, find a church, and offer thanks
their deliverance.

The Portuguese governor of the island, however, did not take kindly
the idea of Spanish ships in Portuguese waters. He ordered the would-
worshipers seized and had them imprisoned. The men were released
y after several days of negotiation, during which Columbus had
show the governor the documents from Ferdinand and Isabella
ich proved him to be an admiral and a viceroy.

A fierce storm was now brewing. But, after the governor's inhospi-
le treatment of his men, Columbus thought it well to get away quickly,
atever the weather. The storm winds were so strong that, even with
e masts, the caravels were driven eastward with perilous swiftness
several days. During this time, the two ships became separated.
lumbus did not see Martin Pinzón again until two weeks later, when,
hin hours of each other the *Niña* and *Pinta* arrived back in Palos.)
n March 4, the *Nina* reached the mouth of the Tagus River on the
st of Portugal. Here the Spanish ship was approached by an armed
tuguese vessel whose captain boarded the *Niña* and demanded
Columbus explain his presence in Portuguese waters. The proud
iral refused to justify himself to a mere ship's captain—particu-
a captain from the country that had spurned his great plan. He

Below: settlers in Haiti began sugar
cultivation and this picture shows
cane being cut. Production of sugar
cane requires a large labor force and
so was suitable for a slave economy.

Below: reproduction of a woodcut
made in 1486 showing the artist's idea
of the *Santa María*. There is a lack of
contemporary information on what the
ship really looked like and here the
artist has simply reproduced a galley.

417

Below: the New World that Columbus
refused to recognize that he had
discovered, stretches far to the
north of the islands where he landed.
Our photograph from space shows the
continent of North America, with the
the Florida coast in the foreground.

Left: in May 1493, in recognition of his discoveries, Columbus was granted this coat of arms. The shield was quartered, with a castle on a green field; a purple lion rampant on a silver field; islands of the sea on a blue field; and the assumed Colombo family arms. Later four anchors were placed in the fourth quarter and the arms removed to the middle base. After the admiral's death a motto encircling the shield was added: "Por Castilla e por Léon Nuevo Mundo hallo Colon." (For Castile and Léon, Columbus, discoverer of the New World.)

simply showed the man his credentials and then dispatched a letter to King John telling him about his voyage.

John, no doubt regretting his lost opportunity to sponsor the voyage, but nevertheless filled with admiration for the brave commander, invited Columbus to visit him at court. There the admiral was treated with every mark of respect. Despite this, he could not resist taunting the king with his success, and mocking him for having thrown away a claim to the wealth of "the Indies." In fact, so outrageous did Columbus' remarks become that John had to restrain his infuriated courtiers from murdering the admiral. John himself kept his temper for the time being. He honored Columbus, dressed his "Indian" natives in fine red cloth, and bade the admiral farewell.

It was March 15 before Columbus reached Palos, and late April before he arrived, by an overland route, at the court of Ferdinand and Isabella. The king and queen were overjoyed at the success of the voyage and the prospects it opened for trade with the Indies. In their gratitude to the brave Admiral of the Ocean Sea, they rewarded and honored him lavishly.

Columbus later undertook three more voyages across the Atlantic, and on all three made important new discoveries. He went on identifying them as Asian lands, however, because, to the end of his days, he believed that he had reached the Orient.

This fact, of course, does not in any way lessen the magnitude of Columbus' achievement. It merely adds further irony to the story of the man whose unswerving faith in himself, his "mission," and his own radical theories opened the way to the New World.

Right: fort at San João do Estoril built to guard the mouth of the Tagus, the longest river in the whole Iberian peninsula, the two branches of which end in a large tidal lake above Lisbon. Columbus swam to the port of Lisbon after the ship in which he was sailing was attacked and caught fire in 1476.

East to Fulfillment

6

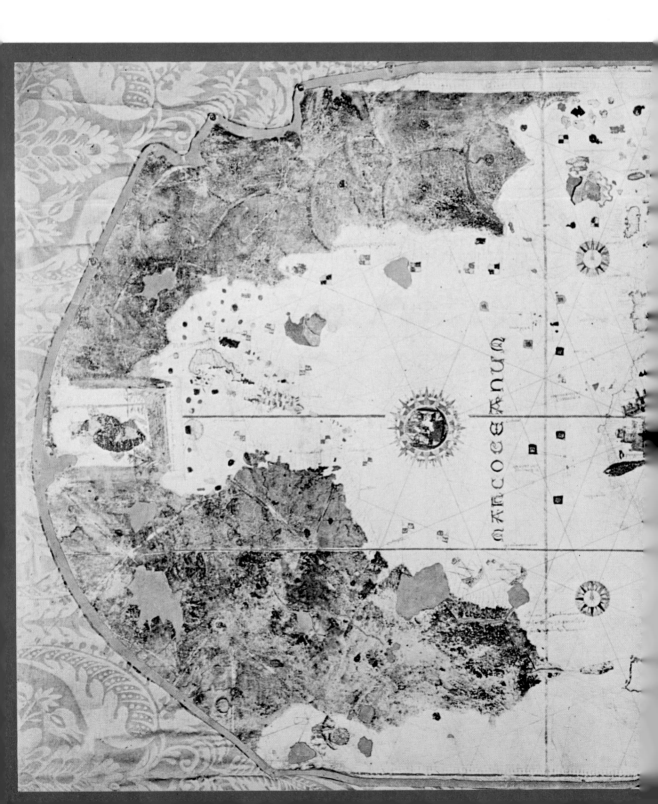

Below: this map of Juan de la Cosa was made in 1500 by Columbus' pilot and is the earliest known map showing the lands discovered by Columbus. The somewhat more accurate outlines of Europe, the Mediterranean Sea, and the African continent are shown in the badly faded center of the map. Also shown is possibly the first record of voyages made by Vincente Pinzón and John and Sebastian Cabot, and Vasco da Gama's arrival in India in 1498.

During his voyage across the Atlantic, Columbus had faced the gravest dangers with calm presence of mind. But at the court of King John he had been neither discreet nor diplomatic. However understandable his boasting may have been in the circumstances, it was exceedingly unwise. In fact, it almost started a war between Spain and Portugal.

It would have been better if Columbus, like Martin Pinzón, had sailed past Portugal to a Spanish port, and there sent a report to Ferdinand and Isabella. If King John had first heard details of the voyage from the Spanish monarchs, instead of from Columbus himself, he

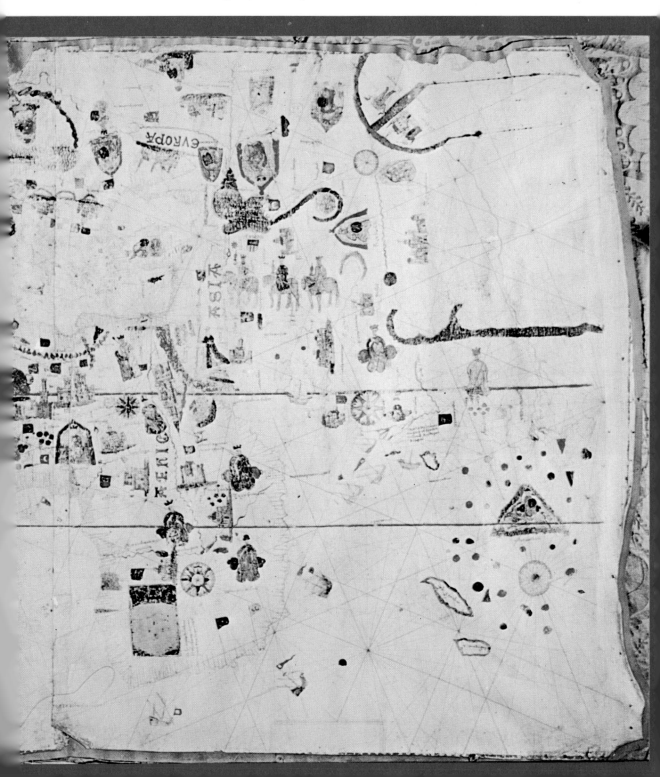

Above: Isabella la Católica (1451— 1504), became queen of Castile in 1474 on the death of her brother. She married Ferdinand of Aragon in 1469. Her high intellect, fierce patriotism, and great religious conviction did much for Spain, raising it to the high standard it reached under "the Catholic rulers." Intuition led her eventually to agree to finance Columbus, and it is said she even offered to pawn her jewelry.

might possibly not have been as angry about the news as he now was.

Indeed, the admiral's impulsive boasting and taunting had so provoked King John that, within a few weeks of Columbus' visit, he was planning to send a fleet of his own across the Atlantic. He deeply resented Spain's entrance into the field of exploration and discovery. As far as he was concerned, Portugal had more than earned a monopoly over it. His plan, therefore, was to cut Spain out before it could make any further gains.

When Ferdinand and Isabella learned of John's proposed expedition, they set in motion the preparation of a war fleet. Meanwhile, having had Columbus' full report, they urged the Admiral to lead a second expedition before John could act.

Yet, even before Columbus had set out on his second voyage, the Spanish king and queen had already taken steps to ensure their rights in the western Atlantic. They had approached the pope—then the final arbiter in such affairs—and requested that Spain be given a monopoly over future transatlantic exploration. On May 3, 1493, the pope granted their request. Spain was to have sole rights to all discoveries made more than 100 leagues west of the Cape Verde Islands. Portugal was to have sole rights to all discoveries made east of that line of demarcation.

This arrangement did not please King John, and there followed a year of tense negotiations. Finally, on June 7, 1494, the two countries signed the Treaty of Tordesillas, which moved the line 250 leagues farther west. This new agreement (which ultimately gave Portugal rights to the part of South America now occupied by eastern Brazil) was more to John's liking.

Meanwhile, Columbus, accompanied by his brothers, Diego and Bartholomew, had embarked on his second expedition. This time the admiral was in command of 17 vessels. The fleet was too large for the little harbor of Palos. So it was from the port of Cádiz that, on September 25, 1493, the expedition set out. In addition to provisions, arms, ammunition, and horses, the ships carried various kinds of seeds, plants, and farm animals, because the main purpose of the expedition was to found a permanent colony in Hispaniola. All told, the fleet carried some 1,500 men. Among them were farmers, craftsmen, missionaries, doctors, and *hidalgos* (men of high birth accustomed to authority).

Columbus did not return from this expedition for nearly three years. During that time, he and his men discovered the islands of Dominica

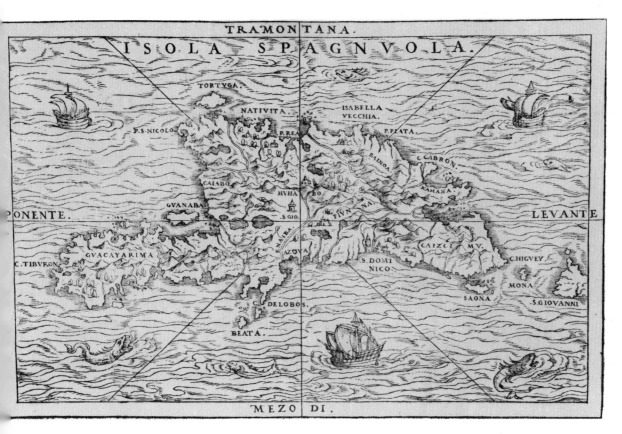

During these first fruitful years of Spanish exploration west of the

uadeloupe, and Mariagalante (islands in the group known as the
sser Antilles, southeast of Hispaniola), as well as Puerto Rico (due
st of Hispaniola) and Jamaica (the island south of Cuba). They also
rther explored Cuba and Hispaniola, and they established the town-
ip of Isabela on its northern coast.

During these first fruitful years of Spanish exploration west of the
rdesillas line, Portuguese exploration east of it did not progress very
pidly. In fact, by 1496, when Columbus returned from his second
yage, the Portuguese had not advanced beyond the point reached
Bartolomeu Dias in 1488.

During this time, King John had been anxiously awaiting word
m Pedro de Covilham, a man he had sent out at the same time as Dias.
Colvilham's mission was to sail to the eastern end of the Mediterra-
n, and from there to proceed overland in search of India and the
d of Prester John.

De Covilham did, in fact, reach India, and even found on his way
re an East African country ruled by a Christian king. This nation,
ich he took to be "the land of Prester John," was Ethiopia. It was some
e, however, before the traveler was able to find a means of getting
tter back to Portugal. Thus, it was not until 1490 or 1491 that King
n had a full report of De Covilham's movements.

his letter, De Covilham described the busy trade in spices that
had witnessed in Calicut (modern Kozhikode) and Goa on India's
t coast. He also said that if Portuguese ships could round the southern
st of Africa, they had only to sail a few hundred miles northward

Below: Prester John, the legendary
Christian monarch of Asia, who
combined the qualities of king and
priest and ruled over huge domains
somewhere in the Far East. His
name was mentioned in ancient
chronicles as early as 1122.

Above: Arab dhow of the type seen by
Portuguese explorers as they sailed
up the east coast of Africa. Dhows
have sailed along this coast for
centuries to and from Arabia. They
sailed with the monsoon winds, which
blow southwest for six months of the
year and northeast for the other six
months. These strange craft were a
source of wonderment to the Portuguese
but it is certain that if the
Portuguese found the Arabs and
their vessels strange, then the Arabs
found the Portuguese equally so.

along its east coast to the port of Sofala (midway along the coast of pr
sent-day Mozambique). There, he wrote, they would meet Arab shi
which regularly voyaged to and from India. De Covilham's letter offer
positive proof that the Atlantic merged with the Indian Ocean. T
sea route to India lay ready for the taking, just as John had hoped.

But the report had reached the king at an inopportune time. John
son and heir had recently been killed in a riding accident, and the ki
himself was ill. Nevertheless, according to Gaspar Correa, a Port
guese historian of the period, John lost no time in preparing a fl
of ships to pioneer the ocean route to India. "He commanded timb
to be cut down, which carpenters and shipwrights ordered for cuttir
and the timber was brought to Lisbon, where three large ships w
at once begun...."

But at this point, John found himself beset by annoyances and
lays. Columbus arrived with the disturbing news that he had reach
the Indies by sailing west, and Portugal and Spain almost came to blo
over the rights to transatlantic exploration. All this was very tryi
for the ailing king. In October, 1495, less than two years after dip
matic bargaining had finally brought about the Treaty of Tordesill
John died.

The throne passed to Manuel I, a distant relation of King John.
was later to become known as Manuel the Fortunate—and fortun
he certainly was. During his reign all the great schemes for Portugu
discovery that had been initiated by Henry the Navigator, nurtu
by Alfonso V, and furthered by John II, reached fulfillment.

King Manuel worked hard to achieve that fulfillment. Only t
months after his accession, he brought the voyage-to-India pro
before his royal council. The scheme he put forward had serious im
cations for Portugal. Clearly, a single expedition would be a wast
money unless it could be followed up by an all-out effort to sec
a sizable share of the Eastern spice trade. But this would alm
certainly lead to fighting with the Moslems who controlled this tr
There might also be trouble with the Venetian Republic, whose p
tion as middleman in the spice trade would suffer if Portugal be
obtaining spices direct from the East. Some councillors were, theref
against the whole idea. But others were willing to accept the risks,
backed by these bolder men, Manuel decided to go ahead with his sche
Within a year he had appointed a leader for the first expedition—V
da Gama.

No one really knows how or why Da Gama was chosen. One contemporary chronicler says that the king, looking down from a balcony, happened to see him crossing a courtyard and took a whim to appoint him. Other accounts offer the more plausible suggestion that Da Gama, having served in previous expeditions, had already been earmarked for the post during John's reign. Apart from these scraps of doubtful information, we know about Da Gama only that he was the son of a government official in the town of Sines; that he had reached his middle or late thirties when he began his great journey; and that he knew enough about navigation to determine a ship's latitude.

It would not have mattered much if Da Gama had known nothing about navigation. This was a task he could leave to the excellent pilots he took with him—pilots who had earlier sailed with Dias. Da Gama's task as commander of the fleet was to steel his men to endure the hardships of a voyage that would be longer than any undertaken before. Beyond this, his mission was to establish friendly relations with Eastern rulers, to open the way for Portuguese merchants and missionaries.

On Saturday, July 8, 1497, Da Gama and the 170 men who were to sail with him walked in procession through the streets of Lisbon to the docks where his four ships lay at anchor. Priests and friars walked with them carrying lighted tapers, "and the people of the city followed, uttering responses to a Litany." Then the abbot of a monastery "made a general confession and absolved... those who might perish in this discovery or conquest." The absolution covered a few convicts under

Below: Vasco da Gama (1469?— 1524), discoverer of the sea route to India, was born at Sines in Portugal. He was given command of the expedition to India in 1497.

425

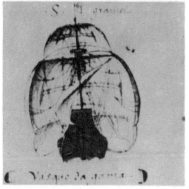

Above: ships specially built for Vasco da Gama's expedition to India, from a manuscript of 1497.

sentence of death, who were to be assigned duties of special danger during the voyage. Having received a final solemn blessing, the fleet then made ready to sail.

Like Columbus' vessels, Da Gama's ships seem terribly small by modern standards. His square-rigged flagship, the *St. Gabriel*, was of only about 200 tons. As was her sister ship, the *St. Raphael*, captained by Da Gama's brother Paulo. The *Berrio*, commanded by Nicolas Coelho, was a lateen-rigged caravel of some 100 tons. The fourth vessel, a store ship, was probably about 400 tons.

Bartolomeu Dias, who supervised the building of the *St. Gabriel* and the *St. Raphael*, had made sure they were of shallow draft, so that they could safely negotiate the shoals off the African coast. The smaller *Berrio*, similar to the caravels used by Henry the Navigator's pioneers, could certainly do so. But, as things turned out, Da Gama was to do very little "coast-hugging" along Africa's western shores.

The fleet had been at sea more than a week and was well south of the Canaries before the African coast was sighted. Then a dense fog closed down, and each vessel lost sight of the others. Another two weeks passed before they reassembled, far to the southwest, near the Cape Verde Islands. Here they agreed to put in for fresh provisions and drinking water. On August 3, they set off again, and followed a southeasterly course for some 800 miles.

After traveling this distance, Da Gama did something quite unheard of. He made a vast semi-circular sweep—first southwestward, then

Left: African villages, such as this one in Dahomey, have changed very little since the time of the early explorers, who found the way of life of the villagers quite incomprehensible. They therefore had great difficulty in deciding how best to treat the native peoples with whom they came into contact.

outheastward—through the Atlantic. It is said that he did so to
void the doldrums and the awkward currents off the Gulf of Guinea,
s well as the bad-weather area which Dias had encountered off south-
vest Africa. These considerations may have been in his mind, but there
nay also have been another. The Treaty of Tordesillas gave Portugal
ne right to explore as far as 350 leagues west of the Cape Verde Islands.
erhaps Da Gama made this westerly sweep through the Atlantic in
ne hope of finding undiscovered lands. He did not succeed in doing
o, but it is interesting to note that, just before he crossed the Tropic
f Capricorn, he was a good deal nearer to Brazil than he was to Africa.

During the course of that colossal westward sweep, Da Gama's
nen were out of sight of land for 96 days. As a result of going so long
ithout fresh fruit and vegetables, many of them began to suffer from
urvy. So it was with joy and relief that at long last they found them-
lves within sight of land—St. Helena Bay, not far north of modern
ape Town. On November 4, even before landing at St. Helena Bay,
ey celebrated their good fortune by putting on their best clothes,
ying flags, and firing the ships' cannons.

After so long a voyage, there was much work to be done—scraping
rnacled hulls, mending torn sails, gathering provisions, filling the
ater-casks, and collecting wood for the cooking stoves. Meanwhile,
me of Da Gama's pilots took an astrolabe ashore to determine the
pedition's exact position. Used by a man standing on firm ground
ther than on the rolling deck of a ship), the instrument could give

Below: Bushmen, the nomadic hunters
and food gatherers found by the
Portuguese at the tip of the African
continent. They are an entirely
separate race of people, fairly short—
the average height being only about
five feet—with prominent cheekbones,
broad noses and flat faces.
Their short hair curls into small
knots all over their heads.

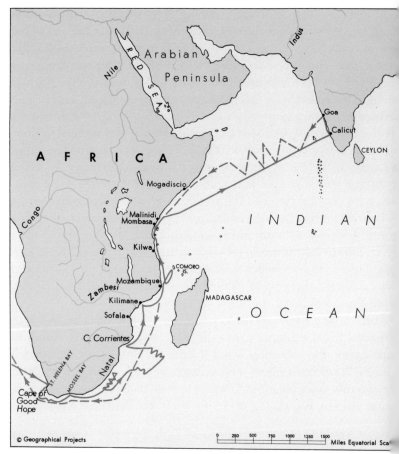

Right: the final part of Vasco de Gama's journey from Europe, crossing the Indian Ocean to the coast of India.

Below: an armlet and a horn or whistle made of ivory, the sort of things for which the Portuguese explorers traded with the inhabitants of the Ivory Coast. Ivory, the very dense substance of which elephant tusks are made, is very easy to work and the gelatinous solution with which it is filled gives it a wonderful polish. Elephants roamed over virtually the whole of the African continent for many years, but the Ivory Coast, between the Grain and Gold Coasts in West Africa, became a great trading center for ivory in the late 1400's.

fairly accurate results. It was not long before the pilots had fixed th latitude and calculated that they were about 120 miles north of the Ca of Good Hope.

Another inland excursion was not so profitable. One of the m took a few hours' leave to visit among the inhabitants of the region Bushmen and Hottentots—whom the Portuguese had encounter for the first time on this voyage. He was invited to share a meal with t natives, but he must have done something to offend his hosts, for soon found himself running for his life, with the natives in hot pursu throwing spears. He made it safely back to his ship, but Da Gama, w had gone to his rescue, was slightly wounded.

The expedition made several stops after leaving St. Helena B On November 22, it rounded the Cape of Good Hope. A week lat it put in at Mossel Bay on the southern coast of Africa. There the m beached the store ship, broke her up, and distributed what remain of the stores among the other vessels. Meanwhile, Da Gama did so trading with the local inhabitants, exchanging little bells and scar caps for ivory bangles. In the course of his negotiations, he ev managed to acquire an ox, which would provide fresh meat for men. This bargaining was accompanied by much merrymakir Everyone was dancing — the natives, the sailors, and Da Gama hims

The stay in Mossel Bay lasted only until the necessary work had b

Above: these African houses, which look very primitive, are nonetheless skillfully adapted to the climatic conditions. The grass thatch keeps out rain and the overhang gives shade to the immediate area around the house. The open sides permit the occasional cool breezes to keep the temperature inside comfortable.

ompleted and the vessels restocked. Then the fleet sailed eastward nce more. By late December, it had reached and passed Algoa Bay, he farthest point attained by Bartolomeu Dias. At last, Da Gama as entering the Indian Ocean. Following the coastline, which now urved northward, the fleet sailed on until Christmas Day, when it put to shore. Appropriately enough, Da Gama named the spot Natal. oday, it is the great port of Durban, South Africa.

On leaving Natal, Da Gama turned eastward, away from the coast. fter several days, however, the fleet ran perilously short of fresh water, d Da Gama was forced to sail west once more to reach the coast and plenish supplies. He landed at the mouth of a small river and, while e crew filled up the water-casks, did some trading with the local inhab-nts, who paid in copper for the shirts he offered.

Next, after rounding Cape Correntes, near the Tropic of Capricorn, Gama sailed almost due north. Had he kept close inshore, he would ve come to Sofala, the town mentioned by De Covilham as a port call for Arab ships on their way to and from India. Standing well t to sea, however, Da Gama's fleet missed Sofala, and went on in-ad to Kilimane, a town several hundred miles north of it, in present-y Mozambique. Kilimane was too small to be an Arab port of call, the Portuguese could learn nothing there about the sea route to India. vertheless, the Kilimane stopover was a useful one for other reasons.

Above: in Renaissance Europe spices were more than just a pleasant flavor to vary what was undoubtedly a most monotonous diet. They were also used, without very much success, to preserve meat through the winter when there was no fresh fodder available to keep animals alive, and all slaughtering had to be done in the fall. It was partly to break the traditional Arab monopoly in the spice trade that led the Portuguese to their voyages of endurance.

Scurvy was beginning to take its toll among the crew, and the sick we comed a few days' rest. In fact, the stopover at Kilimane lasted fro late January to the end of February, 1498. At that time, with the crew rested and the ships repaired and restocked, the fleet set sail once mor

Following the coast northeastward, Da Gama's vessels reached, early March, the port city of Moçambique, some 350 miles north Kilimane. Here the citizens were not amazed—as they been in Ki mane—by the size of the Portuguese vessels. Arab trading ships ha been regular visitors to Moçambique for a long time. For a long tin too, Moçambique had been predominantly Moslem in its religio for where the Arabs traveled, they also spread their faith. This cit 17° south of the equator, was as much a part of Islam as were the souther shores of the Mediterranean. In fact, as Da Gama was soon to fin the Moslem faith was on the increase almost everywhere in the ar around the Indian Ocean.

The men of Moçambique at first took Da Gama's ships to be Ar trading vessels. The fact that their sails were made of cloth instead matted palm leaves, their timbers joined by nails instead of leath thongs, made no difference. Never having seen any but Moslem ship the people of Moçambique assumed that these unusual vessels hail from a Moslem kingdom far away.

Accordingly, the local officials went on board and welcomed th Portuguese heartily. Through Arabic-speaking Portuguese inte preters, the officials talked freely to Da Gama about the other Arab ve sels then in port. These vessels were laden, they said, with spices, go and precious stones. But Da Gama and his men had no wish to sail und false colors. They declared themselves Christians, enquired abo Prester John, and requested pilots to guide them eastward to Ind

This frank admission of their religion and objectives produced immediate change in the attitude of the local officials. They did supp the pilots Da Gama had asked for, but gave them secret instructic to lead the Portuguese astray. Even before the fleet left port, one the pilots, offering to take a party ashore for drinking water, tried lead them into an ambush. Fortunately, the Portuguese were on th guard, and avoided being caught. But Da Gama had to fire his cann before anyone on shore would allow his crew to fill their water-cas This accomplished, the fleet left Moçambique in haste.

On April 7, Da Gama reached Mombasa, 800 miles north of Moça bique, in present-day Kenya. Here, after stating their religion a

their aims, the Portuguese once again met with opposition. Messengers posing as Christians were sent to Da Gama by the local ruler. They offered to supply him with whatever stores he needed, but their real mission was to lull him into a false sense of security and to lure his crews away from their ships. Da Gama was not taken in by their friendly overtures, however. That night, when an armed party attempted to board his ships by force, he and his men were ready for them. When the attack proved unsuccessful, the last Moslem pilots from Moçambique jumped overboard. On April 12, still without clues as to the best route to India, Da Gama left Mombasa.

The next stage of the voyage lasted only three days and brought better

Above: Mombasa, East Africa, where in 1498 Vasco da Gama once more met with hostility in his quest for a route to India. The old harbor shown here, still used by dhows and other native craft, is on the northeast of the coral island on which Mombasa is built and which is connected to the mainland by a bridge.

Left: this is the kind of potentate with whom the Portuguese first came into contact. The Arab lack of enthusiasm for the visitors was understandable. In the first place they represented a threat to the thriving Arab trade and secondly they could not have been the most elegant of figures after many months at sea.

uck: the capture of several Moslems from a small bark sailing just off
hore. On reaching the next coastal town, Malindi (about 50 miles
orth of Mombasa), Da Gama entrusted one of these Moslems with
message for the local ruler. The burden of this message was that Da
ama wished to establish friendly relations and find pilots who could
uide him to India. The Sultan of Malindi responded well. He let Da
ama know that he had nothing but goodwill for Portugal (although
e had probably never heard of it before). He also sent presents, includ-
g a considerable quantity of spices—cloves, ginger, nutmeg, and
epper. In return, the Portuguese commander sent him three copper
owls, some bells, a piece of coral, a hat, and an overcoat.

Partly as a result of this friendly exchange—and partly by holding
ne of the sultan's own servants until matters were arranged to his
tisfaction—Da Gama at last obtained what he most needed: a pilot
ho knew the way to India. Guided by this pilot, the fleet sailed north-
st until May 18. On that day, it reached its goal. At long last, the dream
finding an eastern sea route to India had been fulfilled.

On May 21, the three ocean-battered vessels anchored off Calicut,
najor port on India's southwest coast. Soon the fleet was approached
a number of native boats. The moment for direct negotiations with
e East had arrived. But Da Gama was apprehensive about how the
dians would react to the arrival of foreign traders. He therefore en-
sted the first step in the negotiations to one of the convicts who had
en allowed to sail with him on condition that they undertook partic-
rly dangerous jobs. The man was put on one of the native boats
d taken ashore. There he was conducted to two Moslem traders who
oke Spanish. They were astonished to learn where he came from,
d asked him what Portuguese vessels were doing so far from home.
reply, he summed up 80 years of Portuguese endeavor in a few short
rds. "We come," he said, "in search of Christians and spices."

Below: ancient Calicut, southwest
India, the port at which Vasco da
Gama landed in 1498. It was then a
flourishing city, famed for cotton
weaving. "Calico" originally meant
cloth from Calicut. Da Gama tried
unsuccessfully to set up a trading settlement there. Similar efforts were
made two years later by Pedro Cabral,
but again local hostility caused
destruction of the colony. Da
Gama returned in 1502 and completely
devastated the city in revenge.

Right: an Indian prince surrounded by his ladies in attendance and with his gold cuspidor. This shows the sophistication and splendor of the East which so overwhelmed the Portuguese and which made Vasco da Gama so ashamed of the gifts which the king had given him for the princes and merchants, and which he he had to pretend were his own poor possessions.

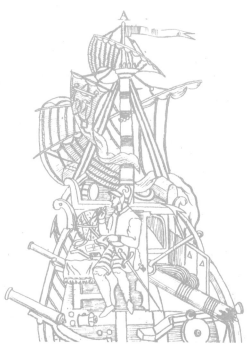

Above: engraving by De Bry from Pigafetta's "Viaggio de Magagliones negli anni 1519/1522 "(Journey of Magellan in the years from 1519—1522), showing Magellan using a globe and dividers to determine the position of his ship.

In fact, Da Gama's stated mission was to open the way for Portugu trade and the spread of Christianity. But he had to return home w positive proof—hopefully in the form of spices—that Portu could profit from the new-found route to India. Otherwise, there wo be no point in sending merchants and missionaries there in future.

In his attempt to obtain spices, Da Gama found himself facing serious obstacles. The first, of course, was the Moslem monopol trade with the East. Moslem traders bought their spices and preci stones on India's southwest coast and then sailed north with then ports on the Red Sea or the Persian Gulf. The precious cargoes t passed into the hands of Moslem caravan traders, who took them o land to the shores of the Mediterranean, where they were purcha by Venetian and Genoese merchants. From India to the Medite nean, therefore, the spices and gems of the East were handled exclus ly by Moslem merchants. Naturally, any outsider's attempt to b into this monopoly would be greeted with dark suspicion and hostility.

On the other hand, the Indian merchants in the Hindu states a the coast were as willing—in principle—to do business with Chris as with Moslems. But they were reluctant to risk offending their Mo clients unless the Christians had something exceptional to offer in way of trade.

Here was the second obstacle facing Da Gama in his quest for sp he had nothing valuable to offer in return. He had brought with only oil, honey, striped cloth, bowls, red caps, shirts, bells, and strings of coral. But while these might interest buyers in Malindi, they met only with contempt in Calicut. In fact, when offering them to the local spice merchants, Da Gama had to pretend they were not the goods provided by his king, but simply odds and ends that he, a poor traveler, had bought and paid for himself.

During his three-month stay in Calicut, Da Gama managed to obtain an audience with the region's wealthy Hindu ruler. At first, the only satisfaction he had from this man was permission to sell his own poor merchandise. There followed a number of unpleasant episodes in which the king of Calicut imprisoned some of Da Gama's men and the Portuguese captured some of the king's. At last, however, just before the fleet sailed, the Hindu ruler relented, and gave Da Gama a letter for King Manuel. In it, he wrote, "In my kingdom there is abundance of cinnamon, cloves, ginger, pepper, and precious stones. What I seek from your country is gold, silver, coral, and scarlet." The way for future trade was thus opened, and Da Gama could go home content.

The homeward voyage was marked by many hardships and perils. After sailing northward to Anjediva, an island south of Goa, the fleet struck out eastward for Africa in early October. Because of calms and contrary winds, the crossing to Mogadiscio (about 600 miles north of Mombasa, in present-day Somalia) took nearly three months. During this time, 30 crew members died of scurvy. Having at last reached the African coast in January, 1499, the fleet began the long southward voyage to the Cape of Good Hope. Along the way, several stops were made to take on water and provisions. On one of these stops, just south of Mombasa, the *St. Raphael* had to be destroyed because there were no longer enough men to handle three ships.

It was late March before the *St. Gabriel* and the *Berrio* eventually rounded the Cape. A month later, near the Cape Verde Islands, the two ships became separated. The *Berrio* sailed directly back to Portugal, but Da Gama, in the *St. Gabriel,* made a stopover in the islands. Thus, the leader of the expedition did not reach home until early September, 26 months after he had set out.

Da Gama was given a magnificent reception at King Manuel's court, and throughout the land his triumphant homecoming was marked by fetes and public rejoicings. Meanwhile, the wheels were set in motion for a full-scale program of eastward voyages. The time had come to capitalize on the hard-won sea route to the Indies.

Below: in the shadow of Table Mountain, at the southernmost tip of Africa, lies Cape Town, the oldest town in South Africa. It has grown from the tiny Dutch settlement founded in 1652 by the Dutch East India Company, to become the main passenger and mail port of South Africa. Da Gama's first landfall for over three months, after he left Cape Verde Islands in August 1497, was at St. Helena Bay, just north of present-day Cape Town.

Below: early map of Cochin, southern India. When in 1498 Da Gama reached the Malabar coast, the rulers of Cochin and Calicut were in conflict. Because Cochin harbor was superior to that at Calicut, the Portuguese sided with the Cochin rajahs. Dom Francisco de Almeida took up residence in Cochin when he became viceroy of Portuguese India in 1505.

Thrusting East and West
7

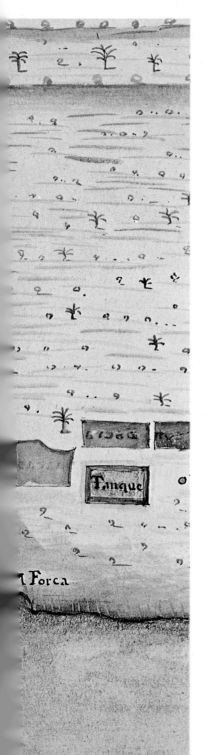

During the early years of the 1500's, Da Gama's discovery of the ocean route to India was followed up with amazing speed and vigor. During the same period, Columbus' discovery of lands across the Atlantic was pursued with equal energy. But the results obtained by the two efforts were in striking contrast. The eastward thrust brought quick and prodigious results; the westward at first brought little but frustration.

On March 9, 1500, less than six months after Da Gama's return, a fleet of 13 well-armed ships laden with trading goods left Lisbon bound for the East. In overall command of the fleet was a nobleman, Pedro Álvares Cabral. With him were several captains, including Bartolomeu Dias and Nicolas Coelho, the captain of the *Berrio* on Da Gama's expedition.

On its way south, Cabral's fleet made a wide westward sweep through the Atlantic—like Da Gama's, but even wider. This tremendous sweep westward brought stunning results: the discovery of Brazil, on the eastern coast of South America. But despite this discovery, Cabral was anxious to get on to India. He did explore a considerable stretch of the Brazilian coast and left two men there to learn all they could about the people and natural resources of the area. Then, having sent one of his ships back to Portugal with the news of this new land, he sailed on.

Off the Cape of Good Hope, the fleet ran into a fierce storm and four ships were lost. (Among them was the vessel captained by Bartolomeu Dias, the first man to have reached the "Cape of Storms.") But the ships that reached India did very well. Because the fleet carried far better merchandise than Da Gama's, Cabral was able to trade more successfully with the ruler of Calicut. And because the fleet also carried better artillery, Cabral was able to attack Moslem vessels which tried to hinder his trading, and even seize their cargoes. Moreover, Cabral succeeded in making commercial treaties with the rulers of Cochin (south of Calicut) and Cannanore (north of Calicut). Cabral returned to Lisbon in July, 1501, his ships heavily laden with quantities of spices, as well as porcelain, incense, aromatic woods, pearls, diamonds, and rubies.

Cabral's remarkable success was soon repeated by many other Portuguese fleets. One of these was a powerful armada of 22 ships which carried several thousand men. This armada, which sailed in 1505, was under the command of Francisco de Almeida, who had been appointed Portugal's first viceroy in India. Under his direction the first permanent Portuguese forts were established in India.

By this time, Portugal was beginning to make a sizable dent in Islam's

Above: the Portuguese who reached India in the 1500's saw many boats like these along the Malabar coast. The Indians rarely sailed far from land. They relied on the Arabs for goods from a distance and this was one of the factors which, until then, had made the Arabs so important as middlemen.

monopoly of the spice trade. Soon after the Portuguese began sailin to India, the Moslem sea trade between India and ports on the Red Se began to fall off noticeably. As a result, so too did the Moslem carava trade between the Red Sea and the Mediterranean. This in turn affecte the Venetian merchants who depended on the Moslems for the spic and other luxury items they marketed to the west. Helpless to rever the trend, Venetian traders watched their cherished position as middl men in the East-West trade slowly but surely being usurped by th Portuguese. Some far-sighted Venetian merchants even began tran ferring their capital from Venice to Lisbon.

Even Egypt felt the effects of Portugal's burgeoning trade wi the East. As fewer and fewer Moslem caravans crossed her lands their way to the Mediterranean, the vast revenues she had derived fro taxing them rapidly diminished. In fact, Portugal's increasing use the sea route to India was beginning to affect the whole pattern of wor trade, and Lisbon, capital of this small but enterprising nation, w fast becoming a mecca for merchants from all over Europe.

But this was only the beginning. Having opened the way to the Ea Portugal was not slow to strengthen her position there. In 1507 or 15 a Portuguese fleet commanded by one Afonso d'Albuquerque co quered Hormuz, the port city that guarded the straits leading into t Persian Gulf. This action enabled the Portuguese to stop Eastern goo brought to Hormuz in Moslem ships, from reaching the merchants w could take them overland through Moslem Syria to the Mediterrane A year or two after the capture of Hormuz, Albuquerque, having s ceeded De Almeida as Portugal's viceroy in India, also seized G then probably the richest port on India's west coast.

Only one major step remained to be taken. India was not the source of spices, it was simply the place where they could be obtained in quantity at a reasonable cost. They actually originated in a group of islands much farther to the east. What Portugal now coveted was a foothold in these islands—islands, it was said, where every kind of valuable spice grew as abundantly as weeds in a neglected garden.

In 1511, Albuquerque sailed east to Malaya, the southernmost peninsula of Southeast Asia. On Malaya's west coast he seized the port of Malacca. This gave Portugal control over the narrow strait between the peninsula and Sumatra, the large island south and west of Malaya. It was through this strait that ships from the Spice Islands passed on their way to India.

The same year (1511), Albuquerque sent out an expedition to explore the Spice Islands themselves. These islands, which today are called the Moluccas, lie roughly midway between the Philippines and Australia. East of them lies the large island of New Guinea, and west, the smaller Indonesian island of Celebes. The vessels sent out by Albuquerque sailed nearly 1,000 miles beyond Java, the Indonesian island southeast of Sumatra, before it reached the tiny Moluccan island of Banda. Here they took on a fine cargo of cloves before setting sail for home.

The expedition of 1511 had failed to reach the richest Spice Islands, Ternate and Timor, which lie several hundred miles away from Banda. By 1520, however, the Portuguese had not only reached these islands, but sailed far north and west of them to China.

By 1520, also, the Portuguese had discovered and explored other islands in and around the Indian Ocean. Among these were Madagascar, off the coast of Mozambique; Ceylon, off the southern tip of India; and Burma, a large kingdom in the Bay of Bengal opposite India. Not only did the Portuguese establish trading stations in these far-flung places, they also often succeeded in forcing the local rulers to pay tribute to King Manuel I. As the fortunes of Portugal approached their zenith, the little nation's power in the Far East became so great that ships from other countries dared not sail into the Indian Ocean without written Portuguese consent.

While Portugal was reaping the tremendous rewards of her eastward expansion, Spain was vainly striving to make some sense—and profit—from her westward claims. In 1498, the year in which Da Gama first reached Calicut, Christopher Columbus made his third Atlantic voyage.

Above: Dom Francisco de Almeida, from a manuscript of the 1500's. Almeida was born in Lisbon in the mid-1400's and became first viceroy of Portuguese India. In March, 1505 he sailed for India, where he conquered Quiloa. He then went on to take Mombasa. In an attempt to maintain Portuguese supremacy, Almeida built forts at Anjediva, near Goa, and at Cannanore. He was killed in a fight with Hottentots on the site of present-day Cape Town in 1510.

439

Above: an old map of Goa, the city seized by Afonso d'Albuquerque in the early 1500's. Goa was the first Portuguese territorial possession in Asia and became the capital of the Portuguese eastern empire, reaching its height of prosperity between the late 1500's and early 1600's. After this it declined and in the 1800's only a handful of priests, monks, and nuns lived there.

On this voyage, the Admiral of the Ocean Sea discovered and nam the island of Trinidad, a few miles off the coast of present-day Venez ela. Strangely enough, though he sailed along the Venezuelan co as far as the mouth of the Orinoco River, he did not make a landing the mainland. Instead, he hastened northward to inspect the new c ony at Hispaniola. He found it in a state of revolt. He and his brothe Diego and Bartholomew (who had been given major responsibilit in governing the colony), handled the situation badly, being som times too lenient, sometimes too quick to resort to the whip and gallows.

News of this trouble in Hispaniola soon reached the ears of Ferdina

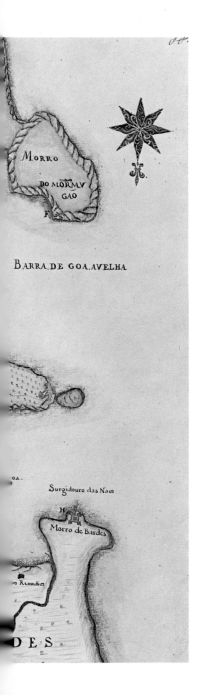

and Isabella. To investigate the charges of cruelty and mismanagement against Columbus, they sent representatives of the crown to Hispaniola. Whether or not these charges were fully justified, it was apparent that Columbus made a better admiral than he did a governor. In October, 1500, he was arrested in Hispaniola, ignominiously brought back to Spain in chains, and stripped of his honors and privileges.

By May, 1502, however, he had partially restored himself to the good graces of his sovereigns, and was allowed to undertake another voyage with four Spanish vessels. Because he had been forbidden to visit Hispaniola, he confined his travels to the area south and west of it. For most of the two years of this voyage, he cruised along the east coast of Central America, from present-day Honduras to Panama. He still believed, of course, that he was on the threshold of Asia. In a letter to Ferdinand and Isabella describing this, his last voyage, he wrote, "On May 13 I arrived in Mango province, which is next to Cathay."

Four years after completing this voyage, Columbus died, never having learned the real truth about his discoveries. Perhaps it is as well that he did not. He had set his heart on reaching the Orient; to have known that he had found something quite different—no matter how

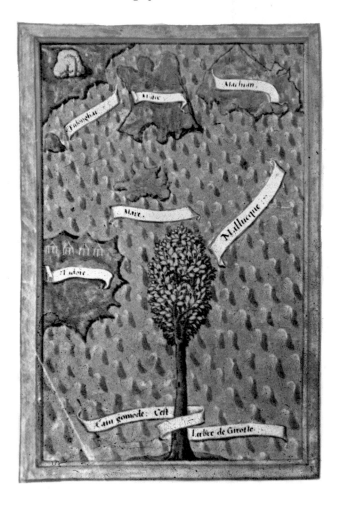

right: illustration showing a clove tree, from Pigafetta's *Relation*, an account of Magellan's first circumnavigation, written in 1524 by Antonio Pigafetta, a volunteer in Magellan's flagship. Pigafetta stressed the interest shown in the clove tree and the desirability of cloves in trading. native of the Moluccas, or Spice Islands, the clove tree is an evergreen, growing to a height of 15 to feet. It has large oval leaves, and groups of crimson flowers the tips of its branches.

Above: branch of a clove tree showing details of buds, flowers, fruit, etc. The clove is the dried, unopened flower bud, which has a very powerful odor and hot taste. It has long been a very desirable spice for trading.

significant the discovery—would have been a cruel disappointment.

In any case, no one at this time possessed sufficient geographical knowledge to say with certainty that the admiral's discoveries were not what he said they were. In fact, until the last years of Columbus' life, few Europeans had any idea of what the real Orient was like. If Columbus saw some vague resemblance between the lands he discovered and the fabulous East described by Marco Polo, who could say he was wrong?

Yet, although Spain continued to call its transatlantic possessions "the Indies," some men had their doubts from the start. One such man was Peter Martyr, an Italian whose enormous correspondence on many subjects was to make him famous. Martyr had seen the natives of Guanahani that Columbus had brought home from his first voyage. The appearance and language of these natives did not agree with Martyr's ideas of how Orientals should look or speak. From May, 1493, onward he wrote numerous letters concerning Columbus and his discoveries, and in one, dated October, 1494, he called the admiral the discoverer of a "New World."

A decade or so after this observation, when the Portuguese were making regular voyages to the East, men were better able to compare Columbus' discoveries with the real Orient. It then became clear that the Admiral of the Ocean Sea had indeed placed a "New World" within Spain's grasp.

Meanwhile, Spanish exploration and colonization around the Caribbean Sea and the Gulf of Mexico were proceeding apace. In 1502 Nicolas de Ovando became governor of Hispaniola. He encouraged large numbers of Spaniards to make their homes there by offering them grants of land and Indian slaves to work it, provided they promised to stay in the island for at least five years. Hispaniola soon prospered under this scheme of colonization.

In 1509, Ovando was succeeded by Columbus' son Diego, who quickly embarked on an ambitious program of expansion. Within months of taking office he sent out an expedition under Alonso de Ojeda to found two new settlements. One of these was in present-day Colombia on the northern coast of South America. The other was just west of it, on the narrow Isthmus of Panama.

Some years after the first settlers arrived in Panama, governorship of the tiny colony passed into the hands of one Vasco Núñez de Balboa. It was he who, in 1513, first gazed out on the great ocean we call the

Above: Trinidad, the most southerly island in the West Indies, the point from which exploration of the rest of the New World began after Columbus' discovery in 1498. Most of the larger West Indian islands were settled by the Spanish in the 1500's. They oppressed the native inhabitants, forcing them into slavery in the fields and mines, and this lasted until the British, Dutch, and French freed them in the late 1800's.

Left: a woodcut made in 1502, from the Journal of Christopher Columbus, showing the presentation of a book to Ferdinand and Isabella. It was in the late 1400's that Columbus started sending his long letters of woe, protesting his supposed mistreatment, to his king and queen.

Left: pearl fishing in America, from an engraving by De Bry in 1594. Pearls found in Caribbean waters were one of the first signs of riches in the New World, other than the few gold ornaments Columbus found on the island of Hispaniola.

Left: in Marco Polo's account of the riches of Cathay, pearl fishing was also mentioned, as shown in this manuscript of 1338, from Les Livres de Graunt Caam. It was this sort of similarity that Columbus clutched at in his determination to believe that he had indeed reached Cathay. Bodleian Library MS Bodley 264. fol. 265.

444

Pacific. The discovery of an ocean stretching away to the west was completely unexpected. Balboa himself could form no conception of the extent of this immense "South Sea." But he did what any good Spaniard would have done in his place. He took formal possession of it for Spain.

Meanwhile, Don Diego was pursuing his expansionist policy in another direction. In 1511, he sent out 300 men from Hispaniola, under the leadership of Diego Velásquez, to conquer and settle Cuba. The conquest of the islanders was easily accomplished, and within a few years Cuba possessed nearly as many Spanish settlers as Hispaniola itself.

It was not long before Velásquez was sending out expeditions of his own. One, led by Francisco Hernandez in 1517, explored the north and west coasts of Yucatán, the bulge of land on Central America's east coast stretching toward Cuba. On this expedition Spaniards in the New World had their first encounter with Indians of an advanced culture. Those they met in Yucatán were not only well clad and well armed, but also proficient builders in stone.

A second expedition was sent out by Velásquez in 1518. Under the command of Juan de Grijalva, it followed the Central American coast many miles westward beyond Yucatán to present-day Mexico. Near where the Mexican city of Veracruz now stands, Grijalva's men encountered Indians whose manner and appearance clearly showed that they were men of wealth and high civilization.

Grijalva's expedition was to have momentous consequences both for Spain and for the world, since it led directly to Hernando Cortes' conquest of Mexico. But in 1518 that great event, which was to make Spain the envy of all Europe, still lay in the future. Meanwhile, all that Spain had thus far gained from the discoveries of Christopher Columbus and his successors was a few scattered farming colonies. While these settlements were not to be despised, they could bear no comparison with the mighty trading empire Portugal had built up in India and southeast Asia.

Nevertheless, Spain maintained a jealous watch over her transatlantic possessions. In the Caribbean and the Gulf of Mexico she had assembled enough ships, men, and arms to make other European nations very reluctant to trespass on her preserves. But it was well known that Spain was unprepared to protect her claims in the regions north and south of the Caribbean. As a result, ships and men from other Euro-

Above: the Panama Canal. World shipping now passes across the narrow neck of land that separates the Pacific Ocean from the Caribbean Sea. The isthmus twists in such a peculiar way that the opening to the Caribbean is actually west of the opening to the Pacific. Alonso de Ojeda founded a colony at Panama, at the southern end of the Canal, in 1499.

pean nations began to travel northwest or southwest across the Atlantic to try their fortunes in other parts of the New World.

It was in 1497 that England first joined in the scramble for oversea territories. Interestingly enough, it was not an Englishman, but a Venetian named John Cabot who sailed the first English ship to the New World. Cabot was living in England when he heard of Columbus' discoveries. John Cabot, with his son Sebastian, set out from Bristol to see if he, too, could find his way to "the Indies." Following a westerly course, he reached Cape Breton Island, off the northern coast

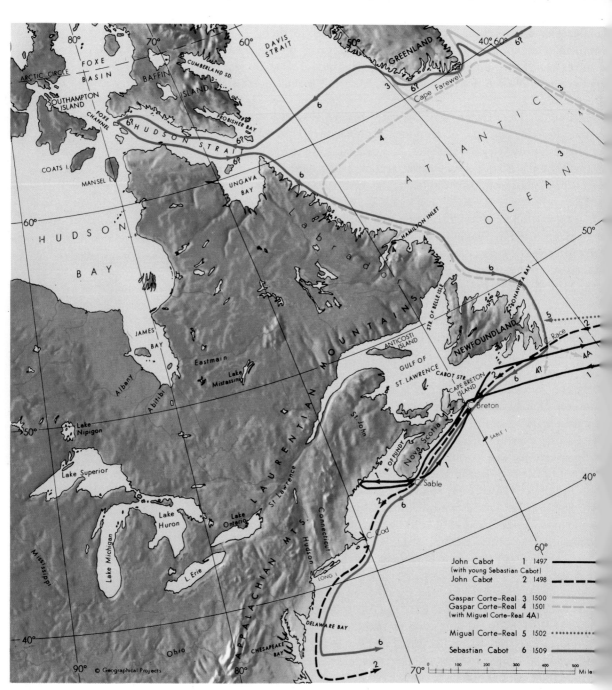

John Cabot	1	1497
(with young Sebastian Cabot)		
John Cabot	2	1498
Gaspar Corte-Real	3	1500
Gaspar Corte-Real	4	1501
(with Miguel Corte-Real 4A)		
Miguel Corte-Real	5	1502
Sebastian Cabot	6	1509

© Geographical Projects

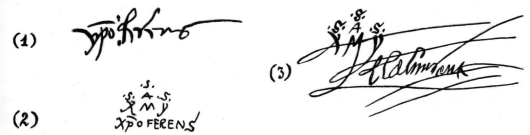

(1)

(2)

(3)

Above: Christopher Columbus' signature. Prior to 1492 he signed himself "Christoferens", which he spelt "Xoferens." After the discovery of America he called himself "Al Almirante."

Left: voyages made by the Cabots and the Corte-Reals to those parts of the New World safely north of Spanish claims. Only the green coastal areas were explored at this time.

of Nova Scotia. He then sailed northeast to the larger island of New-foundland. Having cruised along its southern coast, he returned to England, where he announced that he had found the land of the Great Khan.

The next year, with the blessing and financial backing of England's King Henry VII, Cabot made another journey, this time without his son. He sailed northwest until he reached the coast of Greenland. Then he sailed southward along the shores of Labrador (on Canada's extreme northeast coast) to Nova Scotia. From here he continued south, and possibly had even reached Delaware Bay, more than halfway down the coast of North America, before he sailed for home.

Cabot's was a magnificent voyage, but it produced no spices and no ambassadors from the Great Khan. Disappointed, the English king lost interest in westward exploration. Sebastian Cabot, however, did not. In 1509, he set out once more from Bristol and, according to contemporary accounts, succeeded in sailing through Hudson Strait into Hudson Bay before returning home.

Meanwhile, Portugal, too, was developing an interest in northwest exploration. King Manuel had no wish to break the Treaty of Torde-sillas, of course. But no one knew precisely where the Tordesillas line of demarcation really was, because it was difficult to fix longitude at sea. For this reason, Manuel felt fairly safe in sending Portuguese ships quite a long way west.

Early in 1500, a man called Gaspar Corte-Real, who had probably heard of John Cabot's alleged discovery of the land of the Great Khan, applied to King Manuel for permission to go exploring in the north-west Atlantic. His petition was granted, and that very year he visited the east coast of Greenland, rounded Cape Farewell on its southern tip, and cruised a short distance northwest along its western coast before icebergs forced him to sail back to Lisbon. On this voyage he had the distinction of becoming possibly the first European (other than the Vikings) to meet Eskimos.

The next year, in command of three ships, Corte-Real sailed again, taking his brother Miguel with him. Together they visited Greenland, crossed the Davis Strait to Labrador, and sailed on down the coast of Newfoundland as far as modern Bonavista on its northeast coast. Then, while Gaspar Corte-Real continued southward, Miguel return-ed to Portugal with a number of natives captured in Labrador. Months passed and Gaspar failed to appear. Finally, in May 1502, Miguel sailed

northwest again in search of him. Nothing was ever heard of either brother again.

In 1520, another Portuguese mariner, one João Alvares Fagundes, explored the Atlantic coast from Nova Scotia to Placentia Bay in southeast Newfoundland. The following year he was granted permission to establish a colony in the islands along that coast.

The Cabots, the Corte-Reals, and Fagundes were but a few of the many adventurous men who explored the North Atlantic coast in the early 1500's. As these explorers learned more about the extent of the coast, it gradually became clear that, if ever men were to succeed in sailing west to Asia, they must somehow find their way around a huge continental landmass. It also became clear that any attempt to find a "northwest passage" through the waters of the Arctic Ocean would be extremely difficult, if not downright impossible.

What of trying to reach the Indies by sailing *south*westward? Ultimately, the search for a southwest passage around the tip of South America was to produce one of history's most spectacular voyages: the first circumnavigation of the globe. But that voyage still lay two decades away when, in 1498, the great southern landmass was first sighted by Christopher Columbus. The admiral did not know, of course, what he had discovered when he sailed along the coast of Venezuela. But he did make a rough map of that coast to show the location of the island of Trinidad.

Right: this central American Aztec figure of about A.D. 1500 shows the sophisticated civilization which the Spanish stumbled upon when exploration of the New World got under way.

Left: John Cabot, born in Venice in 1450, leaving Bristol in 1497 carrying letters patent from Henry VII of England. These granted John and his three sons, Lewis, Sebastian, and Santius, "full and free authority, leave and power upon theyr own proper costs and charges, to seeke out, discover and finde whatsoever isles, countries, regions or provinces of the heathen and infidels, which before this time have been unknown to all Christians." They reached Newfoundland before returning to England.

449

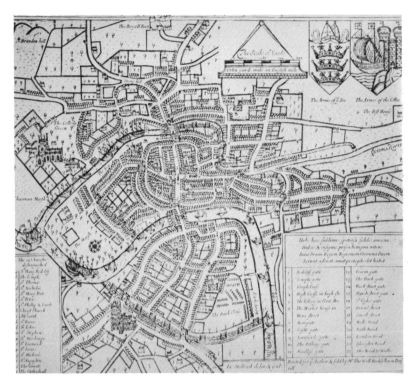

In 1499, a man who had seen that map set out with four small ships to explore the region. This man was Alonso de Ojeda, who later established the colony at Panama. On his 1499 voyage to South America, he took with him a middle-aged Florentine businessman named Amerigo Vespucci. Ojeda and Vespucci sailed to a point on the South American coast near Cape St. Roque on the northeastern tip of Brazil. They then followed the coast westward, far beyond Trinidad to the Gulf of Venezuela, before returning home.

In 1499, Vincente Pinzón, captain of the *Niña* on Columbus' first voyage, sailed to the South American coast and reached Cape St. Roque, a point on the eastern bulge of Brazil. He then proceeded northwest along the coast to the mouth of the Amazon River.

Did Pinzón reach Brazil before April, 1500, when Cabral's westerly sweep through the Atlantic brought him to those shores? Considering that Pinzón set out in 1499, it seems likely that he did, a fact which would give the honor of the discovery to Spain rather than Portugal. But, in fact, the whole question is shrouded in mystery. Many historians believe that the Portuguese knew of the existence of the Brazilian coast several years *before* Cabral reached it. Indeed, some say that it was for this reason that King John II insisted on having the pope's demarcation line moved farther west by the Treaty of Tordesillas. Certainly, it is well known that Portugal tended to keep her discoveries to herself, so the theory may well be correct.

In any case, both Spain and Portugal knew of Brazil by the middle of the year 1500. And, under the Treaty of Tordesillas, both had some claim to explore South America's east coast. Many men were to take part in this exploration during the next few years, and their discover-

Right: ice floes at Kap Dan, Greenland, the largest island in the world, the major part of which is within the Arctic Circle. John Cabot passed the island on his second voyage in 1498 when he reached North America.

Below: the four voyages of Columbus and Vespucci's travels in the Caribbean.

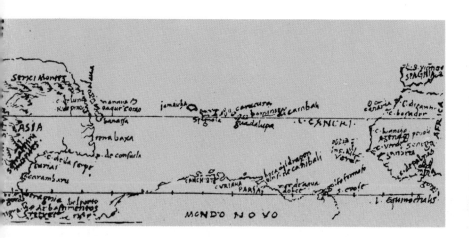

Above: sketch based on a map by Bartholomew Columbus, showing his idea of the world. Spain and Africa can be seen on the right, with the islands of Jamaica, Hispaniola, and Guadelupe in the middle between Africa and Asia. South of these islands is an enormous continent called Mondo Novo—new world.

ies were soon to lead them farther south than Europeans had eve traveled.

In 1501, Portugal's King Manuel sent out an expedition to dete mine how large "Brazil" was, and whether there was a way around which could be used to reach the Indies. Amerigo Vespucci, now the service of Portugal, took part in the expedition. (He was not a experienced seaman, but doubtless his business acumen was consi ered useful in drawing up a report on the resources of the land, so fas could be judged from the coast.) Little is known about what th expedition accomplished, except from the pen of Vespucci himself, an he says that the fleet followed the coast as far as latitude 50° S—only 4 miles from the extreme southern limits of the continent. Few peop accept this statement as true. But, from snippets of information le by others who took part in the voyage, it seems likely that the expediti did reach latitude 32° S, near the present boundary between Brazil ar Uruguay. Vespucci's writings and extravagant claims later made hi famous, and his Christian name, Amerigo, was used in naming bo of the great continents in the New World. Nevertheless, few hist rians today believe that he did half as much exploring as he claim to have done.

The next really vital step in South American exploration was indirect one. It came in 1513, when Balboa first gazed on the "Sou Sea." Although no one yet knew the extent of this new-found oce many men guessed—and rightly—that it extended the whole leng of western America's shores and provided a way west to the Orie

With Balboa's tantalizing "South Sea" in mind, adventurous ma

Above: Bay of Alcantara, near the mouth of the Amazon River. The mighty Amazon—though no one at the time realized just how massive it is—is the great South American river which Vincente Pinzón discovered in 1500. He called it the "Rio Santa Maria de la Mar Dulce," but after its first descent from the Andes in 1541 by Orellana, he gave it the name "Amazonas" after a battle with savages in which the women of the tribe also took part.

Right: Amerigo Vespucci (1451—1512), who gave his name to America, was born in Florence and became a Spanish subject in 1505. He made several conflicting claims of journeys for Spain and Portugal, in one of which, in 1497, he said that he had discovered a new continent, or the New World. Columbus, still imagining that he had reached the Indies, did not dispute Vespucci's claim. The suggestion that the new continent, which was in fact South America, be given Vespucci's name was adopted, for South, and later North, America.

Right: the mouth of the River Plate, on the eastern side of South America, which Juan de Solís entered in 1515 in the hope of finding a passage from the Atlantic to the "South Sea," discovered the year before by Balboa. De Solís was ambushed and killed by Charrua Indians in 1515. The river was given the name Río de la Plata (silver) by Sebastian Cabot in 1526 after he had bartered with the Guarani Indians for silver ornaments.

ners became more anxious than ever to find a southwest passage India. Spaniards in particular became obsessed by the idea, for Spain possessions in the New World were still not paying very high div dends. If they could find a westward route to the South Sea, they cou reach the Spice Islands and challenge Portugal's hold on the East.

It was probably with this object in view that Juan de Solís, a Po tuguese pilot working for Spain, sailed southwest to the Bay of R de Janeiro in 1515. He continued south from this bay until he reach the enormous Río de la Plata estuary, in modern Uruguay. As Solís sailed west into this estuary, he found that the water continu

be salty for many miles. Possibly, therefore, he mistook it for a strait
at would lead directly to the South Sea. It was a natural mistake, but
proved fatal for De Solís and some of his men. Some way along the
inks of the great river, he and eight others went ashore and were cap-
red and killed by cannibals.

Sometime after the survivors of this expedition returned to Portugal,
ord of De Solís' "strait" to the South Sea reached the ears of an ambi-
ous Portuguese mariner named Fernão de Magalhães. The remark-
le voyage he made in pursuit of this strait was one day to make him
mous the world over as Ferdinand Magellan.

Surratte

Around the World

8

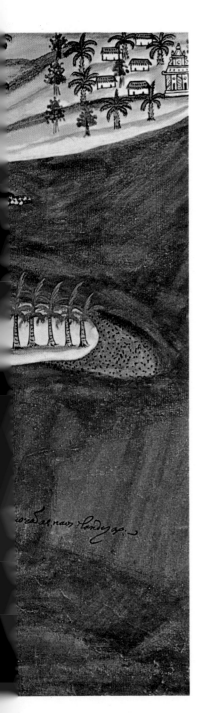

Ferdinand Magellan was born at Sabrosa, in central Portugal, in 1480. His father was one of the less important nobles, and at an early age he became a page in the court of King John II. At 15, he entered the service of John's successor, Manuel I, as a soldier. During the next few years he served on many of the most important of Portugal's first expeditions to the east, and gradually rose in rank.

In 1505, he sailed to India with the great armada of Francisco de Almeida, and was wounded at the battle of Cannanore. He was sent to Sofala, on the African coast, and helped build the first Portuguese fort there. He returned to India, and in 1509 took part in a naval battle against a Moslem fleet off Diu. Later that year, he signed on with the fleet which made the first Portuguese visit to Malaya. This expedition nearly met with disaster. When the Portuguese arrived on the Malay coast, they were greeted with apparent friendliness by the Sultan of Malacca. The welcome he extended, however, was only a trick to disarm the Portuguese. The sultan sent many of his men, secretly armed, to the Portuguese ships in the guise of "traders." Meanwhile, he invited boatloads of the crew ashore to pick up cargo. Suddenly, a signal was given, and the Portuguese were simultaneously attacked on land and sea.

In this dangerous situation, Magellan distinguished himself by

Left: battles between the invading Portuguese, who intended to set up trading compounds, and Arabs, who naturally wanted to protect their monopoly, were frequent. Magellan took part in such a battle early in his career. This particular battle shown was at Surat in Gujurāt, just north of Bombay, India.

Right: Ferdinand Magellan (1480–1521), captain of the expedition which first circled the globe. He made many voyages for Portugal, but, after losing favor with King Manuel, he went to Spain. In 1519 he sailed westward from Spain to find a route to the Spice Islands, on the way discovering the passage from the Atlantic to the Pacific which now bears his name. He was killed in a fight on the island of Mactan in the Philippines.

Below: a fleet of Portuguese carracks such as that in which Magellan sailed to India in 1505 under the command of Francisco de Almeida.

Right: close-up of sailors working on the topmasts of one of the ships.

calmness and bravery. Even before the Malays attacked, he suspected danger and was able to warn his captain in time to save his life and the lives of his crew. One chronicler also relates that Magellan saved another man, Francisco Serrão, who was among the party of men ashore. When the attack began, Magellan, it is said, rowed ashore and rescued Serrão, who thereafter became his lifelong friend.

In 1510, Magellan sailed with a ship bound for Portugal. Off the Laccadive Islands, to the west of Calicut, the ship went aground on a reef and broke up. The ship's boat could hold only a few men, and the officers (of whom Magellan was one) decided to sail them back to India to procure a rescue ship. When the rest of the crew learned that they were to be left behind, they nearly mutinied. Magellan prevented this mutiny by volunteering to remain behind with them.

Back in India once more, Magellan was rewarded for his services with the rank of captain. The following year he again distinguished himself in the Portuguese conquest of Malacca, led by Afonso d'Albuquerque. He then took part in the first Portuguese expedition to the Moluccas, late in 1511. His friend Francisco Serrão was also on this expedition. But after the ships had filled their holds with cloves at the tiny island of Banda, Serrão's ship was wrecked. Fortunately, Serrão

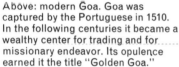

Above: modern Goa. Goa was captured by the Portuguese in 1510. In the following centuries it became a wealthy center for trading and for missionary endeavor. Its opulence earned it the title "Golden Goa."

was rescued by some islanders, and taken to the island of Ternate. When later voyages brought the Portuguese to Ternate, Serrão chose to remain on the island. Via Portuguese merchants he began to send letters to his friend Magellan describing the riches of the islands and urging him to make a voyage there. These letters were to play a significant part in Magellan's decision to pioneer a southwest route to the East.

Meanwhile, Magellan's status as captain had had one unfortunate result. In 1510, Albuquerque called together all his captains to ask them whether or not they agreed that the rich Indian port of Goa should be attacked then or in a year's time. He hoped, of course, that they would all agree to the launching of an immediate attack. Most did, but not Magellan; he urged that the overworked crews be given a rest before undertaking so arduous a campaign.

Some historians suspect that Albuquerque reported unfavorably on this incident to King Manuel. They may well be right, for when Magellan returned to Portugal in 1512, he found himself distinctly out of favor with the king. The way in which Manuel showed his displeasure was by not increasing the pension which Magellan, like all members of the Portuguese nobility, regularly received from the crown. At that time an increase in pension was the customary way of honoring a nobleman who had distinguished himself in the king's service. But on his return to Portugal—after serving bravely in numerous campaigns and expeditions abroad—Magellan received no increase whatsoever. Instead, he was given barely enough to enable him to live in Portugal in genteel poverty. So, after a year, he volunteered for active service once more. He took part in a Portuguese attack on Morocco and, in the fighting, received a lance wound that left him with a permanent limp. But that was not the worst of his luck. Some of the stores he was in charge of disappeared, and he was accused of misappropriating them.

Without awaiting trial—and without obtaining leave—Magellan made his way home to protest his innocence to the king. Although it was obvious from Magellan's previous record that he was a man of honor, Manuel refused to listen to a man who had technically deserted. He sent Magellan back to Morocco to stand trial.

The trial cleared Magellan of all suspicion, but that no longer satisfied him. In Manuel's service he had not only been unjustly accused, but also insufficiently rewarded. It was not enough to be cleared of what he had *not* done; he also wanted recognition for what he *had* done.

Again Magellan went to the king. This time he made three requests. First, he asked for an increased pension as a token of royal esteem. The king refused. Second, he asked to be assigned a mission through which he might gain the king's respect and confidence. Again the king refused. Finally, he asked if he might seek service under some other monarch. To this, the king in effect replied, "Do as you please."

Hurt and annoyed by the king's disinterest, Magellan began casting about for some means by which he could win the honors that had so far eluded him. He made regular visits to the royal library, where maps and charts of the latest discoveries were kept. He had frequent talks with one Ruy Faleiro, a mapmaker who firmly believed that there was a strait between the Atlantic and the Pacific somewhere near latitude 40° S (several hundred miles south of the Plate estuary). And he pored over his letters from Francisco Serrão urging him to visit the Moluccas. Slowly Magellan began to formulate an adventurous scheme that would bring him fame and profit. He would find the strait Faleiro spoke of (and that Juan de Solís had died in search of in 1516) and sail west to the Spice Islands.

No one knew whether the Spice Islands lay in the part of the world which Portugal had rights or in the part to which Spain had rights. The Treaty of Tordesillas had divided the world equally between Por-

Above: detail of a world map made for Henry II of France in the 1500's, showing the Moluccas, or Spice Islands. Spain claimed the islands under the Treaty of Tordesillas, but Portugal bought them in 1528 and they remained Portuguese possessions until the early 1600's when the Dutch took them over.

Above: a dish and a covered cup made of Portuguese silver-gilt, the sort of articles that would have been in use in Portuguese court circles in the 1400's and early 1500's.

tugal and Spain. Therefore, at some point 180° east of the Tordesillas line, Portugal's rights must end and Spain's begin. But because of the difficulty in determining longitude, it was not known exactly where the Moluccas lay in relation to this point. Certainly, they were so far east of Malaya that even Portuguese cosmographers had begun to doubt Portugal's claim to them. Could it be that the richest islands of the East actually lay just beyond Portugal's domain?

If this were so, Magellan reasoned, then Spain had every right to exploit the Spice Islands. But she would have to find a new route there, since only at the risk of war could Spanish ships cross the Portuguese-controlled Indian Ocean. This was why he proposed to find the strait Faleiro spoke of. Once through this strait, a ship had only to sail north-west across the Pacific to reach the Moluccas.

In the fall of 1517, Magellan left his native Portugal, taking several experienced Portuguese pilots with him, to lay his plan before Spain's King Charles. The boyish monarch embraced Magellan's scheme with enthusiasm. By March, 1518, he had drawn up a formal agreement in which he appointed Magellan captain-general of the proposed expedition, promised him ships, made him governor of all lands he might discover, and gave him powers of life or death over all who sailed with him. The five ships Magellan was given were small and ancient, but, under his supervision, the business of patching, refitting, and provisioning them was soon under way, and he was confident that they could be made sufficiently seaworthy for the voyage.

It was a better beginning than Magellan had hoped for. But it was not long before King Manuel of Portugal learned of Magellan's scheme and attempted to sabotage it. His agent in this attempt was Sebastian Alvarez, the Portuguese consul in Seville. Alvarez's first move was to ask King Charles if it were true that Magellan and several other Portuguese seamen were being held in Spain, against their will. Alvarez then hinted that, if Charles *had* detained Magellan, he had done a

Above: painting by El Greco capturing the dignity and pride of Spaniards of rank of the period; a pride that could easily become contempt for foreigners, as Magellan found on his expedition with his captains.

wise thing, for a man who was disloyal to his own country might well be disloyal to another. Alvarez's sinister comments found their mark. King Charles began to treat Magellan with caution. He restricted the number of Portuguese seamen he could take with him and appointed several high-ranking Spanish officials to keep a watch on him during the voyage.

With Magellan, Alvarez used different tactics. He first urged him to save his honor by returning to Portugal, where he could count on King Manuel's forgiveness. Magellan replied that he preferred to keep faith with King Charles. Then Alvarez wished him good luck, and added that he would certainly need it. King Charles, he said, would doubtless suspect his loyalty and surround him with agents who would usurp his authority at the slightest pretext. Moreover, Alvarez said the five ships Magellan proposed to sail in were so decrepit that he, Alvarez, would not risk a voyage to the Canaries in them.

Magellan was not so worried about his ships as worried about the possibility of his authority being usurped. Indeed, he became so afraid of mutiny during the voyage that he never allowed anyone to question his orders. In this way he precipitated a rebellion.

Despite Alvarez's machinations, the preparations for the journey continued. On September 20, 1519, the fleet left Sanlucar de Barramed on the southern coast of Spain, and put out into the Atlantic. The five ships of the fleet were the *San Antonio,* the flagship *Trinidad,* the *Concepción,* the *Victoria,* and the *Santiago.* None of them was of more than 130 tons.

In the way of stores, Magellan had stowed on board essentials such as biscuits, cheese, wine, meat, beans, firewood, lanterns, lamp oil, tools, and utensils of all kinds, and also extras such as mustard, vinegar, almonds, garlic, raisins, medicines, fishing gear, and even musical instruments for the crew's amusement. Charts, instruments, and goods for barter he had in plenty, every item carefully listed. Nothing was lacking except confidence between Magellan and his captains.

All told, the fleet carried some 260 men. The majority of them were Spaniards. Next in number were sailors and pilots from Portugal, followed by a few men from other places. Among these were some Asians who had been brought to Portugal from the East and who might prove valuable as interpreters.

One of the crew members was an Italian named Antonio Pigafetta who later wrote a vivid account of the voyage. Apparently Pigafet

admired and respected Magellan from the outset. "The captain-general," he writes, "was a discreet and virtuous man... and did not commence his voyage without first making some good and wholesome ordinances." These "ordinances" were as follows. The flagship *Trinidad* was always to lead the way, while the other vessels were to keep within easy distance of it, maintaining a lookout for signals from the captain-general regarding making or shortening sail, changing course, and so forth. By night, every ship was to keep three watches, again keeping a sharp lookout for signals from the flagship which would be transmitted by means of flashing lanterns. Pigafetta explains why Magellan, who had never crossed the Atlantic, insisted on leading the way—despite the fact that some of the Spanish captains had more experience. "He did not entirely declare the voyage he was to make, lest men should not, from amazement and fear, be willing to accompany him on so long a voyage."

The Spanish captains must bitterly have resented not being taken into Magellan's confidence. As Pigafetta says, "The captains of the other ships did not love him." But Pigafetta seems not to have understood why. "Of this I know not the reason, except by cause of his being Portuguese, while they were Spaniards or Castilians."

The six-day trip to the Canaries, where the fleet took on more provisions, went smoothly enough. The first signs of trouble came during the ten-week crossing to South America. Instead of sailing directly southwest across the Atlantic, Magellan chose to follow the coast of Africa as far south as Sierra Leone before steering westward. This not only lengthened the distance to be covered, but also, by sheer bad luck, brought the fleet into exceptionally bad weather.

One day, the captain of the *San Antonio* hailed Magellan and asked why he was pursuing this strange course. Magellan, thinking he scented mutiny, replied sharply that no one must question his orders. A few days later, when he called all the captains to a meeting on board the *Trinidad*, the same man repeated his question. When Magellan haughtily refused to answer, the captain declared that he was not prepared to give unquestioning obedience to any and every order. This enraged Magellan, who at once arrested the captain and gave command of the *San Antonio* to another officer.

This incident seems to have had no immediate ill-effects, however, and the fleet sailed on. The ships were now passing through the waters of the southern Atlantic, and Pigafetta records with wonder the sight

of "sharks with terrible teeth, which eat people, dead or alive," and the electrical phenomenon known as St. Elmo's fire, which appeared as flames around the *Trinidad*'s mainmast during tropical storms.

On December 13, the fleet reached the Bay of Rio de Janeiro. It was, of course, in Portugal's domain, but the Portuguese had not as yet established a colony there, so it was safe to rest at anchor in the harbor. After their long voyage, Magellan's men were allowed two weeks of ease, basking in the sun. They found the natives friendly and eager to engage in barter. Pigafetta reports that in exchange for a fishhook a seaman could obtain five or six fowls, while for a mirror he could obtain enough fish to feed 10 men.

On Christmas Day the fleet was still in the bay. The Southern Hemisphere's longest day of the year had come and gone. Moreover, Magellan knew that the farther south he traveled, the less day light sailing hours he would have each day. He was anxious not to waste any more time, and on December 26 gave the order to sail on.

After two weeks, the five ships reached Cape St. Mary on the south east coast of modern Uruguay. They rounded the cape in a storm and found themselves in the comparative calm of the Plate estuary. The next 23 days must have been bitterly disappointing for Magellan. Sailing west up the estuary, his fleet searched long and hard—but in vain—for a way through to the Pacific.

But surely the real strait could not be far away. Magellan decided to press on while the season was still young. The fleet continued southward, therefore, always on the watch for any other deep inlet that might prove to be the strait they were looking for. Late in February, a little south of latitude 40°S, they found the coast tending sharply to the west. Perhaps this was it. But no, they had merely entered the Gulf of San Matias, about a fourth of the way down the coast of present-day Argentina.

Doggedly the fleet continued to follow the coast southward for more than a month, the days always getting shorter, the land looking ever more barren, the temperature steadily falling. As March wore on, even the most optimistic of the men had to admit that winter was

Left: Freetown, Sierra Leone, West Africa, known for centuries as "the white man's grave" owing to the high rate of malaria and tuberculosis was discovered by the Portuguese in the 1460's. As in other places along the coast, they set up trading establishments there.

Above: picture of ships at sea in the 1500's, complete with monsters of the depths. At this period, when so much was unknown, the reality of monsters was as likely as any of the other wonders that were reported by sailors seeing lands not known before. A sea monster is not so different from a hippopotamus, if you happen to be unfamiliar with both.

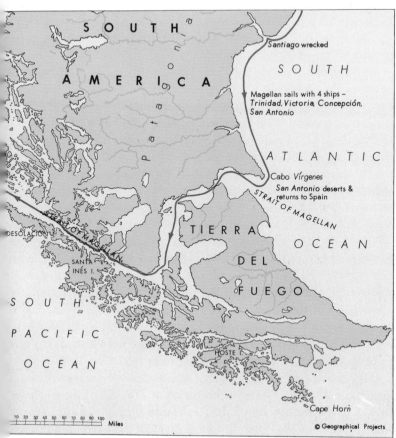

Left: Magellan's route around the tip of South America, weaving through the strait which has been named for him.

467

Above: scarlet cock-of-the-rock, a brilliantly-colored bird found around the Strait of Magellan.

TIERRA DE PATAGÓNES

Above: the naked "giants" reported by Pigafetta in Patagonia. The Tehuelche tribe of this area gained a reputation as giants due to their large stature and physical vigor.

closing in—and still there was no sign of the strait. To continue the search meant facing ever-worsening weather. On March 31, near latitude 50° S, the five ships reached a sheltered harbor, Port San Juliár. Reluctantly, Magellan decided to spend the winter there. Because the coast was barren, all the men would have to be put on short rations for the duration, but the captain-general saw no alternative but to wait until the warm weather returned.

The Spanish captains had long since given up hope of eventually reaching the Moluccas. On their side, the crewmen would gladly have exchanged the doubtful prospect of success for full rations and an immediate return home. But Magellan, already out of favor with the king of Portugal, dared not risk failing in his present mission and thereb earning the displeasure of the king of Spain as well. So, in spite of h men's objections to the plan, he began making preparations for th winter stay at Port San Julián. When it was learned that he would no change his mind, mutiny broke out. Pigafetta tells us that it was led b Juan de Cartagena, conductor of the fleet, and that it included man of the chief officers, who "plotted treason against the captain-genera in order to put him to death." Magellan learned of the mutiny in tim and put a swift and terrible end to it. "Cartagena... was banished wi a priest... in that country called Patagonia" (in Argentina), and the oth ringleaders of the conspiracy were executed and then quartered. Y by the standards of the day, Magellan was not unduly harsh. Many of t crew had been involved in the mutiny; Magellan punished only a fe

Most of the men were now willing to bow to Magellan's authori and for nearly five months, during which some of the men died of t extreme cold, the expedition remained at Port San Julián. The on breaks in the monotony of their existence during this time were t occasional visits paid them by the natives of the surrounding regio

Above: Tierra del Fuego, an island at the tip of South America, separated from the mainland by the Magellan Strait. Magellan named the island to the south "land of fire," because of the custom of the Indians who lived there to build camp fires which could be seen burning everywhere.

Right: this map from Pigafetta's *Relation* shows the Strait of Magellan as being an uninterrupted passage. This is far from the truth, as Magellan discovered. The strait follows a tortuous path, twisting, turning, and dividing around the numerous islands along its length.

Because of their giant stature, the Spaniards named these natives "Patagonians," meaning "big feet."

From late June onward, the nights began to get shorter, and gradually, as the noon sun climbed higher day by day, the cold abated a little. Magellan, anxious to be off, sent the *Santiago* southward to make an advance search for the strait he must find, and report back. Many days passed and the ship did not return. Finally, two exhausted men were sighted staggering along the shore toward the four waiting ships. A sudden squall had driven the *Santiago* aground near Rio de Santa Cruz, some 70 miles to the south. The vessel was beyond repair, and these two men had been sent overland to secure help for the stranded crew.

Rescuing the men of the *Santiago* took time. It was late August before the fleet left Port San Julián, and mid-October before they finally set sail from Rio de Santa Cruz. Just three days later they came to the Cabo Virgenes, where what seemed to be a strait opened out toward the west. This was, indeed, the waterway which Magellan had set out to find so many months before. By evil luck he had wasted a whole winter within 300 miles of it.

There was more ill fortune to follow. This strait, between the mainland and Tierra del Fuego, the large island just south of it, was like one of the great mountain-flanked fiords of Norway. It had many twists and turns, and often it divided into two channels, one running north, the other south. Supplies were running short, and Magellan could not waste the whole fleet's time exploring every channel. At one point, therefore, he decided to divide his fleet in two. The *Trinidad* and *Victoria* were to follow one channel, the *San Antonio* and *Concepcion* another. Some days later the *Concepcion* hurried after the *Trinidad* and the *Victoria* with the good news that the channel it had followed led almost certainly into the Pacific. But the *San Antonio* had disappeared. (She had, in fact, deserted, and was on her way back to Spain with vicious reports about Magellan's conduct, which, her crew alleged, had provoked a justifiable mutiny.)

On November 28, the three remaining vessels emerged from what was named the Strait of Magellan and entered the vast waters of the Pacific. As they did so, all three ships fired a salute and the captain-gen-

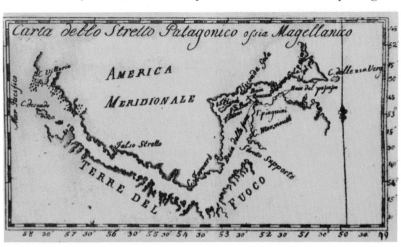

469

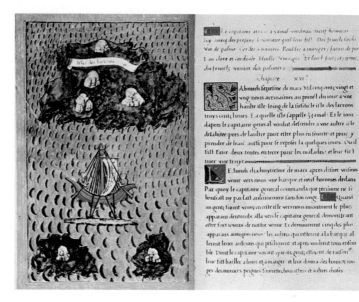

Right: an illustration from Pigafetta's *Relation*, showing the Islas de los Ladrones, "islands of thieves." This name was given to the Marianas by Magellan because, although not unfriendly, the inhabitants stole anything they could from the Spanish.

Below: painting on the ceiling of the church at Cebu in the Philippines, depicting Magellan planting a cross commemorating the first Christian baptism on the island.

eral wept for joy. Magellan had at long last found the southwest passage to the Orient. All that now remained was to voyage steadily northwestward until he reached the Moluccas. He little dreamed how immensely long that voyage would be.

For nearly two months, week followed week with never a sight of land. The remaining provisions dwindled to nothing, the last supplies of water became putrid, and the men were reduced to eating whatever they could find: ox-hides, grub-ridden biscuit, sawdust, and rats. (And even the rats were so few in number that they had to be auctioned of to the highest bidder.) The ravages of scurvy soon took their toll, and scores of men died.

At last, on January 24, 1521, the fleet sighted an island, which Magellan named St. Pablo. But it was barren and uninhabited, and the fleet was forced to sail on. A second island was sighted on February 3, but it, too, was barren. Then, after another agonizing month, the fleet reached some inhabited islands near Guam (about 1,700 miles north east of the Moluccas). Here Magellan's ships anchored. The natives were friendly, but soon took to stealing whatever they could from the Spaniards. For this reason, Magellan named the islands the Ladrones, "islands of thieves." In retaliation for the loss of their possessions the hungry sailors raided the native huts and helped themselves to as much food as they could find.

On March 9, with his crew partially restored to health, Magellan sailed west once more and reached the island of Samar in the Philippines. Here he gave the crew another two-weeks' rest before setting out to trade and preach Christianity in the nearby islands.

Early in April, Magellan reached the Philippine island of Cebu where after doing some trading, he converted the local ruler to Christianity. Magellan then assured the ruler that if he had any enemies, he, Magellan would crush them. The man claimed that he did have enemies on the nearby island of Mactan. Magellan, true to his word, set off with a par

INSVLA MATHAN.

Victoria

Right: the death of Magellan. This map shows Mactan, two of Magellan's ships, islanders offering gifts, and the fight in which Magellan was killed.

Below: detail of the fight between Magellan's crew and the Mactan people.

of men to do battle with them. He was killed in the attempt, on April 27.

Magellan was then less than 1,000 miles northwest of the Moluccas. Had he lived to sail 1,500 miles farther *west,* he would have reached Malaya (where he had been some 12 years before) and become the first man to circumnavigate the globe. As it was, that distinction would belong to one of the Asians who accompanied the expedition as an interpreter.

The failure of the Portuguese to crush the men of Mactan left them wholly discredited in the eyes of the Philippine islanders. The recently converted ruler of Cebu invited several of the fleet's chief officers ashore and had them quietly slaughtered. The forlorn survivors of the expedition then set sail and, after taking on provisions at some nearby islands,

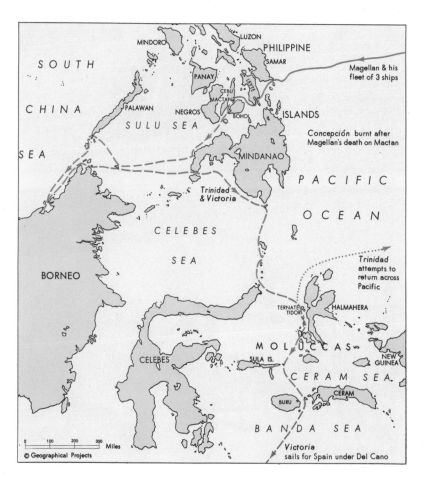

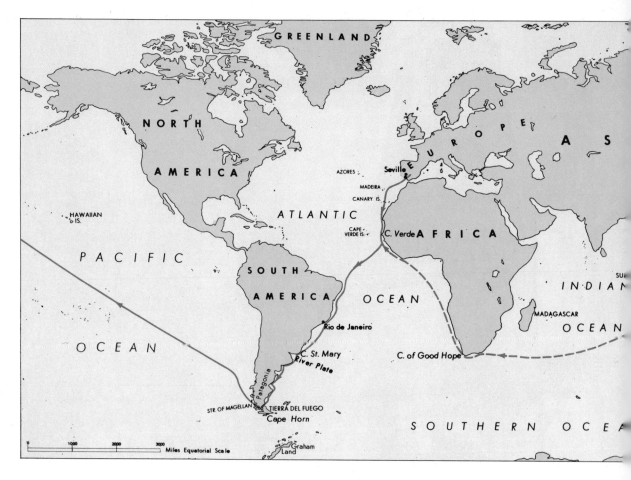

Above: Magellan's magnificent voyage circling the world. The broken line shows the return by the *Victoria* alone.

made for the Moluccas. But of the 260 men who had started on the voyage, only 115 now remained. There were simply not enough crew members to man three ships adequately. Thus it was decided to burn the *Concepción,* the least seaworthy of the three vessels.

Finally, in early November, 1521, the two remaining ships found their way to Ternate and Tidor, the rich Spice Islands to which Francisco Serrão (now dead) had begged Magellan to come. There the tired men of the *Trinidad* and the *Victoria* were received with splendid hospitality. They rested, bought food supplies, and took on heavy cargoes of spices.

When the time came to leave, however, the *Trinidad* was found to be hopelessly unseaworthy. The necessary repairs would take months, so it was agreed that the *Victoria* should sail home ahead of her. In January 1522, therefore, the *Victoria* set off for home alone. Her captain, risen to command as a result of the many deaths among the other officers, was Juan Sebastián del Cano, a former mutineer.

Del Cano might have retraced Magellan's outward voyage, but no one relished the prospect of another Pacific crossing, another passage through the Strait of Magellan, and possibly another winter in Patagonia. Wisely he chose instead to sail westward through the Malacca Strait, across the Indian Ocean, round the Cape of Good Hope, and then north to Spain. He would have to shun Portuguese ports and beware

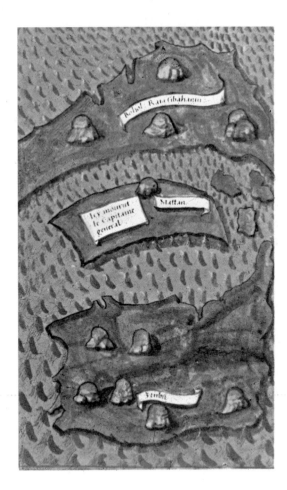

Above: Pigafetta's map of the
Philippine islands of Mactan (where
Magellan was killed), Bohol, and Cebu.
As in most of his maps, Pigafetta
shows south at the top.

f Portuguese ships, but the risks involved in sailing west seemed
nfinitely less great than those involved in sailing east.

Avoiding all well-worn sea paths, therefore, the *Victoria* made her
vay around the second half of the world. As she proceeded west, her
ood and water provisions steadily diminishing, one man after another
ied of hunger, fatigue, and scurvy.

But by mid-May, 1522, in a storm which smashed one of her masts,
he had rounded the Cape of Good Hope, and by early July, she had
eached the Cape Verde Islands. Here, even though he was in Portu-
;uese territory, Del Cano was forced to make a stop. He succeeded in
naking the Portuguese authorities believe, however, that his ship was
n its way back from the New World. The *Victoria*, he said, had been
elayed by a storm, and stood in urgent need of food and water. The
ortuguese, little suspecting the truth, gave the Spanish captain what
e needed, and so made possible the completion of the voyage which
ing Manuel had tried so hard to sabotage.

On Saturday, September 6, 1522, the damaged *Victoria* at last reached
e harbor of Sanlucar de Barrameda with her precious cargo of spices,
1d her exhausted, depleted crew. It closed a chapter. What men had
een hoping for over a century had happened. They had reached the
ast by sailing west, and returned home again. The cost was tremen-
us but it had been proved it was possible.

475

Epilogue

Although he died before the completion of the first voyage round the world, the credit for this historic feat should really have gone to Magellan, for it was he who had made it possible. Indeed, in finding the western ocean route to the Orient, Magellan had achieved what Columbus had tried—and failed—to do. But it was to be many years before the world honored Magellan for the remarkable voyage which had cost him his life.

By the time the *Victoria* reached Spain in 1522, the mutinous officers of the *San Antonio* had long since returned home with their damaging reports about the captain-general. The *Victoria's* captain, Juan Sebastián del Cano, who had taken part in the attempted mutiny at Port San Julián, felt compelled to back their story. As a result, it was he, rather than Magellan, who was accorded recognition for the success of the voyage.

Meanwhile, the first circumnavigation of the globe had produced an interesting consequence for science. According to the crew of the *Victoria* and the ship's logbook, the date of her return was Saturday, September 6. But according to all land calendars it was Sunday, September 7. The reason for this apparent inconsistency, of course, was that the *Victoria* had crossed what we now call the International Date Line. But until this time it had not occurred to anyone that such a line would have to be established.

Strangely enough, the voyage produced no immediate results for navigation. In 1519, when the fleet had set out, Spain's American possessions had seemed of little value compared with the chance of a westward route to the Spice Islands. But by the time the *Victoria* returned, Cortes had completed the conquest of Mexico, and Mexican gold had begun to pour into Spain. This unexpected windfall naturally diminished the Spanish king's interest in spices or in the founding of an Eastern empire. (In any event, it was finally learned that the Moluccas did not lie in Spain's domain, but in Portugal's.) As a result, Magellan's western route to the Spice Islands was not used again for many years.

Yet despite this, the first round-the-world voyage stood out clearly as the culmination of an amazing period in exploration. In fact, it mark-

Right: the tower of Belém, built at the mouth of the river Tagus at Lisbon to act as a landmark and to protect shipping. The tower is incorporated in Lisbon's coat of arms.

476

Cappitaes Mores descubridores antes de
anos Visoreis & Gouernadores.

Annos de Christo

1 — Bertolameu Dias _____ 1496. Descobrio cabo de boaesperança
2 — Vasco dagama desenbridor da Ind.ª 1497. — Tornou as Reyno
3 — D.º Afs. Cabral _____ 1500 — Tornou as Reyno
4 — João da Noua _____ 1501 — Tornou as Reyno
5 — Vasco dagama Almir. da India 1502 — Tornou as Reyno
6 — Afonso de Alburquerque _____ Tornou as Reyno
    Francisco de Alburquerque _____ Perdeose
    Ant.º de Saldanha todos — Tornou as Reyno
    tres capitães mores — 1509
7 Lopo Soares _____ 1504 — Tornou as Reyno

Visoreys Gouernador

			Annos	mezes
Dom Frand.º Alm.º 1.º Visorey	1505	Morreo na offaria gouernão	4	00
Af.º de Alburquerq Gou.º	1509	Morreo na Barra de Goa	6	00
Lopo Soares Gouernador	1515	Tornou a R.º Gouernão	3	00
D.º Lopez de seq.ª Gou.º	1518	Tornou as R.º	3	00
D.º Duarte de Menezes Gou.º	1521	.....	3	00
D.º Vasco da Gama Visorey	1524	Morreo em Cochim	0 — 4
Henrique de Menezes Gou.º	1525	Morreo em Cananor	1 — 1
Mascarenhas Gou.º	1526	Tornou as Reyno	— 00
Lopo Vaz de Sampayo Gou.º	1526	Vez prezo	3 — 20
Nuno da Cunha Gou.º	1528	Morreo no mar vindo prezo	9 — 10
Dom Garcia de Nor.ª Visorey	1538	Morreo em Goa	1 — 7
D.º Estevão da Gama Gou.º	1540	Veo as Reyno	2 — 1

Left: page from an original manuscript of the 1600's recording Portuguese voyages. It shows the names of the captains and the years of their voyages.

Above: Hieronymite Monastery of Jeronimos de Belém. The building was begun in 1500 by João de Castilho, as a monument to Portugal's great seamen. Many of the country's famous men are buried there. Parts of the building have been restored, but the central gateway is original.

ed the end of the beginning. In 1418, when Prince Henry the Navigator had set up his school near Sagres, European seamen had known only the coasts of Europe and the Mediterranean. Now, a little more than 100 years later, they had gained familiarity with the entire coast of Africa and almost all the southern coast of Asia, as well as much of Asia's east coast and many of its adjacent islands. They had roughly charted most of the Atlantic coast of North and South America, and even explored a few stretches of the two continents' Pacific coast.

In a single century, tremendous strides had been taken in discovering and exploring the world beyond Europe's shores. But that discovery and exploration had primarily been limited to the coastline of the world's great continents. In the New World, no Europeans except for Cortes and his soldiers had as yet penetrated far inland. In Asia, the activities of the Portuguese merchants, missionaries, and settlers were still confined to the areas within easy reach of fortified ports. Almost all of the deep interior of Africa was to remain a mystery to white men for more than three centuries to come. Australia, New Zealand, and Antarctica were as yet unknown.

Thus, when the voyage of the *Victoria* brought the first great phase

Above: portrait of young Christopher Columbus from the Franciscan Monastery of La Rábida at Palos, where he lived and studied while he made preparations for his voyage. The canvas itself has been slashed.

of discovery and exploration to a close, the world still containe[d] as much of the unknown as the known. But the daring exploits of me[n] like Dias, Columbus, Da Gama, and Magellan had whetted men's app[e]tite for exploration. And as more and more adventurers left their na[-] tive lands to explore the unknown, it became clear that the "Great Ag[e] of Discovery" had only just begun.

Acknowledgments

Aldus Archives 417(B), 423(B); Arquivo Nacional da Torre do Tombo/Foto-Lafo 389; Associated Press Ltd. 418; Barnaby's Picture Library 445, 466; Bibliothèque de l'Arsenal, Paris/Photo Denise Bourbonnais © Aldus Books 334; Bodleian Library, Oxford 336, 398; Reproduced by permission of the Trustees of the British Museum 324–25, 344, 347, 356, 360, 367, 373, 433, 436, 438, 439, 440, 456, 468(B), 470(T), 478; British Museum/Photo John Freeman © Aldus Books 340, 342, 343, 353(B), 354, 355, 358(BR), 364, 368(T), 368(B), 372, 382, 383, 391(L), 401, 452; British Museum/Photo Michael Holford © Aldus Books 371(B), 385(B), 428(B), 469; British Museum (Natural History)/Photo John Webb © Aldus Books; 370, 442; Bryan & Mullinger Ltd., London/Photo Mike Busselle © Aldus Books 430; Camera Press 353(T); Camera Press/Serge Barton 376(T); Camera Press/G. S. Cubitt 431; Camera Press/R. Douglas 348, 348–49; Camera Press/Goldstein 414; Camera Press/Wim Swaan 417; Camera Press/Sam Waagenaar 406; Photo by J. Allan Cash 346, 349, 369(T), 429, 451(T), 470(B), 479; By courtesy of the City Art Gallery, Bristol 448; Des Bartlett/Bruce Coleman Ltd. 375; Russ Kinne/Bruce Coleman Ltd. 468(TL); Daily Telegraph Color Library 410, 465(T), 480; J. P. de Smidt 397; Geographical Projects Limited, London 330, 339, 365, 377, 390(T), 393, 396, 404, 413, 428(T), 446, 451(B), 467(B), 472, 474; Desmond Harney 387; Based on "Map 8" in Astronomy, 5th edition by John Charles Duncan (Harper & Row, 1954) 358(TR); Photo Michael Holford © Aldus Books 412(T), 423(T), 434(B); Michael Holford Library/Gerald Clyde 341(T), 362; Photo Peter Larsen 390(B); Mansell Collection 333, 335, 338, 351, 361, 374, 395(T), 402, 426(T), 450, 461(T), 463, 467(T), 471(T), 471(B); Mansell Collection/Photo Mike Busselle © Aldus Books 380, 432, 466(B); John H. Moore 453(T), 455; Emil Muench 368(TR); Museo Civico G. Garibaldi, Como 400; Museo del Prado, Madrid/Photo Mas 462, 464; Museu Nacional de Arte Antiga, Liboa/Photo Francisco Marques 350, 392(T); National Maritime Museum, Greenwich 361(B); National Maritime Museum, Greenwich/Photo Michael Holford © Aldus Books 328, 352, 359, 369(B), 412(B), 458, 459; National Maritime Museum, Greenwich/Photo John Webb © Aldus Books 358(BR); The Naval Museum, Madrid/Photo Mas 420; Courtesy of The New York Historical Society 457; PAF International 337; Palacio Real, Madrid/Photo Mas 422; Picturepoint, London 366, 371(T), 378, 379, 384, 385(T), 388, 391(R), 392(B), 417(T), 424, 426(B), 443(T); Popperfoto 332, 348(L), 357, 435, 460, 473, 477; Bernard Quaritch Ltd./Photo John Webb © Aldus Books 405; Radio Times Hulton Picture Library 453; Ann Reading 403; Reiss Museum in Zeughaus Mannheim/Michael Holford Library 449; Royal Astronomical Society 386; Royal Chapel, Granada/Photo Mas 408; British Crown Copyright, Science Museum, London 411; Department of Information, South African Embassy, London 427; India: Paintings from Ajanta Caves (World Art Series, New York Graphic Society by arrangement with Unesco) 434(T); United Press International (U.K.) Ltd. 416; United States Travel Service 415(T); Reproduced by kind permission of the University of the Witwatersrand, Johannesburg 425(T); Victoria & Albert Museum, London/Photo Michael Holford © Aldus Books 461(B); Photo John Webb © Aldus Books 409, 415(B), 443(B), 444(T), 447; Reproduced by permission of Yale University Press from Magellan's Voyage by Antonio Pigafetta, translated and edited by R. A. Skelton © 1969 by Yale University 441, 475.

Index